THE FUTURE OF WORLD TRADE IN TEXTILES AND APPAREL

WILLIAM R. CLINE

The Future of World Trade in Textiles and Apparel

REVISED EDITION

INSTITUTE FOR INTERNATIONAL ECONOMICS
Washington, DC 1987   Revised 1990

William R. Cline is a Senior Fellow at the Institute for International Economics. He was formerly a Senior Fellow at The Brookings Institution; Deputy Director for Development and Trade Research at the US Treasury Department; Ford Foundation Visiting Professor at the Instituto de Planejamento Econômico e Social Aplicado (IPEA) in Brazil; and Assistant Professor at Princeton University.

INSTITUTE FOR
INTERNATIONAL ECONOMICS
11 Dupont Circle, NW
Washington, DC 20036
(202) 328-9000
Telex: 261271 IIE UR
Fax (202) 328-5432

C. Fred Bergsten, *Director*
Linda Griffin Kean, *Director of Publications*

The Institute for International Economics was created, and receives substantial support from, the German Marshall Fund of the United States.

Printed in the United States of America
94 93 92 91 90   5 4 3 2 1

Library of Congress Cataloging-in-Publication Data

Cline, William R.
  The future of world trade in textiles and apparel / William R. Cline.—Rev.
  p. 432 cm.
  Includes index.
  ISBN 0–88132–110–9
  1. Textile industry. 2. Clothing trade.
  3. Textile industry—Government policy—United States. 4. Clothing trade—Government policy—United States. I. Title.
HD9850.5.C55   1990   90-4934
362'.45677–dc20   CIP

  ISBN 0–88132–110–9

Contents

Figures

THE FUTURE OF WORLD TRADE IN TEXTILES AND APPAREL

Preface

Trade policy is a focal point of international economic attention in 1990 and will remain so for the foreseeable future, with the Uruguay Round of multilateral negotiations in the GATT now at a critical stage. One of the central issues in the round is textiles and apparel trade. At the conference in Punta del Este that launched the negotiations, the participating countries committed themselves to work toward "the eventual integration of this sector into GATT." Indeed, some observers believe that the success of the entire round turns on whether a satisfactory solution can be reached in this sector.

Textile trade is replete with paradoxes. The sector comprises almost one-tenth of the volume of world commerce in manufactured products, yet it also faces the most elaborate network of internationally agreed trade restrictions. In the United States, textile and apparel imports have risen steadily even though controls on those imports have tightened substantially. Textiles represents one of the most contentious trade issues internationally, particularly between the industrial and the developing countries, as well as within the United States, where President Reagan vetoed restrictive quota legislation passed by the Congress in 1985 and again in 1987.

The original edition of this study, released in September 1987, analyzed both the domestic and the international dimensions of the textile problem and offered proposals for responding to it. This updated edition assesses the actual flow of textile and apparel imports over the last three years and critically examines the proposals made by the United States and others to try to resolve the issue in the round. It offers a series of recommendations for how best to do so.

The Institute for International Economics is a private nonprofit research institution for the study and discussion of international economic policy. Its purpose is to analyze important issues in that area, and to develop and communicate practical new approaches for dealing with them. The Institute is completely nonpartisan.

The Institute was created by a generous commitment of funds from the German Marshall Fund of the United States in 1981, and now receives about 15 percent of its support from that source. Major institutional grants are now being received from the Ford Foundation, the William and Flora Hewlett Foundation, and the Alfred P. Sloan Foundation. The Dayton Hudson Foundation provides partial support for the Institute's program of studies on trade policy. A number of other foundations and private corporations are contributing to the increasing diversification of the Institute's financial resources. About 10 percent of the Institute's resources in our latest fiscal year came from outside the United States, including about 3 percent from Japan.

The Board of Directors bears overall responsibility for the Institute and gives general guidance and approval to its research program—including identification of topics that are likely to become important to policymakers over the medium run (generally, one to three years) and which thus should be addressed by the Institute. The Director, working closely with the staff and outside Advisory Committee, is responsible for the development of particular projects and makes the final decision to publish an individual study.

The Institute hopes that its studies and other activities will contribute to building a stronger foundation for international economic policy around the world. We invite readers to let us know how they think we can best accomplish this objective.

C. FRED BERGSTEN
Director
June 1990

Acknowledgments

The author gratefully acknowledges the contributions of the numerous individuals from the business, labor, official, and academic communities who participated in the two study group meetings during the preparation of this study. He thanks Bela Balassa, C. Fred Bergsten, Richard N. Cooper, Anne O. Krueger, Charles Pearson, Brian Turner, and Paul Wonnacott for detailed comments on the manuscript, Debby McGuire for typing it, and Jonathan H. Conning for brilliant and tireless research assistance. He thanks Dorsati Madani for research assistance for Chapter 12.   **W.R.C.**

1

Introduction and Summary

Textiles and apparel have received more comprehensive and persistent protection than any other industrial sector, even though the original rationale for their special protection more than two decades ago was to provide temporary relief so that the industries could adjust and become sufficiently competitive to face international competition on their own. Today, industry and labor groups are pressing for still tighter protection, and, in an environment of massive US trade deficits, there is a greater chance than at any other time in the postwar period that Congress will enact restrictive import quotas. The consequences could include the collapse of the international Multi-Fiber Arrangement (MFA) governing trade in textiles and apparel, and perhaps of the new Uruguay Round of multilateral trade negotiations as well.

There are three policy options for textile and apparel trade: to increase the severity of protection immediately and decisively; to drift more slowly toward tighter protection under endless renewals of the MFA; or to reverse this process and set a firm timetable for gradual liberalization of the sectors. This study finds that from the standpoint of the nation as a whole, by far the best policy choice would be gradual liberalization.

The central policy questions may be stated simply: should the American public pay $20 billion or more annually in additional consumption costs in order to preserve approximately 200,000 more jobs in the specific sectors of textiles and apparel (but probably none economy-wide) than otherwise would exist? And should public policy protect people or positions? If the answers are that this cost is excessive, and that known, named people should be sheltered from excessive hardship in adjusting to imports—but that perpetual protection of abstract sectoral positions is not a national goal—then it is time for the policy debate to shift from asking how much more protection is needed to designing a program for dismantling existing protection over time. This study reaches these conclusions on the basis of quantitative models that examine not only the existing cost of protection but also the past and prospective trends of production, employment, and trade under alternative policy regimes.

Industry Health and Foreign Trade

The trade problem in apparel stems from the natural comparative advantage of labor-abundant developing countries in this labor-intensive industry that has proven difficult to mechanize. The underlying trade position of the textile sector is much stronger, because increased capital intensity and mechanization have made this sector internationally competitive at an equilibrium exchange rate. Indeed, in 1979–80 the textile sector achieved a modest trade surplus.

Both textiles and apparel have more robust economic health than might be suspected from the trade policy debate (chapter 2). Neither sector is deindustrializing: although growth has decelerated since the 1960s, domestic production has risen at an average annual rate of 0.45 percent in textiles and 1.1 percent in apparel since the early 1970s. However, because the pace of labor productivity increase has exceeded the rate of output growth, employment has fallen from its peak in 1973 by 31.8 percent in textiles and 19.1 percent in apparel (table 2.1).

Profitability has been surprisingly strong in apparel, where the ratio of profits to capital stock has averaged approximately twice the level for manufacturing as a whole. In textiles, the ratio of profits to capital has typically been below the manufacturing average, although in 1986 profits were considerably higher than that average. Yet the opportunities for technological improvement have been strong in textiles, and investment has been high, often exceeding profits in recent years. In contrast, in apparel only one-third or less of profits has been invested in capital equipment, reflecting the lesser scope for technical change.

The role of imports has remained limited in textiles, at less than 10 percent of domestic consumption (and, if exports are subtracted, the net figure is much lower). For apparel, the degree of import penetration is an intensely debated subject. Advocates of protection commonly cite 50 percent as the share of the market currently held by imports; the best estimate of this study, however, is that in 1986 imports accounted for 31 percent of consumption. It is important to make this calculation on the basis of value rather than physical units because domestic production tends to be of higher unit value; however, it is also important to expand the f.o.b. import values to the wholesale level (by including the insurance, freight, and tariff costs) to obtain an accurate comparison with the wholesale value of domestic output.

Imports have grown rapidly in the 1980s. Improved competitiveness through technological change virtually halted the growth of textile imports from 1971 through 1983, but the overvalued dollar then spurred a surge. In apparel the rise of imports was more steady, from approximately 5 percent of the market in the 1960s and between 10 percent and 15 percent in the 1970s to 20 percent by 1982, even before the more rapid recent increases.

From 1980 to 1986, the real value of textile imports rose by 92 percent; real apparel imports increased by 129 percent, giving average annual growth rates of 11 percent in textiles and 15 percent in apparel. Despite these rapid rates in the 1980s, since the inception of the MFA imports have grown only at about (or below) the 6 percent notional rate embodied in that arrangement in the early 1970s. Measured by square-yard equivalents, imports have grown on average at 4.0 percent annually since 1972 in textiles, and at 7.1 percent in apparel. (The rate for textiles is even lower, 1.8 percent annually, on the basis of real values deflating by wholesale prices; tables 2.4 and 2.6.)

Consumption has grown more slowly than imports, however. After rapid growth associated with new man-made fibers in the 1960s, textile consumption slowed to less than 1 percent annual growth in 1972–86. Apparel consumption has grown at 2.7 percent annually over the same period, about the same rate as GNP. Slow or moderate consumption growth is an important factor in the sectors. However, they are by no means under the same kind of pressure as such industries as steel, where consumption has declined substantially in absolute terms; moreover, alternative data sources suggest higher growth in apparel consumption.

In policy terms, the fact that long-term import growth since the beginning of the MFA has been approximately at or below the 6 percent annual rate envisioned at its outset is of little consolation to representatives of labor and firms in the industry. The reason is that the import growth has been concentrated in the 1980–86 period, after the industry had become accustomed to relatively slow import growth in the initial years under the MFA in the 1970s.

Labor and industry critics maintain that in the 1980s the Reagan administration failed to implement MFA protection in an effective way, and that loose interpretation of the provisions for flexibility in the arrangement permitted an explosion of imports. Hence, the call in 1985 for a Textile and Apparel Trade "Enforcement" Act. As noted below and developed in chapter 9, in 1986 in particular the administration did substantially tighten its restrictive procedures. It is important to recognize, moreover, the surge of imports in the 1980s was at least as much the consequence of macroeconomic forces (and especially the rising value of the dollar) as of any administrative decisions, and in fact the administration of protection successively tightened in several dimensions in the early 1980s. Placed in this context, despite the understandable frustration of textile and apparel labor and industry groups, their appeal for new restrictions loses some of its urgency, because the unfavorable macroeconomic pressures of the early 1980s have begun to reverse.

The Role of Macroeconomic Forces

Protection under the MFA acts as a semipermeable screen that impedes imports but nonetheless does not fully stop their more rapid entry when the underlying economic forces intensify import pressure. Chapter 3 applies a quantitative model of trade, production, and employment to identify the impact of macroeconomic influences such as the real exchange rate and the growth of the economy, trade policy in the form of levels of protection, and microeconomic forces including underlying price trends and long-term foreign supply shifts.

The evidence indicates an important role of the overvalued dollar in the early 1980s as a force in the rapid growth of imports. In textiles, where half of imports are from countries belonging to the Organization for Economic Cooperation and Development (OECD), this influence is more obvious. Even in apparel, however, where nearly 90 percent of imports is from developing countries (especially the East Asian newly industrialized countries [NICs]), the dollar's role was important. Data for 1973–84 clearly show that in periods of dollar strength, US apparel imports from developing countries have risen more rapidly than European and Japanese imports from these countries, while the reverse has been true during periods of dollar weakness (table 3.6). And while the real value of the dollar weighted by shares in US textile and apparel imports rose by nearly 40 percent with respect to OECD suppliers from 1980 to 1985, it also rose by 25 percent to 30 percent with respect to developing-country suppliers (table 3.1).

The model developed in chapter 3 (and appendix A) relates the price of imports to the level of protection, the exchange rate, and the real product price abroad. Imports respond to the import price over a period of two years, to domestic income growth, the state of the business cycle, and a term for outward shifting foreign supply (which follows an S-curve with high initial growth tapering off over time to more moderate rates in the case of apparel imports from developing countries). Domestic consumption responds to population, per capita income, and the weighted product price including domestic and imported goods. Exports are driven by foreign income growth, the real exchange rate, and the underlying domestic product price. Domestic production is determined as the amount required to satisfy consumption and export demand after deducting imports, and employment is determined on the basis of labor/output ratios as adjusted over time for rising labor productivity. In the case of textiles, domestic output includes the amount required as an intermediate input into apparel production. The model as calibrated achieves a high degree of adherence to actual trends over the past 16 years (figures 3.1 through 3.6).

The model explains the rapid rise of imports from 1980 to 1986 as follows. For apparel imports from developing countries, four influences made approximately equal contributions to the increase: dollar overvaluation, secular supply shift, rising US income, and falling foreign prices. Textile imports from developing countries had similar effects, with somewhat greater dollar and foreign price roles and more moderate income and foreign supply shift effects. Thus, even for developing-country supply the overvaluation of the dollar accounted for approximately one-fourth of the rise in apparel imports and one-third of that in textiles. For imports from industrial countries, the dollar was even more dominant, accounting for more than half of the increase in both textiles and apparel (table 3.5).

Policy simulations in chapter 3 indicate that if the dollar had not risen above its equilibrium level (approximately the real 1980 level, when the current account was in balance), the textile sector would have retained a trade surplus rather than moving into substantial deficit, and in apparel imports would have been approximately 20 percent lower in 1986 than their actual level (causing an increase of output and employment by approximately 6 percent). Moreover, abnormally low growth in the United States and abroad in the early 1980s caused output and employment in apparel to be approximately 16 percent lower by 1986 than the levels they would have reached under steady 3½ percent GNP growth (tables 3.3 and 3.4).

The importance of the exchange rate and sluggish economic growth in explaining the difficulties of the textile and apparel sectors in the first half of the 1980s suggests that considerable alleviation of these difficulties should come from the correction of the dollar's overvaluation, if serious new rounds of US and foreign recession can be avoided in the future.

Adjustment

There are two types of industry adjustment to foreign competition: revitalization and downsizing. The analysis in chapter 4 indicates that the textile sector has made important progress in both dimensions, but that adjustment in apparel has been sluggish and limited to moderate downsizing of employment.

Revitalization through investment and technological change has brought rapid growth in labor productivity in the textile sector. Open-end spinning, shuttleless looms, increased fiber polymer extrusion rates, wider looms, and robotics for in-plant transit are examples of technical change in textiles. In contrast, in apparel, sewing has been especially difficult to mechanize, in part because of the difficulty of separating single plies of material. Textile and apparel firms have also sought to adjust through improving delivery time (the quick response effort) relative to imports, and specializing in market niches (such as denim fabric and household textile products).

Ironically, successful revitalization through increased productivity tends to eliminate jobs just as surely as import growth. Decomposition analysis measuring the components of employment decline over the past 25 years indicates that in textiles, productivity growth has typically reduced employment per unit of output at a rate of between 3 percent and 4 percent annually, while import growth has accounted for only about one-third to one-half of a percentage point of employment decline annually. Even in apparel, productivity growth typically cut employment requirements 1 percent to 3 percent annually in comparison with job losses to imports of one-half to 1 percent annually; only in the period after 1982 did the two influences contribute almost equally to employment loss (at about 3½ percent annually; table 4.3).

With annual labor productivity growth of over 4 percent on average in the past 25 years, well above the US manufacturing average of somewhat over 3 percent, the textile sector has made major progress toward revitalization. Apparel has failed to do so, although with its rate of productivity growth up from 1.3 percent annually in the 1960s to 2.8 percent since 1973, the sector has narrowed its lag behind the manufacturing average (table 4.1). In the 1960s neither sector did much labor downsizing, as employment grew almost as fast as that of manufacturing overall; but since 1973, downsizing in the form of employment reduction has also been a major form of adjustment in textiles, and to a lesser extent apparel has downsized employment as well (figure 4.1). For its part, apparel has carried out some adjustment through wage-squeezing, as its average wage has declined from 66 percent of the manufacturing average to 58 percent (table 4.2). Overall, nonetheless, the apparel sector has used the period of special protection much less effectively for adjustment than has the textile sector, and its downsizing has been far more moderate than that in other sectors affected by trade (especially steel and footwear).

The persistence of protection in textiles and apparel, despite its relative ineffectiveness in promoting adjustment (especially in apparel) and its high cost to consumers (as discussed below), reflects the perceived importance and political clout of the two sectors. Together they employ 1.8 million workers, far more than any other manufacturing sector. Previous research has shown a statistical relationship of protection to the absolute number of workers in each sector (as noted in chapter 2). In addition, the two industries have a geographically widespread presence, as well as a concentration in politically pivotal states (including New York, California, Pennsylvania, and

New Jersey in apparel and the Carolinas and Georgia in textiles; chapter 4).

A crucial issue is whether the goal of protection is to perpetuate positions in textiles and apparel or to provide a temporary buffer for existing workers to adjust. There is little basis for the former objective. Macroeconomic policy determines aggregate employment. Fears of deindustrialization are weak grounds for pursuing a specific target of textile and apparel positions in the abstract; US manufacturing output has in fact not been declining over time, and in the specific case of textiles and apparel, wages are in any event not significantly higher than those in the services sectors (such as retail trade) to which workers might be expected to shift. Moreover, the demographics of an end to the labor force entry of the baby-boom generation and decelerating female labor force participation are already expected by the Bureau of Labor Statistics to cut the annual growth rate of the labor force from 2.6 percent annually in 1970–80 to only 1 percent annually in 1990–95. New legislation penalizing employment of undocumented aliens will tighten the labor supply further, especially in low-skill areas. The earmarking of a target number of jobs for the textile and apparel sectors would thus appear to be misguided as an objective of public policy.

In contrast, cushioning the shock for existing textile and apparel workers who lose their jobs is highly germane for policy, considering that the public at large benefits from lower prices under an open trade policy and has some obligation to compensate the groups adversely affected. (This obligation goes beyond that for adjustment to domestic sources of displacement, such as technological change, because there is an explicit national policy decision in the area of trade policy, in contrast to spontaneous market forces domestically.) Survey analysis by the Bureau of Labor Statistics has found, however, that the severity of adjustment difficulty is more moderate than commonly believed. By early 1985, almost three-fourths of textile and apparel workers displaced in the 1980 and 1982 recessions had found new jobs. The median duration of unemployment had been 13 weeks for textile workers and 25 weeks for apparel workers. Contrary to the popular impression, wage losses on the new jobs were minimal. Wages fell 2.5 percent for apparel workers and actually rose 3.3 percent for textile workers on new jobs.

Improved programs of adjustment assistance could help ensure that existing workers do not bear disproportionate pain for the public's benefits from an open trade policy. Trade Adjustment Assistance has become largely moribund under budget cuts in the 1980s, and reviews of previous programs indicate that they were inefficient because of excessive emphasis on supplementary unemployment benefits and inadequate focus on retraining, relocation, and job placement.

Europe, Japan, and the Developing Countries

A cross-country comparison for 1980 (before the period of dollar overvaluation) suggests that US competitiveness is more robust than might be expected from the systematic protection granted to US textiles and apparel. Using the ratio of value added per worker to the average wage, with an index at 100 for the United States, among the major industrial countries only Italy stood out as more competitive than the United States in textiles (120), and only Italy (112) and the United Kingdom (129) in apparel (table 5.4). The results for textiles are consistent with the fact that in 1986 the United States achieved a sectoral trade surplus (table 2.3).

The relative productivity/wage measure shows the somewhat surprising result that US competitiveness is also higher than that of the three developing countries examined (Hong Kong, the Philippines, and India) in both textiles and apparel, although considerably lower than that of Korea. Higher labor productivity thus tends to compensate for higher wages in the United States even in competition with the NICs. While this measure is by no means comprehensive, it does suggest that, at the right exchange rate, the US textile and apparel sectors have a significant chance of meeting foreign competition effectively. Nonetheless, in view of the large US deficit in apparel even in 1980 before dollar appreciation, a more complete analysis of competitiveness would be likely to show a weaker position relative to the NICs in this sector.

A review of the textile and apparel sectors in Europe and Japan (chapter 5) quickly reveals that there has been much more dramatic adjustment through downsizing in these countries than in the United States. Total employment in the two sectors has declined by 50 percent to 60 percent since 1973 in Germany, France, the United Kingdom, and the Netherlands, and by about one-third in Japan. In contrast, the United States is in a more favored tier, together with Italy, with employment cutbacks limited to the range of 15 percent to 20 percent. Contrary to the US experience, downsizing abroad has also taken place in output as well as employment. From 1972–73 to 1983, textile production declined in a range of 1 percent to 1½ percent annually in Germany and Japan and by 4 percent to 5 percent annually in the United Kingdom and the Netherlands. In apparel, output fell by one-half of a percent to 1 percent annually in Japan and the United Kingdom, and by 3 percent to 4 percent annually in Germany and the Netherlands. Italy is the prime exception; its relatively low wage rates (in comparison with those of other industrial countries) have permitted it to achieve rapid output growth in apparel in the 1960s (12 percent annually) and moderate growth in 1972–83 (1.9 percent annually; table 5.7).

Europe and Japan have also carried out adjustment through revitalization in textiles, where (as in the United States) labor productivity growth has been relatively high. With some exceptions, their productivity growth has been slower in apparel (as in the United States), and labor productivity has actually declined over time in apparel production in Japan.

Adjustment programs have been more systematic in Europe and Japan than in the United States. Germany and Japan appear to have had the greatest success. In Japan, the government adopted a program to eliminate capacity, an impressive, conscious decision to cut back an industry that had accounted for one-fourth of manufacturing output and one-half of exports in 1950 (but only about 5 percent of each by the 1980s). Conversion to nontextile products, investment abroad and the shifting of production to Asian NICs, and employment opportunities in affiliated nontextile firms within broader company groupings all played a role in Japan's relatively successful adjustment. In Germany, adjustment occurred through such mechanisms as a shift to foreign processing and a reduction in guest-worker employment, with relatively little government intervention. Government subsidy programs in France and the United Kingdom, in contrast, tended to be costly and had little lasting effect for maintaining employment. In Italy, it was not the official subsidy programs for larger firms but the dynamism of unaided small firms taking advantage of low-cost labor that invigorated the industry.

Overall, the lessons of European and Japanese adjustment experience appear to favor the outright acceptance of the need to downsize and avoidance of subsidies to prop up production and employment. Especially in Japan, which does not formally impose MFA quotas, and Germany, import policy in textiles and apparel appears to have been more open than in the United States, and their rise in imports from developing countries was much more rapid than in the United States (at least for 1972–80, prior to dollar overvaluation; table 5.6). These lessons are relevant to the United States, where the principal means of delaying downsizing has been through protection rather than government subsidies.

In developing countries, exports of textiles and apparel to the industrial countries grew rapidly in the 1960s from a low base (at 11.1 percent for textiles and 21.5 percent for apparel, 1963–73), and continued to grow but at more moderate rates in the 1970s and early 1980s (4 percent annually for textiles, 10 percent for apparel, 1973–84). The developing countries have comparative advantage in apparel in particular; in contrast, industrial countries have maintained a trade surplus in textiles, which are more capital- and technology-intensive and thus suited to industrial country factor endowments.

Explosive export growth from Korea and Taiwan, and later China, has dominated developing-country trade in the two sectors over the past two decades. India and Hong Kong, the traditional suppliers, have lost market shares since the early 1960s to these new exporters. Today the big four East

Asian suppliers (Hong Kong, Korea, Taiwan, and China) account for 45 percent of textile exports to OECD countries and 70 percent of apparel exports. Even so, textile and apparel exports are important to the economies of many other developing countries, and account for more than one-fifth of exports in such countries as Haiti, Bangladesh, Pakistan, Sri Lanka, and the Dominican Republic. The future export prospects for these and other lesser suppliers are hindered by the large market share reserved by the quota regime for the East Asian suppliers. (Even those lesser developed countries not now constrained by quotas, including several African countries, face the prospect of new restrictions if their exports do expand rapidly.)

Evolution and Impact of Protection

The salient feature of international protection of textiles and apparel is its longevity and its seemingly inexorable rise over time. The economic phenomenon underlying this pattern is the historical shift of comparative advantage toward developing countries (at least in apparel) and the corresponding pressure for ever-increasing protection to slow down the natural evolution of trade flows.

The textile and apparel sectors were already among the most highly protected in the 1930s and before. In the postwar period, Japan first placed pressure on industrial country markets. Europe responded with exemptions to liberalization for Japan under special GATT provisions, while the United States negotiated bilateral restraints on Japan in the late 1950s. Following the resulting spillover of supply to new sourcing from Hong Kong, by 1961 the United States led the international negotiation of the Short Term Arrangement (STA) for trade in cotton textiles and apparel, followed in 1962 by the corresponding Long Term Arrangement (LTA). President John F. Kennedy had pledged a new regime of restraints in return for acquiescence of the textile and apparel industries in the launching of the Kennedy Round of trade negotiations, and a key resolution in the General Agreement on Tariffs and Trade (GATT) concerning "Avoidance of Market Disruption" in 1960 paved the way for such a regime.

As trade in man-made fibers mushroomed, by the early 1970s there was intense pressure to extend coverage to noncotton textiles. Financial and trade conflict between the United States and Japan in 1970–71 before the first devaluation of the dollar triggered "voluntary" Japanese export restraints on man-made fiber products, and the United States negotiated similar controls for other East Asian countries. The resulting diversion of supply put pressure on Europe, reversing earlier resistance there to a widening of the multilateral restrictive regime.

By 1974, the new Multi-Fiber Arrangement extended the international regime of restrictions to cover man-made fibers. The Arrangement combined dual objectives: implementing new restraints while at the same time imposing some uniform limits on how severe the restraints could be. This dual liberalizing and restricting nature of the MFA explains many of its seeming contradictions (such as the presence of loopholes in its restrictive network). Under the MFA, as in the LTA and STA before it, the United States and Europe restricted imports from the developing countries and Japan but not from each other, both because of the perceived sources of import pressure and the implicit mutual retaliatory capacity of the two large industrial areas.

Designed mainly to legitimize emerging bilateral restraints, the MFA incorporated compensatory liberalizing moves: the identification of 6 percent annual growth as a target for imports under quota (up from 5 percent under the LTA), and flexibility provisions ("swing" across categories, "carry-forward" over time). The MFA also provided for a phase-down of bilateral European restrictions against Eastern Europe and developing countries. Some analysts judge that the first MFA was thus liberalizing on balance, but if so the change was ambiguous at best considering the much wider product coverage than before and the violation of such basic GATT principles as most-favored-nation (MFN) treatment and prohibition of quantitative restraints.

From the beginning of the MFA, it has been the specific limitations in bilateral agreements negotiated under its auspices with individual supplier countries that have constituted the operational core of the Arrangement. Because the European nations were slow to reach bilateral agreements, by 1977 they contended they had borne a disproportionate burden of imports under MFA-I, and they led the demand for tightening in the 1977 renewal (MFA-II). France precipitated action by briefly imposing unilateral restrictions. At the Europeans' insistence, MFA-II provided for "reasonable departures" from the 6 percent quota growth target of MFA-I, thereby fundamentally backing down on the liberalization compromise originally embedded in the mechanism. The European Community (EC) procedures for the new quotas were considerably more restrictive than before, and included global quotas for product categories considered sensitive. In contrast, under MFA-II the United States eliminated quotas in some categories where they had gone largely unused, and instead instituted a "call" mechanism whereby consultations for new bilateral restrictions could be invoked upon rapid increase in imports.

In the renewal of 1981 (MFA-III), the EC again complained of an undue burden of imports, and sought actual cutbacks of imports from the key East Asian suppliers. GATT analysts subsequently judged that the renewal brought another round of tightening. For its part, the United States tightened procedures in 1983, when it instituted automatic trigger conditions for "calls" to negotiate new bilateral quotas, depending on the size and rate of increase of imports from each exporting country.

By the early 1980s, the United States had bilateral restraint agreements with 34 countries, covering 80 percent of textile and apparel imports from the developing countries. Worldwide, the MFA covered some 14 percent of textile trade and 40 percent of trade in apparel. Other quantitative restraints (such as EC restrictions on East European products) raised the total of trade subject to restraints to approximately 60 percent in textiles and 65 percent in apparel. The remainder of trade, dominated by trade among the industrial countries, was restraint-free but subject to relatively high tariffs.

On the basis of various studies but most importantly evidence on the price of quota rights traded in Hong Kong, chapter 6 estimates the tariff-equivalent of MFA quotas at approximately 20 percent as of 1980, above and beyond the tariff itself. In view of the evolution of the severity of quota protection over time, the chapter estimates the present tariff-equivalent of quotas at 25 percent in apparel and 15 percent in textiles.

Tariff protection also remains high in the sectors. Apparel tariffs in particular have been reduced only marginally through several rounds of trade negotiations, and still stand at some 22 percent (although textile tariffs have subsided further to approximately 12 percent). Europe and Japan have cut tariffs further than the United States (table 6.3).

Industry critics of the MFA charge that it has not restricted imports sufficiently, and stress the rapid increase of US imports in the 1980s. Chapter 7 examines the actual impact of protection to determine whether the MFA did restrain imports. It seems clear that in MFA-I and MFA-II the regime cut back import growth. Thus, the physical volume of textile imports decelerated from annual growth of 16.1 percent in 1961–72 to − 9.1 percent in 1972–77 and − 2.1 percent in 1977–81; for apparel the corresponding decline was from 18.3 percent before the MFA to 2.9 percent during MFA-I and 4.7 percent during MFA-II (table 7.1). Imports only resumed rapid growth under MFA-III in the 1980s—largely, as analyzed in chapter 3, as the consequence of much more intense macroeconomic pressures (in particular, the overvalued dollar). The rise in textile and apparel imports in 1980–86 was part of a much broader surge in US imports generally, associated with macroeconomic factors.

The structure of the MFA has been such (especially as administered by the United States) that there have been loopholes that do permit more rapid import growth when the economic forces increase. The bilateral agreements specify individual product categories subject to quotas. Even for important suppliers, many product categories in the past have not been subject to outright quotas but instead were subject to surveillance and "calls" to negotiate. Some countries do not have bilateral agreements. And for many countries, quota-utilization rates are well below 100 percent. In short, in many country-category combinations, quotas have not been in place or binding.

Upgrading is another systematic means of offsetting MFA restraints. Because quotas are on physical units, the supplier can increase export value more rapidly by improving the quality of the product and receiving higher prices per square yard. One dimension of upgrading has been the shift by developing countries from exports of textiles to apparel, which have higher unit values. More generally, under MFA-I and MFA-II there were clear signs of upgrading. Thus, in contrast to the trend of declining unit values in the 1960s, during the period of MFA-I, US apparel imports showed much more rapid growth in real value (11.1 percent annually) than in physical volume (2.9 percent; table 7.1, using prices for domestic US textiles and apparel as the deflator).

Diversification to new countries and new, uncovered materials were two additional means of responding to restraints. Imports of ramie, silk, and jute products (not covered by the MFA) grew much more rapidly than those of controlled products.

The import surge of the early 1980s was so sharp that further inquiry is warranted. Thus, from 1982 to 1984 textile imports rose by 113 percent in volume. In large part this outcome reflected uncontrolled supply from Europe and the prevalence of relatively loose controls (surveillance) rather than quotas for developing countries. In apparel, where controls were tighter, US imports rose by 40 percent in volume from 1982 to 1984. The increases showed a close fit to the degree of openness by supplier. For imports from the five major industrial countries excluding Japan the rise was 191 percent; at the opposite extreme, the closely controlled big five Asian suppliers achieved an increase of only 23 percent, while groups at intermediate degrees of control (mainly other developing countries) attained an increase of 77.4 percent (table 7.2).

The case of Korea illustrates how imports could rise briskly even from a country with relatively tight controls. Apparel imports rose by 38 percent in value from 1982 to 1984. Categories controlled by quotas in 1982 (representing approximately two-thirds of import value) advanced only 2 percent in quantity but rose 28 percent in value, showing rapid upgrading. Categories subject only to surveillance in 1982 showed, in contrast, a quantity increase of 42 percent and a value increase of 61 percent (table 7.3). In the Korean case, it was neither quota growth nor "adjusted utilization rates" (after provisions for swings and carry-overs) that made the difference, but upgrading where quotas applied and increased volume where looser surveillance existed.

Key changes in the administration of US bilateral agreements in 1986 sharply curtailed the scope for such increases. Already by 1984 the categories subject only to surveillance had been seriously cut back and shifted to quota control. Administrative measures in 1986 extended this process and in addition imposed a system of layered category and subcategory quotas which further removed flexibility. New bilateral agreements with Hong Kong, Korea, and Taiwan cut the annual growth of import quotas to 1 percent or less and extended coverage to Hong Kong silk, linen, and ramie products.

It would be a serious mistake to conclude, on the basis of experience in the early 1980s, that textile and apparel protection has minimal restrictive effect; all indications are that the flexibility that permitted rapid growth in imports in this period has by now been largely eliminated. Moreover, on a global basis the MFA was restrictive even in the early 1980s considering that European imports stagnated in this period (tables 3.6 and 5.4), primarily because of exchange rate considerations rather than any tightening of European restrictions relative to those of the United States. (The appreciation of the dollar relative to European currencies made it attractive for developing-country suppliers to shift their sales from the European to the US market; and, to a lesser degree, the direct competitiveness of the NICs in European markets declined as their exchange rates were partially pulled up by their ties to the dollar.)

Costs of Protection

Protection imposes costs on consumers and the economy at large. Restriction of the supply of imports tends to raise their price. In addition, as import prices rise, the prices of competing domestic goods tend to rise in response; consumers shift demand away from imports and toward domestic goods, and US producers can raise prices when relieved from import competition. The increase in consumer prices causes a transfer of income away from consumers to domestic producers, and thus involves a redistribution of income among domestic groups that would seem unlikely to be consciously chosen if the consuming public were canvassed and asked to vote on the merits of making such a transfer for the purpose of earmarking jobs in the specific sectors of textiles and apparel. In addition, part of the consumer cost accrues not to US citizens but to foreign suppliers, in the form of "quota rents"—the scarcity value of import quotas (as illustrated by the Hong Kong quota premiums noted above). There is a further economic loss from the inefficient allocation of additional resources to produce goods that could be more cheaply purchased abroad.

The net national cost of protection, after deducting transfers to producers (and, in the case of tariff protection, to government revenue), must be compared to the net benefits arising from avoidance of temporary unemployment of workers who would be displaced from the textile and apparel sectors in the absence of protection. This loss from temporary unemployment occurs on a one-time basis, whereas the consumer and efficiency costs recur year after year.

Appendix B develops a model to calculate the consumer and national economic costs (net welfare costs) of protection in apparel and textiles. The model treats imports as partial substitutes for domestic goods, so that prices of domestic goods rise partially but by less than the full percentage by which import prices increase as the result of protection.

The results of the model as applied to 1986 data are shown in table 8.1. Tariff and quota protection raise import prices by an estimated 53 percent for apparel and 28 percent for textiles. Total consumer costs of protection amount to $17.6 billion annually in apparel and $2.8 billion in textiles. Total protection preserves 214,200 direct jobs in apparel and 20,700 jobs in textiles. The average American household thus pays $238 every year to retain some 235,000 jobs in the textile and apparel sectors rather than elsewhere in the economy. The consumer cost per job saved is approximately $82,000 in apparel and $135,000 in textiles. (If the more conservative measure incorporating indirect employment in intermediate inputs is used, the consumer cost is approximately $46,000 per job in apparel and $52,000 in textiles. However, as there would be alternative indirect employment associated with other sectors, if some resources were shifted out of textiles and apparel, the cost per direct job is the more meaningful figure for policy purposes.)

The net welfare costs to all Americans are smaller; after deducting transfers to producers and government, the net national costs annually amount to $7.3 billion in apparel and $811 million in textiles. However, the employment benefits of protection are far smaller than this cost. Evaluated on the basis of average duration of unemployment and average wage, the annualized costs of transitional unemployment resulting from elimination of protection amount to only about 3 percent to 4 percent of the net welfare costs of protection. Of the total net national cost of approximately $8 billion, almost half arises from the transfer of income to foreign suppliers in the form of quota rents.

These estimates of protection costs are broadly comparable to those of other major recent studies. The calculations here should be interpreted as conservative, because they assume that retailing firms pass along to consumers only the absolute cost increase imposed by protection, but do not apply their normal percentage marketing margins to these costs. (Otherwise, the consumer costs could be as much as twice the level estimated here.)

Chapter 8 presents calculations of the income distributional impact of protection in textiles and apparel. Despite the frequent justification of this protection on grounds that it shelters low-income workers, the analysis finds that protection has a regressive income-distribution impact. It reduces the income of the lowest 20 percent of households by 3.6 percent, cuts income by about 1 percent for the next three quintiles, and increases income by one-third of 1 percent for the richest 20 percent (who own the shares of textile and apparel firms). Textile and apparel workers generally fall in the second and third quintiles, and these income classes might be expected to gain; but because of the inefficiency of protection, even these income groups suffer on balance because the gains for textile and apparel workers are smaller than the losses of others in the same income classes.

MFA-IV, Restrictive Proposals, and the Uruguay Round

Despite these consumer and economic costs, in July 1986 the United States and 53 other nations renewed the Multi-Fiber Arrangement for another five years. At US insistence, the renewal provided for new tightening. For the first time, it extended product coverage to ramie, silk blends, and linen. It facilitated measures to guard against import surges. New language opened the door further to outright reductions in quotas from large supplier countries and to departures from the original target of 6 percent quota growth. The renewal also pledges countries to cooperate against fraud, such as falsification of country of origin.

At the same time as the renewal of MFA, the United States concluded new bilateral agreements with Hong Kong, Taiwan, and Korea. As always, the bilaterals were the scene of the real protective content, and the MFA only an umbrella. These new bilaterals broadened product coverage (parallel to the new MFA), and imposed extremely low quota growth rates of one-half of a percent to 1 percent annually. In the case of Taiwan, the agreement actually rolled back imports by 7 percent from the levels reached in the year ending May 1986.

In addition, the Reagan administration tightened implementation of the restraints. It reimposed three tiers of specific restrictions (aggregate, group, and 108 individual product category levels) and largely shifted from consultative provisions to actual quotas, reversing a move to flexibility under MFA-III. In effect, the administration gave the domestic textile and apparel industries a considerable portion of the increase in protection they had been seeking through legislative efforts.

In contrast, the administration opposed those legislative efforts, and blocked the Textile and Apparel Trade Enforcement Act of 1985 by a narrowly sustained presidential veto. This bill called for a sharp rollback of imports from Hong Kong, Taiwan, and Korea, and the imposition of new import quotas (fundamentally shifting from the regime of export restraints by foreign countries themselves) with growth rates constrained to 1 percent annually except for new, minor supplying countries. The model developed in this study is applied in chapter 9 to estimate that the consumer cost of the 1985 bill (as amended) would have been $6 billion annually on a conservative basis (intermediate between the administration's estimate of $9 billion and an estimate by the Congressional Budget Office of $1 billion to $3 billion annually).

The 1985 bill served as a threat to strengthen the hand of the administration in its demands for tightening in MFA-IV negotiations. But the industry remained unsatisfied by the new MFA provisions and the more strict implementation and terms of bilateral agreements, and by early 1987 mounted a new legislative effort to restrict imports. The Textile and Apparel Trade Bill of 1987 calls for global import quotas (for the first time breaking the taboo against restrictions on imports from Europe and Canada), with quota growth limited to 1 percent annually. Representatives of the industry characterized the new proposal as a compromise that did not seek the rollback of the earlier measure. Nonetheless, the new proposal was broader in country coverage, and by imposing global quotas would have choked off the remaining flexibility in the regime for increased total import volume by precluding geographical diversification of production to uncontrolled areas (although flexibility for geographical choice of supply *within* the controlled volume could actually increase).

The models of protection cost (applied in chapter 8) and the model forecasting trade and production (chapter 10) are combined to calculate the consumer cost that would result from the new proposal. The cost is lower at first ($1.3 billion annually for 1987–89) than subsequently. This is true in part because exchange rate correction should cause a slowdown in import growth and thus temporarily limit the difference between the path of imports restricted to 1 percent annual growth and the path they would follow otherwise. However, the cost then mushrooms to magnitudes that would eventually double that of the protection already in place (reaching approximately $10 billion annually in the early 1990s and $20 billion by 1996, at 1986 prices). For the initial 10-year period before the first review of the controls, the average consumer cost of protection from the proposed legislation would be $7.1 billion annually (at 1986 prices; table 9.3).

Enactment of the 1987 proposal would probably mean an end to the MFA. It could also cause a collapse of the Uruguay Round of trade negotiations. This new round of multilateral trade negotiations offers an important forum for negotiating a reversal of the secular trend toward ever-higher protection in the sectors. In particular, it could be the vehicle for reciprocal negotiations that could obtain gradual reduction in protection in the NICs in return for corresponding phase-down of protection in the industrial countries. As indicated in table 9.2, there is considerable protection in the NICs to be negotiated away (with some notable exceptions such as in Hong Kong).

Long-Term Prospects

Representatives of textile and apparel producers and labor groups have justified calls for new restrictions on grounds that otherwise the sectors may be expected to suffer massive losses of output and jobs to growing imports. Burlington Industries commissioned a 1985 study finding that without new protection, the textile and apparel sectors would lose 947,000 jobs by 1990 (as discussed in chapters 9 and 10).

Chapter 10 applies the model of trade, production, and employment developed in the retrospective analysis of chapter 3 to examine the likely course of the industries through the year 2000. The projections investigate three policy regimes: unchanged, more restrictive, and more liberal. For the exchange rate, the projections use the levels reached in January of 1987 for industrial countries (a conservative basis in view of additional depreciation subsequently), and for the developing countries, assume that two-thirds of the appreciation of the dollar from 1980 to 1986 is reversed.

The projections indicate that under current policy, textile production grows at approximately 2 percent annually through the year 2000, while rising labor productivity reduces employment by 1.6 percent annually (137,000 jobs by the year 2000). Imports decline and exports rise significantly in response to correction of the dollar, and by 1995 the textile sector is in trade surplus (as it was in 1979–80). Thus, from 1986 until 1989 when the full effects of dollar depreciation are felt, real textile imports decline by 18 percent and real exports rise by 88 percent. Ironically, the 1987 textile bill could actually boomerang for the textile sector in particular, because foreign retaliation would be likely to choke off export recovery just as dollar depreciation was paving its way.

In apparel, production rises by 2.0 percent in 1987 and 2.5 percent in 1988, but output growth thereafter trends downward to nearly zero by the year 2000. Import growth pauses as dollar correction takes hold but, by the early 1990s, returns to a steady rate of approximately 7 percent in real terms. Apparel employment declines by 17.6 percent by the year 2000, or by 199,000 jobs. Thus, the estimates of this study are that 336,000 jobs would be eliminated in textiles and apparel by the year 2000 (tables 10.1 and 10.2), only about one-third the magnitude of the cutback suggested by the American Textile Manufacturers Institute (ATMI) as soon as 1990.

If instead higher protection is adopted (specified in chapter 10 as an increase in the tariff-equivalent of quotas from 25 percent to 45 percent in apparel and from 15 percent to 60 percent in textiles, reflecting the sharper cutback in textiles proposed in the 1985 bill), by the year 2000 some 24,000 additional jobs would be preserved in textiles in comparison to the base case of present policy, and some 85,000 jobs in apparel. Yet the consumer costs of such protection would be even higher than the $6 billion estimated for the milder, amended 1985 bill (chapter 9).

Under trade liberalization, in contrast (specified as a gradual elimination of quotas and a cut of the tariff to 15 percent in apparel and 10 percent in textiles), by the year 2000 approximately 31,000 additional jobs would be lost in textiles in comparison with the base case of current policy, and some 138,000 in apparel. Thus, in the absence of policy change employment could be expected to decline between 1986 and the year 2000 by 20.5 percent in textiles and 17.3 percent in apparel; import liberalization would raise the employment cutbacks to a total of 25.1 percent in textiles and 29.7 percent in apparel.

The modest difference between the base and liberalization cases in the textile sector reflects the limited import penetration in textiles. The impact of liberalization on the textile sector is moderate even though the calculations include the indirect effects of apparel liberalization on textile production and employment. It is sometimes argued that despite the relatively strong competitive position of textiles, the sector could not withstand a general program of liberalization in textiles and apparel because of the crippling effect on sales of textile inputs into the apparel sector; the analysis here suggests that this concern for the textile sector has been overstated.

The analysis in chapter 11 places the outcome under liberalization into policy perspective. However, the calculations of chapter 10 by themselves clarify that in the textile sector even the differences between the high protection and liberalization cases are relatively minor (11 percent for both employment and output by the year 2000), a finding that is consistent with the numerous elements of information and analysis suggesting that this sector is relatively capable of standing on its own without special protection. In apparel, the gap between future employment under higher protection and liberalization is considerably wider (28 percent, table 10.2). In apparel, the central question is not whether protection makes a large difference, but whether this difference justifies the massive costs to consumers (and net costs to the economy) that it imposes.

The projections of Chapter 10 further clarify that while productivity growth may be expected to erode employment in both sectors, neither one is likely to undergo deindustrialization defined as an absolute reduction of output. Under present policy, textile production stands 34 percent higher in the year 2000 than today, and apparel production 10 percent higher. Even under liberalization textile output grows (by 27 percent); and although apparel production declines, the reduction is limited (8 percent by the year 2000; tables 10.1 and 10.2).

Policy Implications

Chapter 11 draws upon the empirical findings and simulation estimates of this study to obtain implications for trade policy in textiles and apparel. In light of the poor record of adjustment in apparel despite more than a quarter-century of protection; in view of the extremely high and distributionally regressive consumer costs of protection; and considering that the correction of the overvalued dollar should give considerable relief from the rapid import growth of the first half of the 1980s, the chapter proposes that it is time to design a program of gradual liberalization of textiles and apparel.

The evaluation of a program of liberalization first asks whether the industries could survive. The record of relatively high apparel profits, the evidence on broad compensation of lower foreign wages by lower foreign productivity, and the estimates of 10 percent import penetration in textiles and 31 percent in apparel all suggest that neither industry is in danger of imminent collapse. Nor do analogies to the footwear industry suggest otherwise, as examined in the chapter.

A central analysis in chapter 11 demonstrates that the employment reductions projected under the program of gradual liberalization (as simulated with the trade and production model of chapter 10) would be sufficiently moderate to be accommodated by normal attrition from retirement and voluntary quits in the industries. Specifically, under liberalization that phases out quota protection and reduces tariffs to more moderate levels over approximately 15 years, the annual rate of employment reduction would be 1.6 percent in textiles and 2.5 percent in apparel. Because the retirement rate is 2.0 percent annually in textiles and 2.2 percent in apparel, and in addition voluntary quits amount to 1.8 percent annually in textiles and 2.5 percent in apparel, natural attrition would be sufficient to cover the annual employment reductions that would arise in both sectors under a program of gradual liberalization. Indeed, with attrition rates from retirement and voluntary quits totaling 3.8 percent annually in textiles and 4.8 percent in apparel, there would still be room for new recruits to enter the sectors at the annual rates of 1.8 percent of total employment in textiles and 2.2 percent in apparel. New people could still enter the sectors, even though total positions were declining.

Because cutbacks in employment would tend to be more concentrated among the weaker firms (especially in apparel where output would actually decline under liberalization) rather than evenly spread, there should be a program of worker adjustment assistance to retrain and place those workers that were displaced but were not yet retiring. However, eligibility for such assistance would be limited to workers who were already in the industry as of 1987, and a special registration of existing workers would be taken for this purpose. Future workers would enter the industry at their own risk, thereby reducing the distorted signal given by remaining protection inducing new workers to enter the industry. The overall strategy of conscious downsizing of employment coupled with adjustment assistance to cushion the effects for existing individual workers would follow the principle that trade protection should be for people, not positions.

Representatives of labor groups tend to reject the suggestion that employment reduction at below the rate of natural attrition means that adjustment to import liberalization could be feasible. Their concern is that job losses would be highly concentrated in closings of individual plants. While there would almost certainly be a considerable concentration (and thus the need for adjustment assistance as proposed here), it is highly likely that a major portion of the reduction in work force would be widely dispersed. As all firms would face weaker price incentives for expansion or maintenance of production, a generalized reduction of employment in the sector—compared to levels that would attain under higher protection—would be expected. It therefore remains highly relevant that natural attrition rates would equal or exceed the required sectoral employment reduction. Moreover, the American public may reasonably ask at what point the petitions for maintenance of employment in a specific sector become excessive. If even the natural attrition rate is unacceptable to labor groups as a pace of labor reduction, then implicitly the public is being asked to underwrite recruitment of *new* workers to the industry through higher protection, with its associated costs. The public may consider this request excessive, especially if it has already paid for a program of adjustment assistance.

The specific mechanism proposed for gradual liberalization in chapter 11 is as follows. Existing quotas, by country and product, would be transformed into "tariff rate quotas." Countries not now subject to quotas would remain exempt, as would product categories currently not restricted even for countries subject to restraints in other product categories. The tariff rate quota does not place a physical absolute limit to imports but instead imposes a stiff tariff surcharge at a specific quantitative level of imports. At the current volume of quotas under existing bilateral arrangements, a tariff rate surcharge of 15 percent would be applied to any further imports of textiles from controlled countries in controlled categories, and 25 percent for apparel. These rates are designed to match the tariff-equivalent protective effect of existing quotas, and thus the transformation to tariff rate quotas would leave protection initially unchanged.

Gradual liberalization would occur by reducing the tariff rate quota's surcharge by 1.5 percentage points annually, eliminating the surcharge in 17 years for apparel and 10 years for textiles. In addition, the tariff rate would be gradually reduced to 15 percent in apparel and 10 percent in textiles (still above the industrial average). To ensure against disruptive import surges, for major suppliers (those accounting for more than 5 percent of imports), a second-tier surcharge of 10 percentage points would be imposed if imports rose by more than 5 percent in a given year (placing the total surcharge at 35 percent in apparel and 25 percent in textiles).

Revenue from the surcharges under the tariff rate quota mechanism would be channeled to the textile and apparel adjustment program. In principle these revenues would be low or zero, because the surcharges are gauged to replicate existing quota protection and prevent import surges. Accordingly, funding for adjustment assistance would have to come primarily or wholly from other programs, such as the $1 billion proposal for worker adjustment suggested by Secretary of Labor William E. Brock and included by President Ronald Reagan in the budget for fiscal 1988. If the magnitude of imports did exceed the surcharge thresholds by a moderate 10 percent, however, the amount of revenue under the tariff rate quota would reach approximately $300 million annually. This amount would be sufficient to provide two years of retraining, relocation, and placement benefits for the full number of annual jobs lost (an average of 36,000 annually for the two sectors) even if none of the lost jobs were vacated voluntarily through retirements or quits. As noted, because much of the job reduction could be covered by attrition, actual labor adjustment costs could be considerably lower. If so, some funding from the surcharge revenue could also be available for communities in which affected textile and apparel firms were located (and community adjustment funding would be appropriate regardless of the revenue source). As developed in chapter 11, it could also prove useful to make a limited portion of adjustment assistance funding available as loans to those firms that provide advance notice of plant closings (although mandatory advance notification should be avoided because it increases labor rigidity and could inhibit future hiring). Otherwise, adjustment assistance would be limited to workers, not firms, because there is no reason for the public at large to ensure profits for owners of capital, who tend to be in high-income groups.

If representatives of the textile and apparel sectors viewed a tariff rate quota as unacceptable because of uncertainty over the actual level of imports that would enter, the alternative of auctioned quotas could be used instead, with revenue from the auction used for adjustment purposes. In this case, it would be essential to place the magnitude of quotas on a firm timetable of future growth that ensured they would become nonbinding—so large as to be redundant—by the end of the phase-down period. Moreover, it would be undesirable to apply the quotas on a global basis covering all countries, because to do so would increase existing protection. However, it would be appropriate to implement the quotas on an "internationally consolidated" (as opposed to global) basis, aggregating existing country quotas (by product category), for the purpose of auctioning.

It would be desirable to negotiate the program of gradual liberalization in an international context. Adoption of a similar program by other industrial countries would be sought, to avoid concentration of developing-country supply on the US market alone. Moreover, it would be appropriate to seek reciprocal liberalization of textiles and apparel by developing-country suppliers as the counterpart of liberalization by industrial countries. While a delayed timetable for reciprocal liberalization would be appropriate for lower income countries and countries experiencing severe debt-servicing difficulties, for the economically strong East Asian NICs, a timetable for liberalization matching that of the industrial countries would be appropriate. The Uruguay Round would be the natural forum for the negotiation of this program of mutual liberalization.

Chapter 11 outlines one specific approach for achieving reciprocity from supplier countries and parallel liberalization by Europe. The United States would lead an Arrangement for Open Trade in Textiles and Apparel (AOTTA). The program of gradual liberalization described above would be applied to member countries of the AOTTA. The NIC suppliers seeking entry (and therefore the benefits of liberalization) would be expected to provide reciprocal liberalization of their own markets, in the first instance in textiles and apparel but in addition in other sectors to provide full reciprocity. Illustrative calculations in chapter 11 suggest that countries such as Korea and Taiwan could provide ample new opportunities for US exports by offering reciprocal liberalization. To provide a strong incentive for the EC to adopt parallel liberalization and become a member of AOTTA, the opening of NIC markets under reciprocal liberalization would be accorded only to AOTTA members.

In the absence of a concrete program for gradual liberalization, protection in textiles and apparel seems destined to rise over time virtually without limit. The normal evolution of comparative advantage (especially in apparel) toward production abroad by labor-abundant countries means that higher and higher barriers will have to be imposed to hold imports to current levels relative to demand. Consumer costs would rise to ever higher levels over time. As analyzed in chapter 9, persistently increasing protection and consumer costs would be the explicit consequence of the recent legislative initiative to impose a global quota and limit its growth to 1 percent. Although a sideways drift through endless renewal of the MFA would be less restrictive, it too would tend toward rising protection, as suggested by the history of successive tightening of this mechanism.

This study seeks to clarify the stakes involved in these policy choices. If the earmarking of some 200,000 additional jobs for the specific sectors of textiles and apparel beyond levels that would otherwise occur is a conscious goal of the American public, and voters are prepared to impose an annual cost of $20 billion on themselves in higher consumption costs for this purpose (table 8.1), then it would be appropriate to continue current policy. And if voters are prepared to pay up to double this cost by the mid-1990s to add some 150,000 additional sectoral jobs by that time, it would be appropriate to adopt the recently proposed program of increased protection (table 9.3). However, if the public does not attach a high priority to preserving these earmarked jobs in the two sectors specifically, on grounds that overall employment is determined by macroeconomic policies, that most of the adjustment would be manageable through natural retirements and voluntary quits, and that the consumer costs are not only unacceptably high but also distributionally inequitable, then some program of gradual liberalization would appear to be the appropriate policy choice.

2

Economic Performance and the Role of Trade

The textile and apparel sectors date from the earliest stages of industrial development and remain of major importance today. Together they provide 6 to 10 percent of manufacturing output, 4 to 5 percent of GDP, and 12 percent of manufacturing employment in the industrial countries.[1] These industries are widely perceived to be under great stress because of losses to rapidly rising imports, and for more than two decades they have received ever-increasing protection. Yet both industries show signs of more resilience than might be suspected from the broad protection granted and the even wider protection that firms and labor unions have sought.

Profits have been relatively healthy, especially in apparel. In textiles, high investment and mechanization have improved competitiveness, though at the expense of employment. This improvement has been reflected in a favorable performance in foreign trade, prior to the first half of the 1980s when an overvalued dollar caused erosion. In apparel, where production processes are less amenable to mechanization, employment was relatively stable over the two decades 1960–80. Nonetheless, by 1980 employment was 7 percent below its 1973 peak, and by 1986 the cumulative decline had reached 19 percent. Even so, apparel employment contrasted favorably with the more stark reductions in automobiles and steel—two other major industries that have faced serious import competition and have received protection. Indeed, the share of apparel in total manufacturing employment in the United States now exceeds that in Japan as well as Europe.[2]

---

1. Organization for Economic Cooperation and Development, *Textile and Clothing Industries: Structural Problems and Policies in OECD Countries* (Paris: OECD, 1983), pp. 11–14.

2. General Agreement on Tariffs and Trade, *Textiles and Clothing in the World Economy* (Geneva: GATT, July 1984), p. 22.

Apparel faces an adverse long-term trend from the shift of international comparative advantage away from industrial countries toward developing countries. The sector is labor-intensive, and the relatively low cost of labor in developing countries gives them a comparative advantage in the sector. The textile sector is more capital-intensive and competitive. In addition to long-term trends, however, the US textile and apparel industries have faced special pressure in recent years. Recession reduced demand (at least in textiles), and overvaluation of the dollar spurred a sharp rise in imports.

The first challenge to public policy formation is to distinguish correctly between temporary difficulties likely to reverse (as may be the case with problems caused by the overvalued dollar) and more fundamental, long-term trends of erosion. This chapter and the next seek to draw this distinction in quantitative terms. The second challenge is to respond appropriately to the long-term problem. So far the response has been solely to protect the industries against imports. The subsequent discussion of this study reviews the costs and benefits of this response, and considers the appropriate directions for future policy.

Employment, Production, and Profits in Textiles

The textile industry encompasses the production of yarn, fabric (primarily for use in apparel), and finished goods such as bedding and carpets as well as industrial materials such as fabric for tires. The industry has long experienced the pressure of shifting international comparative advantage. The sector was already in decline in industrial countries in 1913–29 as a result of competition from Japan and import substitution in Central Europe and Latin America.[3] From 1933 to 1955, British textile and apparel exports fell by 75 percent as sales to India and other colonial markets lost ground to domestic substitutes.[4]

Two major technological developments have contributed to a revitalization of the industry, however. First, technical changes in chemical production and rapid growth of petrochemical capacity in the 1960s and early 1970s brought a period of declining prices of synthetic fibers, and gave the textile industry a new dynamism. In contrast, US agricultural programs had held

---

3. Ibid, p. 15.

4. Donald B. Keesing and Martin Wolf, *Textile Quotas Against Developing Countries* (London: Trade Policy Research Centre, 1980), p. 9.

Table 2.1   Production, investment, and employment: textiles and apparel, 1960–86
(million dollars and thousand workers)

	Textiles (SIC 22)					Apparel (SIC 23)			
Year	Q	Q*	I	N	Year	Q	Q*	I	N
1960	12,629	21,103	417	874.6	1960	12,999	30,867	86	1,234
1961	12,881	22,192	314	854.8	1961	13,088	29,989	79	1,214
1962	14,036	23,904	372	863.9	1962	13,948	31,269	99	1,234
1963	14,698	30,823	382	862.9	1963	14,818	33,389	128	1,279
1964	15,873	32,039	503	875.3	1964	15,514	34,257	123	1,302
1965	17,080	33,634	618	893.2	1965	16,426	36,271	168	1,335
1966	18,301	36,119	887	927.6	1966	17,308	37,746	205	1,364
1967	18,502	35,529	733	928.7	1967	18,483	37,831	208	1,356
1968	20,514	36,880	690	958.8	1968	19,628	38,478	267	1,356
1969	21,455	37,289	849	968.1	1969	21,045	38,880	311	1,381
1970	21,112	38,110	811	924.5	1970	20,394	34,765	299	1,341
1971	22,438	41,087	872	906.4	1971	21,687	36,510	336	1,319
1972	25,902	46,008	1,127	952.8	1972	23,914	42,192	363	1,368
1973	29,053	46,134	1,121	980.3	1973	25,970	43,335	387	1,400
1974	30,877	42,670	1,169	931.5	1974	26,855	40,595	391	1,317
1975	29,208	41,832	997	835.1	1975	27,098	40,270	381	1,214
1976	34,260	46,115	1,087	875.9	1976	30,019	42,328	423	1,270
1977	38,054	50,050	1,223	875.6	1977	35,323	46,485	457	1,334
1978	40,201	50,945	1,356	861.8	1978	37,845	48,380	514	1,322
1979	42,645	51,265	1,328	842.3	1979	37,350	45,330	524	1,306
1980	44,774	49,423	1,487	817.5	1980	40,293	45,742	608	1,307
1981	47,741	48,146	1,714	783.4	1981	44,074	46,176	646	1,251
1982	44,916	44,916	1,579	717.4	1982	46,681	46,681	654	1,189
1983	50,485	49,812	1,580	723.4	1983	49,423	48,932	n.a.	1,182
1984	52,258	50,065	n.a.	710.6	1984	50,672	49,196	n.a.	1,152
1985	50,147	48,498	n.a.	670.2	1985	50,784	48,551	n.a.	1,142
1986	51,917	49,210	n.a.	668.9	1986	53,323	49,548	n.a.	1,133

Q   production; Q*   real production at constant 1982 prices; I   investment; N   employment; n.a.   not available.
Source: US Department of Commerce, *U.S. Industrial Outlook,* 1987, 1986, 1985, 1974, and 1969.

cotton prices well above international levels, placing cotton textiles at a disadvantage. From 1960 to 1979, the share of synthetic fibers in world fiber production rose from 5 percent to 36 percent; the share of yarn produced with man-made fiber rose from 26 percent to 60 percent in the European

Community (EC), 36 percent to 74 percent in the United States, and 43 percent to 67 percent in Japan.[5] Second, as discussed below, successful mechanization of production reduced labor costs (as well as employment), improving competitiveness.

As indicated in table 2.1, the real value of US textile production nearly doubled from 1960 to 1971. By 1977, however, real output had reached a plateau, and it has actually declined since its peak in 1979. Thus, from 1960–61 to 1972–73 average annual growth was a brisk 6.6 percent, while from 1972–73 to 1985–86 the average was only 0.45 percent. For the Organization for Economic Cooperation and Development (OECD) as a whole, annual growth of textile output fell from a relatively robust 3–4 percent in 1953–73 to less than zero in 1973–82.[6]

Lower economic growth in the period after 1973, marked by the global recessions of 1974–75 and 1980–82, played an important role in this stagnation. However, input costs were important as well. Just as synthetic fibers had spurred the industry in the 1960s, their link to the price of natural gas and oil made them vulnerable to the energy shocks of 1974 and 1980. Dollar prices of synthetic fibers rose by about one-third after the first oil shock, and again by one-half after the second. Moreover, the commodity boom of 1973 caused cotton and wool prices to rise nearly threefold; and although they subsequently lost about half of this gain, by the late 1970s they remained more than twice their level at the beginning of the decade (and about one-fourth higher in real terms).[7] Importantly, synthetic fibers ceased to exert a downward pull on the prices of natural fibers.

The two forces of recession and rising input costs contributed to an erosion in the profit performance of textiles in the period 1973–84. Nonetheless, relative to other sectors, in textiles, profit performance held up fairly well. As indicated in table 2.2, from 1960 to 1973 industry profits averaged 14.8 percent of value added, compared with 19.3 percent in US manufacturing on average. From 1974 to 1979 textile profits averaged somewhat higher, at 15.1 percent of value added, while the US rate rose to 20.0 percent. In 1980 to 1982 (later comparable data are unavailable), the average for textiles fell to an estimated 8.7 percent, while that for US manufacturing fell to 15.3 percent. On the basis of this indicator, the ratio of performance in the textiles sector to the US manufacturing average thus declined from 0.77 in

---

5. OECD, *Textile and Clothing Industries*, pp. 35–38.

6. GATT, *Textiles and Clothing*, p. 16.

7. OECD, *Textile and Clothing Industries*, pp. 36–37; International Monetary Fund, *International Financial Statistics Yearbook 1985*, p. 101.

the first period to 0.65 in the second and 0.57 in the third. This erosion was moderate in view of the rising input costs for textiles. The relative decline was also limited in view of the greater incidence of recession and the high sensitivity of the textiles sector to recession. (Thus, in 1974–75 the profit value-added indicator for textiles fell to only 0.48 of the level for US manufacturing.)

Recent data on textile profits indicate buoyant recovery from the 1982 recession. Data compiled by the American Textile Manufacturers Institute indicate that net profits stood at 6.9 percent of shareholder equity in 1982, well below the manufacturing average of 9.3 percent; but profit performance rebounded to 12.0, 11.2, and 8.6 percent in 1983, 1984, and 1985, respectively, with an average practically the same as that for all manufacturing over this three-year period (11.1 percent). And in the first three quarters of 1986, textile mills outperformed the manufacturing average, with net profits at 13.6 percent of shareholder equity, versus 9.9 percent for manufacturing.[8]

The Retail Industry Trade Action Coalition (RITAC), in opposition to recent proposals for new protection of textiles and apparel, has stressed the strong profitability of the sectors. The group notes that for the first three quarters of 1986 textile profits (pretax) stood 91 percent above the level of the same period in 1985. Textile stocks rose by 30 percent in 1986, outperforming the stock indexes. The Federal Reserve Index of industrial production in textiles rose by 20.9 percent from the first quarter of 1985 to the fourth quarter of 1986, while the increase for manufacturing overall was only 3.7 percent (although as may be seen in table 2.1, the 1985 base had been below the 1984 textile production peak). And in the third quarter of 1986, capacity utilization in textiles stood at 92.6 percent, far above the manufacturing average of 79.9 percent.[9]

From a longer term perspective, declining employment and rising labor productivity have helped sustain profitability despite the influences of rising input costs, recession, and nearly flat production in recent years. Employment peaked at almost 1 million in the boom year of 1973. Since then it has declined to only 668,900, with the sharpest drops coming in the recession years of 1974 and 1982 (table 2.1). After growing at 0.9 percent annually from 1960–61 to 1972–73, employment declined by 2.9 percent annually from 1972–73 to 1985–86 (table 2.1).

A solid pace of investment has enabled the textile sector to achieve rising labor productivity. As shown in table 2.2, the sector has invested a share of

8. American Textile Manufacturers Institute, *Textile Hi-lights,* March 1987, p. 13.

9. Retail Industry Trade Action Coalition, letter sent to members of Congress, 25 June 1987; and *Survey of Current Business,* vol. 67, no. 2 (April 1987), p. S-2.

Table 2.2 Profits[a] and investment in textiles and apparel, 1960–84
(billion dollars and percentage)

Year	Textiles		Apparel	
	Profit	Investment	Profit	Investment
1960	0.65	0.42	0.31	0.09
1961	0.58	0.31	0.35	0.08
1962	0.70	0.37	0.41	0.10
1963	0.73	0.38	0.42	0.13
1964	0.89	0.50	0.53	0.12
1965	1.12	0.62	0.62	0.17
1966	1.09	0.89	0.76	0.21
1967	0.92	0.77	0.76	0.21
1968	1.19	0.70	0.88	0.27
1969	1.04	0.85	0.81	0.31
1970	0.88	0.81	0.75	0.30
1971	0.97	0.87	0.87	0.34
1972	1.02	1.12	1.08	0.36
1973	1.32	1.12	1.23	0.39
1974	0.99	1.17	0.92	0.39
1975	0.72	1.00	1.24	0.38
1976	1.44	1.09	1.42	0.42
1977	1.92	1.22	1.82	0.46
1978	1.92	1.36	1.63	0.51
1979	2.00	1.33	1.62	0.52
1980	1.41	1.49	1.83	0.61
1981	1.30	1.71	2.02	0.65
1982	0.86	1.58	2.18	0.65
1983	1.66	1.58	2.81	n.a.
1984	n.a.	1.92	n.a.	n.a.

Tx   textiles (SIC 22); Ap.   apparel (SIC 23); VA   value added; Cap.   gross capital stock; Inv.   investment; US   US manufacturing; n.a.   not available.
a. Before taxes
Source: US Department of Commerce, *Survey of Current Business,* February 1985, June 1985, July 1985, March 1986, July 1986; US Department of Commerce, *The National Income and Product Accounts of the United States, 1929–76,* Statistical Tables, September 1981; US Department of Commerce, *U.S. Industrial Outlook,* 1987, 1986, 1985.

its profits roughly comparable to that invested by US manufacturing as a whole. Chapter 4 examines investment and productivity growth in greater detail.

In sum, the textile sector has shifted from buoyant growth in the 1960s

Profit/VA			Profit/Cap.			Inv./Profit		
US	Tx	Ap	US	Tx	Ap	US	Tx	Ap
19.1	14.4	6.3	14.3	8.9	25.8	68.5	64.6	29.0
19.2	13.5	7.0	13.9	7.9	29.2	64.8	53.4	22.9
19.1	14.9	7.6	14.6	9.6	31.5	61.5	52.9	24.4
20.3	15.2	7.5	15.7	10.0	28.0	59.2	52.1	31.0
21.1	17.1	8.8	16.7	11.9	33.1	65.1	56.2	22.6
23.3	19.0	9.4	18.8	14.4	36.5	63.1	55.4	27.4
22.7	17.0	10.6	18.2	12.5	38.0	72.9	81.7	27.6
20.3	14.6	10.1	15.3	10.0	34.5	82.0	83.7	27.6
20.6	16.8	10.7	15.3	11.9	35.2	74.4	58.8	30.7
18.2	13.9	9.3	13.0	9.6	28.9	90.0	81.7	38.3
14.1	11.7	8.6	8.9	7.6	22.7	121.8	92.0	40.0
16.1	12.6	9.8	9.8	7.7	24.2	92.2	89.7	39.1
17.4	12.0	11.0	11.1	7.5	27.0	80.7	109.8	33.3
19.5	14.5	11.9	12.8	8.7	27.3	76.3	84.8	31.7
19.7	10.2	8.8	11.1	5.3	16.4	88.6	118.2	42.4
18.2	8.1	11.4	9.6	3.5	20.0	92.9	138.9	30.6
20.6	13.3	11.5	11.5	6.5	20.9	77.4	75.7	29.6
20.8	15.6	13.3	11.7	8.0	23.9	78.4	63.5	25.3
20.8	15.0	11.0	11.3	6.9	18.3	81.2	70.8	31.3
20.5	14.6	10.6	10.9	6.6	16.5	91.8	66.5	32.1
17.5	10.5	11.4	7.8	4.2	16.5	121.9	105.7	33.3
16.9	9.1	11.5	7.9	3.5	16.4	128.5	131.5	32.2
11.4	6.4	12.5	4.7	2.3	17.2	193.1	183.7	29.8
12.8	n.a.	n.a.	5.4	n.a.	n.a.	156.4	95.2	n.a.
13.7	n.a.	n.a.	6.3	n.a.	n.a.	151.3	n.a.	n.a.

to stagnation since the mid-1970s, in the face of recessions and rising costs of synthetic fibers after the oil shocks. Nonetheless, technological change and relatively high investment have sustained industry profitability by reducing labor requirements. Although employment has suffered as a result, the industry still has larger total employment than any other manufacturing sector except apparel, surpassing both automobiles and steel. And in 1986, the industry enjoyed a strong recovery in output and profits, while its employment level stopped declining at least temporarily (table 2.1). As discussed below, the favorable performance of textiles in external trade in recent years (except in 1984–86) tends to confirm that the industry has been making a successful adjustment and is relatively competitive.

Employment, Production, and Profits in Apparel

Real production in apparel has also been relatively flat in recent years, after buoyant growth in the 1960s (table 2.1). From 1960–61 to 1972–73, output grew at 3.1 percent annually, but from 1972–73 to 1985–86 the rate fell to only 1.1 percent. Slower demand growth in the face of recession, as well as rising imports, accounted for the slowdown in domestic output growth. As growth declined, employment shifted from substantial growth to gradual decline. Thus, employment grew at 1.1 percent annually from 1960–61 to 1972–73, but declined at 1.5 percent annually from 1972–73 to 1985–86. Nonetheless, slower productivity growth in apparel than in textiles has meant that the rate of decline in employment since the early 1970s has been much lower in apparel (1.5 percent annually versus 2.9 percent) even though the rate of growth of real output has been relatively close in the two industries (1.1 percent in apparel versus 0.45 percent in textiles).

The investment data in table 2.2 indicate one reason for slow growth of labor productivity in apparel. Although total output in apparel is approximately the same magnitude as in textiles (some $50 billion each), investment in apparel has been only one-third to one-half as large as in textiles.

A striking feature of the apparel industry is that its profits are relatively high, despite the sector's image of great stress. Profits averaged 9.0 percent of value added in 1960–72, 11.2 percent in 1974–79, and 11.8 percent in 1980–82. The ratio of this indicator for apparel to its level for US manufacturing rose steadily, from 0.47 in the first period to 0.56 in the second and 0.77 in the third. Apparel has become more profitable in relative terms, not less. Moreover, if measured from another standpoint more relevant to the incentive to expand activity—the rate of return on capital—profitability in apparel appears high indeed. Before-tax profits averaged 30.4 percent of gross capital stock in 1960–72, 20.5 percent in 1973–79, and 16.7 percent in 1980–82, and stood well above twice the ratio for US manufacturing for the period as a whole.

The data presented in table 2.2 thus indicate what may be called a profits paradox in apparel. Profits appear to have been relatively high and rising, even though the sector is widely considered to have been under stress. The paradox goes further. As noted below, real product prices for apparel have been falling. Deflating by the consumer price index, the price index for product shipments of the domestic industry in apparel declined by 27.5

percent from 1972–73 to 1984–85 in real terms. Using the GDP deflator for manufacturing, the corresponding real price of apparel production shipments declined by 9.3 percent (table 2.7, below).

Two influences appear to be important in resolving the seeming profit paradox in apparel. First, the price of the largest input into apparel—textiles—was also lagging general inflation by the early 1980s compared to the mid-1970s (in part as a reflection of lagging oil prices by 1982). Thus, the price index for apparel product shipments in 1980–82 stood at virtually the same ratio to the corresponding index for textiles as it did in 1974–79 (0.978 versus 0.970, respectively; table 2.7). For a critical input accounting for approximately one-third of the gross output value of apparel, then, costs were not rising more rapidly than product price. (Even for other material costs, the relative price erosion of apparel output was much more limited if, as would seem appropriate, the manufacturing deflator rather than the consumer price index is applied as the relevant yardstick.)

Secondly, there was a systematic wage squeeze in apparel. As analyzed in chapter 4, apparel wages relative to the average wage for manufacturing have fallen steadily since the late 1960s. From the period 1974–79 to 1980–82, the nominal wage in apparel did rise by somewhat more than the nominal price of apparel production (33.9 percent versus 28.6 percent); however, real average labor productivity rose by more than enough to compensate (9.2 percent), so that the dollar value of output per dollar spent on wages actually increased (by 4.9 percent; calculated from tables 2.7 and 4.2).

In summary, lagging costs of textile and labor inputs into apparel have meant that profits have been on a relatively favorable and improving path over time despite the significant lag of apparel product prices behind the overall consumer price index.[10]

With profits high relative to US manufacturing, apparel might have been expected to show high investment and productivity growth. Instead, its investment has lagged that of textiles. Whereas the bulk of profits in textiles have been used for new investment, relatively little reinvestment of profits has occurred in apparel. Thus, table 2.2 shows that investment has averaged only 31 percent of profits for apparel (1960–82), while the same ratio has averaged 88.7 percent for textiles and 88.1 percent for US manufacturing.

These trends suggest that apparel is a sector of comfortably high profit return to capital, in which most of the profit is distributed to shareholders

---

10. Note, however, that in one dimension apparel profitability may be overstated. The capital base considered here refers to plant and equipment but excludes inventories. To the extent that apparel inventories tend to be relatively high, the return on total capital may be less favorable relative to the manufacturing average than is suggested in table 2.2.

instead of being reinvested to improve international competitiveness. Moreover, trade policy appears to have contributed to this posture of the industry. There is some correlation between profit rates and the phasing in of US protection. The three periods of successively higher relative profit performance cited above (1960–72, 1973–79, 1980–82) coincide broadly with phases of successively higher protection (with comprehensive quotas on multi-fiber apparel beginning in 1973, and a tightening of the quota regime in 1977 and again in the early 1980s). High profits associated with high protection are of course precisely the wrong signal for adjustment through reallocation of resources into other sectors; instead, they attract still more resources to the protected sector. Their margin of comfort to firms may also have undermined the incentive to raise productivity by increasing the fraction of profits invested closer to the manufacturing average.

Trends in Trade

Table 2.3 shows US trade, production, and domestic consumption in *textiles* from 1961 to 1986. The data indicate a surprisingly limited role of imports in textiles, despite a surge in 1984 and, to a lesser degree, in 1986. As deflated by the price index for US domestic product shipments (from the Commerce Department), real imports grew at an average annual rate of 7.0 percent from 1961–62 through 1972–73. Then real textile imports actually declined and remained at a lower plateau through 1980. Although they then rose again, by 1983 their level was still only 5.6 percent above the previous 1972 peak. In 1984, in contrast, imports soared by 34.4 percent in real terms. After a relative lull in 1985, when real imports rose by 5.5 percent, they rose rapidly again in 1986—by 20.5 percent. For this whole period 1972–73 to 1985–86, real import value grew at only 4.1 percent annually— actually less than the notional 6 percent rate originally incorporated in the Multi-Fiber Arrangement (chapter 6).

As analyzed in chapter 3, the surge of imports in 1984 was closely related to overvaluation of the dollar. The reacceleration in 1986 also appears to have been related to dollar strength after proper allowance for time lags from exchange rate to price, from price to contracts, and from contracts to trade flows. In addition, preemptive purchasing to beat tighter protection feared from renegotiation of the Multi-Fiber Arrangement may have played a role in the acceleration of import growth in 1986. However, in 1987 import growth in textiles appeared to be slowing down. Data for the first four months indicated that physical volume of imports (square-yard equivalent,

Table 2.3 Trade and domestic consumption: textiles
(million dollars)

Year	Nominal				Real 1982 prices[a]				M/C (per-centage)
	M	X	TB	C[b]	M	X	TB	C[b]	
1961	590	320	−270	13,151	1,016	551	−465	22,657	4.5
1962	699	300	−399	14,435	1,190	511	−679	24,584	4.8
1963	745	307	−438	15,136	1,562	644	−918	31,742	4.9
1964	759	340	−419	16,292	1,532	686	−846	32,885	4.7
1965	858	391	−467	17,547	1,690	770	−920	34,554	4.9
1966	941	405	−536	18,837	1,857	799	−1,058	37,177	5.0
1967	803	377	−426	18,928	1,542	724	−818	36,347	4.2
1968	934	351	−583	21,097	1,679	631	−1,048	37,928	4.4
1969	970	418	−552	22,007	1,686	726	−960	38,248	4.4
1970	1,058	461	−597	21,709	1,910	832	−1,078	39,188	4.9
1971	1,248	465	−783	23,221	2,285	851	−1,434	42,521	5.4
1972	1,345	603	−742	26,644	2,389	1,071	−1,318	47,326	5.0
1973	1,423	926	−497	29,550	2,260	1,470	−790	46,923	4.8
1974	1,407	1,284	−123	31,000	1,944	1,774	−170	42,840	4.5
1975	1,107	1,157	50	29,158	1,585	1,657	72	41,760	3.8
1976	1,392	1,399	7	34,253	1,874	1,883	9	46,106	4.1
1977	1,489	1,345	−144	38,198	1,958	1,769	−189	50,239	3.9
1978	1,855	1,466	−389	40,590	2,351	1,858	−493	51,438	4.6
1979	1,834	2,130	296	42,349	2,205	2,561	356	50,909	4.3
1980	2,034	2,488	454	44,320	2,245	2,746	501	48,922	4.6
1981	2,482	2,326	−156	47,897	2,503	2,346	−157	48,303	5.2
1982	2,225	1,766	−459	45,375	2,225	1,766	−459	45,375	4.9
1983	2,557	1,560	−997	51,482	2,523	1,539	−984	50,796	5.0
1984	3,539	1,541	−1,998	54,256	3,390	1,476	−1,914	51,979	6.5
1985	3,697	1,462	−2,235	52,382	3,575	1,414	−2,161	50,660	7.1
1986	4,322	1,751	−2,571	54,488	4,309	1,660	−2,649	51,859	7.9

M imports; X exports; TB trade balance; C apparent consumption.
Source: See table 2.1.
a. Deflating by textile product shipments price index, US Department of Commerce.
b. Equals production (table 2.1) *plus* imports *minus* exports.

SYE) rose by only 0.7 percent above the level of the same period in 1986, while the dollar value of imports rose 9.8 percent.[11]

As US imports of textiles stagnated through the 1970s, exports rose. The trade balance thus shifted from a deficit of $783 million in 1971 or −3.5

11. US Department of Commerce, "Textile and Apparel Import Report" (Washington: Department of Commerce, 16 June 1987; processed).

percent of output, to a surplus of $454 million in 1980, or + 1.0 percent of output. Only by 1983 did a sizable trade deficit reemerge, at approximately $1 billion. The deficit rose to $2.6 billion (5.0 percent of output) by 1986.

Trade performance in textiles has thus been surprisingly strong for a sector accorded chronic trade protection on grounds of vulnerability to imports. The final column in table 2.3 confirms this pattern, indicating that import penetration was low and stable in a range of 4 percent to 5 percent of consumption from 1961 through 1983, exceeding this range only in 1984–86.[12] As analyzed below, the deterioration of textile trade performance by 1984 was closely linked to the overvaluation of the dollar. Except for this aberration, the trade position of textiles actually strengthened in the 1970s and early 1980s as indicated by the trade balance. Capitalization and labor-saving technological change have been the main reasons for the industry's ability not only to withstand imports but also to expand its export base.

The growth of imports is even smaller if judged by alternative measures. Table 2.3 estimates real imports by deflating current dollar values by the price index for domestic industry product shipments, under the assumption that prices for constant-quality imports rose at rates identical to those of domestic output. The alternative of deflating by unit values of imports would probably be misleading because quota protection gave an incentive for upgrading—raising observed import unit values without implying an increase in price for imports of unchanged quality. Table 2.4 reports the physical volume of imports in square-yard equivalents as measured by the US International Trade Commission (USITC) in its monitoring of textile-apparel trade. These data refer to products covered by the Multi-Fiber Arrangement, accounting for the bulk, but not all, of textile and apparel products. On this basis, real imports fell by one-half from their 1972 peak to 1980, and by 1986 stood at 72.1 percent above the 1972 level (as opposed to 80.4 percent on the measure used in table 2.3). However, because of product upgrading, the square-yard equivalent measure probably under-states real import growth; and the rising role of fibers not covered by the MFA until mid-1986 (silk, ramie, jute) may further understate import growth in the SYE data.

A third alternative measure also shows lower import growth than the central measure used in table 2.3. If general wholesale prices are used as the deflator (table 2.4), real imports by 1986 stood at only 27.6 percent above their earlier 1972 peak (rather than 80.4 percent above it). The divergence

---

12. The table uses Department of Commerce data for import penetration. As discussed below in the context of apparel, alternative definitions can give somewhat higher import penetration estimates.

stems from the fact that textile prices have lagged substantially behind general wholesale prices. This alternative measure also probably understates import growth, however, because it implies that import prices rose more sharply than domestic textile prices, which is unlikely given the relatively stable share of imports in consumption.

The divergences between the data in table 2.4 for physical volume and real value reflect in part the process of product upgrading. From 1964–65 to 1971–72, the physical volume (SYE) of imports rose by a multiple of 3.36 while the real value of imports (domestic output deflator basis) rose by a multiple of only 1.45. In this period, the average real value per square yard thus declined by 57 percent, in part because of the rapid rise of man-made fibers and the declining real price of these new materials. After 1972—when bilateral US quotas inaugurated the regime of protection formalized in the 1973 MFA—this process reversed sharply. Faced by quantitative limits, foreign suppliers upgraded their products. From 1971–72 to 1979–80, the physical volume of imports fell by 49.5 percent, while their real value declined by only 4.8 percent, indicating a rise of 88.6 percent in the real value of imports per square-yard equivalent.[13]

In sum, consideration of the physical volume of imports as well as their real value measured by alternative deflators confirms that textile imports have risen relatively slowly through most of the past two decades, with the exception of a surge in 1984 and, to a lesser extent, 1986. Part of this slow growth may be explained by protection, even though the process of product upgrading has moderated the restrictive effect of quotas. However, in view of the industry's improving export performance through much of this period, the industry's increasing competitiveness may be as relevant as protection in explaining the general absence of rapid import growth.

The *apparel* industry has experienced far more pressure from rising imports than the textiles sector. From 1961–62 to 1972–73, real imports grew at 15.5 percent annually—much more rapidly than domestic consumption (3.6 percent annual growth; table 2.5). From 1972–73 to 1981–82, in the face of new protection the growth of real imports slowed to 9.7 percent annually, on a basis of values deflated by the price index for domestic industry product shipments. In the same period real consumption slowed to annual growth of 1.7 percent. Then in 1983–85, as the US economy recovered and the dollar became severely overvalued, the real value of imports surged, by 16.5 percent in 1983, 37.4 percent in 1984, and 10.4 percent in 1985 (while real consumption rose by a total of 16.1 percent over the same period, a rapid

---

13. Chapter 7 presents a more complete analysis of the process of upgrading, taking account of different coverage of the *Industrial Outlook* data and the MFA-based *Major Shippers* data, both issued by the US Department of Commerce.

Table 2.4 Alternative measures of real textile imports, 1964–86

Year	Million square yards (MFA category imports)			Million dollars at 1982 prices Textile deflator		
	Amount	Index 1982 = 100	Percentage change	Amount	Index 1982 = 100	Percentage change
1964	963	37.7	n.a.	1,532	68.9	n.a.
1965	1,380	54.1	43.3	1,690	76.0	10.3
1966	2,024	79.3	46.7	1,857	83.5	9.9
1967	1,695	66.4	− 16.3	1,542	69.3	− 17.0
1968	2,145	84.0	26.5	1,679	75.5	8.9
1969	2,105	82.5	− 1.9	1,686	75.8	0.4
1970	2,772	108.6	31.7	1,910	85.8	13.3
1971	3,853	150.9	39.0	2,285	102.7	19.6
1972	4,010	157.1	4.1	2,389	107.4	4.6
1973	3,035	118.9	− 24.3	2,260	101.6	− 5.4
1974	2,473	96.9	− 18.5	1,944	87.4	− 14.0
1975	1,751	68.6	− 29.2	1,585	71.2	− 18.5
1976	2,560	100.3	46.2	1,874	84.2	18.2
1977	2,511	98.4	− 1.9	1,958	88.0	4.5
1978	2,834	111.0	12.9	2,351	105.7	20.1
1979	1,968	77.1	− 30.6	2,205	99.1	− 6.2
1980	2,000	78.3	1.6	2,245	100.9	1.8
1981	2,626	102.9	31.3	2,503	112.5	11.5
1982	2,553	100.0	− 2.8	2,225	100.0	− 11.1
1983	3,537	138.5	38.5	2,523	113.4	13.4
1984	5,437	213.0	53.7	3,390	152.4	34.4
1985	5,713	223.8	5.1	3,575	160.7	5.5
1986	6,902	270.4	20.8	4,309	193.7	20.5

n.a. not available

Source: US International Trade Commission, *The History and Current Status of the Multifiber Arrangement,* USITC Publication 850, January 1978, and *US Imports of Textile and Apparel Products Under the Multifiber Arrangement,* USITC Publication 1863, June 1986; IMF, *International Financial Statistics, Yearbook 1986;* US Department of Commerce, *U.S. Industrial Outlook,* 1987, and by communication.

post-recession increase but still much smaller than the percentage rise in imports).

By 1986, apparel imports were still growing rapidly, although at a pace well below that of the 1984 surge. The principal measure of real apparel imports (value deflated by domestic product shipments price index) increased by 13.2 percent in 1986; physical volume in SYE also rose at this

	Million dollars at 1982 prices Wholesale deflator	
Amount	Index 1982 = 100	Percentage change
2,399	107.8	n.a.
2,659	119.5	10.8
2,822	126.8	6.2
2,403	108.0	− 14.8
2,727	122.6	13.5
2,726	122.5	0.0
2,869	129.0	5.2
3,275	147.2	14.1
3,381	151.9	3.2
3,161	142.1	− 6.5
2,631	118.2	− 16.8
1,895	85.2	− 28.0
2,277	102.3	20.1
2,295	103.1	0.8
2,652	119.2	15.6
2,330	104.7	− 12.1
2,264	101.8	− 2.8
2,532	113.8	11.8
2,225	100.0	− 12.1
2,525	113.5	13.5
3,414	153.4	35.2
3,583	161.1	5.0
4,314	193.9	20.4

rate. Rapid growth continued into early 1987, when for the first four months the physical volume of imports stood 12.5 percent above the level of the same period in 1986, and the dollar value of imports rose by 21.2 percent. The lagged effects of a strong dollar and possible preemptive buying related to MFA renegotiation in 1986 and threatened quota legislation in 1987 appear to have dominated the still high rate of import growth. Note in addition that the spread between quantity and dollar value growth appeared to be reflecting the initial phase of the J curve, as a lower dollar meant higher dollar price for imports.

Apparel exports showed a surprising dynamism from 1973 to 1980, as they grew at 16.2 percent annually in real terms. However, the larger base

Table 2.5   Trade and domestic consumption: apparel
(million dollars)

Year	Nominal M	Nominal X	Nominal TB	Nominal C[b]	Real 1982 prices[a] M	Real 1982 prices[a] X	Real 1982 prices[a] TB	Real 1982 prices[a] C[b]	M/C (percentage)
1961	283	159	−124	13,212	648	364	−284	30,273	2.1
1962	374	152	−222	14,170	838	341	−497	31,767	2.6
1963	400	158	−242	15,060	901	356	−545	33,934	2.7
1964	481	196	−285	15,799	1,062	433	−629	34,887	3.0
1965	568	177	−391	16,817	1,254	391	−863	37,135	3.4
1966	637	188	−449	17,757	1,389	410	−979	38,726	3.6
1967	692	207	−485	18,968	1,416	424	−992	38,823	3.6
1968	900	220	−680	20,308	1,764	431	−1,333	39,811	4.4
1969	1,149	242	−907	21,952	2,123	447	−1,676	40,555	5.2
1970	1,286	250	−1,036	21,430	2,192	426	−1,766	36,531	6.0
1971	1,574	258	−1,316	23,003	2,650	434	−2,216	38,726	6.8
1972	1,967	300	−1,667	25,581	3,470	529	−2,941	45,133	7.7
1973	2,261	381	−1,880	27,850	3,773	636	−3,137	46,472	8.1
1974	2,465	593	−1,872	28,727	3,726	896	−2,830	43,425	8.6
1975	2,775	603	−2,172	29,270	4,124	896	−3,228	43,498	9.5
1976	3,912	740	−3,172	33,191	5,516	1,043	−4,473	46,801	11.8
1977	4,393	859	−3,534	38,767	5,796	1,133	−4,663	51,148	11.3
1978	5,722	1,035	−4,687	42,352	7,315	1,323	−5,992	54,372	13.5
1979	5,902	1,387	−4,515	41,865	7,163	1,683	−5,480	50,810	14.1
1980	6,543	1,604	−4,939	45,232	7,428	1,821	−5,607	51,349	14.5
1981	7,752	1,628	−6,124	50,198	8,122	1,706	−6,416	52,592	15.4
1982	8,516	1,236	−7,280	53,961	8,516	1,236	−7,280	53,961	15.8
1983	10,018	1,049	−8,969	58,392	9,918	1,039	−8,879	57,812	17.2
1984	14,001	1,026	−12,975	63,647	13,632	999	−12,633	61,968	22.0
1985	15,711	991	−14,720	65,424	15,044	949	−14,095	62,646	24.0
1986	17,744	1,102	−16,642	69,965	17,035	1,044	−15,991	65,539	25.4

M imports; X exports; TB trade balance; C apparent consumption.
Source: See table 2.1.
a. Deflating by apparel product shipments price index, US Department of Commerce.
b. Equals production (table 2.1) *plus* imports *minus* exports.

of imports meant that, even with slower growth, their absolute increase caused the trade deficit in apparel to rise (from 6.8 percent of production in 1973 to 11.3 percent in 1980). Then from 1980 to 1985 apparel export performance reversed, and real exports fell by half while the trade deficit widened to 29.1 percent of domestic output. In 1986, real apparel exports reversed and rose by 10 percent (perhaps reflecting a shorter lag than imports in response to the dollar's decline). Nonetheless, the trade deficit widened further to 32.3 percent of output.

The final column of table 2.5 summarizes the sector's trade difficulties in a constantly rising ratio of import penetration (imports relative to consumption). Imports rose from the range of 2–3 percent of consumption in the early 1960s to 6–8 percent in the early 1970s, 9–11 percent by the mid-1970s, and 14–17 percent in 1978–82. With the import surge beginning in 1983, the import penetration ratio rose to 17.2 percent in 1983, 22.0 percent in 1984, 24.0 percent in 1985, and 25.4 percent in 1986.

Two paradoxes emerge in the estimates here. The first is that the apparel sector was able to obtain import protection at such low rates of initial import penetration. Cotton products have been protected since 1962, when import penetration was only 2.6 percent. Much broader protection began in 1972, when import penetration was less than 8 percent. Even allowing for differences under other measurements of import penetration (as discussed below), the sector's ability to secure special (and extensive) protection at such low rates of import penetration is a testimony to the perceived importance and political clout of this industry, the largest employer among all US manufacturing sectors.[14]

The second paradox is that real apparel imports have risen at relatively rapid rates despite protection. The Multi-Fiber Arrangement originally envisioned 6 percent annual growth in imports, and its subsequent renewals have provided for much lower growth. Yet, as noted, the real value of imports grew at an average annual rate of 9.7 percent in the period 1972–73 to 1981–82 even before the 1983–84 surge.

A major part of the explanation of this second paradox is that the MFA is structured in terms of limits on physical quantities of imports, whereas product upgrading has made it possible for the real value of imports to rise more rapidly than their physical volume. In fact, the physical volume of apparel imports actually declined from 1972 to 1974 and by 1977 still remained at its 1972 level (SYE, table 2.6). Although the physical volume of imports then began to grow again, for the period 1972–73 to 1981–82 it grew at an average annual rate of only 4.7 percent, well below the notional 6 percent of the MFA. Then the physical volume of imports began to rise rapidly, at 15.3 percent, 20.9 percent, 8.6 percent, and 13.2 percent in 1983 through 1986, respectively. By 1986, the rapid growth in the 1980s had raised the cumulative average growth rate of the physical volume of apparel imports to 7.1 percent annually since 1972, modestly above the original MFA target of 6 percent.

---

14. Elsewhere I have presented statistical tests showing the important roles of sectoral employment size, on one hand, and import penetration, on the other, in explaining which industrial sectors receive protection. William R. Cline, *Exports of Manufactures from Developing Countries: Performance and Prospects for Market Access* (Washington: Brookings Institution, 1984).

Table 2.6　Alternative measures of real apparel imports, 1964–86

Year	Million square yards (MFA category imports)			Million dollars at 1982 prices Apparel deflator		
	Amount	Index 1982 = 100	Percentage change	Amount	Index 1982 = 100	Percentage change
1964	561	16.6	n.a.	1,062	12.5	n.a.
1965	684	20.2	21.9	1,254	14.7	18.1
1966	777	23.0	13.6	1,389	16.3	10.8
1967	877	25.9	12.9	1,416	16.6	1.9
1968	1,152	34.1	31.4	1,764	20.7	24.6
1969	1,520	44.9	31.9	2,123	24.9	20.4
1970	1,686	49.9	10.9	2,192	25.7	3.3
1971	2,098	62.0	24.4	2,650	31.1	20.9
1972	2,226	65.8	6.1	3,470	40.7	30.9
1973	2,090	61.8	− 6.1	3,773	44.3	8.7
1974	1,937	57.3	− 7.3	3,726	43.8	− 1.2
1975	2,077	61.4	7.2	4,124	48.4	10.7
1976	2,428	71.8	16.9	5,516	64.8	33.8
1977	2,466	72.9	1.6	5,796	68.1	5.1
1978	2,905	85.9	17.8	7,315	85.9	26.2
1979	2,671	79.0	− 8.1	7,163	84.1	− 2.1
1980	2,884	85.3	8.0	7,428	87.2	3.7
1981	3,136	92.7	8.7	8,122	95.4	9.3
1982	3,382	100.0	7.8	8,516	100.0	4.9
1983	3,899	115.3	15.3	9,918	116.5	16.5
1984	4,714	139.4	20.9	13,632	160.1	37.4
1985	5,120	151.4	8.6	15,044	176.7	10.4
1986	5,796	171.4	13.2	17,035	200.0	13.2

n.a. not available.
Source: See table 2.4.

The differences between the slower growth rates of physical volume and the more rapid growth of real value, especially in earlier years, represented product upgrading. Chapter 7 examines this phenomenon in detail. It also analyzes a second reason for the paradox of rapid import growth despite MFA protection: flexibility in this protection, including incomplete coverage of products and countries by quotas as well as scope for temporary swings in controlled imports.

The difference between growth in real value and physical volume of imports narrows substantially if the general wholesale price index is used, rather than the domestic apparel output deflator, to deflate the current value

| | Million dollars at 1982 prices | |
| | Wholesale deflator | |
Amount	Index 1982 = 100	Percentage change
1,520	17.8	n.a.
1,760	20.7	15.8
1,910	22.4	8.6
2,071	24.3	8.4
2,628	30.9	26.9
3,229	37.9	22.9
3,488	41.0	8.0
4,131	48.5	18.4
4,944	58.1	19.7
5,023	59.0	1.6
4,609	54.1	−8.2
4,750	55.8	3.1
6,398	75.1	34.7
6,770	79.5	5.8
8,182	96.1	20.9
7,499	88.1	−8.3
7,284	85.5	−2.9
7,908	92.9	8.6
8,516	100.0	7.7
9,894	116.2	16.2
13,506	158.6	36.5
15,228	178.8	12.8
17,712	208.0	16.3

of imports (table 2.6). On this basis, from 1972–73 to 1981–82 real import value grew at only 5.7 percent, instead of the 9.7 percent estimated using the domestic apparel output deflator. Even more than in the case of textiles, however, it is unlikely that prices for imported apparel of constant quality increased relative to domestic prices, given the rapid rise of import purchase. Accordingly, the domestic output deflator appears more appropriate than the wholesale price index. As in the case of textiles, the divergence between the two indicates that apparel prices (for both imports and domestic output) lagged substantially behind general wholesale prices.

To recapitulate, apparel imports have grown relatively rapidly despite protection. In terms of real value, imports grew at over 15 percent annually in the 1960s and early 1970s; at nearly 10 percent annually from the mid-

1970s to the early 1980s; and at over 20 percent annually in the 1983–84 surge, before returning to an average annual rate of about 12 percent in 1985–86. This persistent growth has increased import penetration from only 2 percent of consumption in the early 1960s to 25 percent by 1986 (under a narrow measure before expansion of import value from f.o.b. to wholesale-levels). Product upgrading in the face of physical quota limits has been a major source of the growth of real import value, and indeed for most of the MFA period the physical volume of imports has grown at rates below the 6 percent rate originally envisioned in the mechanism. Flexibility in the MFA (now disappearing) allowed the surge of imports beginning in 1983 as pressure from the overvalued dollar became intense (chapters 3 and 7).

Trends in Consumption

Trade and employment problems in the textile and apparel sectors have been aggravated in recent years by slow growth in domestic consumption. On the basis of tables 2.3 and 2.5, from the period 1961–62/1972–73 to the period 1972–73/1985–86 real consumption growth decelerated from 6.5 percent to 0.65 percent annually for textiles and from 3.6 percent to 2.7 percent for apparel. Rapid growth in textiles consumption in the first period may have been in response to falling real prices attributable to the rising role of synthetic fibers at declining costs. Thus, deflating by the consumer price index, textile output prices fell by 28.8 percent from 1961–62 to 1972–73 (table 2.7).

Relative textile prices continued to decline in 1972–73 to 1984–85 (by 28.8 percent, table 2.7) but consumption growth fell sharply. In this period a dominant influence was the deceleration of growth in apparel production (from 3.1 percent to 1.1 percent annually)—considering that apparel is a major source of demand for textile products. Technological changes, such as the shift to radial tires (and the reduction in demand for tire fabric), may also have contributed to the relative deceleration in textile demand. In addition, because the textile cycle tends to move with the cyclical movement of total consumer demand, the more severe recessionary experience in the period following 1973 than in the previous decade may also be a factor in the slowdown of growth in textile consumption. Nonetheless, the size of this deceleration remains to some extent an enigma.[15]

---

15. Recent GATT and OECD studies on the textile sector find it more difficult to analyze textile demand than that for apparel, in part for lack of meaningful data. For example, fiber consumption understates demand growth because of technical change reducing fiber input per unit of textile and clothing output. GATT, *Textiles and Clothing*, pp. 28–33; OECD, *Textile and Clothing Industries*, pp. 28–35.

Table 2.7   Relative prices of textiles and apparel, 1960–85
(1980 = 100)

	Textiles			Apparel		
Year	Nominal deflator	Price[a] A	Price[a] B	Nominal deflator	Price[a] A	Price[a] B
1960	59.8	195.1	140.4	42.1	137.3	98.8
1961	58.0	187.3	135.8	43.6	140.8	102.1
1962	58.7	187.4	136.2	44.6	142.3	103.5
1963	47.7	150.3	112.8	44.4	139.9	105.0
1964	49.5	154.2	116.7	45.3	140.9	106.8
1965	50.8	155.4	118.4	45.3	138.5	105.6
1966	50.7	150.7	116.0	45.9	136.4	105.0
1967	52.1	150.6	116.0	48.9	141.2	108.9
1968	55.6	154.3	119.1	51.0	141.5	109.2
1969	57.5	151.5	120.0	54.1	142.5	112.9
1970	55.4	137.7	111.2	58.7	145.8	117.9
1971	54.6	130.2	106.0	59.4	141.6	115.3
1972	56.3	129.9	108.1	56.7	130.8	108.8
1973	63.0	136.8	120.0	59.9	130.2	114.1
1974	72.4	141.6	126.6	66.2	129.5	115.7
1975	69.8	125.2	106.9	67.3	120.7	103.1
1976	74.3	126.0	109.1	70.9	120.3	104.1
1977	76.0	121.1	105.4	75.8	120.7	105.1
1978	78.9	116.8	104.0	78.2	115.7	103.0
1979	83.2	110.6	103.2	82.4	109.6	102.2
1980	90.6	106.1	103.8	88.1	103.2	100.9
1981	99.2	105.2	104.3	95.4	101.3	100.3
1982	100.0	100.0	100.0	100.0	100.0	100.0
1983	101.4	98.2	99.7	101.0	97.9	99.3
1984	104.4	97.0	101.9	102.7	95.4	100.2
1985	103.4	92.8	101.0	104.6	93.9	102.0
1986	105.5	92.8	102.8	107.6	94.7	104.8

Source: IMF, *International Financial Statistics, Yearbook 1986;* US Department of Commerce, *U.S. Industrial Outlook* 1986 and 1987, and by communication; Council of Economic Advisers, *Economic Report of the President* (Washington: CEA, February 1986), pp. 264–65, and 1987, pp. 264–65.
a. Deflating by consumer price index (A) or GDP deflator for manufacturing (B).

In apparel, consumption was more in line with what would have been expected from population and income growth, combined with price movements. From 1961–62 to 1972–73, real consumption of apparel grew at 3.6

percent annually, or at a rate or 2.4 percent in per capita terms, while per capita income grew at 2.9 percent. In 1972–73 to 1984–85, real consumption grew at 2.6 percent annually and per capita consumption at 1.6 percent, while per capita income grew at 1.8 percent.[16] Accordingly, the apparent income elasticity of demand for apparel (with respect to per capita income, and before taking account of price effects) was approximately 0.85 over the full period. Apparel consumption has been growing at the rate of population growth (approximately 1 percent) plus almost the full growth rate of per capita income.

Houthakker and Taylor have estimated the long-term income elasticity of demand for apparel at 0.51.[17] The OECD argues that because of Engels' law on the declining relative demand for basic goods, the income elasticity for clothing is well below unity—although its empirical estimate for the elasticity rises from 0.4 unadjusted to 1.0 after adjusting for demographic change.[18] Rapid growth in demand in the 1960s and early 1970s was related importantly to the arrival of the postwar baby-boom cohorts to the teen and young-adult years. The apparent income elasticity of unity in the last two decades represents a true income elasticity of perhaps 0.5 to 0.7, plus the added effect of demographic patterns and declining relative prices for apparel. Thus, from 1961–62 to 1972–73, apparel output prices deflated by general consumer prices declined by 7.8 percent; from 1972–73 to 1984–85 there was an additional decline of 27.5 percent (table 2.7).

In sum, consumption of textiles has grown slowly, and that of apparel has grown only at about the rate of total income (per capita income plus population growth). Growth in textile demand weakened substantially in the last decade after rapid growth in the 1970s; and while apparel growth has been steadier in relation income growth, the sector has relatively low income elasticity of demand. As a result, annual consumption growth has averaged only about two-thirds of 1 percent annually for textiles and some 2½ percent for apparel since the inception of the MFA in the early 1970s. Moreover, much of this growth was associated with declining relative prices, suggesting that at constant prices demand growth would have been slower.

---

16. Real per capita income growth is calculated from real GNP and population as reported in IMF, *International Financial Statistics, Yearbook 1985* and February 1987.

17. H.S. Houthakker and Lester D. Taylor, *Consumer Demand in the United States: Analyses and Projections* (Cambridge, Mass.: Harvard University Press, 1970), pp. 166. Note that the authors find a higher short-term income elasticity: 1.14. In fact, they describe clothing as a "consumer durable," for which purchases depend on the existing stock. For such goods (automobiles, for instance), the short-run income elasticity tends to be high because purchases can be put off during bad years and accelerated during good.

18. OECD, *Textile and Clothing Industries*, pp. 29–30.

With imports growing faster than consumption (especially in apparel), the scope for domestic output growth declined below the already slow growth of consumption.

An alternative data source for apparel consumption suggests more rapid growth. Estimates by the Bureau of Labor Statistics (BLS) for consumption at the household level (for the category "apparel less footwear"), as deflated by the corresponding component of the consumer price index, indicate that from 1961–62 to 1973–72 real consumption of apparel grew at 4.2 percent annually (rather than 3.6 percent based on the data of table 2.5), and from 1972–73 to 1984–85 the rate was 4.7 percent (rather than 2.6 percent).[19] If the BLS estimates for the latter period are correct, the apparent income elasticity of demand would be a high 2.1 (3.7 percent per capita consumption growth divided by 1.8 percent per capita income growth).

Because the analysis of this study requires compatible data relating imports to domestic production, consumption, and exports, the industry-based (Standard Industrial Classification, SIC, category 23) data reported in table 2.5 are considered the principal source for consumption estimates. Nonetheless, the alternative BLS series suggests that the basic consumption growth estimates used here may be understated. This possibility is especially important for the long-term projections of chapter 10. In effect, the use of the lower rates of growth for apparel consumption means that the projections of chapter 10 may overstate future job losses in the sector, because they may understate consumption growth and therefore the growth of production and employment.

Measuring Import Penetration

The debate on US trade policy in textiles and apparel has been marked by controversy over the actual degree of import penetration. Advocates of the 1985 bill to cut back imports maintained that in 1984 imports rose to 50 percent of US apparel consumption.[20] Press reports variously indicated apparel import penetration at 30 percent to 43 percent on the basis of estimates by industry analysts.[21] However, the leading opponent of the 1985 bill, Representative Sam Gibbons (D-Fla.), countered that Commerce De-

19. Calculated from US Department of Commerce, *Survey of Current Business,* various issues, and Bureau of Labor Statistics indexes of consumer prices for apparel less footwear, Data Resources, Inc., database.

20. Fiber, Fabric, and Apparel Coalition for Trade, "The Import Crisis in the Fiber, Fabric and Apparel Industries" (Washington: FFACT, 15 March 1985), p. 1; and Amalgamated Clothing and Textile Workers Union as quoted in *New York Times,* 23 July 1985.

21. *New York Times,* 23 June 1985, 10 October 1985; *Journal of Commerce,* 10 July 1985.

partment data showed that imports accounted for only 14 percent of textile and apparel consumption in 1984.[22]

The public debate has tended to imply that, in the absence of imports, domestic producers could provide the previously imported amounts to the market. Implicitly, advocates of protection suggest that US apparel output and employment could virtually double in the absence of imports. While the degree of import penetration is certainly germane in assessing the state of domestic production, it would be highly misleading to infer that US production could rise fully to replace imports. Closure of the market would raise prices and cut back the quantity demanded by the public. Prices would have to rise to induce domestic firms to expand their output. Total sales would be less than before, so that only a portion of the imports eliminated would be replaced by sales of domestic products.

Even if measured accurately, then, the import penetration ratio must be interpreted with care. Unfortunately, the commonly cited measures are often misleading in economic terms. The high estimates—that imports claim half of the US apparel market—refer to physical quantities: millions of square-yard equivalents. On this basis, the best estimate appears to be that in 1984, imports accounted for 33 percent of US consumption of apparel.[23] Considering that from 1984 to 1986 the physical SYE of imports rose by 23 percent (table 2.6) while the physical volume of total consumption seems unlikely to have risen by much more than the approximate magnitude of 6 percent indicated by the estimated real value of consumption (table 2.5), by 1986 the import penetration ratio based on square-yard equivalents was probably in the range of 38 percent.[24] However, because imports tend to be of cheaper products, square-yard equivalents overstate the real economic value of imported goods relative to domestic output.

---

22. *Journal of Commerce,* 11 October 1985.

23. In 1984, total US production of apparel was 10.1 billion square-yard equivalents (SYE). Imports were 4.7 billion SYE, and exports were 0.5 SYE. Apparent domestic consumption was thus 14.3 billion SYE, and the import penetration ratio was 33 percent. US Department of Commerce, by communication.

24. Note that experts from the American Textile Manufacturers Institute (ATMI) have obtained similar estimates for apparel import penetration in the 1984–86 period based on square-yard equivalent volumes. By communication. It may be noted, however, that Frederick B. Dent, President of the Mayfair Mills textile firm of Arcadia, South Carolina, reports that a June 1986 survey of 22 department stores (regionally dispersed) found that of the inventory count of apparel, 60 percent was imported (with the ratio at 57 percent for women's and 63 percent for men's). By communication, 26 June 1986. This high ratio may nonetheless be compatible with the estimates here if the garment count corresponds more to physical volume than to value (and thus would be comparable to the 38 percent volume penetration ratio noted here rather than the 31 percent value ratio calculated below), and if the added uncertainties of supply cause retailers to hold relatively larger inventories relative to sales for imports than for domestically produced garments.

Table 2.8 Adjusted import penetration ratios, value basis[a] (percentage)

Period	Textiles	Apparel	Textiles and apparel
1961–65[b]	6.0	3.7	4.9
1966–70[b]	5.7	6.0	5.9
1971–75[b]	5.8	10.7	8.2
1976–79[b]	5.2	16.3	10.8
1980	5.6	18.4	12.1
1981	6.3	19.5	13.2
1982	5.9	19.9	13.7
1983	6.0	21.6	14.4
1984	7.9	27.3	18.6
1985	8.5	29.6	20.5
1986	9.5	31.1	22.0

Source: Tables 2.3 and 2.5; see text; IMF, *International Financial Statistics*, 1986.
a. US Department of Commerce Import Data (customs value) adjusted upward for insurance and freight and for import duties. Import penetration ratios are equal to adjusted imports divided by apparent consumption (domestic output plus adjusted imports less exports).
b. For multiple years: averages.

The more appropriate measurement of import penetration is on a basis of import value relative to domestic production value. However, the data presented earlier report imports on a customs value basis—essentially their prices as received by foreign exporters. To these values, it is necessary to add insurance and freight to arrive at values relevant to importers (c.i.f.). In addition, it is necessary to incorporate the cost of import duties to reach the price relevant for domestic consumption. In 1984, imports of textiles and apparel on a c.i.f. basis were approximately 7.5 percent more costly than on a customs valuation basis.[25] In recent years tariffs have averaged approximately 27 percent for apparel and 15 percent for textiles (table 6.3). Import values inclusive of tariffs, insurance, and freight have thus averaged approximately 37 percent above customs valuation of imports for apparel and 24 percent for textiles.

Table 2.8 reports the adjusted import penetration ratios. For apparel, the ratio rose from approximately 4–6 percent in the 1960s to 11 percent in the early 1970s, 16 percent in the late 1970s, and 18–20 percent by the early 1980s. Following the surge of imports beginning in 1983, the ratio reached

25. US Department of Commerce, *Highlights of US Export and Import Trade*, FT 990, October 1985, pp. C-6 to C-9.

27.3 percent in 1984, 29.6 percent in 1985, and 31.1 percent in 1986. The best estimate is thus that imports now account for somewhat less than one-third of the value of US apparel consumption. Even if the less meaningful measure of physical units is used, the ratio is less than two-fifths (38 percent, as noted above), still well below the estimate of one-half commonly cited by advocates of import restrictions. For textiles, the import penetration ratios are much lower, standing at slightly less than 10 percent in 1986 (value basis, including adjustment for insurance, freight, and duties).[26]

The adjusted import penetration ratios estimated here are close to those estimated by the World Bank, which placed import penetration in the US apparel market at 16.7 percent in 1980 and an average of 7.7 percent in

26. The method here obtains consumption by adding imports to domestic output and subtracting exports. In comments on an early draft of this study, ATMI experts objected that this procedure overstates consumption by not reducing gross output by the amount used for intrasectoral intermediate inputs. The "product shipments" concept used by the US Department of Commerce in its *Industrial Outlook* (OUTL) is smaller than gross sectoral output including intrasectoral use, however. In 1977, the one year for which data are available both from OUTL and from the US Input-Output table (I-O), the apparel sector showed product shipments of $35.23 billion (SIC 23); while in the I-O table (sector 18), it showed gross output of $41.43 billion, of which $8.64 billion was used as an input into the industry itself. Similarly, textile-product shipments amounted to $38.05 billion (SIC 22), compared to gross output according to the I-O table (sectors 16, 17, and 19) of $45.81 billion, of which $14.55 billion was in inputs from the textile industry into itself. Thus, in apparel the OUTL product data are already closer to a net rather than gross production concept (standing 15 percent below the gross I-O figure and only 7.5 percent above the net figure). For textiles, the OUTL product figure is approximately halfway between the gross and net concepts in the I-O table. Thus, there would appear to be little distortion in the consumption estimates from this source, especially in the apparel sector (considering that the data used for output are already close to a net concept). More fundamentally, intraindustry use is a legitimate source of total demand for the product, and probably should be included in calculating the "consumption" against which imports are to be compared. On this basis, the divergence between the I-O gross output figures and the SIC product shipments figures might suggest that "consumption" as estimated here is underestimated rather than overestimated as feared by the ATMI analysts. US Department of Commerce, *Survey of Current Business*, vol. 64, no. 5 (May 1984), p. 53, and *U.S. Industrial Outlook, 1987*, pp. 41-2 and 42-2.

ATMI experts also argue that the OUTL domestic production figure is overstated relative to imports, because domestic product-shipments data include a significant portion of imported goods purchased by US producer firms themselves (for example, to round out their product lines). Census Bureau experts queried on this point indicated doubts that these amounts would be large. They noted that the questionnaires for the Annual Survey of Manufacturers explicitly instruct firms not to include finished goods purchased elsewhere (including from abroad) in reported product shipments, but instead to report them separately as goods for resale. The only instance where imports explicitly become comingled with domestic product shipments data is in the case of tariff code 806–807 products. These are goods for which the intermediate inputs are exported from the United States, processed abroad, and reimported with duty only applied to the value added abroad. These flows remain a small portion of total imports, however. By communication, 13 February 1987.

1970–74.[27] The estimate here for total import penetration in textiles and apparel, 22.0 percent in 1986, is also closer to the 14 percent figure cited by Representative Gibbons (as noted above) than is the apparel penetration estimate (31.1 percent) to the 50 percent figure often used in the debate.

Trends in International Trade and Comparative Advantage

Textiles and apparel are important sectors in international trade. In 1982, total world exports amounted to $52 billion in textiles, $41 billion in apparel, $16 billion in fibers, and $10 billion in textile machinery. The complex thus accounted for 9 percent of world trade in manufactures and 5 percent of total world merchandise trade.[28] For developing countries the textile-apparel group is especially important. In 1982, its shares in total and manufacturing exports, respectively, were: 18 percent and 35 percent for low-income countries; 12 percent and 20 percent for middle-income oil-importing countries; and 9 percent and 18 percent for upper middle-income countries.[29]

Trade in textiles and apparel has grown rapidly. From 1963 to 1973 international trade in the two sectors grew at 11.5 percent annually in real terms. From 1973 to 1982, after the advent of the MFA, trade growth slowed to 4.8 percent annually, but still remained well above growth in production in industrial countries.[30]

Although trade policy has tended to be uniform for both textiles and apparel, the two sectors differ sharply in terms of the competitiveness of industrial countries, including the United States. The developed countries tend to have a trade surplus in textiles, while in apparel they have a trade deficit and the developing countries have the comparative advantage. Table 2.8 shows trade in textiles and apparel in 1984 for major industrial and developing countries. The EC and Japan had trade surpluses in textiles, and, although in this year the United States was in deficit, it had shown a textile-trade surplus in 1979–80 (table 2.3). As a group the industrial countries were in surplus in textile trade in 1984, while the developing countries were in deficit. These data suggest that the MFA regime of quota protection of textiles against imports from developing countries is somewhat of an anomaly: protection of a product in which industrial countries already have a trade surplus.

---

27. GATT, *Textiles and Clothing*, appendix IV, p. 61.

28. GATT, *Textiles and Clothing*, p. 35.

29. World Bank, *World Development Report 1985* (Washington: World Bank, 1985), pp. 192–93.

30. GATT, *Textiles and Clothing*, p. 36.

Within the industrial countries, Japan and Italy stand out as relatively large net exporters. Among developing countries, Hong Kong has a conspicuously large trade deficit in textiles, indicating that this country imports textiles for processing into apparel.

In apparel, the industrial countries run a sizable trade deficit. Italy is an important exception, accounting for about 10 percent of world apparel exports but less than 1 percent of imports. In the other major industrial countries, apparel imports range from approximately twice exports in Japan and the EC excluding Italy to over 15 times exports in the United States (table 2.9).

The developing countries have a strong revealed comparative advantage in apparel, with exports more than twice as large as imports and an aggregate trade surplus approximately equal to the trade deficit of the industrial countries (the balance being supplied by a surplus in the Eastern bloc countries). Again the distinction between Hong Kong, on the one hand, and Korea and China, on the other, is informative. Hong Kong has sizable apparel imports but much larger exports—a pattern of intraindustry trade reflecting an open market; in contrast, Korea and mainland China have large exports and negligible imports.

The present dominance of developing countries in apparel trade is the result of persistent and rapid growth in their exports. Table 2.10 shows a constant rise in the share of non-OECD countries in the supply of apparel imports to the US market over the past two decades. This share rose from 30 percent in 1962–63 to 90 percent in 1982–83. Even Italy has not escaped the loss of the US market to developing countries; its share fell from 21.5 percent in 1962–63 to only 3.4 percent in 1983–84, indicating that its large volume of exports is directed primarily to Europe rather than the United States. In textiles, the share of non-OECD countries in US imports has risen more slowly but from a higher base, from approximately one-third to one-half over the same period.

The data for Japan warrant special comment. In the early 1960s, Japan was the principal source of import pressure for the United States, and the first voluntary quota restraints were on Japan. By the 1970s Japan was losing comparative advantage to the developing countries. Although Japan's share of US textile imports declined only modestly, from approximately 25 percent in the early 1960s to 19 percent in the early 1980s, its share of apparel imports plummeted from approximately one-third to only 3 percent over this period. Not surprisingly, a protective regime initially established to deal with Japan soon broadened to restrain imports primarily from developing countries.

The central reason for the secular rise of developing countries in apparel trade is that this industry is labor-intensive and well suited to the relative

Table 2.9   Trade in textiles and apparel: major countries and regimes, 1984

(billion dollars)

	Textiles			Apparel		
	X	M[a]	TB	X	M[a]	TB
EC	20.21	18.47	1.74	13.17	16.87	− 3.69
France	2.67	3.18	− 0.51	1.76	2.46	− 0.70
Germany	5.55	4.84	0.71	2.63	7.01	− 4.38
Italy	4.37	2.27	2.10	4.83	0.66	4.17
United Kingdom	1.92	3.58	− 1.66	1.34	2.69	− 1.35
United States	2.38	4.61	− 2.23	0.85	14.60	− 13.75
Japan	5.34	1.93	3.41	0.78	1.95	− 1.17
Developed[b] countries	30.9	29.4	1.5[c]	15.6	30.8	− 15.2[d]
(Intra-EC)	(11.3)	(11.3)	(0)	(7.8)	(7.8)	(0)
Hong Kong	1.10	4.16	− 3.06	5.96	1.48	4.48
Korea	2.60	0.60	2.00	4.50	0.02	4.48
China	3.52	0.93	2.59	2.54	0.01	2.53
Developing[b] countries	15.5	17.5	− 2.0	19.7	7.0	12.7
Eastern bloc[b]	5.2	4.6	− 0.6	5.7	3.3	2.4

X   exports; M   imports; TB   trade balance; EC   European Community.
Source: GATT, *International Trade 1984/85*, table A-15; GATT, *Textiles and Clothing in the World Economy*, pp. 40–41.
a. Imports are c.i.f. for individual countries and EC; f.o.b. for broad groupings.
b. Data are for 1982.
c. Sum of EC, United States, and Japan with imports at c.i.f.: $2.92 billion.
d. Sum of EC, United States, and Japan with imports at c.i.f.: $ − 18.61 billion.

"factor endowment" of these countries. Physical and human capital are relatively scarce in these countries, while unskilled labor is abundant. Correspondingly, they tend to have a strong comparative advantage in products that require relatively large amounts of unskilled labor and small amounts of capital and skilled labor. Thus, among the 81 International Standard Industrial Classification (ISIC) divisions at the 4-digit level, in 1978 the apparel sector (3220) ranked last in capital intensity measured by physical capital per worker, and sixty-fifth in human capital intensity measured by the ratio of average wage to the wage for unskilled labor

Table 2.10 Sources of US imports, 1961–84
(million dollars)

	Textiles (SITC 65)				
Year	Total	OECD	Japan	Italy	United Kingdom
1961	521	342	129	39	51
1962	646	422	138	46	57
1963	680	404	161	48	56
1964	683	417	174	42	58
1965	799	491	219	52	64
1966	909	547	246	48	59
1967	812	476	213	45	50
1968	963	611	270	71	57
1969	1,019	622	285	62	53
1970	1,135	778	302	75	72
1971	1,392	961	376	66	100
1972	1,527	981	354	80	99
1973	1,580	660	302	100	104
1974	1,629	842	278	76	74
1975	1,233	693	271	61	57
1976	1,653	856	354	94	79
1977	1,790	982	388	123	97
1978	2,304	1,258	492	209	132
1979	2,293	1,138	395	198	129
1980	2,542	1,200	393	212	132
1981	3,072	1,424	538	265	127
1982	2,852	1,408	553	240	118
1983	3,276	1,584	609	247	124
1984	4,617	2,273	704	438	179

n.a. not available.
Source: OECD, *Foreign Trade by Commodities,* series C, vol. 2, various years.

(operatives) in the sector.[31] As discussed in chapter 4, most of the operations of apparel production have been difficult to mechanize, so that industrial countries have had little success at "factor reversal" toward capital intensity as a means of improving competitiveness. In this light, the persistent growth

31. Unpublished data base for variables discussed in William R. Cline, *Exports of Manufactures,* pp. 70–71. Note that for the ratio of physical capital per worker, the average in apparel was only 12.8 percent of that for manufacturing overall. For the human capital variable, the measure for the apparel sector stood at only 67.8 percent of the average for manufacturing. Data are for 1972.

		Textiles (SITC 65)		
Non-OECD	India	China	Korea	Taiwan
179	116	n.a.	n.a.	2
224	134	n.a.	n.a.	7
276	173	n.a.	3	5
266	161	n.a.	4	6
308	187	n.a.	7	8
362	181	n.a.	8	8
336	169	n.a.	10	8
352	170	n.a.	11	9
397	197	n.a.	11	10
357	137	n.a.	14	12
431	165	.2	21	19
546	218	3	25	n.a.
920	188	11	20	25
787	215	28	31	35
540	119	33	28	37
797	165	47	47	61
808	177	36	44	72
1,046	191	67	63	86
1,155	201	69	66	80
1,342	232	149	119	114
1,648	202	257	170	170
1,444	152	245	186	167
1,692	150	255	245	225
2,344	208	392	312	309

of developing-country exports of apparel may be seen as a historical process of shifting production to its area of comparative advantage as international transportation costs have declined and infrastructure (such as arrangements with industrial country retailers for design and quality control) has developed. The process of rising protection may be understood as a political reaction to delay this shift from the pace it would follow on economic grounds.

The contrast between textiles and apparel is that textiles have been much more resistant to the reallocation of production to developing countries. The chief reason is that, as analyzed below, in textiles it has been possible to mechanize production. The capital intensity of textile production has risen

Table 2.10   (Continued)
(million dollars)

Year	Apparel (SITC 84)				
	Total	OECD	Japan	Italy	France
1961	269	113	82	45	11
1962	363	249	107	68	15
1963	392	275	100	95	15
1964	452	306	113	99	18
1965	543	349	141	101	18
1966	608	385	169	102	18
1967	649	371	160	103	18
1968	855	448	191	127	19
1969	1,056	556	255	128	21
1970	1,269	586	277	109	24
1971	1,521	574	275	93	28
1972	1,883	648	302	103	36
1973	2,167	649	249	119	55
1974	2,323	548	182	107	64
1975	2,551	497	154	102	81
1976	3,613	615	242	130	94
1977	4,123	686	234	155	103
1978	6,124	910	313	198	140
1979	6,355	788	199	200	129
1980	6,943	746	215	188	114
1981	8,118	832	292	200	95
1982	8,791	852	269	216	94
1983	10,418	1,105	361	279	110
1984	14,598	1,937	527	580	175

so substantially that today it is approximately average among industrial
sectors (although there is wide variation between firms that have modernized
and those that have not).[32]

Even in apparel, however, labor intensity is not the sole explanation of
rising exports from developing countries. If it were, the dominant suppliers
would be low-income countries such as India. Instead, it is the middle-
income East Asian countries that dominate the market (Hong Kong, Taiwan,
and Korea), and although their wage levels are low compared to those of
industrial countries, they are relatively high compared to those of countries

---

32. OECD, *Textile and Clothing Industries*, p. 87.

Apparel (SITC 84)			
Other	Hong Kong	Taiwan	Korea
156	46	3	n.a.
114	62	8	n.a.
117	63	7	4
146	83	9	3
194	115	11	11
223	126	15	14
278	147	26	28
407	201	50	62
500	244	88	94
683	266	148	118
947	333	256	178
1,235	402	n.a.	237
1,518	435	367	246
1,775	479	418	287
2,054	594	437	387
2,998	990	618	663
3,437	1,065	709	695
5,214	1,478	1,090	1,060
5,567	1,592	1,173	1,054
6,197	1,780	1,391	1,129
7,286	2,027	1,480	1,412
7,939	2,120	1,662	1,517
9,313	2,417	1,931	1,786
12,661	3,200	2,482	2,447

such as India and Bangladesh.[33] The development of high quality control and arrangements with multinational corporations appear to explain the dominance of the East Asian exporters despite the availability of much lower cost labor in other developing countries.

Table 2.11 shows the concentration of apparel trade in a few supplier countries. Together, Hong Kong, Taiwan, Korea, and China accounted for 66.9 percent of US apparel imports in 1983. This concentration in a few countries with limited political influence (with the exception of mainland China) is no doubt one reason why the regime of protection has progressed so

33. See table 5.4.

Table 2.11 Principal suppliers of US textile and apparel imports, 1983

Textiles		Apparel	
Country	Share of total import value (percentage)	Country	Share of total import value (percentage)
Japan	18.6	Hong Kong	23.2
China	7.8	Taiwan	18.5
Italy	7.5	Korea	17.1
Korea	7.5	China	8.1
Taiwan	6.9	Japan	3.5
Hong Kong	4.9	Philippines	3.3
India	4.6	Italy	2.7
United Kingdom	3.8	India	2.4
Canada	3.7	Singapore	2.0
Brazil	3.5	Mexico	1.8
Germany	3.5	Dominican Republic	1.4
France	3.0	Macau	1.4
Pakistan	3.0	Sri Lanka	1.3
Bangladesh	2.5	Thailand	1.3
Mexico	2.3	France	1.1
Belgium	1.9	Canada	1.0
Switzerland	1.3	United Kingdom	1.0
Netherlands	1.2	Haiti	0.8
Thailands	1.0	Indonesia	0.8
Peru	1.0	Costa Rica	0.6
Portugal	0.9	Romania	0.5
Spain	0.9	Germany	0.4
Philippines	0.9	Colombia	0.4
Colombia	0.7	Uruguay	0.4
Egypt	0.6	Pakistan	0.3

Source: OECD, *Foreign Trade by Commodities,* series C, vol. 2, 1983.

far. (Notably, Italy and other industrial countries are exempt from protection under the MFA.) Ironically, because quotas are determined on a basis of historical market shares, it is possible that under free trade the East Asian countries would lose a portion of their market share to new suppliers from other developing countries. Indeed, this consideration tends to give the East Asian countries a vested interest in the quota regime. Trends in trade shares among developing countries are examined further in chapter 5.

3

Causes of Trade, Output, and Employment Trends: A Quantitative Analysis

This chapter attempts to quantify the relative roles of the various economic influences on the performance of the textile and apparel industries over the past several years. The analysis here focuses on the role of macroeconomic factors: the overvaluation of the dollar in the period 1980–85, and the impact of slower economic growth in the 1970s and early 1980s. A quantitative model of textiles and apparel incorporates, in addition, the influence of productivity growth on employment and the impact of protection on imports, output, and employment. The subsequent chapter investigates in more detail the issues of productivity growth and adjustment. Together, the two chapters seek to divide the industry's problems into two basic components: macroeconomic adversities and microeconomic problems of competitiveness.

In some other protected sectors, especially steel, possible "unfair trade" is a third influence that must be taken into account. However, in textiles and apparel, foreign subsidies and dumping have not been major issues; the underlying competitiveness of developing countries in labor-intensive goods has meant that their resort to these measures typically has been unnecessary. There are some areas of fraudulent trade, as discussed in chapter 9, but this source of difficulty also appears to have been limited.

The Role of the Dollar

The rapid increase in imports of textiles and apparel in recent years, documented in the previous chapter, has not occurred in isolation from the rest of the economy. The first half of the 1980s was a period of rapid import growth for the entire US economy, largely as the result of a strengthening exchange rate. From 1980 to 1986, the value of US nonoil imports rose from $180 billion to $349 billion in nominal terms, an increase of 94.1 percent.[1]

---

1. Calculated from International Monetary Fund, *International Financial Statistics,* July 1987. Imports are c.i.f.

In comparison, the nominal value of US imports of textiles rose by 112.5 percent, while imports of apparel increased by 171.2 percent (tables 2.3 and 2.5). To a significant extent, the increase in textile and apparel imports was part of a general rising tide of imports overall in response to an overvalued dollar.

In textiles, the increase in nominal value of imports in the past six years was not greatly in excess of that of general nonoil imports, and a sensitivity (elasticity) to import price somewhat above the average would be sufficient to explain most of the difference. In apparel, however, other forces appear to have been at work as well. With the percentage increase in import value nearly twice that for nonoil imports overall, apparel seems likely to have been subject to additional, special influences, most probably a process of the shifting of supply sourcing to developing countries, even at constant prices, as transportation, communication, and distribution channels improved. Nonetheless, even in apparel the overvaluation of the dollar appears to have played a key role in rising imports.

An intuitive grasp of the relevance of dollar overvaluation may be obtained by consideration of the real exchange rate relevant for textile and apparel trade. Several East Asian countries are important in this trade, and it is not immediately obvious that the patterns resulting from dollar overvaluation generally in the early 1980s would apply to trade with these countries as well. However, as indicated in table 3.1, the real exchange rate weighted by US imports in textiles and apparel, respectively, did appreciate sharply not only for trade with members of the Organization for Economic Cooperation and Development (OECD) suppliers but also for trade with the developing-country suppliers.

As indicated in the table, from 1980 to 1985 the dollar appreciated in real terms by approximately 35 percent for textile imports and by 24 percent for apparel imports. These real rates are based on nominal rates (foreign currency per dollar) as deflated by foreign and US wholesale price indexes. For textile and apparel imports from the five major OECD suppliers (listed in table 3.1), the real exchange rate appreciated by approximately 37 percent. For imports from the nine largest developing-country suppliers, the appreciation was smaller but still substantial: approximately 28 percent. The overall appreciation for textiles was greater than for apparel, because of the larger weight of OECD supply in textiles.

The rise of the dollar relative to the yen and European currencies is well known. The rise of the dollar in real terms relative to the currencies of major developing-country suppliers of textiles and apparel was as follows (1980–85): Taiwan, 22 percent; Hong Kong, 11 percent (and 22 percent for 1980–83); Korea, 28 percent; China, 90 percent; Mexico, 24 percent; India, 27

**Table 3.1   Real exchange rates for trade in textiles and apparel:
United States, 1973–85**

Year	Textiles			Apparel		
	OECD[a]	LDCs[b]	Total	OECD[a]	LDCs[b]	Total
1973	111.40	95.30	103.82	109.86	107.91	107.57
1974	108.80	89.75	99.84	106.81	95.23	95.94
1975	111.51	96.99	104.68	109.54	104.02	104.05
1976	116.49	103.85	110.58	115.33	102.74	103.48
1977	111.11	102.63	107.17	111.03	103.35	103.57
1978	100.57	102.08	101.35	101.59	102.90	102.20
1979	100.76	101.87	101.35	100.61	101.90	101.21
1980	100.00	100.00	100.00	100.00	100.00	100.00
1981	114.83	107.24	111.31	116.66	104.14	104.84
1982	125.94	118.98	122.74	128.00	113.16	114.05
1983	129.79	124.04	127.17	132.27	120.65	121.18
1984	137.35	127.70	132.88	139.55	120.40	121.70
1985	136.27	133.52	135.08	139.11	123.18	124.12
1986	105.45	132.32	118.27	107.17	120.55	118.52

Source: Calculated from IMF, *International Financial Statistics,* various issues; OECD, *Foreign Trade by Commodities,* series C, vol. 2, various years.
a. France, Germany, Italy, Japan, United Kingdom.
b. Bangladesh, China (PRC), Hong Kong, India, Korea, Mexico, Philippines, Singapore, Taiwan.

percent; and Bangladesh, 19 percent. The dollar failed to rise against the currencies of only two important suppliers: Singapore and the Philippines.[2]

Modeling Trade, Production, and Employment

In order to examine the influence of macroeconomic factors on the textile and apparel sectors more fully, it is helpful to construct a model capable of simulating production, employment, and trade experience under actual conditions and under alternative macroeconomic scenarios. The analysis here focuses attention on two influences at the macroeconomic level: the exchange rate and the pace of economic growth. In addition to the adverse effect of dollar overvaluation as just discussed, production and employment

2. Calculations are from IMF, *International Financial Statistics,* various issues.

in the two sectors were affected by the general environment of slow growth in the early 1980s, plagued by the worst recession since the 1930s.

Appendix A develops a model of trade, production, and employment that permits a diagnosis of the respective roles of the dollar and slow economic growth in explaining the levels of employment and production in textiles and apparel in the early 1980s. The model provides separate estimates for textiles and apparel. All data are in terms of constant real values at 1982 prices (that is, the real output, import, and export estimates shown in tables 2.1 through 2.4).

The model begins with imports, disaggregated between supply from OECD countries and that from all other (primarily developing) countries. With 1970 as a base year, the growth in imports each successive year is a function of the growth of GNP (income) in the United States, the state of the business cycle (actual GNP relative to trend), and the change in real import price. The change in the import price is composed of the change in foreign real price, the change in protection, and the change in the real exchange rate. In the absence of price data for textiles and apparel in foreign countries, it is assumed that the foreign real price moves identically with the domestic US real price, which has declined over the past two decades (chapter 2). Failure of foreign real prices to accompany this decline would be inconsistent with the strong performance of US imports.

Lags are important in the import estimates. Import volumes are assumed to respond to changes in import prices in the previous year, as the result of time required for new order decisions based on new prices, and for shipping. In turn, the current year's import price change is assumed to reflect the change in the exchange rate in both the current and the previous year, with weights of 0.4 and 0.6, respectively. The lag from exchange rate movement to import price change reflects the fact that firms may accept temporary profit reductions before eventually passing on higher dollar prices corresponding to a given yen price (for example) following dollar depreciation. (Similarly, when the dollar is rising, foreign suppliers may enjoy temporarily bloated profit margins that require time to induce new entrants who will drive down the margins through competition, as investors wait to see whether the changes are permanent.) The reluctance of firms to lose market shares contributes to this behavior. Even after all lags are exhausted, the model assumes that there is a pass-through ratio of 80 percent from real exchange rate changes to import price changes. This ratio assumes that some portion of the exchange rate change is permanently absorbed in varying profit margins of foreign suppliers.

The exchange rate lag is important in understanding why little import relief was evident by 1986. In that year, the average real exchange rate for apparel imports from OECD sources (for example) showed a depreciation of the dollar by 23 percent from 1985 (table 3.1). Yet imports of apparel from the OECD rose by 10.8 percent in real terms (figure 3.3). The change in 1986 imports was responding to the 1985 change in import prices, not the 1986 price change; and the 1985 import price change, in turn, was responding to the exchange rate change in 1985 and in 1984. Thus, a turnaround in real imports based on the 1986 exchange rate was not expected to begin until 1987, and would take until 1988 to be completed on the basis of these lags.

Protection also influences the import price. The import price *equals* the world price *plus* the tariff for OECD supply. In the case of non-OECD supply only, the increment from world to import prices includes in addition the extra tariff-equivalent of nontariff barriers. The level of this protection is discussed in chapter 6. In general, however, for apparel the tariff level has been in the range of 25 percent over several years, while the tariff-equivalent of quotas (above and beyond the tariff) has risen from a range of 5 percent in the 1960s to 15 percent by the mid-1970s, 20 percent by the late 1970s and early 1980s, and 25 percent beginning 1982. Protection levels for textiles have been lower. Rising protection has exerted a restraining effect on imports by raising their price.

The model applies a price elasticity of -1.3 for imports of textiles (a 1 percent decline in import price causes a 1.3 percent rise in the quantity of imports). For apparel, the price elasticity is -2.5 for imports from the OECD and -1.5 for imports from the rest of the world. As discussed in appendix A, these values are consistent with several past estimates and with the best fits obtained through iterative examination of the model.[3]

In addition to the price factors determining imports, there is an important term for long-run growth of import supply. Changing tastes, improved

---

3. As the primary focus of the quantitative analysis of this study is policy simulation rather than statistical estimation of new econometric results, the approach here is to draw upon the existing econometric literature to establish the boundaries of parameter values used in the models. Specific parameters are then selected from within these ranges on the basis of internal consistency of the specific model formulation (see the discussion of "cross-elasticity" values in appendix B, for example), a priori reasoning and institutional features of the sectors, and, importantly, the closeness of adherence of the simulated variables to actual historical data in 1970–86. This research strategy takes account of the risks involved in direct application of specific statistical regression results to the policy model. (Classical difficulties include the problem that colinearity can falsely attribute excessive influence to one variable while understating that of another, and that "simultaneity" of two or more sets of relationships of the variables involved, to each other or to still other variables, can distort the meaningfulness of the parameters estimated for the particular relationship being tested.) The process of model validation judged by historical fit could be more formalized, for example through a very large number of iterative "backcasts" with a summary criterion (such as sum of squared residuals estimated from actual values) for each one. An alternative approach would be constrained estimation of the equations by maximum likelihood technique, with acceptable upper and lower bounds specified for each parameter.

Table 3.2   Imports of apparel from non-OECD sources as percentage of US apparent consumption[a]

Year	Actual	Three-year moving average	Predicted[b]	Percentage change, predicted
1971	3.7	3.6	3.6	23.2
1972	4.4	4.4	4.4	22.1
1973	5.0	5.0	5.3	20.8
1974	5.8	5.8	6.3	19.3
1975	6.7	7.0	7.4	17.6
1976	8.6	7.9	8.6	15.8
1977	8.3	9.0	9.8	13.9
1978	10.3	9.8	10.9	11.9
1979	10.9	10.9	12.0	10.0
1980	11.5	11.6	13.0	8.2
1981	12.5	12.2	13.9	6.6
1982	12.5	12.9	14.6	5.2
1983	13.7	14.3	15.2	4.0
1984	16.7	n.a.	15.6	3.0

n.a. not available.
a. Imports on customs value basis, excluding insurance, freight, and duties.
b. Based on regression estimate of logistics curve. See appendix A.

international communication and transportation, and the movement of importers (especially retailing firms) abroad to develop foreign sources of supply for products made to order, have all probably contributed toward a rising tendency to purchase more abroad even at unchanged foreign price and domestic income. Moreover, the available data may not fully capture foreign price declines associated with outward-shifting foreign supply curves (as discussed in appendix A).

In apparel, imports from developing countries have grown rapidly from a small base, and tapered off to more moderate and sustainable growth rates after several years. This pattern of growth is sufficiently typical of new activities that a special mathematical relationship has been used to characterize it: the "logistics curve." This profile is one of an S-shaped curve showing imports rising gradually (in absolute terms) at first, then rapidly, then rising by declining absolute amounts as they approach some ceiling. In such a curve, the percentage growth at any given time is a declining function of the level of imports.

Table 3.2 shows the ratio of imports of apparel from developing countries to total US consumption (using the customs value basis for imports, with no increment for shipping and tariffs) from 1971 to 1984. The second column indicates a three-year moving average of this import penetration ratio. The third column reports a "predicted" import penetration ratio based on a statistical regression relating the percentage change in import ratio to the level of this ratio (appendix A), and the final column indicates the corresponding predicted percentage change in the penetration ratio. The statistical estimates confirm the pattern of a logistics curve for apparel import penetration from developing countries. This pattern is important in itself, because it indicates that the pace of this import growth has been decelerating relative to domestic consumption growth. This deceleration suggests that difficulties imposed by growth in these imports should be less in the future than in the past. For purposes of the model of imports, this logistics pattern is applied to the estimate of imports from the other factors (import price, US income, and cyclical status) to obtain the final estimate of imports (as discussed in appendix A).

The term for long-term (secular) growth is quite different for apparel imports from OECD countries. These imports have been losing market share to competition from developing countries, and a negative time trend for import penetration is imposed on the equation for them (and in addition their income elasticity of demand is set at a lower level; appendix A).

Domestic consumption is estimated as a function of per capita income, population, price, and cyclical state of the economy. For its part, the price of consumption is a weighted average of the price for domestic output, imports from the OECD, and imports from developing countries. Exports are estimated as a function of the price of exports (driven by the real exchange rate in the current and previous year) and the growth and cyclical status of the OECD economies outside the United States.

For textiles, consumption is divided into two components. The first is the use of textiles as an intermediate input into the apparel sector. On the basis of the 1977 US Input-Output table, $1.00 of gross output in the apparel sector requires $0.33 in inputs from the textiles sector.[4] Thus, for this component of textile consumption, actual apparel output is multiplied by this coefficient to determine required textile supply. The second component of textile consumption is determined in the same way as in the general formulation of consumption growth as outlined above (driven by income

---

4. In 1977 the total requirement from textiles (Input-Output sectors 16, 17, and 19) into apparel (sector 18) amounted to $0.418 for each dollar of apparel delivered to final demand, while the corresponding requirement from the apparel sector itself was $1.262 (that is, 26 cents of apparel output was used as an intermediate input into the apparel sector for each dollar of apparel delivered to final demand). The corresponding coefficient for textile inputs per unit of gross apparel output was $0.33 (or $0.418/1.262). US Department of Commerce, *Survey of Current Business*, vol. 64, no. 5 (May 1984), p. 69.

and population growth, price, and the business cycle). The model thus captures the key interindustry relationship linking demand for textiles to domestic output of apparel, while at the same time recognizing that approximately two-thirds of textile output goes to the market directly rather than as an input into textiles.[5]

Given the estimates of imports, consumption, and exports, domestic output is estimated as the amount required to meet consumption after considering availability of imports net of exports. The model applies a labor coefficient (which declines over time with technical change) to calculate the amount of employment associated with the estimated level of production. In years of estimated output reduction (sectoral recession), employment is a weighted average of the labor coefficient divided into the current and previous year's output levels, with a heavier weight for the preceding year to reflect the practice of retaining redundant workers during recession rather than incurring the costs of separation and subsequent rehiring.

As discussed in appendix A, the model applies parameters (mainly "elasticities") drawn from existing empirical estimates but also calibrated to give a close fit of estimated to actual values. Once the model is estimated, it is possible to investigate the influence of the exchange rate and domestic growth on the textile and apparel sectors by simulating the values of trade, production, consumption, and employment under alternative macroeconomic conditions.

Simulation Results

Figures 3.1 through 3.6 for apparel illustrate the model's predictive power for historical levels of trade, consumption, production, and employment since 1970. The best performance is in the trade sectors, the subject of the principal focus of this study. The model's simulated estimates of imports and exports closely track the actual paths of these flows. The model successfully captures the sharp increases in imports from both the developing countries and the OECD from 1980 to 1986, and similarly predicts with relative accuracy the decline in US apparel exports over the same period.

---

5. Thus, in 1986, the estimated intermediate use of textiles into apparel was $16.35 billion (equal to apparel output, $49.55 billion, multiplied by 0.33), or 33.2 percent of total textile output ($49.21 billion). Note that the simulated past levels of textile output apply actual rather than simulated values of apparel output to determine this interindustry consumption (to avoid transmitting simulation error for apparel into the textile estimates). For the counterhistorical simulations of equilibrium exchange and higher growth, the actual level of apparel output is multiplied by the ratio of simulated-hypothetical to simulated-actual to obtain the hypothetical apparel output level for computation of the corresponding scenario cases in textiles.

Figure 3.1 Apparel imports from OECD countries

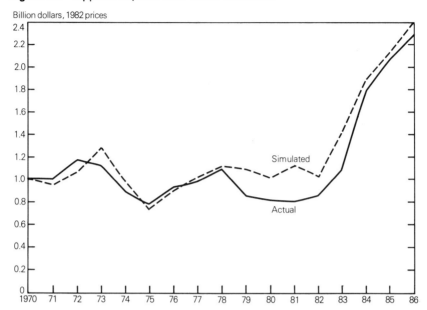

Billion dollars, 1982 prices

Simulated

Actual

Figure 3.2 Apparel imports from developing countries

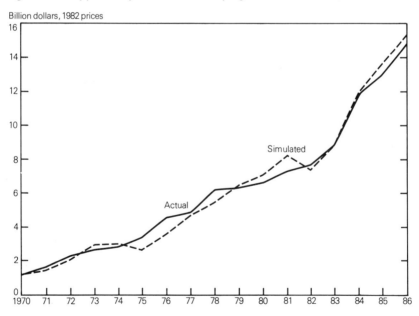

Billion dollars, 1982 prices

Simulated

Actual

Figure 3.3 Apparel consumption

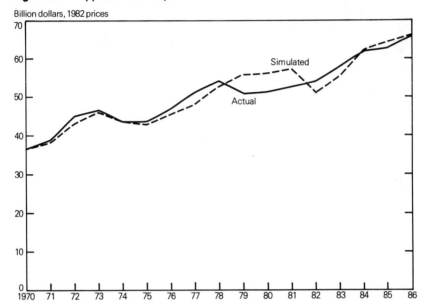

Billion dollars, 1982 prices

Figure 3.4 Apparel employment

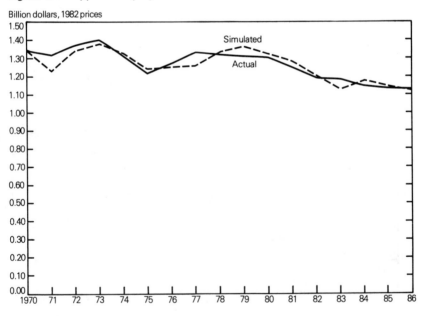

Billion dollars, 1982 prices

Figure 3.5 Apparel output

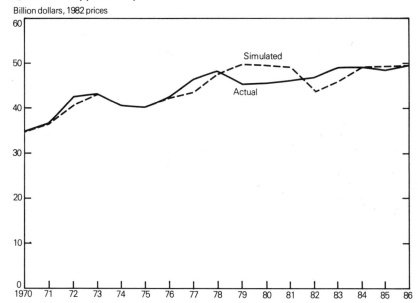

Billion dollars, 1982 prices

Figure 3.6 Apparel exports

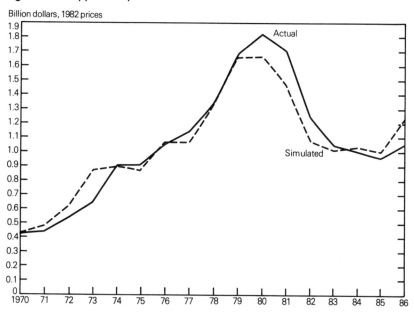

Billion dollars, 1982 prices

The predictions for consumption (figure 3.3) also broadly adhere to historical experience, although they significantly overstate the level in the period 1979–81. After rising rapidly in 1977–78, actual consumption declined in real terms by 6.6 percent in 1979 with no apparent cause from the underlying economic forces measured here (price, income, business cycle). It is not until the recession year of 1982 that the predicted level of consumption falls to a path more consistent once again with actual consumption. The decline of apparel consumption in 1979–81 drives a corresponding reduction in actual output (figure 3.5) that also is not captured well by the model, although by 1984 the predicted value is once again close to the actual value. Predicted employment (figure 3.4) adheres more closely to actual employment, because of the phenomenon of overhead labor. Thus, actual employment does not drop as sharply as output in 1979, but instead stays closer to the path predicted by the model.

Table 3.3 presents the principal magnitudes estimated in the model for textiles in the period 1980 to 1986. The first column reports actual values (millions of dollars at 1982 textile prices and thousand workers). The second shows the corresponding "simulated" estimates calculated by the model. The simulated values are generally close to actual values.

In conducting the experiments to measure the influence of macroeconomic policies, it is necessary to identify an appropriate benchmark for comparison with actual exchange rates and economic growth. Williamson has estimated that the real US exchange rate in 1980 was approximately 3 percent below the equilibrium level associated with modest and sustainable capital inflows, and that thereafter the dollar rose far above its equilibrium rate.[6] Thus, the analysis here considers what would have happened in the apparel sector if the (apparel-based) real exchange rates of the dollar (with respect to both OECD and developing-country suppliers) had been 3 percent stronger than it actually was in 1980 but had then remained unchanged rather than rising sharply through 1985.

For a benchmark appropriate to domestic economic growth, it is useful to recall that in the decade of the 1960s real US GNP grew at approximately 4 percent annually. During the 1970s the rate averaged 3.2 percent. Thus, a reasonable rate for long-term US growth might be 3.5 percent annually. In contrast, actual growth averaged only 1.8 percent in 1980 through 1984.[7]

---

6. John Williamson, *The Exchange Rate System*, POLICY ANALYSES IN INTERNATIONAL ECONOMICS 5, rev. (Washington: Institute for International Economics, June 1985), pp. 98–99.

7. Council of Economic Advisers, *Economic Report of the President* (Washington: CEA, February 1986), p. 254.

Table 3.3 **Textiles: simulated effects of dollar overvaluation and slow growth** (million 1982 dollars and thousand workers)

| | | Simulated | | |
	Actual	Actual	Equilibrium exchange rate (EER)	Higher growth (HG)	EER and HG
Output					
1980	49,423	50,939	50,846	54,732	54,632
1981	48,146	50,733	50,880	56,220	56,384
1982	44,916	47,030	48,008	60,068	61,243
1983	49,812	49,384	51,081	61,244	63,344
1984	50,065	52,141	54,642	61,338	64,310
1985	48,498	52,462	55,529	62,953	66,726
1986	49,210	53,484	56,616	64,594	68,596
Employment					
1980	818	858	857	910	908
1981	783	816	816	901	904
1982	718	770	776	929	947
1983	723	736	762	913	944
1984	711	750	786	882	925
1985	670	727	770	873	925
1986	669	715	757	864	917
Imports					
1980	2,245	2,427	2,427	2,741	2,741
1981	2,503	2,540	2,570	3,017	3,053
1982	2,225	2,157	2,139	3,307	3,279
1983	2,523	2,753	2,506	4,019	3,658
1984	3,390	3,464	2,947	4,627	3,937
1985	3,575	3,701	3,034	5,132	4,207
1986	4,309	4,186	3,326	5,886	4,676
Exports					
1980	2,746	2,573	2,496	2,750	2,667
1981	2,346	2,245	2,399	2,540	2,714
1982	1,766	1,664	2,444	1,985	2,914
1983	1,539	1,556	2,648	1,838	3,128
1984	1,476	1,563	2,967	1,770	3,358
1985	1,414	1,476	3,124	1,704	3,605
1986	1,660	1,784	3,256	2,120	3,870

Table 3.3 reports the simulated values of trade, output, and employment in the textile sector under these "benchmark" macroeconomic conditions. The first simulation is for an equilibrium exchange rate and actual growth; the second, actual exchange rate and benchmark growth; and the third, equilibrium exchange rate and benchmark growth. Comparison of these simulated values with those calculated by the model under actual exchange rate and growth conditions provides a measure of the influence of these macroeconomic disturbances on the textile and apparel sectors in the first half of this decade.

The results shown in table 3.3 indicate that both the exchange rate and lackluster domestic growth have played important roles in lagging output and employment in the apparel sector in the early 1980s. If the exchange rate had been at equilibrium levels, by 1986 real textile imports would have been 21 percent lower than their actual level, while exports would have been 83 percent higher. The sector would have had a trade surplus in 1982–85 instead of a deficit. (All comparisons are relative to the "simulated" values under actual conditions.) As a result, domestic production and employment would have been higher than their actual values by 5.9 percent. This calculation indicates that the overvalued dollar was responsible for a loss of 42,000 jobs in direct textile production.

The calculations for different GNP growth show even larger results. If US growth had averaged 3.5 percent in 1980–85, by the end of the period domestic output and employment would have been 21 percent above their actual level—even though imports would have been 41 percent above their actual level. Higher growth would have meant more domestic consumption and production.

The final column of table 3.3 reports the combined influences of an equilibrium exchange rate and more rapid domestic growth. Under these conditions imports would have been 12 percent larger in 1986 than their actual value, but production and employment would have been larger than their actual values by 28 percent.

These calculations indicate that macroeconomic conditions (including the overvalued dollar) have indeed had a substantial adverse effect on the textile industry in the first half of the 1980s. The overvalued dollar artificially stimulated imports and depressed exports, while slow domestic growth further limited production and employment by retarding the growth of consumption. In the absence of dollar overvaluation, the textile sector would have retained the status of net exporter (which it had finally attained in 1979–80; table 2.3) instead of falling again into trade deficit status.

Table 3.4 reports the corresponding estimates for apparel. In this sector also, dollar overvaluation and mediocre growth of the economy have had a severe adverse impact. If the dollar had been at equilibrium levels, by 1986

Table 3.4 Apparel: simulated effects of dollar overvaluation and slow growth (million 1982 dollars and thousand workers)

		Simulated			
	Actual	Actual	Equilibrium exchange rate (EER)	Higher growth (HG)	EER and HG
Output					
1980	45,742	49,534	49,482	53,099	53,043
1981	46,176	49,197	49,248	54,259	54,315
1982	46,681	43,562	44,084	55,030	55,661
1983	48,932	45,931	47,087	56,331	57,817
1984	49,335	49,300	51,358	57,406	59,922
1985	48,551	49,264	51,959	58,276	61,731
1986	49,548	49,710	52,641	59,044	62,928
Employment					
1980	1,307	1,324	1,324	1,413	1,412
1981	1,251	1,281	1,280	1,406	1,407
1982	1,189	1,205	1,209	1,388	1,403
1983	1,182	1,127	1,155	1,382	1,419
1984	1,152	1,177	1,227	1,371	1,431
1985	1,142	1,146	1,208	1,355	1,435
1986	1,133	1,124	1,191	1,336	1,423
Imports					
1980	7,428	8,109	8,109	9,131	9,131
1981	8,122	9,323	9,435	11,028	11,160
1982	8,516	8,418	8,461	12,772	12,839
1983	9,918	10,300	9,530	14,883	13,775
1984	13,632	13,902	11,854	18,393	15,687
1985	15,044	15,769	12,876	21,640	17,676
1986	17,035	17,698	14,255	24,615	19,833
Exports					
1980	1,821	1,661	1,609	1,787	1,731
1981	1,706	1,455	1,560	1,675	1,795
1982	1,236	1,071	1,603	1,316	1,969
1983	1,039	1,009	1,762	1,237	2,160
1984	999	1,031	2,016	1,211	2,369
1985	949	987	2,164	1,185	2,598
1986	1,044	1,220	2,294	1,516	2,849

real apparel imports would have been 19.5 percent below their actual (simulated) level. Exports would have been 88 percent higher (from a small base). With an improved trade balance, apparel production and employment would have been 5.9 percent higher than their actual levels. Thus, direct employment in apparel would have been 67,000 jobs above its actual level.

If growth in the United States and the OECD had averaged 3.5 percent, demand would have been sufficiently larger by 1986 to have increased production and employment in apparel by 18.8 percent from their simulated actual levels, even though with higher demand and an uncorrected exchange rate US imports of apparel would have been 39 percent higher than their simulated actual level. If both areas of macroeconomic distortion had been improved, with 3.5 percent growth as well as an equilibrium value for the dollar, US production and employment in apparel would have been 27 percent higher than their simulated actual levels. Employment in apparel would have been higher by 299,000 jobs (thereby remaining at a level virtually unchanged from the hypothetical high-growth level in 1980, rather than declining by over 200,000 jobs). And these favorable results would have been possible despite a rise in real imports by 12.1 percent from their actual level—the net consequence of larger import demand associated with higher GNP growth, on the one hand, and lower import demand from the standpoint of higher price associated with nonappreciation of the dollar, on the other.

It is possible to obtain an overview of the causes of rapid import growth in the first half of the 1980s by decomposing the rise in imports into its component contributions from the underlying influences traced by the simulation model. For example, the contribution of exchange rate change to the rise in imports is identified through multiplication of the resulting import price change by the import elasticity. Table 3.5 sets forth this compositional analysis for the total increase of textile and apparel imports from OECD and developing countries over the period 1980 to 1986.

In the case of apparel, the real value of imports from the OECD rose by 181.5 percent in this period, and from non-OECD countries (mainly developing countries) by 122.9 percent. The model captures most of these large increases (estimating them at 136.8 percent and 115.8 percent, respectively). The components of the simulated import increases show that for apparel imports from developing countries, four factors have played approximately equal roles: the rising exchange rate, the declining real price in the foreign countries, growth of US income, and the secular (long-term) outward shift in the supply sourcing in accordance with the S-curve analysis. Each effect contributed an increase of between 22 percent and 27 percent.[8] In contrast,

---

8. Note that in the case of the price variables—exchange rate and real home price in the foreign country—the percentage change in imports exceeds the amount that would

Table 3.5 Composition of US real import increase, 1980–86
(percentage)

	Textiles		Apparel	
	OECD	Non-OECD	OECD	Non-OECD
Total				
Actual	100.1	84.7	181.5	122.9
Simulated Actual	63.0	81.7	136.8	115.8
Sources (simulated):				
Exchange rate	32.6	26.0	77.0	22.0
Real foreign price	22.8	24.0	46.0	27.0
Protection	2.6	− 3.0	0.0	− 5.0
US income	18.7	18.7	15.5	27.2
Business cycle	− 7.6	− 7.6	− 7.6	− 5.4
Secular supply shift	− 11.4	9.3	− 14.1	22.1

the severity of the 1982 recession yielded a small net decrease in imports from the business cycle influence, while a modest further tightening of quotas cut imports by an estimated 5 percent.

For apparel imports from the OECD, the price effects were more dominant, reflecting a higher import elasticity and a sharper appreciation of the dollar relative to the currencies of these countries. Thus, from 1979 to 1985 real appreciation of the dollar relative to OECD apparel suppliers was 38.3 percent, while the increase was only 20.9 percent for developing-country suppliers; and the model applies an import elasticity of − 2.5 for imports from the OECD as opposed to − 1.5 for those from developing countries. Overall, appreciation of the dollar played by far the largest role in increasing US imports of apparel from the OECD from 1980 to 1986 (a rise of 77 percent); the decline of foreign home prices was also important (46 percent import rise), while US income growth induced only moderate increases and the business cycle and secular trend variables reduced these imports from levels they otherwise would have reached.

---

be calculated merely by applying the price elasticity to the total full-period price change. Thus, the real import price from developing countries for apparel declines from 1979 to 1985 by 24.7 percent, while the total contribution to increased imports equals 47 percent (1.22 x 1.27 x .95 = 1.47 for the three price components—exchange rate, foreign price, and protection). This increase exceeds the total price change *times* the elasticity (− 24.7 x − 1.5 = 37.0). The reason is that each year's price reduction enlarges the import base somewhat, so that the cumulative effect is larger than that which would occur if the full period price change occurred in the first year and were applied to the original base. (In terms of equation 5 of appendix A, the cumulative effect of a chain of percentage increases in imports involves higher-powered terms of the elasticity as the consequence of sequential multiplication.)

For textiles, the compositional analysis of table 3.5 indicates the following patterns. For imports from developing countries, exchange rate change and decline in the imputed real price abroad are the leading influences, with approximately equal importance. US income growth is next (although the business cycle on balance reduces import demand). Higher protection causes a modest cutback of 3 percent in demand. Secular growth in imports from developing countries accounts for a 1½ percent increase annually—significant but considerably less important than in apparel. For textile imports from industrial countries, the exchange rate effect is more pronounced, while the other influences are similar to those found in imports from developing countries (with the exception of secular trend, set at a decline of 2 percent annually).

The model presented here could be used as well to examine the impact of past protection on trade, production, and employment, and indeed in chapter 11 the model is applied to determine the impact of alternative trade policies on the future evolution of the sectors. However, for a detailed examination of the role of existing protection, chapter 8 develops a separate model oriented specifically to this purpose.

Further Evidence on Exchange Rate Effects

The findings of this chapter place considerable emphasis on the role of the overvalued dollar in explaining the trade problems of textiles and apparel so far in the 1980s. The compositional analysis above attributes to the dollar's rise approximately one-fourth of the 1980–86 increase in apparel imports from developing countries, more than half of the increase in apparel imports from industrial countries, approximately one-third of the rise in textile imports from developing countries, and nearly one-half of the increase in textile imports from industrial countries. Significant controversy exists, however, over the influence of the dollar's strength during this period. Some analysts place far more emphasis on institutional factors (such as the development of international sourcing networks) and less on the exchange rate.

A recent study by Economic Consulting Services (ECS) argues that the strong dollar had little effect on US imports of textiles and apparel from low-wage countries. The study surveys imports from the 25 largest supplier countries. It finds that textile and apparel imports from developing countries that depreciated relative to the dollar actually rose more slowly than those from a benchmark group of 6 countries that had stable exchange rates with the dollar. However, the study does attribute an important influence to the overvalued dollar in the rapid growth of US imports from industrial countries.[9]

---

9. Economic Consulting Services, Inc., *The Impact of Exchange Rate Changes on US Imports of Textiles and Apparel* (Washington: July 1986).

In contrast, a study carried out for the US Chamber of Commerce has found that "industry representatives contend that the rise in the value of the dollar during the first half of the 1980s accounts for a large portion of the exponential growth in U.S. textile and apparel imports." In response to the study just cited, the Chamber study points out that of the six countries in the benchmark group, only one, Taiwan, was a major supplier. It notes that the ECS study itself concludes that the dollar exchange rate had some impact or a major impact on US imports from 14 of the 25 countries surveyed: Hong Kong, Korea, Italy, Pakistan, Canada, Germany, Mexico, Indonesia, India, the Philippines, Brazil, the United Kingdom, France, and Spain.[10]

Other difficulties with the ECS conclusion that the overvalued dollar had little influence on imports from low-wage countries include the following. First, as noted above, the dollar did appreciate in real terms relative to the currency of Taiwan from 1980 to 1985, yet Taiwan is the one major supplier in the ECS "stable currency" benchmark group. Second, that group includes primarily small suppliers whose export growth is rapid from a low base (Singapore, Dominican Republic, Malaysia, Egypt, and Haiti). It would not be surprising that the major developing-country suppliers would have had slower export growth to the United States than some of these suppliers, even if the exchange rate were substantially accelerating the growth of imports from the major suppliers beyond what it otherwise would have reached. Third, and more fundamentally, the ECS analysis omits the influence of dollar overvaluation on the reallocation of developing-country exports from the European and Japanese markets to the US market even in the absence of any change in the real exchange rate between the dollar and the currency of the supplier country itself. This factor is examined below. In short, the "control group" methodology of the ECS study appears inadequate to examine the question that study seeks to answer. Ideally, the impact of the dollar's strength on imports from each of several major supplier countries would be examined by an import model for each one, with the bilateral US-supplier real exchange rate appearing as one variable, the weighted average real exchange rate between the dollar and the currencies of this supplier's other major markets appearing as another variable, and with other relevant variables (including US income growth) included as well.

As an additional source of evidence on the relevance of the exchange rate, it is useful to consider the following question: did imports of textiles and apparel into Japan and Europe also surge during the early 1980s, or was this boom strictly a US phenomenon? And more generally, has there been any pattern of import behavior into Europe and Japan during periods when US imports appear

---

10. William Davidson, Charles Feigenoff, and Fariborz Ghadar, "International Competition in Textiles and Apparel: The U.S. Experience" (Washington: National Chamber Foundation, 1986; processed), pp. 5, 12.

to have accelerated simultaneously with an overvalued dollar? If the answers to these questions indicate that US import surges have merely been part of a worldwide deluge of supply from developing countries, it could be appropriate to conclude that the overvalued dollar has had little influence. If, instead, European and Japanese imports have grown slowly just when US imports have soared in the presence of an overvalued dollar, there is additional support for the hypothesis that the dollar's strength matters.

Table 3.6 shows that indeed there has been a positive correlation between the relative import growth of the United States from developing countries relative to that of the other industrial areas, on the one hand, and the strength of the dollar, on the other. Thus, in 1981–84 when the dollar was strong, US imports of apparel rose by 104 percent in dollar value while Japan's imports declined by 24 percent and Europe's fell by 12 percent. But when the dollar was weak in 1978–80, US apparel imports rose only 19 percent, far less than the 74 percent increase in Japan and the 58 percent increase in Europe. The other corresponding comparisons in the table (for textiles, and for earlier periods of a strong versus weak dollar), generally show the same pattern. Importantly, these data indicate that it would be difficult to explain differential import growth for Europe and Japan versus the United States by supposed tighter protection; conversely, the exchange rate explanation neatly fits the evidence. Moreover, these data refer to imports from non-OECD countries, a more severe test of the exchange rate hypothesis than in the case of imports from industrial countries (where even the ECS study recognizes the exchange rate effect).

Skeptics of the role of the exchange rate stress that imports of textiles and apparel did not decline in 1986 even though the dollar had fallen significantly from its 1985 high. As discussed above, the explanation for this paradox is that there are lengthy lags, involving delay in price change in response to exchange rate change as suppliers temporarily adjust profit margins waiting to see if the exchange rate movement is permanent, and the time elapsed from the actual change in import price to changes in purchase orders and ultimately arrival of the shipped good. Various models of US trade indicate lags of some two years, and there is little reason to believe that the lags are shorter in textiles and apparel.[11]

---

11. In a recent research project conducting coordinated simulations across seven different models of the US external sector (including some from official entities), lags of two years are typically encountered. Brookings Institution, Workshop on US Current-Account Imbalance, 20 January 1987. Note also that preliminary calculations in a study at the Institute for International Economics on adjustment of the US external imbalance suggest a two-year lag from exchange rate to trade change. Thus, if the US trade balance is normalized by dividing by trade turnover (imports plus exports), then for nonoil trade (with exports to OPEC excluded on the export side) this ratio reached a peak in the fourth quarter of 1981, eight quarters after the real

Table 3.6 Relative growth of imports into the United States, Europe, and Japan in response to dollar strength, 1973–84
(percentage change)

	I 1973–75	II 1976–77	III 1978–80	IV 1981–84
Relative position of dollar	Weak	Strong	Weak	Strong
Average real effective exchange rate	103.9[a]	105.2	96.3	123.6
Increase in imports from non-OECD countries[b]				
Textiles				
United States	−0.6	49.5	66.0	74.5
Japan	119.3	15.7	92.6	30.4
Europe[c]	82.8	45.6	76.7	−22.9
United States/Japan	−54.7	29.2	−13.8	33.8
United States/Europe[c]	−45.6	2.7	−6.1	126.3
Apparel				
United States	66.4	153.9[d]	18.9[e]	104.3
Japan	122.8	72.2[d]	73.8[e]	−24.4
Europe[c]	150.6	65.7[d]	58.0[e]	−12.0
United States/Japan	−25.3	47.4[d]	−31.6[e]	170.2
United States/Europe[c]	−33.6	53.2[d]	−24.7[e]	132.2

Note: Entries of United States/Europe and United States/Japan refer to percentage changes in the ratios of dollar values of imports into these areas, respectively.

Source: Real exchange rate, John Williamson, *The Exchange Rate System*, POLICY ANALYSES IN INTERNATIONAL ECONOMICS 5, (Washington: Institute for International Economics, 2d ed. June 1985), pp. 98–99; trade, calculated from OECD, *Foreign Trade by Commodities*, series C, vol. 2, DRI data base.

a. 1973:Q3 to 1975:Q4.
b. Dollar value in final year of period over amount in final year of previous period, percentage.
c. OECD-Europe.
d. 1978 over 1975.
e. 1980 over 1978.

---

value of the dollar reached a trough in 1979:Q4; similarly, the preceding trough of this trade-balance measure in the first quarter of 1978 occurred seven quarters after the peak of the dollar's real value in the first quarter of 1976. Unpublished analysis for William R. Cline and Stephen Marris, *Correcting the US Trade Deficit: the Global Impact* (Washington: Institute for International Economics, forthcoming).

Overall, the evidence suggests that the overvalued dollar did play a major role in the rapid growth of US imports of textiles and apparel in the first half of the 1980s. A judgment on this issue is of central importance; requests for additional protection in the two sectors could be seen as less urgent if the view is accepted that the dollar's strength substantially increased imports, considering that the dollar has now declined sharply. As discussed below, it is necessary to take account of the broad absence so far of dollar depreciation against the East Asian and other developing countries. However, table 3.6 suggests that some moderation of import growth from these countries as well could be expected even in the absence of real appreciation of their rates against the dollar, because of the probable shift of their supply to the now more lucrative (in dollars) markets of Europe and Japan. Indeed, in this regard the simulation model of this chapter is conservative in its implications for future improvement in the US trade balance in textiles and apparel, because in estimating imports from developing countries the model confines the analysis to consideration of the direct exchange rate relationship between the dollar and the currencies of the developing-country suppliers, without including the additional influence of the redirection of developing-country supply away from the US market to the Japanese and European markets as the dollar declines against the currencies of the industrial countries.

Implications

A central implication of these findings is that conditions in the textiles and apparel sectors could improve as the macroeconomic distortions of slow growth and dollar overvaluation are corrected. The dollar has already declined substantially from its high in early 1985, and after a lag of some two years there should be a corresponding reduction in imports and increase in exports. The International Monetary Fund (IMF) index of the nominal exchange rate of the dollar (based on its multilateral exchange rate model, MERM) declined from 150.2 in 1985 to 122.5 in 1986 as a whole and to 107.8 by April 1987, a reduction of 28.2 percent from the 1985 level.[12]

The real exchange rates applicable to textile and apparel imports had declined by less (table 3.1). Thus, by 1986 the average rate for textiles had fallen by 12.4 percent from the 1985 level, and the rate for apparel had declined by only 4.5 percent. These smaller corrections, especially that for apparel, were attributable to the fact that the real exchange rate with

---

12. IMF, *International Financial Statistics*, June 1987.

developing-country producers has not declined in tandem with the real value of the dollar relative to the yen and European currencies.[13]

An important, and open, question is whether the exchange rates for the newly industrialized countries (NICs) will appreciate in real terms relative to the dollar. Some appreciation can probably be expected, especially after the decline in oil prices (which is strongly favorable for the external accounts of Korea, Taiwan, and Hong Kong). And in the past decade the rates of the major developing-country exporters of textiles and apparel have tended to move similarly with most of the major OECD suppliers against the dollar (table 3.1). At the very least it should be likely that the currencies of major textile and apparel suppliers will not continue to depreciate relative to the dollar in real terms as they did in the period 1980–85.

As for economic growth, the outlook is less certain. The decline in oil prices, interest rates, and inflation should set the stage for more robust long-term growth than in the early 1980s, although failure to correct the US fiscal deficit could jeopardize this potential.

The estimates of this chapter also suggest that exchange rates and GNP growth have by no means been the sole factors in the rise of US imports in the 1980s. From 1980 to 1986 the real value of apparel imports rose by 123 percent from developing countries and by 182 percent from industrial countries, while real textile imports rose by 85 percent from developing countries and 100 percent from industrial countries. The rise in the strength of the dollar accounted for about one-half of the increase in these imports from industrial countries, but only some one-fourth to one-third for imports from developing countries.

A secular trend of rising imports from developing countries was just as important as the exchange rate in the case of apparel (but not textiles). The model estimates also indicate that declining real prices of textiles and apparel even in the absence of exchange rate change played an important role (although it should be reiterated that these foreign "home" prices are assumed to parallel US domestic real price, not observed directly).

---

13. Thus, from 1985 as a whole to 1986 as a whole, the dollar fell in real terms (deflating by wholesale prices) by 24.4 percent against the Japanese yen, 23.5 percent against the French franc, 23.0 percent against the Italian lire, 26.3 percent against the German mark, and 19.9 percent against the British pound. In contrast, it declined in real terms by only 8 percent against the Taiwan dollar, 6.2 percent against the Hong Kong dollar, 2.7 percent against the Singapore dollar, and 1.2 percent against the Chinese yuan. The US dollar actually appreciated in real terms by 0.8 percent against the Korean won, 18.7 percent against the Mexican peso, and 6.9 percent against the Philippine peso. Calculated from IMF, *International Financial Statistics*, January 1987.

The future trend of imports should depend importantly not only on the real exchange rate but also on long-term trends in shifting supply and in international production prices for textiles and apparel. As developed in this chapter, the pace of outward shifting supply from developing countries (important in apparel imports to date) seems likely to have slowed down following an S curve characteristic of many such processes of initial growth from a small base, so that this factor should be less important in the future. Similarly, there is no reason to expect the real international production prices of textiles and apparel to continue to decline in the future.

The model developed here is applied to projections to the year 2000 in chapter 11. The analysis there considers not only the effects of future exchange rates, growth, and secular trend, but also the impact of alternative trade policy regimes for textiles and apparel.

4

Productivity and Adjustment

The macroeconomic influences of an overvalued dollar and recession adversely affected the textiles and apparel sectors in the first half of the 1980s, but over the longer term it is the microeconomic response to changing comparative advantage that will determine their health. This response, or "adjustment," takes two principal forms: productivity growth through modernization, and industry contraction ("downsizing") both in output and employment. Nonadjustment may also persist but only with the aid of rising protection to forestall the market effects of changing comparative advantage.

This chapter first traces the experience of the textile and apparel sectors in modernization and productivity growth, and compares that experience to the performance of the manufacturing sector in general. The analysis examines the issue of allocating employment changes to the distinct components of demand growth, productivity growth (which reduces employment requirements), and changes in foreign trade. The discussion also considers the extent to which downsizing has featured in the adjustment record of the two sectors. The analysis then combines productivity growth and downsizing in an overall review of adjustment. The discussion concludes with a brief examination of the process of adjustment: the obstacles to and prospects for reallocation of workers from the textile and apparel sectors to other sectors of the economy.

Modernization

The dispersed structure of production has probably impeded modernization. There are approximately 6,000 textile mills in the United States; in apparel, there are some 15,000 firms and 21,000 separate plants.[1] Domestic production

1. US Department of Commerce, *U.S. Industrial Outlook 1985* (Washington: Department of Commerce, 1985), p. 45-1; William Davidson, Charles Feigenoff, and Fariborz Ghadar, *International Competition in Textiles and Apparel: The US Experience* (Washington: National Chamber Foundation, 1986; processed), p. 6.

is approximately $50 billion in each sector (table 2.1), so average output per plant is on the order of $12 million in textiles and $3 million in apparel, and median size would be smaller. Expensive machinery might seem to be beyond the reach of a sizable percentage of firms.

Nonetheless, in textiles technological change in the past three decades has worked toward industrial concentration and mechanization. Mass production methods spurred integration of spinning and weaving in cotton textiles and increased the minimum efficient scale. In fabrics, there has been a trend toward dualism, as thousands of small to medium firms produce specialized products while a few extremely large firms account for a large share of the market across a wide range of products. In natural and man-made fibers, production is knowledge- and capital-intensive, and the structure of production is concentrated, typically in multinational chemical companies. Thus, although the average number of employees per textile mill is approximately 110 workers, two-thirds of employment is in firms of 250 or more workers.[2] As noted below, the two largest textile firms alone employ 86,000 workers. In short, concentration and dualism mean that, within textiles, there are large firms capable of massive investment despite the large number of smaller firms.

In apparel, small size is more pervasive. Economies of scale are much more limited than in textiles, and technological change has been relatively scale-neutral. While cutting is subject to greater efficiency at larger volume, sewing apparently is not. The need to gear production closely to fashion tends to limit production runs, and flexibility in production tends to be more important than cost reduction through larger volume operations. Because of the lesser scale requirements and lower barriers to entry, the apparel sector has remained less concentrated than that of textiles.[3]

As noted in chapter 2, investment for modernization has been relatively high in textiles but low in apparel. The difference has reflected not only industrial structure but also technological opportunity. In the 1970s a new generation of technology emerged in textile production. Open-end spinning permitted a quadrupling of the rate of production of yarn in comparison with the older ring spinning technique and sharply reduced the number of steps required to produce some types of yarn. In fabric weaving, the wooden fly shuttle that moved back and forth across the loom was replaced by shuttles driven by air or water jets. These shuttleless looms tripled speed

2. OECD, *Textile and Clothing Industries: Structural Problems and Policies in OECD Countries* (Paris: OECD, 1983), p. 25; National Research Council, *The Competitive Status of the US Fibers, Textiles and Apparel Complex* (Washington: National Academy Press, 1983), pp. 8–9; US Department of Commerce, *Industrial Outlook 1985*, p. 44-1.

3. OECD, *Textile and Clothing Industries*, pp. 25–27; National Research Council, *The Competitive Status*, p. 13.

and multiplied fabric output even more because of the increased fabric widths possible; they were also safer and quieter.[4]

In the production of fiber polymers, advances in the 1970s enabled speeds of extrusion to multiply some 10-fold over rates in the 1950s, and spindle speeds on texturing machines some 40-fold. In weaving, even conventional looms increased width, with two or three fabrics woven side by side. Operating speeds increased in knitting, in some cases with the assistance of minicomputer controllers. In carpet-making, high-performance synthetic yarns made possible looms with speeds more than double those of the 1960s.[5]

Automation and computer controls are illustrated by Burlington Industries' denim plant in Erwin, North Carolina. Cotton and synthetic fiber are fed into machines where they are shredded and then twisted into thin strands of yarn by high-speed rotors. After computer coding, the pallets of yarn are moved by truck to a new $45 million weaving plant. Machines unload the yarn, and a robot sorts it and places it on a conveyer belt, which moves it to driverless carts for delivery to weaving machines when the machines signal computers that more yarn is needed. The 350 Swiss-made weaving machines do the work of 1,000 old shuttle looms, with the help of constant computer monitoring.[6]

If increased speed and quality are common themes to these technological changes, so is the reduction of labor requirements. Fewer operators are necessary in spinning and weaving, especially in material-handling functions.[7] As illustrations, from 1978 to 1985 Burlington Industries invested $1.5 billion in advanced textile machinery, while cutting its work force from 66,000 to 53,000; J.P. Stevens invested over $480 million in equipment from 1980 to 1985 while reducing its employment from 41,400 to 32,700.[8]

The push toward mechanization and technological advance in textiles in the last two decades appears to have been spurred by innovations introduced by manufacturers of textile machinery, especially those in Germany, Switzerland, and Japan. The United States now imports approximately half of its textile machinery.[9]

---

4. Davidson, Feigenoff, and Ghadar, *International Competition*, p. 10.

5. OECD, *Textile and Clothing Industries*, pp. 20–21.

6. *New York Times*, 23 June 1985.

7. General Agreement on Tariffs and Trade, *Textiles and Clothing in the World Economy* (Geneva: GATT, 1984), p. 35.

8. *New York Times*, 23 June 1985.

9. Davidson, Feigenoff, and Ghadar, *International Competition*, p. 40; NRC, *The Competitive Status*, p. 42.

In apparel, the pace of technological change has been far slower. Although there have been advances in automating and integrating design and cutting, with computerized machines for cutting various grades of patterns available by the late 1960s and laser-beam cutting by the 1970s, sewing has been difficult to mechanize. Faster machines have helped only marginally, as the bulk of a machine operator's time is spent loading and unloading fabric. Separating a single ply of fabric and guiding it through the sewing machine remains almost strictly manual because of the difficulty of mechanization.[10]

Research efforts continue in an effort to overcome the difficulty of apparel mechanization. Apparel firms, their textile suppliers, the Amalgamated Clothing and Textile Workers Union, and the US government have created the Textile Clothing Technology Corporation (called TC²) to fund automation research. The union has joined in the effort because labor leaders prefer the maintenance of a reduced work force in an automated industry to still greater job losses in the absence of improved competitiveness.[11] Even though garment-making robots may be years away, the General Agreement on Tariffs and Trade (GATT) notes that prospective technological developments in sewing could profoundly change apparel employment, and that this process will be stimulated by the likely shortages of skilled sewers and by rising wages.[12]

The need to stay in close touch with rapidly changing fashion imposes a constraint on apparel mechanization, however. These changes can require frequent adjustments of equipment,[13] and tend to lead to batch production rather than long production runs.

In both apparel and textiles, some US firms are pursuing supplemental strategies to improve competitiveness. One is to exploit the natural comparative advantage of location within the US market by concentrating on delivery with short lead times. It has typically required approximately a year to translate retailers' orders to delivery of apparel. Some textile firms are seeking integrated systems with apparel producers and retailers to cut this lead time to approximately five months. Shorter response time would mean lower inventory costs for retailers, and greater ability of the domestic industry to compete with foreign suppliers. The time for ocean shipping and delays associated with transacting business abroad tend to mean unavoidably long lead times for imports, with the consequence that by the time of their arrival they are often behind the fashion and must be sold at discounts. However, analysts expect the accelerated delivery systems to

---

10. OECD, *Textile and Clothing Industries*, p. 22.

11. *Wall Street Journal*, 7 August 1986.

12. GATT, *Textiles and Clothing*, p. 35.

13. US Department of Commerce, *Industrial Outlook 1985*, p. 45-2.

require substantial investments in computer-controlled equipment for design, cutting, and even sewing. Moreover, some apparel executives have expressed concern that the commitments of textile firms to expensive equipment such as high-speed looms designed to produce long runs of individual types of cloth may be efficient but inflexible, whereas the short-response strategy will require flexibility.[14]

Another strategy involves specialization in particular market segments in which US comparative advantage may be high. For example, one firm has multiplied its varieties of denim fabrics, adding such high-margin lines as fashion stretch denim and velour-line fabric marketed under specific trade names.[15] Textile firms have also focused efforts on the home furnishings market, including upholstery, bedding, and carpets. They regard this market as less volatile and less subject to import competition than the apparel market. In apparel, firms have emphasized fashion products, including sportswear, woven dress shirts, and tailored clothing.[16]

Overall, the performance of productivity improvement is widely regarded as favorable in textiles, but less so in apparel. As examined below, productivity growth in textiles in the last 25 years has exceeded that of manufacturing industry generally, whereas productivity growth in apparel has been below the average. One group of experts judges the US textile industry to be the most productive in the world, with the greatest competitive edge in fabrics and man-made fibers, and high productivity as well in floor coverings, hosiery, and knit goods.[17] Another reaches the same conclusion concerning strong US comparative advantage in man-made fibers and yarn based on advanced technology, and cites in addition such high-productivity areas as sheets and towels in textiles and, in apparel, denim and corduroy products. Styling and distribution advantages contribute to strong competitiveness in these and other areas.[18]

Despite the advances in textile technology and productivity, considerable room for improvement remains. Thus, of more than 200,000 looms in use in US textile mills, only about 30 percent are the modern, shuttleless type.[19] More fundamentally, there is a basic policy paradox inherent in adjustment through mechanization and labor-saving technological change. The political justification for protection is that it will save jobs. Yet if protection prompts

---

14. *Wall Street Journal*, 17 December 1985.

15. *New York Times*, 23 June 1986.

16. Davidson, Feigenoff, and Ghadar, *International Competition*, p. 41.

17. NRC, *The Competitive Status*, p. 380.

18. NRC, *The Competitive Status*, p. 38.

19. *New York Times*, 23 June 1985.

sharp employment reduction through mechanization, it ends up saving firms and profits but not jobs. The evaluation of adjustment, below, returns to this paradox.

Productivity Growth and Wage Adjustment

The technological developments and characteristics of industrial structure described above would lead to the expectation that productivity growth would have been relatively high in textiles but lower in apparel. Ideally, productivity would be measured as the ratio of production to total factor inputs, including capital as well as labor. However, meaningful capital data are difficult to obtain, and productivity is usually measured by the ratio of output to employment. This "labor productivity" measure must be understood to reflect "capital deepening" (rising capital per worker) as well as "pure" technical change (in which output rises both per unit of capital and per worker). Economic efficiency is enhanced the most by pure technical change, although it may also rise (as measured by profitability) from capital deepening in the context of relatively cheap capital and expensive labor.

As measured by labor productivity (output per worker), the expected pattern has indeed occurred. Productivity growth in textiles has been relatively rapid while that in apparel has been relatively slow, especially in the 1960s and early 1970s. Table 4.1 reports estimates of annual labor productivity growth in textiles, apparel, and US manufacturing overall from 1961 through 1985. To avoid the problem of selecting representative base and terminal years for computation of these growth rates, the estimates are based on statistical regressions using annual data over the whole period.[20]

---

20. The regressions are based on the equation:

(1) $q_t = e^{[K + kD]} e^{at} e^{bD(t - T)}$,

where q_t is output per worker in year t, K is a constant, D is a dummy variable with value 1 beginning in 1973 and zero before, e refers to the base of the natural logarithm, T is the value of t at the end of the first period ($T = 12$ for 1972), and the terms k, a, and b are regression coefficients. When expressed in logarithmic form, this equation provides a linear regression in which productivity growth during the first period equals "a" and during the second period equals "$a+b$," with the constant term K during the first period and $K+k$ during the second. If the terms k and b are significantly different from zero, the constant terms and productivity growth differ significantly between the two periods; otherwise they do not. Data are from table 2.1 for textiles and apparel (output expressed in constant 1982 dollars divided by total employment) and from Council of Economic Advisers, *Economic Report of the President 1986* (Washington: CEA, February 1986), pp. 298, 304, for US manufacturing (total manufacturing employees and manufacturing production index). The estimated productivity growth coefficients and their t-statistics in parentheses are as follows. For textiles: $a = .0488$ (10.1), $b = -.0118$ (1.7). For apparel: $a = .0128$ (4.9), $b = .0147$ (4.0). For US manufacturing: $a = .0351$ (16.0), $b = -.0061$ (2.0).

Table 4.1 Growth of labor productivity: textiles, apparel, and US manufacturing, 1961–85 (annual percentage)

	Textiles	Apparel	US manufacturing
1961–72	4.88	1.28	3.51
1973–85	3.71	2.75	2.90

Source: Calculated by statistical regression; see text.

The regressions apply dummy, or shift, variables to capture changes in productivity growth between the two sub-periods, 1961–72 and 1973–85.

The productivity growth rates shown in table 4.1 confirm the expectation that performance in textiles has been above the manufacturing average, ·while that in apparel has been below the average. However, these divergences were much sharper in the 1960s and early 1970s than in the remainder of the 1970s and the early 1980s. In the period 1973–85, the rate of productivity growth in apparel in particular doubled, while that in manufacturing generally fell by one-fifth. As a result, in this second period there was much less difference between the two. And although textile productivity growth remained well above that of apparel and overall manufacturing, the divergence was smaller (about 1 percentage point) than in the period 1961–72 (3½ percentage points above apparel and 1⅓ percentage points above manufacturing).

Despite the relative improvement for apparel in the past decade or so, its productivity growth has remained at best middling—no greater than the manufacturing average. Yet for a sector to adjust to import competition through rising productivity ("revitalization," as designated below), it would be expected to achieve productivity growth rates well above the manufacturing average. Thus, about the most that can be said for performance in apparel in relation to trade policy is that tighter protection in the period of the Multi-Fiber Arrangement (MFA, 1973 to the present) has not lulled the sector into lower productivity growth than before (and indeed that growth has even accelerated). It does not follow that the industry's productivity performance has been adequate for successful adjustment. In contrast, a much better case for adjustment through revitalization can be made in the case of textiles, which has sustained a significantly higher productivity growth rate than has manufacturing generally.

Profitability and thus survivability of the industry depend not only on the productivity of labor but also its cost. The record shows that the apparel sector has to a considerable degree compensated for its slower productivity growth by the squeezing of labor costs through wage erosion. Table 4.2 reports indexes of annual labor productivity and of the sectoral average

Table 4.2 Labor productivity and relative wages in US textiles and apparel, 1960–84 (indexes, 1972 = 100, and dollars per hour)

Year	Textiles Real output per worker	Wage[a]	Relative wage[b]	Apparel Real output per worker	Wage[a]	Relative wage[b]
1960	49.4	1.64	99.7	80.5	1.56	104.2
1961	53.1	1.68	99.5	79.5	1.59	103.5
1962	56.6	1.72	98.9	81.5	1.65	104.2
1963	73.1	1.77	99.3	84.0	1.70	104.8
1964	74.9	1.82	98.8	84.7	1.73	103.2
1965	77.1	1.91	100.6	87.4	1.78	103.0
1966	79.7	1.99	100.9	89.0	1.82	101.4
1967	78.3	2.10	102.3	89.8	1.99	106.5
1968	78.7	2.24	102.3	91.3	2.15	107.8
1969	78.9	2.36	101.7	90.6	2.24	106.0
1970	84.4	2.48	101.7	83.4	2.27	102.3
1971	92.8	2.62	100.8	89.1	2.41	101.9
1972	100.0	2.78	100.0	100.0	2.53	100.0
1973	97.3	2.99	100.5	100.4	2.67	98.6
1974	93.2	3.27	101.7	99.2	2.82	96.3
1975	102.7	3.56	101.3	107.8	3.06	95.7
1976	107.6	3.80	100.0	108.1	3.22	93.1
1977	117.7	4.07	98.5	112.7	3.56	94.6
1978	120.5	4.41	98.2	116.8	3.80	93.0
1979	124.5	4.75	97.4	112.1	3.97	89.5
1980	122.6	5.18	97.9	111.8	4.25	88.3
1981	124.4	5.58	96.0	118.0	4.53	85.6
1982	129.4	5.99	96.8	127.9	4.90	87.1
1983	142.1	6.32	98.4	131.5	5.07	86.7
1984	143.2	6.56	98.2	124.1	5.35	88.0
1985	152.3	6.80	98.3	124.7	5.59	88.7

Source: Table 2.1; US Department of Commerce, *US Industrial Outlook 1985,* pp. 44-4, 45-7; 1986; pp. 42-1, 43-1; and by communication; Council of Economic Advisers, *Economic Report of the President,* 1986, p. 300.
a. Average hourly earnings.
b. Relative to average gross hourly earnings, US manufacturing (note: = $3.82 in 1972).

wage relative to the manufacturing average. As indicated, the ratio of textile wages to the manufacturing average has remained almost unchanged over the past quarter century (at about 72 percent). In contrast, in apparel the trend has been toward declining relative wages. From 1972 to 1985, the apparel wage relative to the manufacturing wage declined from an index of 100 to 88.7, or from 66.2 percent of the manufacturing average to 58.7 percent.

Wages in apparel have been consistently below those in textiles and falling steadily in relative terms. From 1972 to 1985 the wage in apparel fell from 91 percent of that in textiles to only 82 percent, a reduction of about 10 percent in the relative wage. During the same period, output per worker in apparel fell by about 12 percent relative to that in textiles (at 2.75 percent annual growth instead of 3.71 percent). As a result, declining relative wages in apparel approximately compensated for falling relative labor productivity, in comparison with textiles.

Data on the share of total labor costs in gross output value indicate a similar tendency toward moderation of differential productivity growth, but with the compensation through relative wage erosion less complete. Thus, from 1972 to 1985 total payroll costs declined from 23.4 percent of gross output value in textiles to 18.4 percent (a cutback by the proportion 0.21); in apparel, the reduction was from 30.2 percent to 25.4 percent (a decline by the fraction 0.16).[21]

The lag of apparel wages behind textile wages appears to reflect two forces: what the market will bear, and skill composition. With slower productivity growth, apparel has less room for wage increases than textiles. In addition, the mechanization and modernization of textiles has meant a changing composition of its labor force, as lower-skilled workers in such operations as in-plant materials transporting have been eliminated while computer technicians and operators of sophisticated machinery have been added. (Indeed, it may be that a proper measure of constant-skill wages in textiles would find that they have declined relative to the manufacturing average because of more rapid skill upgrading in textiles than in manufacturing overall.)

In short, since the mid-1970s, wage erosion in apparel has enabled the sector to attain a performance in cost reduction that is closer to that of textiles than would be expected on a basis of their respective rates of growth of labor productivity. Indeed, if the basis for comparison is the manufacturing average rather than textiles, the apparel sector has probably achieved some modest improvement in competitiveness. That is, from 1972 to 1985 the rate of growth of labor productivity was practically equal for apparel and for manufacturing overall, while the wage in apparel declined by approximately 11 percent relative to that in manufacturing (table 4.2). Improving relative cost performance translated into modestly declining relative price without a corresponding reduction in profitability. Thus, on the basis of

---

21. Calculated from US Department of Commerce, *U.S. Industrial Outlook 1987* (Washington: Department of Commerce, 1987).

national accounts price deflators, from 1972 to 1985 inflation in apparel averaged 5.1 percent annually, in textiles 5.3 percent, and in all manufacturing, 5.8 percent; at the same time, apparel avoided any decline (and appears in fact to have achieved an increase) in its profitability relative to that of manufacturing overall.[22]

Overall, the textiles sector appears to have achieved considerable adjustment through productivity growth in the past two decades. In part because of the greater difficulty of mechanization, the apparel sector has achieved lesser results in productivity growth, but in partial compensation has squeezed labor costs through relative wage erosion. As a result, even apparel appears to have modestly outperformed manufacturing on average in terms of labor cost, at least in 1972–85. However, it is unclear that the combined effects of adjustment through productivity growth and through wage restraint have been sufficient to boost apparel, and even textiles, into such high relative cost performance that their overall pace of adjustment is adequate to enable them to confront import competition. In apparel particularly, the relative improvement overall is at best modest, if the basis for comparison is the US manufacturing average. Moreover, it is possible that another relevant standard for comparison—production costs in major foreign competitor countries—would show less favorable performance than the benchmark of US manufacturing, calling further into question the adequacy of cost adjustment.

Sources of Employment Decline

The other side of the coin of rising labor productivity is declining labor requirements per unit of output. Unless demand for the product is growing sufficiently, productivity growth can cause falling employment. The level of employment has indeed declined in both textiles and apparel. Textile employment peaked at 980,300 workers in 1973 and by 1986 had fallen to 668,900 workers; in apparel, the reduction has been from a peak of 1,400,000 workers in 1973 to 1,133,000 in 1986 (table 2.1). The percentage decline from peak employment has been less than two-thirds as large in apparel (19.1 percent) as in textiles (31.8 percent). Not only has productivity growth been faster in textiles; in addition, total output growth has been more rapid in apparel.[23]

Since at least the 1960s, the policy debate has tended to attribute employment problems in textiles and apparel to rising imports. Economists

---

22. Ibid; Council of Economic Advisers, *Economic Report of the President 1986*, pp. 264–5; and table 2.2.

23. At constant prices, textile output rose by 5.1 percent from 1973 to 1985, or 0.4 percent annually, while apparel output rose by 12.0 percent, or 0.9 percent annually. Calculated from table 2.1.

have periodically pointed out, however, that job losses must also be attributed to mechanization and rising labor productivity.[24] In the mid-1970s Charles R. Frank, Jr. proposed a method for identifying the respective contributions of import expansion and productivity growth to total employment performance, as well as those of demand growth and export expansion. His method is a definitional decomposition that states that the percentage change of employment must equal a weighted average of the percentage changes of demand and exports (positive), as well as imports and labor productivity (negative).[25] Applying the approach to US industrial data for 1963–71 at the level of 19 Standard Industrial Classification (SIC) 2-digit categories, Frank found that only four sectors had experienced declining employment (textiles, apparel, leather products, fabricated metal products), and only in leather was the impact of trade important. Rising labor productivity and stagnant growth in domestic demand were found to be far more important than trade influences. Krueger obtained similar results with more detailed analysis for the period 1970–76.[26] She found that in 10 of the 19 SIC 2-digit categories employment had declined, but in only one (leather products) did import-related losses exceed those attributable to domestic demand or productivity growth. At the 4-digit SIC level, employment declined in 22 of the 44 categories, but imports contributed significantly to employment loss in only five, of which two were in apparel (children's outerwear, men's and boys' suits).

Some authors have criticized this "accounting decomposition" approach as mechanical and devoid of economic causation. Thus, Grossman has argued that the only way to detect the influence of imports on employment is through a comprehensive econometric model that can be simulated to replicate history on the one hand and a hypothetical counterexample without import pressure, on the other.[27] Similarly, Martin and Evans have criticized the technique for failing to recognize that productivity growth could be

---

24. In particular, Peter Isard, "Employment Impacts of Textile Imports and Investment: A Vintage-Capital Model," *American Economic Review*, vol. 63, no. 3 (June 1973), pp. 402–16.

25. Charles R. Frank, Jr., *Foreign Trade and Domestic Aid* (Washington: Brookings Institution, 1977), p. 27. Frank's equation is:

$$r_e = r_d(D/Q) + r_x(X/Q) - r_m(M/Q) - r_p,$$

where r_e is the rate of growth of employment, r_d is the rate of growth of domestic demand, r_x is the rate of growth of exports, r_m is that of imports, and r_p is the rate of growth of labor productivity; D is domestic demand, Q is domestic output, X is exports, and M is imports.

26. Anne O. Krueger, "Protectionist Pressures, Imports and Employment in the United States," *Scandinavian Journal of Economics*, vol. 82, no. 2 (1980), pp. 133–146.

27. Gene M. Grossman, "The Employment and Wage Effects of Import Competition in the United States," National Bureau of Economic Research Working Paper, no. 1041 (Cambridge, Mass., December 1982).

endogenous, an induced response to import pressure—in which case the role of imports in reducing employment would be understated by the accounting attribution based on import growth and import share.[28]

In practice, the principal risk of misinterpretation of the accounting approach is that it will fail to attribute productivity changes to pressures arising from import competition. Statistical regressions for textiles and apparel in the period 1961–85 fail to find a significant influence of the import penetration ratio on labor productivity,[29] however, so it would appear useful to apply the decomposition technique to examine the relative roles of demand, productivity growth, and trade in explaining the stagnation and eventual decline of employment. Treatment of productivity growth as independent of import pressure appears warranted institutionally as well for textiles, where the driving force has been the development of new technology and where imports have remained in the range of 10 percent of the market or less. In apparel, the a priori case for causation running from imports to productivity growth might be greater, given the higher and rising import share; but the fact that productivity growth in apparel has been less than or barely equal to that for manufacturing overall lends institutional support to the statistical finding that imports have played no special role.

Application of the employment decomposition technique to textiles and apparel (using the method of footnote 25) yields the results indicated in table 4.3. Growth rates for the individual variables, and their respective weights, are calculated from the trade, consumption, and output data presented in chapter 2 (tables 2.1 through 2.5).

Table 4.3 indicates, first, that like many industries with stagnant or declining employment, textiles (especially) and apparel have slowly growing consumption. After rapid growth in the 1960s, textile consumption rose by only about 1 percent annually from 1972–86 (despite a surge in the recovery from the 1982 recession), contributing only about the same annual growth in potential employment. Against this slow consumption growth, rapid productivity growth in textiles contributed substantially to employment erosion. Thus, in the weighted composition of employment change, productivity growth has reduced employment by an average of 3.25 percentage

---

28. John P. Martin and John M. Evans, "Notes on Measuring the Employment Displacement Effects of Trade by the Accounting Procedure," *Oxford Economic Papers,* vol. 33, no. 1 (March 1981), pp. 154–64.

29. This test augments the equation of note 20 by the multiplicative terms w_t^i and m_{t-1}^q where w is the real wage (deflating by wholesale price index) and m is the import penetration ratio (imports divided by consumption). Estimated for the period 1961–85 for textiles and apparel separately, the resulting equation yielded insignificant coefficients for the wage term and for the import penetration term. Specifically, lagged import penetration has the following coefficient (and t-statistic): textiles, 0.0225 (0.27); apparel, -0.063 (-0.51).

points annually since 1972.[30] In contrast, at least until 1982, trade in textiles had little effect on the evolution of employment. The shift of exports from a small but positive contribution before the early 1980s to a negative impact as exports declined in 1982–85 is noteworthy. As for imports, they actually had a favorable effect in 1972–77 as they declined, and even in their worst period (1982–85) their negative contribution to textile employment change was only about one-sixth as large as the negative contribution from productivity growth. In short, in textiles the decomposition approach supports the view that productivity growth and slow growth of consumption have dominated declining employment, while import growth has played only a minor role.

In apparel, this approach yields a larger role for imports, but still finds productivity growth to be the more dominant source of declining employment. Consumption demand in apparel has grown more rapidly than that in textiles, averaging 3.0 percent annually in the period 1972–85. Stagnant demand is thus much less of a problem in apparel than in textiles. In the same period, productivity growth has contributed an average of 2.9 percent annually to the decline of employment. Apparel exports have had only small effects on employment because of their limited size. However, imports have had a persistently growing and negative effect on apparel employment. From an annual negative contribution of approximately 0.4 percent in employment growth in the 1960s, the impact of imports rose to an annual employment decline of about 1 percent in 1972–82 and surged to an impact of 3.25 percent job loss annually during the import boom of 1982–85. Even so, it was not until this final period of extremely rapid import growth that the employment-reducing effect of imports came to rival that of productivity growth. And, as noted in chapters 3 and 7, there are strong reasons to doubt that the rapid growth of apparel imports in the period 1982–85 will continue into the future.

In sum, the decomposition approach indicates that for textiles in virtually all periods and for apparel at least until the 1970s and even prior to 1982, the adverse effect of imports on employment has been much more limited than that of labor productivity growth (and, in the case of textiles, slow growth in demand). While the import surge of 1982–85 temporarily pushed the negative employment effect of imports in apparel to a magnitude almost equal to that of productivity growth, the pace of this import growth is unlikely to continue.

---

30. Note, however, that the rates discussed here are simple averages from the periods of table 4.3 and, because they are based on end-point calculations, less meaningful than the regression-based productivity growth rates of table 4.1.

Table 4.3 Decomposition of employment growth, 1961–85[a]
(percentage growth rates)

	Textiles				
	1962–67	1967–72	1972–77	1977–82	1982–85
Actual growth rates					
Output	8.82	3.91	1.98	−0.38	1.46
Consumption	8.85	4.01	1.40	−0.56	3.05
Exports	7.21	4.65	12.84	2.37	−11.76
Imports	8.65	6.37	−3.97	4.20	12.91
Employment	1.54	0.03	−1.19	−3.08	−2.79
Sources of employment growth					
Consumption	9.07	4.12	1.44	−0.56	3.03
Exports	0.17	0.10	0.28	0.09	−0.51
Imports	−0.41	−0.30	0.21	−0.17	−0.65
Productivity	−7.28	−3.86	−3.19	−2.70	−4.27
Total	1.54	0.05	−1.25	−3.34	−2.40

Source: Calculated from tables 2.1, 2.3, and 2.5.
a. Periods are for two-year base and terminal average, in each case including year prior to named year (example: 1961–62 to 1966–67).

The broad policy implication of the earlier Frank and Krueger findings was that, because domestic demand and productivity growth rather than imports were primarily responsible for stagnant or declining employment, calls for protection on grounds of job displacement by imports were unwarranted. In the case of textiles today, the same conclusion is appropriate. The impact of trade on employment in this sector is simply too limited to justify demands for additional protection; and indeed, with the decline in the dollar the trade impact on textile employment could well be positive in the near term.

In apparel, recent experience has been that imports have indeed been a source of important employment erosion. The impact of imports in the period 1972–82 seems more relevant over the longer term than that during the aberrational period of overvaluation in 1982–85. If so, the broad range of employment erosion attributable to import growth would be in the vicinity of 1 percent annually. The policy question, then, is whether employment reduction on this scale from the source of import growth is compatible with domestic adjustment without excessive pain, or whether instead tighter import restrictions are appropriate—and, if so, at what cost

Apparel				
1962–67	1967–72	1972–77	1977–82	1982–85
4.20	0.81	2.42	0.89	1.76
4.46	1.57	3.11	1.68	5.22
3.36	2.88	16.30	6.03	− 13.74
12.71	15.60	12.29	7.72	18.15
2.11	− 0.24	− 0.63	− 1.30	− 2.06
4.52	1.61	3.31	1.86	5.99
0.04	0.03	0.20	0.15	− 0.44
− 0.31	− 0.58	− 0.95	− 0.98	− 3.25
− 2.10	− 1.04	− 3.05	− 2.22	− 3.79
2.15	0.02	− 0.50	− 1.20	− 1.49

to consumers. Despite the construct of the accounting approach in which productivity growth reduces employment, there would be little merit in recommending as a policy course that labor productivity growth be slowed down. That growth surely contributes to the long-term ability of the industry to achieve competitiveness at some threshold of a reduced but relatively stronger production base.

In one important dimension, the appropriate policy would be to go slowly in productivity growth. Policies that artificially stimulate investment for productivity growth may be misguided and inferior to a course of reducing production while leaving labor productivity at a more slowly growing level. This is especially true if the investments to be stimulated are large and would sharply increase nonlabor costs. Of course, protection itself is an artificial stimulus to investment, but it is also an artificial stimulus to employment in the industry. Perhaps the worst policies are those that, in the name of preserving employment, would actively erode it by lowering the relative price of capital compared to labor and promoting the replacement of labor by capital more rapidly than would occur under market signals, even when the market is distorted by the presence of protection.

Downsizing and Overall Adjustment

It is natural for firms and governments in industrial countries to seek "adjustment" to import pressure through modernization and productivity growth in the domestic industry, or what may be called "revitalization." However, there is another side of adjustment that should also be present: a conscious process of orderly retreat from the industry as resources are reallocated to other sectors in which the economy has more favorable comparative advantage. Indeed, the Multi-Fiber Arrangement provides that:[31]

This Arrangement shall not interrupt or discourage the autonomous industrial adjustment processes of participating countries. Furthermore, actions taken under this Arrangement should be accompanied by the pursuit of appropriate economic and social policies, . . . required by changes in the pattern of trade in textiles and in the comparative advantage of participating countries, which policies would encourage businesses which are less competitive internationally to move progressively into more viable lines of production or into other sectors of the economy. . .

The reallocation of resources to more productive sectors may be called downsizing. As measured by the allocation of labor resources to production, there has been considerable downsizing in US textiles and, to a lesser degree, apparel. Thus, as noted above, from the peak in 1973 these sectors have experienced reductions in employment by approximately one-third and one-fifth, respectively. Measured by total factor allocation including capital resources, downsizing would be more modest, with the difference especially marked in textiles where investment has been high. An even stronger test of downsizing would be the level of real output. However, total output could continue to grow slowly even as total factors devoted to the sector declined, because of rising total factor productivity. In fact, the level of total output in the textile and apparel sectors has been relatively stagnant in recent years. Real output in textiles peaked in 1979 at $51.3 billion (in 1982 prices), and after a sharp reduction in the 1982 recession, was still 4.0 percent below the peak by 1986. In apparel, real output has risen but slowly (table 2.1).

A graphical summary facilitates an overview of sectoral adjustment through revitalization and downsizing.[32] Figure 4.1 shows average annual growth

---

31. *Arrangement Regarding International Trade in Textiles,* Article 1, paragraph 4.

32. The first statement of this approach is in William R. Cline, "U.S. Trade and Industrial Policy: The Experience of Textiles, Steel, and Automobiles," in *Strategic Trade Policy and the New International Economics,* edited by Paul R. Krugman (Cambridge, Mass.: MIT Press, 1986), pp. 212–39.

Figure 4.1 Adjustment through revitalization and downsizing

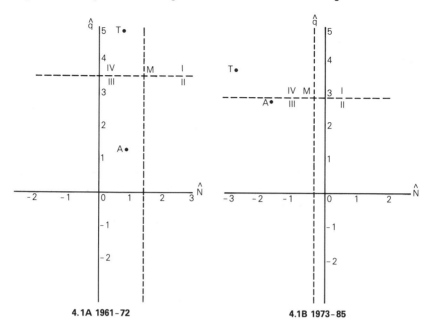

rates of labor productivity and of employment for two periods, 1961–72 and 1973–85, for textiles (T), apparel (A), and US manufacturing overall (M). The performance of US manufacturing may be used as a benchmark for "normal" productivity and employment growth. If a sector achieves above average productivity growth, it may be considered to be carrying out adjustment through revitalization. If a sector experiences slower employment growth than the manufacturing average, it may be considered to be implementing downsizing.

In the figure, a supplemental set of axes drawn through the position of US manufacturing (M) serves to demarcate revitalization and downsizing from nonadjustment in the respective dimensions of productivity growth and total labor resources. Points above the supplemental horizontal axis (in quadrants labeled IV and I) indicate the presence of revitalization, or productivity growth more rapid than the manufacturing average. Points to the left of the supplemental vertical axis (in quadrants labeled IV and III) indicate a process of downsizing, as employment growth falls short of the average for manufacturing. Sectors located in quadrant I would be achieving revitalization with expansion (above average labor growth), while those in quadrant IV would be revitalizing while at the same time downsizing. Sectors in quadrant III would be failing to revitalize (productivity growth below average) but would at least be adjusting through downsizing. Sectors in quadrant II would be failing to adjust at all: they would be neither revitalizing nor downsizing.

Figure 4.1 indicates that the textile sector has been carrying out both types of adjustment for the past 25 years. Its productivity growth has been well above the manufacturing average (revitalization), while its employment growth has been below the average (downsizing), placing it in quadrant IV in both the earlier and more recent periods. Indeed, in the period 1973–85 the downsizing aspect of textile adjustment has become pronounced, as its employment growth has turned sharply negative (− 2.8 percent annually, versus + 0.8 percent in the earlier period). Note that in the later period, total US manufacturing employment was also declining (at a rate of 0.3 percent annually, versus positive annual growth of 1.4 percent in the earlier period). The diagram thus suggests that adjustment in textiles has been relatively brisk, in both forms.

Adjustment in apparel has been more sluggish. In the first period the sector was not only failing to revitalize but was not even keeping up with average US productivity growth. And although its employment growth was below the manufacturing average, placing it in quadrant III where the sector was at least accomplishing downsizing adjustment, employment growth was still positive (0.9 percent) so that in an absolute as opposed to relative sense downsizing was not taking place. In the more recent period, the apparel sector has begun to downsize both absolutely and relatively, as its employment declined at an average rate of 1.5 percent annually. However, it has still been unable to implement adjustment through revitalization, as its productivity growth has still, if just barely, lagged behind the manufacturing average. The graphical analysis does not take account of the further dimension of adjustment through wage compression, as discussed above. Nonetheless, the basic message of the diagram remains accurate: overall adjustment has been relatively rapid in textiles but slow in apparel, although the difference between the two sectors has declined in recent years.

The analysis here judges revitalization on the basis of productivity growth relative to the US manufacturing average. It might be objected that the more germane standard would be productivity growth of the same industries abroad in the countries of principal competitors. While the same technological changes that have facilitated textile productivity growth have been available internationally, the very definition of comparative advantage concerns relative efficiency among the array of domestic industries. For this reason, it is highly relevant to consider the productivity growth of the individual textile and apparel sectors in comparison with that of US manufacturing on average. Other things being equal, the above average productivity growth of the textile sector should have tended to make this sector relatively more efficient compared to other US industries over the past two decades, while the lagging rate in apparel would have made that sector relatively less efficient. In the first instance, then, comparative advantage would have shifted toward US textiles and away from US apparel over this period.

A more complete examination of international productivity might find that in countries such as Korea and Hong Kong productivity growth in textiles had also been high. But in that case, it would also require the finding that this productivity growth had exceeded the average of manufacturing in Korea and Hong Kong to reverse the conclusion of improving comparative advantage for US textile producers. For those countries too, it is the relative efficiency compared to other domestic industries that determines the path of comparative advantage over time. Moreover, because the technological changes in textiles have been capital-intensive and capital is relatively more abundant in the United States than in countries such as Korea (where the rate of return on, and cost of capital are considerably higher), the mere availability of the same technologies to all foreign producers would be unlikely to have neutralized the gain in comparative advantage for US textile producers implied by the sectoral productivity analysis above.

Some analysts have judged the US adjustment experience under textile and apparel protection a success.[33] A recent study prepared for the National Chamber of Commerce judges that the textile and apparel industries had made extensive efforts to adjust to import competition and that during the 1970s "this adjustment process, at least in the textile industry, proceeded relatively smoothly" and, although the apparel sector fared less well, imports increased at moderate levels. The study notes that in the 1980s, in contrast, imports grew much more rapidly because of the overvalued dollar and "the arrival of the NICs as important and permanent participants." The authors find that the US textile industry has "performed strongly in comparison to the industries of Europe and Japan" and that apparel has done no worse than in other industrial countries.[34]

Because protection has remained high in textiles (where more restrictive quotas have at the least offset negotiated tariff reductions) and has risen consistently in apparel, however, it would appear erroneous to conclude that adjustment has been successful. The relevant test of adjustment success

---

33. Thus, Stanley Nehmer, a former US official who helped design textile restrictions in the 1970s, and a coauthor write: "By stabilizing world markets somewhat, the MFA has encouraged competitive responses by domestic manufacturers through investment, innovation, and consolidation." Stanley Nehmer and Mark W. Love, "Textiles and Apparel: A Negotiated Approach to International Competition," in *US Competitiveness in the World Economy*, edited by Bruce R. Scott and George C. Lodge (Boston, Mass.: Harvard Business School Press, 1985), p. 230.

34. Davidson, Feigenoff, and Ghadar, *International Competition*, pp. 35, 43.

is the reopening of the market. Just as legitimate infant-industry protection in developing countries should be subject to time limits so, too, should adjustment of declining industries in the industrial countries. Yet today US protective barriers in textiles are as high as they were a quarter of a century ago, and in apparel they are substantially higher.

The underlying economic performance suggests adjustment success in textiles, where the US trade balance actually turned to a surplus immediately before the erosion under an overvalued dollar in the early 1980s. In this sector, policy appears to have lagged behind economic performance, as protection has not declined accordingly and is on no timetable toward phasedown.

In apparel, the underlying economic performance would appear to be less favorable. The evidence suggests that in this sector, which is difficult to mechanize and remains labor-intensive, future reestablishment of US comparative advantage is doubtful. In this sector, the more relevant type of adjustment is downsizing rather than revitalization. Yet it is precisely in apparel where downsizing has been limited, and ever-higher protection has been the response instead. Thus, a decline of 19 percent in employment from the previous historical peak is meager in comparison with much sharper cutbacks in apparel employment in other industrial countries (chapter 5), and even in comparison with the textile sector in the United States. Apparel downsizing of employment also looks sluggish when compared with the cutbacks of employment in other sectors that have faced import pressure. Thus, in the steel sector, employment peaked in 1965 at 584,000 and by 1984 had declined by 59 percent to 242,000.[35] In footwear, employment peaked at 260,600 in 1941 and declined from 242,600 in 1960 to 116,100 in 1984.[36]

Labor Adjustment

It is crucial that the public policy process more explicitly address the objective of protection in textiles and apparel: is the goal to protect people or positions? If the goal is to limit adverse effects of imports on existing employees in the sectors—that is, to protect people who have names and are known—then the relevant question is how to accomplish sectoral adjustment while limiting the pain for these individuals. If the goal is to preserve "positions" in the sense that it is a national objective to ensure

35. William R. Cline, "U.S. Trade and Industrial Policy," pp. 212–13.

36. Bureau of Labor Statistics, *Employment and Earnings, U.S. 1909–78*, Bulletin 1312–11, July 1979, pp. 697–98, and *Supplement to Employment and Earnings*, June 1985, pp. 116–17.

that in the year 2000 and beyond there are some 2 million jobs in textiles and apparel even though most of the workers at that time are not yet in the labor force, then the task is quite different. It amounts instead to acceptance of ever-rising consumer and efficiency costs as protection mounts indefinitely for this purpose.

Representatives of labor groups implicitly tend to advocate the latter formulation of US policy in the two sectors. This approach seems to subscribe to two notions: that workers displaced from specific manufacturing sectors would find employment only in the services sectors, and that US manufacturing jobs are better than the service sector jobs. The view of "position preservation" appears to hold that there must be some location for manufacturing workers with modest skills, to absorb lower-tier workers in an equitable society.

US farm policy has long made costly transfers to the agricultural sector in part because of a similar belief that farm jobs were important to preserve for their own sake. Those concerned about the "deindustrialization of America" appear to support similar national transfers to sustain positions in the manufacturing sector on the implicit assumption that manufacturing jobs are somehow superior to those in the services sector, the locus of employment expansion in the past two decades.[37]

Three facts would seem to contradict this vision of the importance of textile-apparel employment per se as part of a desire to sustain and raise manufacturing employment. The first is that the available evidence suggests that in fact almost one-half of workers displaced from manufacturing jobs and subsequently reemployed obtain new jobs in the manufacturing sector.[38] Secondly, service-sector wages are not much, if any, lower than those in the textile and apparel sectors. Thus, in 1985 the average hourly wage for production workers was $6.80 in textiles and $5.59 in apparel.[39] These rates were well below the manufacturing average of $9.65 per hour, and in fact were close to the average for retail trade, $6.03 per hour.[40]

---

37. From its peak in 1973, US manufacturing employment has declined from 20.2 million workers to 19.4 million in 1985, virtually the same level as in 1966. Over the same period (1973–85), employment in the service industries (transportation and public utilities, wholesale and retail trade, finance, insurance, real estate, government, and other services) has risen from 51.9 million workers to 72.6 million, an increase of 40 percent. Compared with the levels of two decades ago, manufacturing employment has remained unchanged, while that in services has risen by 78 percent. Council of Economic Advisers, *Economic Report of the President 1986*, pp. 298–99.

38. As found by the Bureau of Labor Statistics in its study of displaced workers over the period 1980–83. Richard M. Devens, "Displaced Workers: One Year Later," *Monthly Labor Review*, vol. 109, no. 7 (July 1986), p. 41.

39. US Department of Commerce, *U.S. Industrial Outlook 1987*.

40. Council of Economic Advisers, *Economic Report of the President 1986*, p. 300.

Indeed, service jobs in the retail sector paid more highly than apparel manufacturing jobs. (Retail service jobs are probably the most relevant subsector with available data; overall averages for service sector wages can be misleading, because they include such highly paid professional categories as doctors and lawyers.) Supposed superiority of manufacturing jobs over service-sector employment would thus appear to have little foundation in textiles and apparel.

The third fact that should be taken into account is that demographic changes already in process are likely to reduce the relative availability of labor in the 1990s and beyond. The Bureau of Labor Statistics (BLS) estimates that the US civilian labor force, which grew at 2.6 percent annually in 1970–80 and had already slowed to a pace of 1.5 percent in 1980–84, will decelerate further to a growth of 1.3 percent annually in 1984–90 and only 1 percent annually in 1990–95. This sharp slowdown is the consequence of a shift from new entry into the labor force by the baby-boom generation in the 1970s, and from rapid increase in female labor force participation, to a phase of labor force entry by the post-baby-boom cohorts and moderation in the increasing female participation rate.[41] Moreover, recent legislation imposing penalties on employers of undocumented aliens will aggravate this emerging relative scarcity, especially at the low end of the skills spectrum.[42] Thus, public creation of jobs for specific sectors at a direct or indirect cost to the general public may be a policy that is especially inappropriate for the coming decades.

More generally, the concern about deindustrialization has been exaggerated. Careful analyses of the issue stress that US manufacturing is not declining in terms of production levels. Instead, the principal phenomenon is that the share of the manufacturing sector in total employment has declined as rising labor productivity enables an approximately constant manufacturing labor force to produce a rising level of production, while the service sector absorbs a growing share of employment. Thus, from 1959 to 1985, the share of manufacturing in US employment fell from 25.8 percent to 18.0 percent, while the share of services (excluding construction) rose

---

41. Howard N. Fullerton, Jr., "The 1995 Labor Force: BLS' Latest Projections," *Monthly Labor Review*, vol. 108, no. 11 (November 1985), pp. 17–25. With respect to the baby boom, the figures are as follows: annual US births rose from 2.6 million in 1940 and 2.9 million in 1945 to 3.6 million in 1950 and 4.3 million in 1960, but then retreated to 3.5 million in the late 1960s and only 3.1 million in the early 1970s (although by the early 1980s the rate had returned to some 3.6 million annually). US Department of Commerce, *Statistical Abstract of the United States 1985* (Washington: Bureau of the Census, 1984), p. 57.

42. By mid-1987 there were already growing reports that textile and apparel workers were in scarce supply because of the new immigration law, especially in California. Some firms were seeking to import Philippine workers to fill jobs. *Washington Post*, 5 July 1987.

from 50.8 percent to 67.8 percent. However, the share of manufacturing in gross national product did not decline but actually rose slightly, from 20.7 percent to 21.7 percent, while the share of services in GNP rose by considerably less (from 60.0 percent to 66.7 percent) than the service sector's share in employment. And despite absolute declines of production in some individual sectors (including steel, leather, and tires), real manufacturing production in the aggregate rose by 162.5 percent from 1959 to 1984 (and by 15.9 percent from 1979 to 1986 despite the recessions of 1980 and 1982).[43]

Overall, there would seem to be little merit to the goal of preserving abstract job numbers, or "positions," in the textile and apparel sectors. Instead, the more germane concern is for "people," those workers currently employed in the sector who face potential displacement if adjustment through downsizing is rapid and deep. One, rather extreme, view would be that because most of these workers entered the sectors when it was already apparent that textiles and apparel were declining and receiving artificial assistance through protection, they did so at their own risk and incorporated in their decisions the probability-weighted costs of subsequent job loss.[44] A more pragmatic approach would be the more traditional view that because the public at large benefits from open trade through lower consumer costs and improved production efficiency, there are grounds for compensation from the public to the individuals displaced through trade liberalization. In this approach, the relevant constraint on a reversal toward liberalization in textiles and apparel would be not the number of jobs that such a policy might eventually eliminate, but the efficiency and fairness of the mechanisms for facilitating the transfer of workers to other sectors.

Labor adjustment in textiles and apparel is complicated by geographic and demographic factors. After having migrated from New England to the Southeast in search of low-cost labor beginning as long ago as the late nineteenth century, the textile industry is currently heavily concentrated in a few states. North and South Carolina together account for more than half of US textile employment, and the sector is concentrated in Georgia as well. Apparel production is also relatively concentrated, with 60 percent of firms located in New York, California, Pennsylvania, and New Jersey and tending to specialize in higher fashion and tailored products. The remainder of the

---

43. Council of Economic Advisers, *Economic Report of the President 1987* (Washington: CEA, January 1987), pp. 257, 282, 290, 296. Also see Robert Z. Lawrence, *Can America Compete?* (Washington: Brookings Institution, 1984).

44. On these grounds, Leamer argues that unemployment due to wage rigidities in the face of import competition is not an adjustment cost to be considered in trade policy. Edward Leamer, "Welfare Computations and the Optimal Staging of Tariff Reductions in Models with Adjustment Costs," *Journal of International Economics*, vol. 10, 1980, pp. 21–36.

apparel sector is located primarily in the South and Southwest, and tends to produce work and casual clothing.[45]

Geographical concentration raises labor adjustment costs by reducing the likelihood that the worker will find alternative employment without relocating, perhaps at great distance. Mutti and Rosen identify three groupings of states by performance of manufacturing employment in 1973–79. In the first, employment rose in most industries. Sunbelt and energy states were in this category. In the second, net manufacturing employment rose but there were significant declines in some sectors. Several states in the southeast were in this group. In the third group of states, manufacturing employment actually declined. This group included snow- and rustbelt states (Illinois, Indiana, Michigan, Ohio, Maryland, New Jersey, New York, Pennsylvania). The authors note that adjustment costs should be the highest in the third group, because of the increased difficulty of obtaining new employment in the same region. Research by the Congressional Budget Office (CBO) has confirmed that dislocated workers unemployed for more than 26 weeks have been concentrated in the rustbelt manufacturing states of the North.[46]

The primary concentration of the textile industry is thus in three states (the Carolinas and Georgia) that are in the intermediate category—presence of job losses in some sectors but expanding manufacturing employment overall. At the state level, then, labor adjustment in textiles should not be unusually difficult; indeed, in the first quarter of 1986, unemployment in the Carolinas and Georgia was 6.1 percent, below the 7.1 percent US average.[47] Nonetheless, problems can arise at the local level, because often the textile mill is located in a small town and is its sole major employer.[48]

In apparel, one of the prominent producing states—California—is in the sunbelt area with rising manufacturing employment. However, three states (New York, Pennsylvania, and New Jersey) are in the category with overall declines in manufacturing employment, and thus, relatively greater adjustment difficulties.

Demographic factors add to adjustment difficulties for the sectors. In textiles, women account for over half of employment and minority groups for 22 percent. In apparel, women constitute 81 percent of the work force and minorities account for 27 percent of employment.[49] While the national

---

45. *Journal of Commerce*, 5 September 1985; US Department of Commerce, *Industrial Outlook 1985*, pp. 44–1, 45–1.

46. John Mutti and Howard F. Rosen, "US Labor Market Adjustment," in Gary Clyde Hufbauer and Howard F. Rosen, eds., *Domestic Adjustment and International Trade* (Washington: Institute for International Economics, forthcoming).

47. *Washington Times*, 1 July 1986.

48. *New York Times*, 23 June 1986.

49. Davidson, Feigenoff, and Ghadar, *International Competition*, pp. 6–7.

unemployment rate for women is not significantly higher than the overall average, often female workers are spouses of the primary household earner and are therefore less mobile and less able to relocate. Minority group unemployment rates, for their part, tend to be about twice the national average.[50] An additional difficulty is that many of the displaced are in their 50s and 60s and have worked all their lives for the textile mill, although with a proper adjustment program workers in their 60s might appropriately take early retirement.

In January 1984, the Bureau of Labor Statistics conducted a household survey to examine the problem of adjustment of displaced workers. It found that in the recessions of 1980–81 and 1982–83, 11.5 million workers lost their jobs. Of these, 5.1 million workers were found to be displaced workers—defined as those who had lost a job they had held three or more years. Half of the displaced workers were in manufacturing, and half in other sectors (including services). Of the 5.1 million displaced workers, approximately half had lost their jobs because the plants or businesses they worked in had closed down or moved.

The study's findings for textiles and apparel were as follows. First, plant closings or the moving of plants accounted for 72 percent of labor displacement in textiles and 61 percent in apparel. Second, the number of workers identified as displaced stood at 80,000 for textiles and 132,000 for apparel (or 10.6 percent and 10.1 percent, respectively, of 1980 employment in the two sectors; see table 2.1). Third, the median time spent by displaced workers before obtaining another job was 13.3 weeks in the textile industry and 24.8 weeks in apparel. Fourth, by January 1984, 59.8 percent of the displaced textile workers had found new jobs, 13.9 percent had left the labor force, and 26.2 percent remained unemployed; in apparel, the corresponding rates were 63.0 percent reemployed, 22.8 percent leaving the labor force, and 14.2 percent unemployed. Fifth, the median salaries on the new jobs found by the reemployed were actually higher than earnings on the original jobs by 3.3 percent for textile workers, and were only lower by 2.5 percent for apparel workers. Finally, an update of the same group of workers (for all industries) found that by January 1985, 71 percent had found new jobs (up from 61 percent a year earlier), and that of these, 60 percent had obtained salaries equal to or higher than their original earnings.[51]

The BLS findings suggest that the severity of adjustment to job displacement in textiles and apparel has been more moderate than might be surmised from the trade policy debate. A wide majority of the displaced workers in

---

50. Council of Economic Advisers, *Economic Report of the President 1986,* p. 293.

51. US Department of Labor, Bureau of Labor Statistics, *Displaced Workers, 1979–83,* Bulletin 2240, July 1985; and Richard M. Devens, Jr., "Displaced Workers," pp. 40–43.

these sectors managed to find new jobs (almost three-fourths, based on the 1984 figures as adjusted upwards by the rise from January 1984 to January 1985 for all industries). The duration of unemployment was relatively short for textile workers (although considerably longer—nearly six months—for apparel workers). And, contrary to the widespread impression, wage losses on the new jobs found by the reemployed appear to have been minimal (and wages actually rose for the displaced and reemployed textile workers).

The central thrust of these findings is that labor adjustment in textiles and apparel is by no means an impossible task. For purposes of trade policy, however, it is important to consider the role that official programs can play in facilitating the adjustment process.

US programs for labor adjustment have in the past achieved relatively limited success, and at the present time are minimal. Trade Adjustment Assistance (TAA) under the Trade Expansion Act of 1962 provided only small funding, primarily because of the restriction that assisted workers had to have been displaced as the result of a prior import liberalization. The revised and liberalized program under the Trade Act of 1974 generated much larger assistance, and at its peak in 1980 allocated $2.2 billion at an average of $4,400 per worker assisted.[52]

It is widely judged, however, that this program failed to achieve significant retraining or relocation, and that instead its funding amounted to financial relief above normal unemployment benefits.[53] By the early 1980s, in any event the TAA program contracted sharply as the Reagan administration included it as a prime target for cutbacks in domestic expenditure.

In short, labor adjustment programs in the past have probably been inadequate, and to make matters worse, the difficulty of adjustment may be unusually high for textile and apparel workers because of geographic and demographic factors. Nonetheless, as the estimates of chapter 8 demonstrate, the costs of protection per job preserved appear to be enormous. Other analysts have tended to find, similarly, that the benefits of liberalization vastly exceed the labor adjustment costs.[54]

If trade policy in textiles and apparel is to break out of its downward spiral toward ever-increasing protection, a meaningful mechanism of support

---

52. James A. Orr, "US Policies for Displaced Workers," in Hufbauer and Rosen, *Domestic Adjustment and International Trade.*

53. OECD, *Textile and Clothing Industries,* p. 115; and James A. Orr, "US Policies for Displaced Workers." A study by James and Ann Orr found that fewer than 40 percent of TAA recipients had been even aware that job retraining and reallocation services were available. Ibid.

54. Thus, Baldwin, Mutti, and Richardson found that the welfare benefits from a 50 percent tariff cut in the Tokyo Round of trade negotiations would exceed adjustment costs by a ratio of 50 to 1, although they did find negative net effects in a limited list of sectors. As cited in Mutti and Rosen, "US Labor Market Adjustment."

for labor adjustment will almost certainly have to be present. On the basis of evaluation of past TAA programs, James Orr recommends the following key elements of such a mechanism. Assistance should be targeted to those permanently displaced, omitting those only on temporary layoff and expected to be rehired. The focus of assistance should be retraining, employment, and relocation services, not income maintenance (which can actually prolong unemployment). Within training, the most efficient approach is on-the-job rather than classroom training. Orr suggests that with this reorientation, adjustment assistance could more effectively facilitate reemployment at a lower cost per worker than that experienced under TAA in the late 1970s.[55]

Overview

In summary, there has been considerable adjustment through revitalization in the textile sector, spurred by important technological innovations and implemented with heavy investment. Adjustment through productivity improvement has been slow in apparel, however, in part because technological change has been slower and mechanization more difficult. The apparel sector has adjusted somewhat more through wage compression, but it has not carried out the other major form of adjustment—downsizing—to nearly the extent experienced in textiles. Instead, rising protective barriers have validated the more sluggish adjustment in apparel. Recourse to protection has been a major response in both sectors, even though the role of trade has been minimal in employment losses in textiles and limited even in apparel except for the early 1980s when the dollar was overvalued. Instead, mechanization and rising labor productivity have driven employment cutbacks in textiles and to a lesser extent in apparel, and slow growth of textile consumption has been an additional factor.

Labor adjustment obstacles in textiles and apparel are substantial. While apparel is concentrated in the Southeast where manufacturing employment has fared better than in the Northern rustbelt, the labor force in both sectors is heavily female and minority group, and plants are often in towns without alternative industrial employment. Past and, especially, current adjustment assistance programs have been inadequate to provide the kind of support that would seem essential if a meaningful move toward reversal of the spiral toward increased protection is to begin. A revitalized adjustment assistance program should deemphasize income maintenance and stress retraining (especially on-the-job) and relocation services.

In his study of the clothing industry in industrial countries, de la Torre identifies seven modes of adjustment: technical change, increased scale and

---

55. James A. Orr, "US Policies for Displaced Workers."

concentration, wage moderation, product and market shifts, foreign assembly and subcontracting, foreign direct investment, and exit and diversification. He notes that in apparel some processes are not amenable to mechanization, and that developing-country producers also have access to new technology; and that the clothing industry is fragmented and movement toward concentration and scale has been slow. He suggests that wage adjustment has been the preferred response in the OECD, through domestic migration of the industry to low-wage regions and through the use of female, immigrant, and minority labor. He finds that moving "up market" to fashion and specialty products has been a successful strategy for some parts of the industry. Some US foreign assembly (especially in the Caribbean) takes place under section 807 of US trade legislation, although German and Dutch firms have pursued this option more fully. Similarly, US firms have not used foreign investment as a response whereas Japanese investment in Asian countries has been substantial.[56]

Downsizing is perhaps the most fundamental form of adjustment, however.[57] Labor force downsizing may result from modernization and replacement of labor by machines, but absolute reduction of output may also be necessary. A fundamental problem of protection as an instrument for promoting adjustment is that it gives exactly the wrong market signal to accomplish production downsizing: it increases the price rather than allowing it to decrease in response to changing comparative advantage. The higher price attracts still more resources into the sector rather than indicating that they should be reallocated to other sectors. It is difficult to see how the US industry will adopt decisive adjustment measures, especially in the mode of planned output reduction, as long as corporate planners do not seriously

---

56. José de la Torre, *Clothing-Industry Adjustment in Developed Countries* (London: Trade Policy Research Centre, 1984), chapter 3.

57. Robert Z. Lawrence and Paula R. DeMasi provide evidence for the view that adjustment usually requires downsizing in their examination of the history of US escape clause (Section 201) actions. They reason that adjustment has been "successful" in those sectors that have gone through a period of temporary escape clause protection and subsequently have not been granted further protection. By this definition, of 16 industries that have undergone escape clause protection, 12 have successfully adjusted while for the other four it is too early to judge the outcome. Of the 12 that have adjusted, only one—bicycles—managed to do so while expanding output, with the help of new styling and favorable demand. Nine of the adjusting sectors (ball bearings; nuts, bolts, and screws; color television; footwear; pianos; sheet glass; stainless steel flatware; watches; and Wilton and velvet carpets) did so through contraction of both output and employment, often in a strategy of focusing on a market segment. In two sectors, adjustment was through exit; in ferrochromium and CB radios, foreign costs were so low (and demand changes so adverse) that firms terminated production. Robert Z. Lawrence and Paula R. DeMasi, "Do Industries with a Self-Identified Loss of Comparative Advantage Ever Adjust?" in Hufbauer and Rosen, eds., *Domestic Adjustment and International Trade.*

anticipate eventual reduction in the wall of trade barriers that have successively grown around the two sectors.

If, as would seem appropriate, the policy objective of protection is to vouchsafe people rather than preserve positions, downsizing of both employment and output should be an integral part of the national strategy for adjustment. However, it should be accompanied by meaningful mechanisms of labor retraining and relocation; otherwise the "people"—existing workers in the sectors (but not future, unknown workers who would enter the sector at their own risk)—will bear a disproportionate burden. The costs of protection are so high that the community as a whole can well afford to lighten this burden.

5

Europe, Japan, and the Developing Countries

Evaluation of proper policy for the international trade regime for textiles and apparel, as well as an understanding of the performance and prospects of the sectors in the United States, require at least a summary view of the industry in other major producing and trading nations. This chapter reviews trends in production, trade, and adjustment in Europe and Japan, and briefly examines evolving comparative advantage among the developing countries.

Industry Performance in Europe and Japan

In Europe, textiles and apparel have long been declining industries. Japan too has become like Europe and the United States in facing the need to adjust in textiles and apparel, after having been the principal competitive threat to the rest of the industrial world earlier in the postwar period.

The most striking feature of the sectors in Europe is the extent to which their employment has declined. At the same time, the number of people still working in textiles and apparel remains large and continues to give an important political dimension to trade and industrial policies in the sectors. There are major differences among European countries. At the policy level, Germany and the Netherlands have tended to allow market forces to reduce production and employment, while in France, the United Kingdom, and Italy the governments have intervened more in attempts to sustain the industries. At the level of industry performance, Italy has become the largest net exporter of textiles and apparel in the world, while the other major European countries run sizable deficits. These differing approaches and circumstances bring tensions to the process of trade policy formation, which is at the level of the European Community (EC) as a whole.

Table 5.1 Shares of textiles and apparel in manufacturing value added and employment (percentage)

	Textiles		Apparel	
	Value added	Employment	Value added	Employment
United States				
1963	3.8	6.3	3.6	7.0
1981	2.9	5.0	2.6	5.8
Germany				
1963	6.0[a]	7.4	4.0[a]	5.0
1983	2.4	3.9	1.7	2.7
France				
1963	7.7	9.5	3.5	6.7
1983	3.3	5.2	2.2	4.8
Italy				
1963	8.3	14.0	2.6	5.1
1981	6.6	8.5	3.3	5.1
United Kingdom				
1963	n.a.	9.3	n.a.	5.2
1982	3.1	5.1	2.0	4.1
Japan				
1963	8.7	14.2	1.3	2.8
1983	4.0	6.9	1.5	4.3

n.a. not available.
a. Allocated between textiles and apparel on basis of employment shares.
Source: United Nations, *Yearbook of Industrial Statistics, 1983; The Growth of World Industry 1971 Edition.*

In the last two decades, employment in textiles and apparel in the European Community has declined from 4.1 million to 2.0 million, or by 51 percent.[1] As indicated in table 5.1, the combined share of the two sectors in total manufacturing employment in Europe has declined from an average

1. Calculated from United Nations, *Yearbook of Industrial Statistics,* 1983 and *The Growth of World Industry, 1971 Edition.* Refers to Germany, France, Italy, United Kingdom, Belgium, and the Netherlands. Note that employment data are to some extent misleading because the industrial statistics apparently exclude substantial numbers of "outworkers" who work at home (estimated as high as 500,000 in Italy). Donald B. Keesing and Martin Wolf, *Textile Quotas Against Developing Countries* (London: Trade Policy Research Centre, 1980), p. 114.

of approximately 16 percent in 1963 to approximately 10 percent in 1983. The corresponding share in total value added—approximately 11 percent on average in 1963 and 6 percent in 1983—is much smaller than the employment share, reflecting the above-average labor intensity of the sectors.

Table 5.2 shows the annual levels of employment and output in textiles and apparel for 1963 to 1983, for major European countries and Japan. The sharp reductions in employment shown in the table have resulted from foreign competition, first from Japan and then from the developing countries; and, even more importantly, from rising labor productivity (as examined below). The generally more severe declines in textile employment than in apparel reflect the greater incidence of technological change in textiles (as explored in the US case in the previous chapter).

Table 5.3 summarizes the changes in employment in the past two decades, with the midpoint set at the average for 1972–73 to limit distortion from the industrial boom in 1973. The table includes employment changes for the United States. For all seven countries examined, employment trends are distinctly worse in the most recent decade than from the mid-1960s to the mid-1970s. The employment declines exceeded one-third in the decade 1972/73 to 1983 for textiles in Germany, France, the United Kingdom, the Netherlands, and Japan; and for apparel in Germany, the United Kingdom, and the Netherlands. The largest decline in employment occurred in the Netherlands (from 1963 to 1982, by 74 percent in textiles and 88 percent in apparel).

The employment data indicate that contraction in the US textile and apparel sectors has been distinctly less severe than in all other major industrial countries with the exception of Italy. The level of employment in textiles and apparel combined declined by 50 percent to 60 percent from 1972–73 to 1983 in the Netherlands, France, and the United Kingdom, and by nearly 50 percent in Germany. Employment in the two sectors fell by nearly one-third in Japan, as declines in the much larger textile sector swamped modest gains in the apparel sector. By contrast, Italy and the United States emerged as favored countries in terms of employment maintenance, with overall declines in the range of 15 percent to 20 percent for the 1972–73 to 1983 period. Placement of the United States in the top of these three tiers of employment outcome is ironical in view of the common impression that the Italian and Japanese industries are much more favorably situated than that in the United States, and the absence of any general recognition that Europe has had far worse employment declines than the United States. The divergence at the micro level in the textile and apparel sectors, both of which bulk large in overall manufacturing employment, is consistent with the more widely recognized contrast between high overall unemployment in Europe and more favorable employment experience in the United States over the past decade.

Table 5.2 Trends in employment and output in Europe and Japan, 1963–83

	Germany		France		Italy	
	N	Q	N	Q	N	Q
Textiles (ISIC 321)						
1963	573	78	545	n.a.	n.a.	100
1967	490	78	496	n.a.	420	94
1968	489	91	463	n.a.	410	93
1969	508	99	461	n.a.	422	100
1970	501	100	451	n.a.	424	100
1971	481	105	732	n.a.	402	98
1972	458	108	736	n.a.	386	106
1973	434	108	725	n.a.	382	115
1974	394	102	697	n.a.	365	113
1975	357	99	364	n.a.	357	104
1976	342	107	346	n.a.	340	123
1977	343	104	333	n.a.	329	120
1978	331	103	316	n.a.	312	114
1979	323	105	304	n.a.	306	129
1980	317	103	297	n.a.	296	136
1981	296	97	278	n.a.	275	136
1982	273	92	268	n.a.	n.a.	133
1983	256	92	258	n.a.	n.a.	121
Apparel (ISIC 322)						
1963	388	79	388	n.a.	n.a.	n.a.
1967	371	83	363	n.a.	152	n.a.
1968	367	93	338	n.a.	162	n.a.
1969	382	102	340	n.a.	184	n.a.
1970	379	100	338	n.a.	197	n.a.
1971	372	103	n.a.	n.a.	222	n.a.
1972	272	107	n.a.	na.	219	n.a.
1973	360	100	n.a.	na.	222	n.a.
1974	310	92	n.a.	n.a.	217	n.a.
1975	288	93	304	n.a.	213	n.a.
1976	277	101	298	n.a.	204	n.a.
1977	244	100	292	n.a.	198	n.a.
1978	239	100	282	n.a.	183	n.a.
1979	236	98	274	n.a.	275	n.a.
1980	228	94	272	n.a.	272	n.a.
1981	211	86	249	n.a.	249	n.a.
1982	191	79	244	n.a.	244	n.a.
1983	175	77	238	n.a.	238	n.a.

N thousands of workers; Q index of production, 1970 = 100; n.a. not available.
Source: United Nations, *Yearbook of Industrial Statistics,* 1971, 1976, 1983.

United Kingdom		Netherlands		Japan	
N	Q	N	Q	N	Q
817	84	102	87	1,392	55
734	94	81	83	1,384	78
723	97	75	94	1,361	83
727	101	85	97	1,309	91
697	100	82	100	1,349	100
586	100	75	100	1,293	104
553	103	68	97	1,277	105
561	106	62	96	1,261	114
550	97	59	94	1,167	100
517	92	54	85	1,093	94
495	94	49	90	1,055	102
481	94	45	85	986	100
472	91	41	80	968	102
432	87	36	81	950	103
351	75	34	76	916	102
301	68	30	71	765	100
276	66	27	68	749	99
n.a.	67	n.a.	65	733	99
458	92	132	98	272	n.a.
423	95	117	93	307	86
420	97	112	102	320	85
424	97	71	105	391	94
402	100	67	100	364	100
363	105	62	104	372	103
356	109	57	95	408	103
355	117	51	84	438	117
347	115	44	81	496	105
339	116	36	73	467	97
330	113	32	69	478	105
321	120	29	61	467	105
318	123	27	58	480	106
301	126	25	55	473	107
277	113	21	51	466	104
239	103	18	52	456	105
222	102	16	61	459	105
n.a.	103	n.a.	63	457	103

Table 5.3 Changes in employment in major industrial countries, 1963–83
(percentage)

	Textiles	Apparel	Combined
United States			
1963–72/73	12.0	8.2	9.8
1972/73–1983	− 25.2	− 14.0	− 18.6
Germany			
1963–72/73	− 22.2	− 5.7	− 15.5
1972/73–1983	− 42.6	− 52.2	− 46.9
France			
1963–72/73	34.0	− 17.5[a]	12.5
1972/73–1983	− 64.7	− 25.6[a]	− 52.8
Italy			
1967–72/73	− 8.6	45.1	5.6
1972/73–1981	− 28.4	7.9	− 15.1
United Kingdom			
1963–72/73	− 31.8	− 22.4	− 28.5
1972/73–1982	− 50.4	− 37.6	− 54.6
Netherlands			
1963–72/73	− 36.3	− 59.1	− 49.1
1972/73–1982	− 58.5	− 70.4	− 63.9
Japan			
1963–72/73	− 8.8	55.5	− 0.4
1972/73–1983	− 42.2	8.0	− 29.7

Source: See table 5.2.
a. Estimated.

Competitiveness

Data compiled by the United Nations according to International Standard Industrial Categories (ISIC) provide a basis for comparing the relative size and labor productivity of the textile and apparel sectors among the principal industrial and developing-country producers. Because value data are in national currencies, these comparisons can be misleading in years of severe exchange rate misalignments. Table 5.4 reports major indicators of industry size and performance for 1980, a year chosen as the most recent for which the dollar was not seriously overvalued. National values are converted to dollars at average 1980 exchange rates. Output refers to gross production value at producer prices. The table also reports trade data. Among the principal developing countries, data are included for Hong Kong, Korea, the Philippines, and India. Taiwan is omitted because the United Nations does not report data for it, China because its exchange rate, product prices, and wages seem unlikely to have been determined by market processes in 1980 and thus would convey limited information.

The estimates of gross production shed light on the relative size of the textile and apparel sectors across countries. The five major European countries combined represented textiles production of $63.4 billion in 1980, in the same range of magnitude as the US production of $56.8 billion.[2] The Japanese textile industry is about two-thirds as large as either the US or the European industry, at $40.8 billion. In Hong Kong and Korea, production might appear smaller than expected (given their salience as suppliers), at $3.7 billion and $5.6 billion, respectively. However, these amounts represent 16 percent of the size of US output for the two Asian countries combined, far greater than their relative size in terms of gross national product (3.4 percent).[3] For its part, the Indian industry is large ($7.6 billion) but supplies primarily the populous domestic market.

In apparel, the US industry is more dominant in relative size. The combined production of the five major European countries ($33.4 billion) is 10 percent smaller than that of the United States ($37.7 billion), while Japanese production ($10.8 billion) is less than one-third as large. As indicated in table 5.2, the Japanese apparel industry was even smaller in relative terms in the past. Japan's specialization in textiles rather than apparel is also evident in the fact that the country's trade balance was positive in textiles but negative in apparel in 1980. Once again, in apparel the size of the industry in Korea and Hong Kong might seem modest in absolute terms but is large relative to the size of their economies. The small figures for the Philippines and especially India suggest that much of what might be classified as apparel production in industrial countries is reported as textiles.

2. Note that the US figures differ from those of chapter 2 because of the differences between the ISIC and the US Standard Industrial Classification.

3. This contrast reflects the intense specialization of the Hong Kong and Korean industries in exports. Thus, the ratio of exports to production is 39 percent for textiles in Korea, and exports actually exceed reported output in Korean apparel (probably reflecting classification as apparel of some products treated as textiles in industrial output data, as well as exchange rate valuation difficulties). In Hong Kong, apparel exports amount to 89 percent of output. The extreme orientation of these industries toward exports makes them vulnerable to foreign protection.

Table 5.4 Indicators of industry size and competitiveness, 1980

Country	Output (billion dollars)	Employment (thousand)	Exports (billion dollars)	Imports[a] (billion dollars)	Trade balance[a] (billion dollars)
Textiles					
United States	56.80	986	3.62	2.54	1.08
Germany	19.09	317	6.25	6.81	−0.56
France	15.07	297	3.41	4.10	−0.69
Italy	15.73	296	4.11	2.61	1.50
United Kingdom	13.49	351	3.11	3.55	−0.44
Japan	40.85	916	5.10	1.65	3.45
Hong Kong	3.66	128	0.91	2.97	−2.01
Korea	5.65	393	2.20	0.41	1.79
Philippines	0.57	144	0.07[b]	0.16[b]	−.09[b]
India	7.59	1,695	1.20[c]	0.80[b]	0.40
Apparel					
United States	37.70	1,150	1.22	6.94	−5.72
Germany	10.12	228	2.91	8.37	−5.46
France	8.99	272	2.31	2.64	−0.33
Italy	7.23	172	4.63	0.80	3.83
United Kingdom	7.03	277	1.87	2.85	−0.98
Japan	10.76	466	0.50	1.53	−1.03
Hong Kong	5.24	264	4.64	0.69	3.95
Korea	1.81	186	2.95	0.01	2.94
Philippines	0.25	195	0.35[b]	0.00[b]	0.35[b]
India	0.31	51	0.80[b]	0.00[b]	0.80[b]

Source: United Nations, *Yearbook of Industrial Statistics*, 1983; IMF, *International Financial Statistics, Yearbook 1985;* GATT, *International Trade 1982/83,* table A-7.
n.a.   not available.
a. f.o.b.   b. 1981.   c. 1982.

Table 5.4 also reports value added per worker, average wage, and their respective levels relative to those of the United States. The broad picture that emerges is that differences in productivity tend to offset differences in wage rates across countries. Thus, Korea has only about one-fifth the value added per worker that is attained in the United States, but its wage level is also only about one-fifth as high.

The final column of the table provides a rough measure of competitiveness. It indicates the ratio of the country's relative value added per worker

Wage (dollars per year)	Value added per worker (dollars per year)	Relative wage	Relative value added per worker	Relative value added per worker/ relative wage
11,268	23,357	1.00	1.00	1.00
14,040	22,022	1.25	0.94	0.75
n.a.	21,515	n.a.	0.92	n.a.
9,141	22,689	0.81	0.97	1.20
9,052	15,442	0.80	0.66	0.82
8,729	17,325	0.77	0.74	0.96
4,377	8,430	0.39	0.36	0.92
2,065	5,079	0.18	0.22	1.22
640	1,229	0.06	0.05	0.83
714	1,077	0.06	0.05	0.83
8,365	17,200	1.00	1.00	1.00
11,003	22,127	1.32	1.29	0.98
n.a.	14,618	n.a.	0.85	n.a.
8,036	18,587	0.96	1.08	1.12
7,132	12,260	0.55	0.71	1.29
6,289	11,376	0.75	0.66	0.88
4,285	7,042	0.51	0.41	0.80
1,639	3,667	0.20	0.21	1.05
411	564	0.05	0.03	0.60
466	843	0.06	0.05	0.83

(compared to the US base) to its relative wage.[4] These ratios would appear to conform relatively well to competitive positions among the industrial countries. Thus, the strongest competitor, Italy, has a ratio (to the United States) of 1.2 in textiles and 1.12 in apparel. On this measure, the United

4. At an equilibrium exchange rate, the ratio of relative labor productivity to relative wage rate should be a good indicator of relative product price at international values. Differences from nonlabor costs would tend to be neutral if lower real interest rates

States was considerably more competitive in textiles in 1980 than Germany or the United Kingdom, and was even slightly more competitive than Japan. In apparel, the United States lagged behind the competitiveness of Italy and the United Kingdom in 1980, but was at about the same level as Germany and in a stronger position than Japan. These estimates tend to confirm the view that US competitiveness in the textile sector was relatively strong before the period of dollar overvaluation; they also suggest a relatively less favorable but by no means sharply laggard position in apparel.

The indicator of relative productivity divided by relative wage gives the surprising result that for both textiles and apparel, the United States tends to be competitive with the developing countries. Higher productivity offsets higher US wages, even for apparel. Of course, this indicator gives only a partial view of competitiveness; nonetheless, the estimates here do suggest a much greater ability of the textile and apparel industries in the United States (and other industrial countries, especially Italy) to stand up to competition from the developing countries than would be expected from the progressive recourse to greater protection under the Multi-Fiber Arrangement (MFA).

Finally, table 5.4 indicates trade flows in 1980 for the 10 countries examined. Among the industrial countries, Italy and Japan had a strong surplus in textiles, and Italy also had a surplus in apparel (although Japan had a deficit). In 1980 the United States also had a sizable trade surplus in textiles, although its deficit in apparel was large. The clearest division of comparative advantage along North-South lines was in apparel, where the industrial countries except Italy all had trade deficits and the four developing countries all had surpluses. In contrast, in textiles, Hong Kong in particular had a large trade deficit, indicating its openness to imports and its use of imported textiles for processing into apparel for exports.

The broad thrust of the comparisons in table 5.4 is that the textile and apparel industries are more robust in the United States and other industrial countries, relative to some of the leading developing countries, than might be thought from the protective regime. The relative sizes of the industries, the productivity performance compared to relative wage costs, and the trade flows in textiles (but not apparel), all suggest a picture rather different from the familiar image of sectors in the North on the verge of decimation by powerful new competition from the NICs (newly industrialized countries).

---

in industrial countries approximately offset higher capital applied per unit of output. Note, however, that at an overvalued exchange rate the measure here overstates the country's competitiveness. Nominal increases of value added and wage cancel each other out in the ratio, while these increases from a stronger exchange rate boost the country's price relative to those of its competitors.

This observation applies fully to the United States as drawn in the 1980 economic profile here, although dollar overvaluation in the early 1980s eroded the US position.

Trends in Trade and Import Penetration

The contrast between the competitiveness indicators just examined and the dismal experience of the industrial countries in employment in textiles and apparel over the past two decades as reviewed above raises the same question examined in chapter 4: what is the relative role of productivity growth as opposed to rising imports in explaining the decline of employment in these sectors? Table 5.5 sheds light on this issue. The table indicates import penetration ratios for the six major industrial countries for 1970 and 1980. In addition, it indicates the trade balance of each country in the two sectors, expressed as a percentage of consumption (the same base as used for the import penetration ratio). Alternative measures of import penetration for the United States are discussed in chapter 2; for the purposes of table 5.5, it is useful to use definitions comparable to those used in the available estimates for other countries.[5]

The estimates in table 5.5 show a relatively moderate role of rising imports in textiles for the United States, Germany, Italy, and Japan over the 1970s. In these four countries imports rose in the decade by less than four percentage points of consumption (and, in the United States, practically not at all). The principal exception was the United Kingdom, where the share of imports in textile consumption more than doubled. The estimates of trade balance relative to consumption show an even more favorable trend for the United States, where the balance shifted from a deficit of 2 percent of consumption to a surplus of equal size. In Germany, textiles shifted from a small surplus (3 percent of consumption) to a small deficit (2.8 percent). The balance remained unchanged at a strong 10 percent of consumption in Italy, while declining from 15 percent to 10 percent in Japan. In the United Kingdom, the trade balance ratio eroded by approximately 10 percentage points of consumption, more modest than the 18 percentage point erosion suggested

---

5. For the United States, the United Kingdom, and Japan, the estimates in table 5.5 are drawn from World Bank calculations as reported in General Agreement on Tariffs and Trade, *Textiles and Clothing in the World Economy* (Geneva: GATT, 1984), appendix IV, p. 61. For the other countries, the data developed in table 5.4 are the source of the trade ratios. These data compare industrial output statistics from the United Nations with trade data from GATT. This approach tends to understate the import penetration ratio by omitting the writeup from f.o.b. import values to wholesale values; nonetheless, for some of the countries, the ratios are high. Possible biases in the levels of the ratios should not preclude identification of meaningful trends over time.

Table 5.5 Trends in import penetration and net trade balance:
major industrial countries, 1970–80 (percentage)

	Textiles		Apparel	
	m/c	(x-m)/c	m/c	(x-m)/c
United States				
1970	4.5	− 2.0	6.4	− 5.3
1980	4.4	2.1	16.7	− 14.0
Germany				
1973	27.2	3.0	32.1	− 35.0
1980	34.7	− 2.8	53.7	− 20.6
France				
1980	26.0	− 4.4	28.3	− 3.5
Italy				
1973	15.2	10.4	12.5	73.0
1980	18.3	10.5	23.5	112.6
United Kingdom				
1970	14.1	7.1	13.5	− 1.2
1980	32.9	− 2.4	38.6	− 14.1
Japan				
1970	4.0	14.9	4.4	18.5
1980	7.4	10.1	10.7	− 7.2

m imports; c apparent consumption; x exports.
Source: Calculated from table 5.4; GATT, *Textiles and Clothing,* 1984, appendix IV, p. 61; GATT, *International Trade 1982/83,* table A-7; and United Nations, *Yearbook of Industrial Statistics,* 1976.

by the import penetration ratio alone. It should be noted that the tendency in Europe toward high import penetration ratios but more modest trade balance ratios reflects a higher degree of intraindustry trade there than in the United States or Japan.

In apparel, rising import penetration was more pronounced. On both the import and trade balance ratios, trade accounted for a deterioration of some 10 percentage points of consumption in the United States. The trade balance ratio declined by 13 percentage points of consumption in the United Kingdom. The sharpest erosion from trade, however, was in Japan, where the trade balance in apparel declined from a surplus equal to 18 percent of consumption to a deficit of 7 percent, a swing equal to one-fourth of consumption. This analysis once again reveals a pattern not widely recognized: Japan experienced the largest relative trade erosion in the apparel sector among industrial countries in the 1970s.

The trends for Germany and Italy vividly illustrate the difference between gross import trends and net trends as the consequence of intraindustry trade. On the import penetration ratio alone, both countries experienced substantial erosion over the 1970s, as the ratio nearly doubled in Italy and rose by two-thirds in Germany. However, exports rose relatively more than imports, so that the trade balance actually improved by 14 percentage points of consumption in Germany. In Italy, the performance was dramatic: the trade surplus in apparel rose from three-fourths of domestic consumption in 1970 to 113 percent in 1980.

In short, trends in import penetration ratios and trade balances relative to consumption in the decade 1970 to 1980 reveal only moderate pressure from the source of foreign trade in textiles for the major industrial countries with the exception of the United Kingdom. In apparel, the experience of these countries is more divided. Japan faced sharp erosion in its trade balance, and more limited deteriorations occurred for the United States and the United Kingdom. In contrast, there were substantial improvements on a trade-balance basis in apparel for Germany and Italy.

Import penetration data are not available for more recent years. They would tend to show a sharply rising ratio for the United States, as imports rose briskly in association with the overvalued dollar. For Europe and Japan, import penetration ratios through 1985 would tend to stay constant or rise moderately; while their weak currencies tended to limit import growth, the valuation of domestic output at these rates would tend to depress the measure of consumption while dollar value of imports remained relatively unchanged. By 1986, import penetration ratios for these countries would be reduced, as exchange rate valuation went in the opposite direction.

The estimates here tend to generalize the conclusion reached for the United States in chapter 4: at least through 1980, foreign trade played only a limited role in the erosion of employment in textiles and apparel in the industrial countries, and indeed for Italy (and to some extent Germany) trade has been a source of expansion.

In addition to the evolution of total import penetration and trade balances, it is useful to review that of imports from the countries subject to protection under the MFA. Table 5.6 reports the dollar value of imports into the principal industrial countries from non-OECD (Organization for Economic Cooperation and Development) supplier countries in the past 15 years. These imports broadly encompass trade with countries subject to the MFA, considering that it is the industrial countries (primarily OECD) that have restraint-free market access under the Arrangement. They refer primarily to imports from developing countries, although they include socialist and other non-OECD countries as well.

Table 5.6 Imports of major industrial countries from non-OECD sources, 1970–85 (million dollars)

	United States	Europe[a]	Germany	France	Italy	United Kingdom	Japan
Textiles[b]							
1970	356	686	179	44	79	161	99
1971	428	808	261	48	60	199	122
1972	544	1,051	328	90	91	212	216
1973	619	1,596	484	135	173	292	719
1974	787	1,994	489	211	203	374	532
1975	541	1,921	567	201	177	308	473
1976	797	2,389	723	256	255	379	617
1977	808	2,796	863	295	289	437	547
1978	1,046	3,165	1,053	346	279	529	1,048
1979	1,154	4,266	1,381	507	473	695	1,378
1980	1,342	4,940	1,582	601	586	634	1,053
1981	1,647	3,840	1,176	481	420	545	1,068
1982	1,443	3,669	1,025	488	454	506	1,050
1983	1,691	3,638	1,080	431	424	540	983
1984	2,341	3,807	1,062	454	477	567	1,372
1985	2,469	3,908	1,054	499	536	606	1,312
Apparel[c]							
1970	682	651	267	25	6	147	64
1971	946	920	395	42	7	226	92
1972	1,235	1,365	621	93	17	285	114
1973	1,519	2,081	927	136	39	444	463
1974	1,775	2,712	1,219	173	85	502	673
1975	2,054	3,420	1,519	251	69	630	405
1976	2,998	4,360	1,889	341	93	733	633
1977	3,437	4,905	2,143	414	122	745	659
1978	5,215	5,668	2,567	436	123	957	941
1979	5,568	7,478	3,257	720	194	1,390	1,350
1980	6,198	8,954	3,834	922	326	1,572	1,095
1981	7,287	8,580	3,537	905	325	1,645	1,380
1982	7,940	7,977	3,269	917	287	1,440	1,419
1983	9,314	7,496	3,252	851	251	1,246	1,150
1984	12,664	7,881	3,430	855	245	1,403	1,611
1985	13,755	7,764	3,274	988	298	1,306	1,646

Source: OECD, *Foreign Trade by Commodities*, series C, vol. 2, DRI data base.
a. OECD-Europe.   b. SITC 65.   c. SITC 84.

As analyzed in chapter 2, these data show the reversal in import growth rates associated with the shift in relative dollar strength. Imports into OECD-Europe peaked in dollar terms in 1980 and then actually fell as the dollar strengthened. The rising dollar encouraged suppliers to shift their focus to the US market, and European goods became more competitive with those from developing countries that tended to move their exchange rates with the dollar. The pattern of declining or stagnant imports after 1980 is also evident for Japan (although in textiles the peak was in 1979, and in apparel Japanese imports rebounded in 1984–85). In contrast, US imports doubled from 1980 to 1984.

If again 1980 is chosen as a more germane base for longer term analysis, the absolute magnitudes of imports reveal important patterns. They show far higher textile imports into Europe from the developing countries than into the United States. Even in apparel, in 1980 Europe's imports from developing countries exceeded those of the United States by nearly one-half, although by 1984 the reverse was true. These data thus show no particular tendency for Europe to screen out imports from developing countries more tightly than does the United States.

For Japan, the same conclusion would appear to apply for textiles, in which Japan's imports from developing countries in 1980 were nearly 80 percent the US level despite a smaller domestic market. In contrast, Japan's imports of apparel from developing countries have been small relative to those of Europe and the United States (in 1984, only 13 percent of the US level and 20 percent of the European level). The divergence between textiles and apparel is in the opposite direction from what would be expected on grounds of relative factor cost: to the extent that textiles are more capital-intensive and apparel labor-intensive, it might be expected that Japan would tend to import apparel relatively more heavily from developing countries (unless the types of textiles imported are traditional, labor-intensive goods). While Japan does not formally apply MFA quota restraints on textiles and apparel, the relatively low level of its apparel imports from developing countries raises doubts about the effective openness of its market in these goods. It should be noted, however, that the growth rate for Japanese imports of apparel from developing countries from 1970 to 1980 was identical to that of Europe and higher than that of the United States.

The relative positions of individual European countries may also be examined using the data of table 5.6. The sharpest divergences may be seen in apparel imports from developing countries. In these products, Germany's import level is approximately 4 times that of France, 13 times that of Italy, and over twice that of the United Kingdom. These comparisons tend to confirm the stylized facts about strategy and competitiveness within Europe. They indicate a high degree of openness of the German market and a relatively more restrictive market in France. The contrast with Italy may be explained by the greater competitiveness of Italian apparel (based on Italy's export performance). The United Kingdom is in an intermediate position, with perhaps a less open market in effective terms than that of Germany but more open than that of France.

Adjustment through Downsizing and Productivity Growth

The trends in trade and import penetration suggest that in Europe trade has not been the dominant force of pressure on the textile and apparel industries, especially in the early 1980s as the strong dollar brought a slowdown in imports. For Japan, trade was a greater source of pressure in the apparel sector on the basis of trends in trade balance relative to consumption; nonetheless, apparel imports remain relatively low in Japan. These patterns suggest that the principal force behind sharp reductions in employment has been rising productivity. Table 5.7 summarizes annual growth rates of production, employment, and productivity for five European countries, the United States, and Japan in the period 1963–83.

The analysis of chapter 4 indicated that for the United States, adjustment in textiles had taken place through increasing labor productivity, with downsizing in employment but not in production. US adjustment in apparel was more limited, with lower productivity growth, smaller employment reduction, and rising rather than declining production. Table 5.7 suggests that in Europe and Japan, adjustment has been more rapid than in the United States in both dimensions: labor productivity growth and sectoral downsizing. The contrast is more vivid in production downsizing. Thus, in textiles US output grew at a positive annual rate of 0.7 percent in 1972–73 to 1983, while output actually declined in Germany (− 1.5 percent annually), the United Kingdom (− 4.8 percent), the Netherlands (− 3.7 percent), and Japan (− 1.0 percent). In apparel, US production grew at 1.3 percent annually in this period, while production declined on average in Germany (− 2.8 percent per year), the United Kingdom (− 1.1 percent), the Netherlands (− 4.0 percent), and Japan (− 0.6 percent). Italy is the exception; its output of textiles grew 2.4 percent and apparel 1.9 percent annually, as the country emerged as the industrial nation specializing in textiles and apparel (aided by unrestricted entry into other industrial countries in contrast to quota restrictions on other major suppliers).

Europe, except Italy, and Japan were thus downsizing more radically than the United States, because they were cutting output levels in addition to reducing employment. In addition, the alternative form of adjustment—productivity growth—also proceeded more rapidly on average in Europe and Japan than in the United States. In the decade ending in 1983, textile productivity grew at 3.7 percent annually in the United States. The rate was

Table 5.7   Average growth rates: output, employment, and labor productivity, industrial countries, 1963–83

	Textiles		Apparel	
	1963–72/83	1972/73–83	1963–72/73	1972/73–83
United States				
Q	4.2	0.7	2.6	1.3
N	1.2	− 2.8	0.8	− 1.4
q[a]	4.9	3.7	1.3	2.8
Germany				
Q	3.4	− 1.5	2.8	− 2.8
N	− 2.6	− 5.3	− 0.6	− 7.0
q	6.1	3.8	3.5	4.2
France				
Q	n.a.	n.a.	n.a.	n.a.
N	3.1	− 9.9	− 2.0	− 2.8
q	n.a.	n.a.	n.a.	n.a.
Italy				
Q	2.9[b]	2.4[c]	12.0	1.9
N	− 1.6[b]	− 3.9[c]	6.8	0.7
q	4.6[b]	6.4[c]	5.3	1.1
United Kingdom				
Q	2.3	− 4.8[d]	2.2	− 1.1[d]
N	− 4.0	− 7.4[d]	− 2.7	− 5.0[d]
q	6.3	2.6[d]	4.8	3.9[d]
Netherlands				
Q	1.1	− 3.7[d]	− 1.0	− 4.0[d]
N	− 4.7	− 9.2[d]	− 9.4	− 12.8[d]
q	5.8	5.6[d]	8.5	8.8[d]
Japan				
Q	7.2	− 1.0	4.5	− 0.6
N	− 1.0	− 5.2	5.8	0.7
q	8.2	4.3	− 1.4	− 1.4

Q   output; N   employment; q   labor productivity.
Source: Calculated from tables 2.1, 4.1; United Nations, *Yearbook of Industrial Statistics,* 1971, 1976, 1979, 1983.
a. 1961–72 and 1973–85.   c. End-year 1982.
b. Base year 1967.   d. End-year 1982.

faster in four countries (Germany, 3.8 percent; Italy, 6.4 percent; Netherlands, 5.6 percent; and Japan, 4.3 percent) and slower in only one (United Kingdom, 2.6 percent). The relative US performance was somewhat more favorable but still below average in apparel, in which US productivity growth (2.8 percent annually) lagged behind that of three countries (Germany, 4.2 percent; United Kingdom, 3.9 percent; Netherlands, 8.8 percent) but exceeded the rate in two (Italy, 1.1 percent; Japan, −1.4 percent).

The most dramatic case of adjustment in Europe has been that of the Netherlands, where both productivity growth and output downsizing have been the highest overall. Germany and the United Kingdom form a second tier of rapid adjustment, again with brisk paces of both product downsizing and labor productivity growth in the decade ending 1983.

The case of Italy is the one instance of adjustment with output expansion in Europe. The country's record in textiles was one of high productivity growth coupled with moderate output growth, so that downsizing did take place in employment (quadrant IV of the adjustment diagram introduced in chapter 4). Italy's experience in apparel was more remarkable; in the 1960s, output growth was so rapid (12 percent) that it was possible to achieve high productivity growth along with rapid employment growth, placing this period for Italy as virtually the sole example of adjustment with productivity growth and employment expansion (the unusual quadrant I in the adjustment diagram). By the 1970s, however, Italy's output growth in apparel had slowed to only 1.9 percent, and employment continued to rise slowly only because productivity growth also dropped sharply (to 1.1 percent). The employment and productivity estimates might be biased if industrial statistics increasingly covered out-workers not reported in the 1960s. In any event, the poorer performance of productivity growth in the second decade raises questions about the permanence of Italy's comparative advantage in the sector, although Italy remains the low-cost supplier within Europe.

Overall the trends in European and Japanese performance suggest more rapid adjustment than in the United States. This experience, and especially its combination with the relief afforded in the early 1980s by the strong dollar, seem to have brought the EC close to the point of favoring a more liberal position on the MFA in its fourth renewal in 1986. However, by the time of the final negotiations the decline in the dollar had brought new pressure on the European industry, and EC negotiators opted for the more restrictive approach urged by the United States (chapter 9).

The Adjustment Process in Europe

The OECD Secretariat has criticized adjustment policies in textiles and apparel in the industrial countries, including Europe. It notes that protection has acted as a signal to firms to expand capacity. At the same time, industrial policies aimed at modernization, sometimes with subsidized investment, have stimulated the replacement of labor by capital. Employment has not expanded along with capacity, and industrial policy has conflicted with manpower policy. The retraining aspect of European programs has been limited. Thus, in 1979 the EC's European Social Fund provided only some $15 million in retraining for approximately 15,000 workers. More generally, manpower policies have placed excessive emphasis on preventing the displacement of workers rather than reducing the adjustment cost for those displaced through retraining and relocation.[6]

Philip Hayes of the London-based Trade Policy Research Centre has examined the adjustment policies followed in the EC in textiles and apparel.[7] He notes that countries entered the Community with sharply differing trade regimes for the sectors, and wide differences remain today. Different national quotas still remain on imports from outside the EC (as opposed to EC-wide quotas), and freedom of movement of these products within the Community is proscribed under Article 115 of the Treaty of Rome, which blocks such indirect imports. National laws requiring origin marking, intensified administrative controls at intra-EC borders, and other obstacles hamper trade in the sectors within the EC. Of the large countries only Germany has tended toward a free trade policy; in the United Kingdom even the Conservative government of Mrs. Margaret Thatcher has tended toward pragmatism compatible with the strong political position of the industry, which is highly concentrated in Lancashire.[8]

Official adjustment policies in the EC in recent years have included the following. Governments have provided investment assistance for rationalization plans (United Kingdom, Netherlands, France, Belgium, and Italy in the late 1970s). They have provided concessional loans for investment (Netherlands, France).

The EC Commission has sponsored sector programs to limit capacity (as in synthetic fibers in 1977). National governments have offered programs of retraining and technical assistance (United Kingdom, France). The EC Commission and national governments have sponsored common programs of research and development (EC for clothing in 1975 and 1979; United Kingdom for clothing, 1977; France for textiles, 1981). Governments have adopted labor mobility programs. They have offered loans or grants to

---

6. OECD, *Textile and Clothing Industries: Structural Problems and Policies in OECD Countries* (Paris: OECD, 1983), pp. 119; 127–28.

7. Philip Hayes, *Trade and Adjustment Policies in the European Community (with Special Reference to Textiles and Clothing)* (London: Trade Policy Research Centre, 1983; processed).

8. Ibid, pp. 5, 9, 16.

maintain employment (Italy, Netherlands, Belgium, and United Kingdom, in the period 1974–78). They have reduced social security payment obligations in return for employment undertakings by firms (Italy, France). In France, "solidarity" contracts have sought to maintain employment. And governments have undertaken regional investment in infrastructure and aid to depressed regions (France and Netherlands, 1978).[9]

The EC Commission has sought to impose discipline on the national adjustment programs, to ensure that they do not adversely affect other EC members. In 1971 the Commission issued a "framework for aids to the textile industry." It provided that modernization programs should not lead to increases in capacity, and that aids to facilitate elimination of excess capacity should be temporary and require a substantial cost contribution by the beneficiaries. The Commission's guidelines have sometimes placed it at odds with member governments, as in the instance of interest free loans from the Belgian government in 1977. The Commission initiated proceedings under Article 93(2) of the Treaty of Rome, and obtained Belgian agreement that beneficiary firms would have to accept a timetable for reconversion, that a general government program for the sector would be announced within six months, and that the loans could not be compounded with other assistance programs. The Commission has also played a role in setting forth longer term strategy for trade and industrial policy in the EC, as in a 1981 Communication that postulated that production "should not fall below the level of the last few years" and, accordingly, any increase in imports should be balanced by an increase in exports; and that "all the main types of production" should be sustained to avoid the "danger of whole industries emigrating."[10]

One dominant theme of earlier European adjustment was the attempt to move toward large scale and mass marketing through mergers, particularly in the United Kingdom and France. This strategy met with poor results, as it tended to create inflexible organizations biased toward mechanization and slow to respond to fashion. The relatively greater successes in adjustment appear to have been in Germany, where a relative absence of the federal government led to a slimming down of the industry to a stronger but smaller base; and in Italy, where the sector of small firms has been the most dynamic.[11]

De la Torre has concluded that adjustment policies in Europe have come full circle. In the 1950s and 1960s, the dominant approach was to allow the

---

9. Ibid., pp. 34–37.

10. Ibid., pp. 38–39, 43–44, 52.

11. William Davidson, Charles Feigenoff, and Fariborz Ghadar, *International Competition in Textiles and Apparel: The U.S. Experience* (Washington: National Chamber Foundation, 1986; processed), p. 30.

market to determine adjustment, with government support limited to general development programs and the negotiation of orderly marketing agreements with first Japan and then developing countries. Adjustment was relatively painless as employment continued to grow. In the first half of the 1970s, however, accelerating import competition, productivity gains, and stagnation in demand combined to intensify the adjustment problem. Governments then shifted from general programs to sectoral assistance. In 1975–77 annual subsidies to preserve jobs reached $300 million in Italy and the Netherlands and $200 million in the United Kingdom; yet these employment subsidies did little to avoid job losses, while adding competitive difficulties for the stronger firms not aided. France was an exception in its focus on technological advance as the response.[12]

By the late 1970s, governments began to seek more permanent solutions through industrial restructuring. Government-industry studies proliferated, and governments formed agencies to carry out their plans. But funds were limited, strategies and priorities were unclear, labor unions opposed the job losses implied, and industry was more interested in securing additional import protection than in implementing the plans. By the early 1980s, the restructuring plans were broadly rejected as too complex, and a neoliberal approach began to dominate. The new approach acknowledged the role of some degree of protection, the responsibility of the government to provide alternative employment opportunities in sectors with greater comparative advantage, and the need to minimize worker adjustment costs through retraining, relocation, and job-search services.[13]

Country Experience

The differing adjustment experiences of the principal European countries and Japan provide a further basis for evaluating alternative strategies.

United Kingdom

The UK experience illustrates two approaches with relatively poor records. One was the strategy of merger for achievement of scale and mass marketing. In the early 1960s, the two largest producers of man-made fibers (Courtauld and ICI) vied for acquisitions and enlargement to obtain economies of scale and market power, under the assumption of protection from low-cost

---

12. José de la Torre, *Clothing-Industry Adjustment in Developed Countries* (London: Trade Policy Research Centre, 1984), pp. 208–09, 219–21.

13. Ibid., pp. 223–26.

Commonwealth suppliers. By the early 1970s it was becoming evident that the merger strategy was not successful, as it diverted attention from specialization and marketing and led to overcapacity.[14] The second approach pursued in the United Kingdom was that of government subsidies. In the late 1970s the Temporary Employment Subsidy (TES) of £20 per week covered as many as 200,000 workers, half of them in the textile and apparel industries (10 percent of the sectors' employment). The government terminated the program in 1979. The net effects of the TES were ambiguous, but there was evidence that firms that saw their future as tied to capital-intensive production went ahead with dismissals rather than seeking the subsidies, while subsidized firms often had to dismiss workers once the subsidies ended.[15]

A recent study for the US Chamber of Commerce notes that productivity in the UK industry is only about half the level of that in the United States, and that the process of industry concentration has continued.[16] Lower productivity than in the United States is confirmed in the estimates of table 5.4 (but by a narrower margin). However, it should be recognized that the United Kingdom has carried out a great deal of adjustment already in terms of industry downsizing, and that its performance in productivity growth in at least apparel has been relatively favorable in recent years (table 5.7).

France

Government intervention in the sectors in France began in the 1950s when small business remained dominant, and the government extended support for modernizing equipment in small firms. A second wave of intervention occurred in the 1960s, when larger producers had gained influence and the policy thrust was toward modernization through mergers. In a third phase the government bureaucracy replaced industry associations in the design of policy. By the mid-1970s the French response to rising imports was to curtail imports by negotiation or unilaterally; even after establishment of a more coordinated EC position during the negotiation of MFA-II (chapter 9), French restrictions appear to have remained especially tight as reflected in low imports (noted above).[17]

---

14. Davidson, Feigenoff, and Ghadar, *International Competition*, pp. 24–25, 41, 43.

15. OECD, *Textile and Clothing Industries*, p. 117.

16. Davidson, Feigenoff, and Ghadar, *International Competition*, p. 25.

17. Ibid., p. 26; Philip Hayes, *Trade and Adjustment Policies*, pp. 18–22.

Italy

The Italian experience is of special interest in view of the country's successful trade performance in recent years (table 5.5). Ironically, the Italian success appears to have been driven by the economics of comparative advantage from low-cost labor within a broadly protected industrial country market, rather than by government policy. The government has tended to intervene in the form of acquiring direct state ownership of bankrupt and failing companies. Large firms have tended to receive the bulk of the government's subsidies. The costs to the government have been high and would have been higher in the absence of EC restraints on aid. In contrast, the small-firm sector has thrived in Italy, in considerable degree because of its greater access to low-cost labor (especially through out-hiring) as it avoided high labor costs imposed on large firms by legislation and labor unions. In woolen fabrics, knitting, and clothing the benefits of low-cost labor in small firms have outweighed any scale economies (which are presumably limited for operations difficult to mechanize). In short, textiles and apparel have been successful in Italy because of a flourishing but largely unaided small-firm sector, despite government assistance to their competitors in large, moribund firms.[18]

Germany

The German government has taken a noninterventionist position toward the textile and apparel industries. The domestic industry came under pressure in the late 1960s as Asian countries expanded exports to Germany in the face of restraints in the United States and the United Kingdom. Several large firms neared or reached bankruptcy, and although the federal government did not intervene, the provincial (*Land*) governments did provide subsidies. Part of the German response was to shift to outward processing, with subcontracting of processing to East German and other countries. Eventual strains with other EC members over entry of these goods contributed to German acquiescence in a restrictive stance of the Community on the MFA.[19]

As indicated above, employment has declined sharply in the textile and apparel sectors in Germany over the past two decades. Nonetheless, adjustment has been relatively smooth, as the declines occurred during periods

---

18. Davidson, Feigenoff, and Ghadar, *International Competition*, pp. 22–24; Philip Hayes, *Trade and Adjustment Policies*, pp. 24–26.

19. Ibid., pp. 24, 32.

of rapid overall economic growth and a basis of relatively even geographical distribution. Attrition in employment of foreign guest workers also facilitated adjustment. An open trade, market-oriented approach resulted in rapid growth of both exports and imports, and by 1983 nearly half of Germany's production was exported (placing Germany, behind Italy, as the second largest exporter in the world). Overall, most analysts judge Germany's experience as an important case of successful adjustment without major government intervention.[20]

Japan

The Japanese textile and apparel industries are characterized by a small-firm structure. In textiles in particular the Japanese industry has smaller scale than in other industrial countries. Thus, in the early 1980s there were some 47,000 textile establishments in Japan, as opposed to 6,600 in the United States and 2,900 in Italy. The average number of workers per establishment was only 15.7 in Japan, compared with 101 in the United States and 94 in Italy. In apparel, Japanese production was also at small scale, an average of 18 workers per establishment compared with 47 in the United States and 95 in Italy. Even allowing for the fact that an uneven distribution means that a major portion of production and employment is in establishments larger than these averages in all three countries, the fact remains that the Japanese industry structure is dispersed.[21]

As indicated in table 5.5, Japan has experienced a loss in comparative advantage in textiles and apparel, with the greatest decline in apparel. Japan had been virtually the only exporter in East Asia in the 1950s, and it faced increasing trade barriers in Europe and the United States through the 1960s. These restrictions became less relevant by the 1970s, however, as rising wages and a stronger yen undermined Japan's competitiveness. The textile and apparel industries fell from their earlier dominant position in Japanese industry and trade. According to one estimate, the sectors accounted for 23.4 percent of total manufacturing shipments and 48.2 percent of total exports in 1950; the output and export shares then declined to 7.7 percent and 12.5 percent, respectively, by 1970, and to 5.2 percent and 4.8 percent by 1980.[22] Moreover, the disappearance of Japan's comparative advantage coincided with greater pressure from imports from developing countries, as MFA restrictions

---

20. Davidson, Feigenoff, and Ghadar, *International Competition*, pp. 20–22.

21. The estimates are from United Nations, *Yearbook of Industrial Statistics,* 1983, and US Department of Commerce, *U.S. Industrial Outlook 1987* (Washington: Government Printing Office, 1987).

22. Davidson, Feigenoff, and Ghadar, *International Competition,* p. 27.

in other industrial countries shifted supply to the Japanese market. Thus, in 1978 after the much tighter renewal of the Arrangement (MFA-II), Japan's textile imports from non-OECD countries doubled (table 5.6).

The government's response to decline in the textile and apparel industry was in the Japanese tradition of government-business cooperation and conscious formulation of industrial policy. The private sector itself had begun adjustment in the form of shifting production abroad through direct foreign investment elsewhere in Asia. The government focused its attention on the scrapping of outdated and excess capacity. In the early 1970s, various legislative and administrative measures provided well over 100 billion yen (nearly $400 million) for the programs of purchasing and scrapping redundant capacity. The government also provided low interest loans for structural improvement.[23] The official thrust toward reducing capacity meant a forthright acceptance of downsizing as a means of adjustment. The negative growth rates for Japanese production since the early 1970s (table 5.7) reflect this strategy.

The 1979 law for "Structural Improvement to the Textile Industry" provided for additional adjustment efforts. The textile and apparel manufacturers worked closely together in research projects and product development. The strategy included vertical integration and conversion to nontextile business. Thus, the largest textile company (Asahi Chemical) achieved more than two-thirds of its sales in nonfiber products, and the next two largest firms approximately one-third. The most difficult challenge arose in dealing with the large number of tiny firms. Approximately half were already associated with large producers of synthetic fibers, but the other half had especially poor production facilities. The 1979 law provided tax and financial incentives to small firms that entered into vertical cooperation projects under MITI (Ministry of International Trade and Industry) guidelines. Restructuring efforts included the scrapping of outdated machinery, development of differentiated products, and the use of small-batch technology for product variety.[24]

Japan did not choose the route relied upon heavily by most of the other industrial countries: protection. Japan has not resorted to import quotas. In part the lack of formal barriers has reflected greater competitiveness. It may also have reflected the difficulty of entering the Japanese market without Japanese partners, for example because of the nature of the distribution system and the interrelationships among Japanese firms.[25]

---

23. OECD, *Textile and Clothing Industries*, p. 114.

24. Davidson, Feigenoff, and Ghadar, *International Competition*, pp. 27–29.

25. Donald B. Keesing and Martin Wolf, *Textile Quotas Against Developing Countries* (London: Trade Policy Research Centre, 1980), p. 55.

Most observers judge the Japanese adjustment effort in textiles and apparel to have been successful.[26] One study summarizes the reasons for this success as follows. Japanese firms made deliberate decisions to upgrade and streamline production. They pursued changing comparative advantage by investing abroad and moving production to Korea, Taiwan, and ASEAN countries, and they played a role in the emerging industry in China. Their vertical integration meant that they could shift their fabric operations abroad while continuing to supply them with domestically produced fibers. And the fact that textile producers belonged to larger groupings of firms provided alternative employment opportunities that facilitated scrapping of domestic capacity and movement of production abroad.[27]

Evolving Comparative Advantage among Developing Countries

The discussion in chapter 2 highlighted the rapid rise of the developing countries as suppliers of textiles and apparel to the US and world markets. It also noted that the most pronounced comparative advantage of the developing countries has emerged in apparel. In textiles the industrial countries actually have maintained a trade surplus, while the developing countries are in deficit (table 2.9).

Table 5.8 shows the dramatic rise in imports of textiles and apparel from the developing countries. The data here are for 25 major exporting nations. Imports into OECD countries from these suppliers rose from under $600 million in 1963 to $2.8 billion in 1973 and $8.7 billion in 1984, in textiles, and from less than $300 million to $4 billion and $22.5 billion, respectively, in apparel. If these nominal values are deflated by an index of unit values of exports from industrial countries,[28] the annual growth rates in real terms were 11.1 percent for textiles and 21.5 percent for apparel in 1963–73, and 4.0 percent for textiles and 10.0 percent for apparel in 1973–84. The extremely high growth rates in the 1960s were from low initial base levels. Growth in the 1970s was relatively slow for textiles, but remained relatively high in apparel. In comparison, overall manufactured exports from developing countries (defined narrowly to exclude processed foods and copper) grew in real terms at 15.6 percent annually from 1965 to 1973 and 12.4 percent

---

26. Davidson, Feigenoff, and Ghadar, *International Competition*, p. 29; GATT, *Textiles and Clothing*, p. 172.

27. National Research Council, *The Competitive Status of the US Fibers, Textiles and Apparel Complex* (Washington: National Academy Press, 1983), pp. 60–61.

28. With 1963 = 100, this index rose to 159 in 1973 and 315 in 1984. IMF, *International Financial Statistics, Yearbook 1983* and September 1986.

from 1973 to 1980 (before slowing to 4.1 percent in 1980–82).[29] Because of rapid growth in the 1960s and relatively slower growth of raw materials exports, the share of textiles and apparel in total exports of the upper-middle income developing countries rose from 5 percent in 1965 to 9 percent in 1982.[30]

In the early 1960s, India and Hong Kong dominated developing-country exports of textiles, while Hong Kong alone provided three-fourths of apparel imports from these countries into the OECD nations. Then, in the 1960s and early 1970s, South Korea and Taiwan achieved extraordinary export growth to capture, in each case, approximately one-sixth of exports of apparel from developing countries and 10 percent of textile exports.[31] In a third distinct phase, mainland China emerged forcefully in the market to capture nearly 9 percent of developing-country exports of apparel and 18 percent of their textile exports by 1984 (up from 3 percent and 12 percent in 1973, respectively). By 1984, Hong Kong's share of apparel imports into OECD countries from developing countries had declined from 74 percent in 1963 to 27 percent, largely as the result of a sharp rise in the shares of Korea, Taiwan, and China.

It is clear from table 5.8 that there has been no similar explosive growth in these exports from countries other than Korea, Taiwan, and China. On the contrary, there have been major declines in shares (for India, from 52 percent of textiles in 1963 to 8 percent in 1984; for the Philippines, from 9 percent of apparel in 1963 to 3 percent in 1984). By region, the five East Asian countries doubled their share in textiles from 1963 to 1984 to nearly half of the export market, and together retained the large share of some three-fourths in apparel previously held by Hong Kong alone. In contrast, the rest of Asia including India experienced a decline in trade share from 59 percent of developing-country exports in textiles in 1963 to only 22 percent in 1984, and retained only about a 10 percent share in apparel exports. In Latin America, only Brazil achieved a relatively large share of textile exports (although in proportionate terms growth was high in Peru as well), while Latin America's share of apparel exports remained extremely low. For their part, the Mediterranean countries of Europe held relatively constant market shares, at approximately one-fifth of developing-country

---

29. William R. Cline, *Exports of Manufactures from Developing Countries* (Washington: Brookings Institution, 1984), pp. 122–23.

30. World Bank, *World Development Report 1985* (Washington: World Bank, 1985), p. 193.

31. Keesing and Wolf note the dramatic benefits to these economies from such export expansion. In Korea, from 1967 to 1976 clothing output increased 16 times and textiles output 8 times; and from 1972 to 1976 apparel employment rose from 76,000 to 201,000 while textile employment rose from 223,000 to 357,000. Keesing and Wolf, *Textile Quotas,* p. 121.

Table 5.8 Imports into the OECD from 25 developing countries, 1963, 1973, and 1984

(million dollars, percentage shares in parentheses)

| | \multicolumn{6}{c}{Textiles (SITC 65)} | | | | | |
	\multicolumn{2}{c}{1963}	\multicolumn{2}{c}{1973}	\multicolumn{2}{c}{1984}
China	30.6	(5.2)	329.0	(11.6)	1,542.1	(17.8)
South Korea	4.4	(0.8)	303.3	(10.7)	1,038.5	(12.0)
Taiwan	7.4	(1.2)	221.2	(7.8)	734.6	(8.5)
Hong Kong	72.5	(12.3)	306.4	(10.8)	545.0	(6.3)
Singapore	n.a.	(n.a.)	26.7	(0.9)	31.6	(0.4)
Subtotal	114.9	(19.5)	1,186.6	(41.8)	3,891.7	(45.0)
Pakistan	35.7	(6.0)	267.3	(9.4)	534.4	(6.2)
Bangladesh	n.a.	(n.a.)	44.2	(1.6)	255.0	(2.9)
India	308.3	(52.2)	423.3	(14.9)	706.3	(8.2)
Sri Lanka	0.2	(0.0)	0.5	(0.0)	7.8	(0.1)
Thailand	0.6	(0.1)	45.8	(1.6)	246.2	(2.8)
Indonesia	0.4	(0.1)	4.0	(0.1)	119.8	(1.4)
Philippines	2.7	(0.5)	17.8	(0.6)	37.6	(0.4)
Subtotal	347.8	(58.9)	802.9	(28.3)	1,907.0	(22.0)
Haiti	2.9	(0.5)	6.7	(0.2)	15.9	(0.2)
Dominican Rep.	0.0	(0.0)	0.1	(0.0)	3.2	(0.0)
Costa Rica	0.0	(0.0)	0.4	(0.0)	1.4	(0.0)
Colombia	1.4	(0.2)	38.9	(1.4)	56.2	(0.6)
Peru	0.3	(0.0)	2.6	(0.1)	115.0	(1.3)
Brazil	1.9	(0.3)	144.7	(5.1)	573.3	(6.6)
Argentina	2.3	(0.4)	9.8	(0.3)	11.1	(0.1)
Uruguay	1.4	(0.2)	2.7	(0.1)	22.6	(0.3)
Subtotal	10.2	(1.7)	205.8	(7.2)	798.8	(9.2)
Greece	6.4	(1.1)	122.9	(4.3)	411.3	(4.8)
Portugal	58.7	(9.9)	262.1	(9.2)	575.1	(6.6)
Spain	29.1	(4.9)	109.9	(3.9)	451.8	(5.2)
Turkey	2.5	(0.4)	78.1	(2.7)	467.9	(5.4)
Yugoslavia	20.7	(3.5)	72.9	(2.6)	152.6	(1.8)
Subtotal	117.3	(19.9)	645.9	(22.7)	2,058.8	(23.8)
Total	590.2	(100)	2,841.2	(100)	8,656.3	(100)

n.a. not available.
Source: OECD, *Foreign Trade by Commodities,* series C, vol. 2, DRI data base.

Apparel (SITC 84)					
1963		1973		1984	
3.7	(1.3)	105.1	(2.6)	1,960.3	(8.7)
4.1	(1.4)	642.3	(16.1)	4,364.1	(19.4)
8.8	(3.0)	663.7	(16.6)	3,387.8	(15.1)
215.9	(74.0)	1,394.3	(34.9)	5,990.3	(26.6)
n.a.	(n.a.)	115.4	(2.9)	426.8	(1.9)
232.6	(79.7)	2,920.9	(73.2)	16,129.4	(71.7)
0.6	(0.2)	18.2	(0.5)	158.5	(0.7)
n.a.	(n.a.)	0.0	(0.0)	58.5	(0.3)
1.3	(0.5)	79.9	(2.0)	750.6	(3.3)
0.0	(0.0)	0.6	(0.0)	310.3	(1.4)
0.1	(0.0)	31.1	(0.8)	412.6	(1.8)
0.0	(0.0)	2.1	(0.1)	266.6	(1.2)
27.2	(9.3)	61.0	(1.5)	630.2	(2.8)
29.2	(10.0)	193.0	(4.8)	2,587.2	(11.5)
0.2	(0.1)	12.1	(0.3)	108.5	(0.5)
0.0	(0.0)	2.3	(0.1)	182.9	(0.8)
n.a.	(n.a.)	7.5	(0.2)	82.2	(0.4)
0.0	(0.0)	17.0	(0.4)	47. 8	(0.2)
0.0	(0.0)	1.3	(0.0)	21.8	(0.1)
0.0	(0.0)	44.1	(1.1)	154.4	(0.7)
0.3	(0.1)	17.7	(0.4)	27.8	(0.1)
0.0	(0.0)	7.6	(0.2)	96.3	(0.4)
0.6	(0.2)	109.6	(2.7)	721.6	(3.2)
1.6	(0.5)	126.8	(3.2)	721.2	(3.2)
8.2	(2.8)	200.1	(5.0)	855.7	(3.8)
7.9	(2.7)	116.5	(2.9)	234.0	(1.0)
0.1	(0.1)	49.0	(1.2)	592.8	(2.6)
11.5	(3.9)	275.9	(6.9)	633. 1	(2.9)
29.4	(10.1)	768.3	(19.2)	3,066.8	(13.6)
291.8	(100)	3,991.8	(100)	22,504.9	(100)

exports of textiles and 10 percent to 15 percent exports of apparel to OECD countries.

Inspection of table 5.8 reveals the still highly skewed distribution of textile and apparel exports from developing countries to the industrial countries. The big four suppliers (Hong Kong, Korea, Taiwan, and China) in 1984 accounted for 44.6 percent of these exports in textiles and 69.8 percent in apparel. This extreme concentration raises significant policy issues. In particular, it means that insofar as the protection regime gives rise to quota rents for suppliers, these rents are highly concentrated in the four East Asian countries. It seems unlikely that income transfers channeled through more conscious mechanisms such as official development assistance would go to these countries in this degree of concentration, if at all. This consideration lends some logic to the recent US position (and that adopted in the MFA renewal of 1986; chapter 9) that there should be a relative expansion of import quotas for countries other than the big four East Asian suppliers (although the risk is that industrial countries will freeze imports from these suppliers without according liberal treatment to imports from other developing countries).

The dominance of the four East Asian suppliers in developing-country exports of textiles and apparel does not mean that the sectors are unimportant for other developing countries. In 1984 the combined exports of textiles and apparel amounted to 69 percent of total exports in Haiti, 34 percent in Bangladesh, 27 percent in Pakistan, 22 percent in Sri Lanka, 21 percent in the Dominican Republic, 15 percent in India, 13 percent in the Philippines and in Uruguay, 9 percent in Thailand, and 8 percent in Costa Rica.[32] Although textiles and apparel account for only 2 percent to 4 percent of exports in Indonesia, Colombia, Peru, and Brazil, their weight in manufactured exports is higher, and in view of weak commodity markets in recent years opportunities for manufactured exports are important.

The case of China warrants special mention. As is evident in table 5.8, China's exports of textiles and especially apparel have accelerated rapidly in recent years. US authorities have tended to be more accommodating to China than to the other large East Asian suppliers, on two grounds. First, they have recognized that China was a late entrant and started from a small base (although now it is the largest developing-country supplier of textile products and the fourth largest supplier of apparel; table 5.8). Second, China is in a much stronger political position to threaten retaliation against restriction. Thus, the final version of the 1985 bill for textile quotas in the United States omitted China from the large cutbacks to be imposed on the other three large East Asian suppliers because legislators were concerned

---

32. Calculated from table 5.8 and IMF, *International Financial Statistics*, September 1986.

that China would close its own market.[33] Previously, China had succeeded in repelling tighter restriction by threatening to cut off imports of agricultural products from the United States.[34]

Africa is absent from the list of the top 25 developing-country suppliers of textiles and apparel. However, open trade in these products could be especially important to many low-income countries in Africa. These sectors are among the few for which the unsophisticated level of industrial production in these countries permits exports. While African nations typically do not face quotas today, the scope for future growth of their exports is necessarily constrained by the overall regime of textile and apparel protection, which probably already discourages investment for export expansion by posing the threat of quota imposition if exports do rise substantially.

In a regime of open trade, relatively rapid growth of textile and apparel exports from latecomers among the developing countries could be expected. There would probably be a natural evolution away from concentration of these exports among Korea, Taiwan, and Hong Kong (although it could be longer before China's expansion would peak). In a regime of protected global trade in textiles and apparel, policymakers play a major role in allocating the scarce resource of an export market among the many claimants in the developing world. It is not clear that the present method of this allocation is either the most equitable or the most efficient.

---

33. *Washington Times,* 1 July 1986; *New York Times,* 11 October 1985.

34. See I.M. Destler and John Odell, *The Politics of Anti-Protection: Changing Forces in United States Trade Politics,* POLICY ANALYSES IN INTERNATIONAL ECONOMICS 21 (Washington: Institute for International Economics, September 1987).

6

The Evolution of Protection in Textiles and Apparel

Textiles and apparel are the most systematically and comprehensively protected sectors in the world today. The unique degree of their protection dates from at least the late 1950s, when new restrictive regimes began to emerge even as overall protection of manufactures was beginning to decline through successive postwar tariff negotiations. Multilateral coordination of protection in the sectors began in the early 1960s for cotton textile products. A decade later, major trading nations expanded coverage to man-made fiber products under the Multi-Fiber Arrangement (MFA). First negotiated in 1974 and renewed in 1977 and again in 1981, the MFA most recently acquired an additional five-year term under a renewal agreement reached in July of 1986.

In many ways the most important feature of the special regime for textiles and apparel protection is its seeming permanence. In other sectors, protection has come and gone (and in cases, come again). Color television sets, footwear, and automobiles are examples of sectors that have experienced US protection in recent years but are currently free from overt barriers (except for a truly voluntary restraint on Japanese autos). Steel protection has also fluctuated, and currently appears to be in a phase of tightening of restrictions.

With continuous restrictive regimes since the early 1960s, the textile and apparel sectors are preeminent in durability of import protection. An important reason for this durability is the persistent view that in the absence of international regimes (the MFA), protection in the United States and abroad could be even more severe.

The Short and Long Term Arrangements on Cotton Textiles

After World War I, British textiles still dominated the industry internationally, but through protection the United States had already become a major producer in the late nineteenth century. The US Tariff Acts of 1922 and

1930 established unusually high tariffs for the industry under the prevailing view that it was of special importance and could not survive without protection. Thus, in 1930 the average US tariff on cotton goods was 46 percent and on woolen goods 60 percent, compared with 35 percent for metal manufactures and 31 percent for chemicals.[1]

During the Great Depression, textile trade fell sharply even as competition from Japan rose. The United Kingdom applied imperial preferences in response, while other nations began the widespread use of quotas. By the late 1930s a major portion of Japan's textile exports was subject to quantitative restrictions as well as high tariffs internationally. For its part, in 1936 the United States induced Japan to enter a "gentlemen's agreement" restricting exports—a precursor of the most widespread form of quantitative restrictions today, the voluntary export restraint.[2]

By the 1950s, the remaining welter of restrictions from the 1930s began to yield to postwar negotiations for US-European trade, but restraints on Japan, Eastern Europe, and the developing countries continued or tightened. When Japan applied for membership in the General Agreement on Tariffs and Trade (GATT) in 1955, many member countries chose to continue restricting imports from the country under Article XXXV adopted for that purpose. Although the United States did not invoke this article, the Eisenhower administration did propose in 1955 that Japan voluntarily limit its exports of selected cotton textiles. Section 204 of the Agricultural Act of 1956 authorized the President to negotiate limitations of textile exports from other countries, and in the same year Japan adopted a five-year limitation to begin in 1957.[3]

What followed inaugurated a cycle that has plagued textile protection ever since: the spillover of imports from controlled to uncontrolled areas. Under self-restraint, Japan's share of US imports of cotton textiles fell from 63 percent in 1958 to 26 percent in 1960, while the share of Hong Kong rose from 14 percent to 28 percent; imports also surged from several other countries. Moreover, US agricultural policy aggravated import competition for a decade after the 1956 act, by forcing domestic textile mills to purchase cotton at an artificially high support price while foreign producers could buy exported US cotton at a lower price.[4]

---

1. F. W. Taussig, as cited in Donald B. Keesing and Martin Wolf, *Textile Quotas Against Developing Countries* (London: Trade Policy Research Centre, 1980), p. 11.

2. General Agreement on Tariffs and Trade (GATT), *Textiles and Clothing in the World Economy* (Geneva: GATT, 1984), pp. 62–63.

3. Ibid, p. 64; United Nations Conference on Trade and Development, Programme of Cooperation among Developing Countries, Exporters of Textiles and Clothing, *Manual for Textile Negotiators*, vol. 1 (Geneva: UNCTAD, 1983), p. 8.

4. Keesing and Wolf, *Textile Quotas*, pp. 14–15.

Led by US negotiators, GATT discussions in 1959 and 1960 developed the concept of "market disruption," defined as instances of sharp import increases associated with low import prices not attributable to dumping or foreign subsidies. In November 1960 GATT adopted the Decision on the Avoidance of Market Disruption. This concept made important changes going beyond the existing Article XIX safeguard mechanism. It provided that restrictions could be applied even if actual injury had not taken place, and against individual countries responsible for the import surge rather than on a most-favored-nation basis. It also established the presence of a price differential between imports and comparable domestic goods as a basis for determining the need for restriction. In adopting the Short Term Arrangement (STA) in 1961 the GATT applied the concept of market disruption, and it remained a cornerstone of textile and apparel protection thereafter in the Long Term Arrangement (LTA), and then the MFA. Although the original Decision adopting the concept in 1960 did not intend to limit it to textiles and apparel, GATT has not spread its application to other sectors.[5]

After having pledged support for the textile industry in his campaign, in 1961 President Kennedy called for an international conference to avoid disruption to the sector. In July 1961 an international Short Term Arrangement authorized one-year restrictions at base period (mid-1960 to mid-1961) levels for 64 categories of cotton textiles, to avoid market disruption until a more permanent mechanism could be negotiated. In February 1962, 19 major trading nations adopted the Long Term Arrangement Regarding Cotton Textiles. This arrangement, renewed in 1967 and 1970 through 1973, provided for bilateral consultations and automatic annual increases of 5 percent in restraint levels in the absence of agreement otherwise (with zero growth, but not actual reductions, permitted in exceptional cases).[6]

In short, by 1962 an international regime was in place that tended to limit volume growth of imports to 5 percent annually for the bulk of cotton textiles and apparel. Ironically, the US trade deficit remained a low 4 percent of value added in the sectors in 1963, while the European Community (EC) actually had a surplus. Yet political reality encouraged preemptive action. The textile and clothing industries employed 17 percent of manufacturing labor in the industrial countries, while the countries restricted under the LTA—Japan and the developing countries—had little bargaining power in the GATT. Moreover, President Kennedy needed the LTA to persuade the textile interests in the United States to acquiesce in the launching of the

---

5. GATT, *Textiles and Clothing,* pp. 5, 65.

6. Keesing and Wolf, *Textile Quotas,* p. 16; William Davidson, Charles Feigenoff, and Fairburtz Ghadar, *International Competition in Textiles and Apparel: The US Experience* (Washington: National Chamber Foundation, 1986), pp. 33–34.

Kennedy Round of multilateral trade negotiations, just as the MFA in 1973 may be viewed as one price President Nixon had to pay to obtain congressional authority to begin the Tokyo Round. And, as in the later case of the MFA, proponents were able to argue that the LTA was the lesser of two evils: multilateral agreement or unilateral restraint, and that the arrangement would actually promote trade by ensuring that its growth was orderly. A recent GATT study notes that in the case of Europe, which had more extensive restraints than the United States, the LTA probably did have a liberalizing influence by specifying criteria for quotas and providing for some quota increases.[7]

MFA-I

Import growth persisted despite the LTA. Thus, at 1982 prices US imports of textiles rose from $1.02 billion in 1961 to $2.4 billion in 1972, while imports of apparel rose from $648 million to $3.5 billion (chapter 2, tables 2.3 and 2.5), for an average annual growth rate of 11.5 percent for the two sectors combined. Import growth was focused in textiles and apparel of man-made fibers not covered under the cotton textile arrangement. Thus, from 1960 to 1970 US imports of man-made fiber textiles rose from 31 million pounds to 329 million pounds.[8] By the late 1960s and early 1970s an increasingly overvalued dollar aggravated import pressure.

The response to the rise of man-made fiber goods was a resort to bilateral quantitative restrictions outside the auspices of either the GATT or the LTA, especially by the United States and Canada. In 1971 and 1972 the United States negotiated bilateral agreements restricting imports of man-made fiber and wool products from Hong Kong, Japan, Korea, and Taiwan.[9]

The political context of these bilateral agreements was one of considerable domestic US pressure to extend LTA quota coverage to man-made fiber and woolen products. In the 1968 presidential election, Richard Nixon won support of the textile and apparel industries with a pledge to develop an international agreement covering these products. By 1970 an initiative along these lines met with cool response from European officials, while Japan had refused to adopt voluntary restraints over the broader range of products. In response to rising industry and labor pressure, Representative Wilbur D.

---

7. Keesing and Wolf, *Textile Quotas,* pp. 14–18; GATT, *Textiles and Clothing,* p. 7.

8. Davidson, Feigenoff, and Ghadar, *International Competition,* p. 34.

9. GATT, *Textiles and Clothing,* p. 7; Davidson, Feigenoff, and Ghadar, *International Competition,* p. 34; OECD, *Textile and Clothing Industries: Structural Problems and Policies in OECD Countries* (Paris: OECD, 1983), p. 107.

Mills (D-Ark.) submitted a bill to impose quotas on imports of textiles, apparel, and footwear. The House of Representatives passed the bill in late 1970, but the Senate rejected it. By 1971, however, the entire trade relationship with Japan had become more contentious with the issue of whether Japan and European countries would revalue their currencies. Following the 10 percent import surcharge of August 1971, President Richard M. Nixon threatened to restrict imports of textiles and apparel unilaterally under the "Trading with the Enemy Act." On the day these restrictions were to enter into force, October 15, Japan agreed to comprehensive restraints.[10]

By 1972, with bilateral agreements restricting US imports from Japan and other major Asian suppliers, the resulting diversion of exports exerted pressure on European governments to go along with a new multilateral mechanism covering man-made fibers and woolen goods. As in the earlier episode with the LTA and, to a considerable degree, the renewals of the MFA subsequently through 1986, precursor bilateral restrictions were perhaps the more important reality that the international agreements subsequently ratified and at best sought to moderate rather than roll back.

Following its negotiation in 1973, the Arrangement Regarding International Trade in Textiles, known as the Multi-Fiber Arrangement, entered into force on January 1, 1974. The Arrangement was a general framework for determining the conditions under which textile and apparel trade could be controlled. Its most important part was Article 4, which established norms for the bilateral export-restraint agreements that in practice implemented the arrangement.

US policymakers sought the MFA as a means of providing legitimacy for the extension of quota protection to man-made fibers and woolen goods. They preferred an international arrangement over strictly bilateral measures because they considered that the result would do less damage to the multilateral trade apparatus under GATT, that it would ensure a sharing of the import burden by Europe, and that it would avoid still more restrictive and permanent quotas that might otherwise be enacted by Congress. These same motives have remained through successive renewals of the Arrangement and help explain its longevity.

Because the MFA would provide legitimacy for extension of textile controls, US authorities were prepared to offer concessions in the degree of protection that had been afforded to cotton textiles under the LTA and bilateral agreements on man-made fibers emerging in the early 1970s. Thus, the MFA provided for annual quota growth at 6 percent instead of 5 percent (with lower but still positive rates permissible for exceptional cases). It

---

10. UNCTAD, *Manual,* pp. 47–48.

instituted quota flexibility through "swing" adjustments that permitted the transfer of quotas across categories, "carry forward" allowances that permitted borrowing against a future year's quota, and "carry over" adjustments that allowed for unused quotas to be added to subsequent years' imports. The arrangement also created a Textiles Surveillance Body (TSB) to monitor implementation of the arrangement. Importantly, in implementation the Europeans applied the phase-out mechanism of the arrangement to eliminate many restrictions on Eastern Europe and developing countries. For these reasons, many observers conclude that the establishment of the first MFA in 1974 was a move toward liberalization.[11] Nonetheless, the increase in coverage of quotas to include man-made fibers and woolen goods meant that at best this liberalization was ambiguous.

Despite the dominant but arguable policy view at the time that the establishment of the MFA was on balance liberalizing compared to the realistic alternatives, the arrangement was an embarrassing breach of GATT principles, not unlike the earlier glaring exception to these principles in GATT's dispensations granted to agricultural trade. The MFA violated the most-favored-nation principle by permitting discriminatory treatment among supplier countries. It broke the general GATT mandate of applying tariff rather than quota protection. It undermined the principle of assured market access through tariff binding by making access contingent.[12] Importantly, the MFA also established a precedent of imposing quantitative restrictions against developing countries (and in this case Japan as well) but not against industrial countries.

MFA-II

The potential of the Multi-Fiber Arrangement for tighter protection became more apparent in its renewal in 1977. While the United States had been the

---

11. Keesing and Wolf, *Textile Quotas,* pp. 39–41; GATT, *Textiles and Clothing,* pp. 8, 86. Similarly, Aggarwal makes the judgment that while the formal MFA arrangements did not represent much of a change away from or toward protection in comparison with the LTA (because increased coverage offset more liberal terms), actual behavior at the national level did shift in a liberalizing direction with the advent of the MFA. He then stresses that under subsequent renewals of the arrangement, ostensibly in a liberalizing direction, national implementation of bilateral agreements brought a systematic increase in protection. Vinod K. Aggarwal, *Liberal Protectionism: The International Politics of Organized Textile Trade* (Berkeley: University of California Press, 1985), p. 24.

12. Gerard Curzon, José de la Torre, Juergen B. Donges, Alasdair I. MacBean, Jean Waelbroeck, and Martin Wolf, *MFA Forever?* (London: Trade Policy Research Centre, 1981), p. 32.

principal protagonist in the mechanism's creation, by the late 1970s Europe was leading the drive for increasing its restrictiveness. European markets were under considerable pressure, as total imports of textiles and apparel rose from $14.8 billion in 1973 to $22.0 billion in 1976 (an increase of 49 percent). US imports rose nearly as much in proportionate terms (40 percent, from $3.7 billion to $5.3 billion) but from a much smaller base. Much of the rise in European imports was in intraregional trade associated with further development of specialization within the European Community, but the pace of increased imports from nonoil developing countries was also rapid: from $1.9 billion in 1973 to $3.9 billion in 1976 (an increase of 106 percent), compared with an increase in the United States from $2.1 billion to $3.6 billion (by 75 percent).[13]

The standard interpretation of the EC position on MFA-II was that it was a response to the EC's experience in the formation of the first MFA, when it had lagged behind in developing a common position and its imports had begun to surge before it had worked out Community-wide restraint agreements with major suppliers. Thus, the first EC bilateral agreements were in 1975 (with Hong Kong and Korea), two years after the MFA entered into force.[14] While this factor was no doubt prominent, the data cited above suggest an additional reason for greater protectionist pressure in the EC in this period. The increase of EC imports even in intraregional trade was large in this period (with the increase of imports from Organization for Economic Cooperation and Development (OECD) members four times as large in absolute terms as that from non-OECD suppliers). The adjustment stress associated with rising specialization within the EC thus may well have added significantly to the impact of rapidly growing imports from countries controlled by the MFA.

Three influences appear to have placed the United States in a less aggressive posture than the EC with respect to tightening in the renegotiation of the MFA. First, the sizable depreciation of the dollar in 1971–73 had improved the competitiveness of the US industry. Second, the United States had more thorough protection already in place, as the result of its bilateral agreements that preceded MFA-I and its prompt implementation of new agreements upon adoption of that arrangement. Third, production was rising and productivity increasing only slowly in this period in the United States so that employment was not declining rapidly, while in Europe employment fell by approximately one-sixth in 1973–77.[15]

---

13. GATT, *International Trade 1976/77* (Geneva: GATT, 1977), tables A and D.

14. Keesing and Wolf, *Textile Quotas*, p. 57.

15. OECD, *Textile and Clothing Industries*, p. 107.

Within the EC, intense industry and labor pressure for protection, the shift of the United Kingdom to France's position favoring tighter restrictions, and the threat of imposition of individual member-country restrictions (as occurred in France in mid-1977) pressured the EC authorities to insist on a more restrictive arrangement as the price of MFA renewal. The alternative threat was an end to the Arrangement and more restrictive EC protection unilaterally. EC negotiators insisted in particular on more flexibility to depart from the 6 percent norm for quota growth. Previously, departures had required the relatively difficult demonstration that adherence to the norm would cause "market disruption" or "damage to . . . minimum viable production" (Annex B of the Arrangement). Thus, over the opposition of developing countries a crucial change in the language of MFA-II permitted "jointly agreed reasonable departures" from the terms of the MFA regulating export restraints.[16]

In December 1977 the signatory countries renewed the MFA for four years. It is widely agreed that the allowance of "reasonable departures" proved to be the key change in the arrangement that paved the way for its subsequent implementation in a manner that at best led to a further tightening of the instrument and at worst also violated its original intent. This clause pushed the MFA still further toward an arrangement that mattered far less than the implementing bilateral agreements under its aegis. The departures most commonly negotiated in these agreements were deviations from the norms set forth in Annex B of the Arrangement, primarily reductions of quotas or growth at less than the 6 percent standard, and denial of flexibility under swing and carry-over provisions. The bilateral agreements negotiated by the EC (as well as Sweden) used these departures the most extensively.[17]

The EC bilateral agreements negotiated in late 1977 divided MFA products into 114 categories and five groups. Group I contained the eight most sensitive categories, and the agreements brought rollbacks in this group. Thus, Hong Kong agreed to cut back exports in this group to the EC by 8.4 percent from 1976 to 1978. The EC maintained, however, that it was preserving the opportunity for overall 6 percent growth for each supplier by allowing more generous quota increases in the nonsensitive groups. The EC also instituted member-country subquotas based on 1976 imports from MFA supplier countries (although analysts have pointed out that the opportunity for substitution by intra-EC suppliers combined with free intraregional trade has meant that these subquotas were relatively mean-

---

16. Keesing and Wolf, *Textile Quotas*, pp. 60–62.

17. GATT, *Textiles and Clothing*, p. 81.

ingless). In addition, it adopted a "basket extractor" mechanism whereby any uncontrolled country whose exports exceeded a threshold share (such as 1 percent) of total EC imports would become subject to controls.[18]

An important change in EC practice under MFA-II was to identify global ceilings of imports from all "low cost" countries in the sensitive groups (especially group I), under the concept of "cumulative market disruption." The significant shift in interpretation was away from the previous bilateral approach, whereby action would be taken against a country only if its individual exports could be blamed for injury, toward a comprehensive approach in which even small suppliers would be restricted because disruption would be defined globally.[19]

US bilateral agreements under MFA-II also tended in a more protective direction, although to a lesser degree. The US approach provided more latitude than the highly elaborated EC system, as might be expected for a single country as opposed to a grouping where intramember positions had to be negotiated. In the period 1978–80 the United States renegotiated bilateral agreements, tightening up swing and carry-over provisions for Hong Kong, Korea, and Taiwan. For categories where quotas had gone unused to a considerable degree, some of these agreements abolished the quotas but instituted a "call" mechanism whereby consultations on new quotas would be triggered if imports rose above specified levels that in practice were lower than the magnitudes that would have been permitted under the previous quotas. Total quotas from the big three suppliers were frozen in 1978 at the 1977 levels, and allowed to grow only at rates well below 6 percent thereafter. There was some tendency in US bilateral agreements to provide more leniency on the new, smaller supplying countries, however.[20] The same theme of seeking to freeze imports from the big three suppliers while providing scope for growth of imports from new suppliers resurfaced in both of the subsequent renewals of the MFA.

Overall, the effect of the various bilateral agreements under MFA-II was to reduce access to US and European markets. However, the incidence of unilateral restrictions did decline as the coverage and restrictiveness of bilateral agreements under the MFA increased.[21]

---

18. Keesing and Wolf, *Textile Quotas,* pp. 64–67; Carl Hamilton, "Follies of Policies for Textile Imports in Western Europe," *World Economy 8,* no. 3 (September 1985), pp. 219–33.

19. Gerard Curzon et al., *MFA Forever?* p. 6.

20. Keesing and Wolf, *Textile Quotas,* pp. 74–77; 63.

21. OECD, *Textile and Clothing Industries,* p. 108.

MFA-III

Negotiations in 1981 for the second renewal of the MFA continued the trend toward tightening. The EC once again complained of burden sharing, and maintained that its per capita imports of low-cost textiles were much higher than those of the United States and Japan. In fact, however, if net trade deducting exports was taken into account, the EC's net imports from developing countries excluding southern Europe were approximately the same as those of the United States (some $4 billion in 1979).[22] Nonetheless, the principal objectives of the EC in the renegotiation included outright cutbacks in quotas of the dominant suppliers (primarily Hong Kong, Taiwan, and Korea) and limitation of quota growth for other countries to well below 6 percent annually on grounds that domestic demand was stagnant or growing much more slowly. In the negotiations the United States also indicated that the original terms of Annex B in terms of growth (6 percent) and flexibility were no longer realistic. Domestically, textile interests stressed that President Reagan's letter to Senator Strom Thurmond (R-SC) during the 1980 campaign had pledged to "strengthen" the MFA when it expired at the end of 1981 by "relating import growth from all sources to domestic market growth." However, US negotiators assured suppliers that they did not seek actual rollbacks in quota levels.[23]

For their part, the developing countries sought greater discipline in MFA III, and elimination of the clause permitting "reasonable departures" from the norms on export restraints in particular. The Protocol finally negotiated did omit renewed reference to reasonable departures. However, on the protective side it incorporated an "anti-surge" provision (paragraph 10) providing for special restraint in the face of sharp increases of imports of sensitive products with previously underutilized quotas. In addition, its language on supplier "goodwill" (paragraph 6) reflected the EC demand for cutbacks in some quotas for dominant suppliers.[24]

Once again, the implementation mattered more than the MFA language. The GATT subsequently judged that implementation of MFA-III brought "further tightening" of restrictions.[25] As an illustration in the US case, in December 1983 the Reagan administration adopted new procedures for "calls" for consultation on imposing quotas. Such discussions would be automatically triggered whenever imports reached at least 20 percent of

---

22. Gerard Curzon et al., *MFA Forever?* p. 26.

23. UNCTAD, *Manual,* pp. 25–28, 52.

24. Ibid., pp. 25–31; GATT, *Textiles and Clothing,* p. 8.

25. Ibid.

production or had risen by 30 percent in the previous 12 months.[26] Nonetheless, in an evaluation of MFA-III a group of exporting countries organized with support from the United Nations Conference on Trade and Development (UNCTAD) concluded that it had helped "return to the framework of the MFA"; that participants "viewed the Arrangement as a balanced instrument capable of regulating international trade in textiles in an equitable manner"; and that the MFA was helpful in particular because while it permitted importers to apply quantitative restrictions, these rights were "balanced by the obligation to observe certain rules and norms of quota management prescribed notably in Articles 4:3, 5 and Annex B."[27] With even the exporters thus blessing the MFA for fear of what might happen without it, the instrument's durability was understandable.

MFA Coverage

By the early 1980s, the formation and successive renewals of the MFA had established it as a comprehensive mechanism for the control of international trade in textiles and apparel. There are currently 43 signatories to the MFA, representing 54 countries.[28] The United States has bilateral agreements with 34 countries under the MFA, and some 80 percent of US textile and apparel imports from developing countries are limited by quotas under these agreements.[29] The EC has maintained bilaterally negotiated restrictions on imports from some 25 countries, along with unilateral restraints on Taiwan and some Eastern European countries.[30]

There are notable exceptions to MFA country coverage. Although eight major industrial countries are members (United States, Canada, Japan, EC, Austria, Finland, Sweden, Switzerland), two—Australia and New Zealand—are not. And despite their membership, Japan and Switzerland do not maintain quotas under bilateral agreements as permitted by the MFA. On the exporting side, Taiwan and East European countries are not members, and the People's Republic of China joined only in 1984.

Nonmembership does not of course exempt Taiwan and Eastern Europe from quantitative restrictions, whether bilaterally negotiated (US) or uni-

26. Ibid., p. 102.

27. UNCTAD, *Manual*, pp. 41–42.

28. GATT, "Extension of Multifibre Arrangement Agreed," Press Release 1390, 5 August 1986.

29. Jim Berger, "US Textiles and Apparel: Is Protection a Solution?" *Policy Focus* No. 6 (Washington: Overseas Development Council, 1985), p. 7.

30. Gerard Curzon et al., *MFA Forever?* p. 7.

lateral (EC). Conversely, by far the largest bloc of textile and apparel trade that takes place unfettered is among the industrial countries themselves, whether members of the MFA or not. The exception is Japan as a supplier country; it remains subject to MFA restrictions on a number of textile and apparel categories, in considerable part because of the historical context in which it was the principal source of import pressure in the 1930s and again in the 1950s.

There are other areas of textile trade unencumbered by quantitative restrictions. They have included EC preferential treatment to Mediterranean basin countries, which are granted access free of quantitative restraints or, since 1978, with far fewer restricted categories than for imports from other developing countries and Eastern Europe. The EC has also avoided restrictions on imports from the 66 African, Caribbean, and Pacific countries of the Lomé Convention. Offshore processing enjoys duty-free entry for imports corresponding to intermediate inputs originally obtained from the importing country. US practice accords no special quota treatment to offshore processing, however, and while in some bilateral agreements the EC identifies quotas for these imports separately, it is unclear whether their special status increases the total volume of quotas from levels that would otherwise be permitted.[31]

Table 6.1 presents a broad decomposition of world trade in textiles and apparel by coverage of nontariff trade restraints. As indicated, approximately 43 percent of world trade in textiles and 35 percent of total trade in apparel are free from nontariff restraints: the trade among the industrial countries themselves, with the exception of their imports from Japan. Coverage under MFA restraints is shown in the second portion of the table. Broadly, the MFA restrains trade from Japan and the developing countries into the industrial countries. The volume of these flows amounts to 3 percent and 11 percent, respectively, of world textile trade, and 1.4 percent and 38.5 percent of world apparel trade. The remainder of world trade in the sectors is generally subject to other quantitative restraints, unilaterally or through bilateral agreements. Essentially this remaining bloc of non-MFA, but restricted, trade encompasses industrial country imports from the Eastern area countries, and imports of developing countries and Eastern area countries from all sources.

The estimates of table 6.1 are only approximate. They treat all industrial country imports from Japan and the developing countries as controlled under the MFA, whereas in fact there are numerous combinations of supplier countries and product categories that are not constrained by quotas. Nonetheless, because the MFA framework provides for potential protection for

---

31. GATT, *Textiles and Clothing*, pp. 104–106; Keesing and Wolf, *Textile Quotas*, p. 69.

Table 6.1 Shares of world trade in textiles and apparel subject to MFA and other restraints (percentage)

Importing area	Supplying area	Textiles	Apparel	Total
1. Free of restraints				
Industrial countries	Industrial countries except Japan	42.8	35.1	39.2
2. MFA restraints				
Industrial countries	Japan	3.0	1.4	2.3
	Developing countries	11.0	38.5	23.9
	Subtotal	14.0	39.9	26.2
3. Bilateral or national restraints				
Industrial countries	Eastern area	3.6	5.0	4.3
Developing countries	All sources	30.8	12.8	22.4
Eastern area	All sources	8.7	7.2	8.0
Subtotal		43.1	25.0	34.7
Subtotal, restrained	(2 + 3)	57.1	64.9	60.8
Total		100.0	100.0	100.0
Memorandum: value (billion dollars)		53.5	46.0	99.5

Source: GATT, *International Trade 1984/85*, table A39; OECD, *Trade by Commodities*, series C, vol. 2, 1984.

virtually this entire subset of suppliers, the estimate here is useful for policy purposes. The table also does not distinguish the imports of Australia and New Zealand (approximately \$2 billion in 1984, of which most was from non-OECD sources) from imports into other industrial countries, although for these two markets the controls should be grouped under other restraints rather than the MFA. In addition, there is some overstatement of the flow of trade under other restraints by treating all developing country and Eastern bloc imports in this category. Thus, Hong Kong has sizable restraint-free imports. Nonetheless, the table provides an approximate gauge of the division of world trade into restraint-free, MFA, and other-restraint groupings.

These estimates indicate that the MFA covers approximately one-fourth of world trade in textiles and apparel. However, the coverage is much higher for apparel (40 percent) than for textiles (14 percent), reflecting the larger role of developing-country suppliers in apparel than in textiles. The estimates also bring out other important patterns. First, there is probably a larger share of world trade restrained by national and other non-MFA restrictions than by the MFA. Second, the developing countries account for an impressive share of world imports: 30.8 percent of textiles and 12.8 percent even in apparel. This large market, especially in textiles, should serve both as a base for developing-country negotiating power on one hand, and as a significant target for industrial country efforts toward multilateral trade liberalization on the other. Third, although the MFA itself is much more heavily oriented toward protection against apparel than against textiles (because it restrains imports from developing countries and their comparative advantage lies more in apparel than textiles), if other bilateral and national restraints are taken into account the share of world trade subject to such protection is close to 60 percent for both categories of products.

Functioning of the MFA

Critics from both sides assail the MFA. Exporters from developing countries, representatives of some consumer groups, and many economists criticize the Arrangement as causing excessive protection, high costs to the consumer, and inefficiency in resource allocation. Representatives of textile-producing firms and labor unions charge that the MFA is ineffective as a mechanism for restraining imports because of loopholes and inadequate enforcement.[32] Chapter 7 examines the question of whether the arrangement has indeed restrained imports; chapter 8 considers its costs; chapters 4 and 5 reviewed the influence of the MFA in terms of the adjustment of industry to trade pressures under its aegis, and chapter 10 presents estimates of the economic effects of alternative broad strategies toward the MFA and textile-apparel protection over the next two decades. However, at this point in the discussion of the evolution of the MFA it is useful to highlight certain central issues concerning its broad effectiveness as a policy instrument.

At a fundamental level, from the outset there has been a tension in the MFA between the ideal of liberalization and the operational objective of restraint. Thus, the language of the MFA provides "that the basic objective shall be to achieve the expansion of trade, the reduction of barriers to such trade and the progressive liberalization of world trade in textile products . . ." (Article 1:2).[33] Yet the reality, as outlined above, has been one of successive tightening of practices under the MFA and the creation of a protective regime of unrivaled longevity and scope.

The dual nature of the MFA—as a mechanism for both restraint and restraint on restraint—has numerous operational manifestations. One of the

---

32. Edward B. Rappaport, "Textile Imports Under the Multi-Fiber Arrangement," (Washington: Congressional Research Service, Issue Brief, 25 June 1986), p. 1.

33. GATT, "Arrangement Regarding International Trade in Textiles," *GATT Basic Instruments and Selected Documents, 21st Supplement* (Geneva: February 1975), pp. 3–19.

more controversial is the resulting loose yoke of quotas under the Arrangement. For many supplying countries and in many categories, the existing quotas are not binding because they are not fully utilized. Thus, Keesing and Wolf noted that in 1976, while the three largest East Asian exporting countries filled 99.8 percent of their combined quotas, four other Southeast Asian suppliers filled only 54 percent of theirs, while the ratio was 61 percent for four Latin American countries and less than 15 percent for Egypt.[34] The authors stressed that the effect of the quotas was still restrictive, both because there were important instances of binding quotas even in the countries with underutilization overall, and because the very presence of the quota discouraged investment for exports.

In application over the past 12 years the MFA has generated numerous quota levels that exceed actual imports. The initial structure of the arrangement provided for 6 percent annual growth, and where country exports lagged behind this pace, a gap of unused quota levels developed. In addition, in other categories importing countries have not experienced sufficient pressure to negotiate quotas at all. Table 6.2 reports the portion of textiles and apparel imports covered by quotas, and the average degree of quota utilization, for all supplier countries that account for 1 percent or more of US imports of textiles or apparel (from table 2.11). It is clear from the table that the "big three" exporters—Korea, Taiwan, and Hong Kong—are tightly controlled in both the share of trade subject to quotas and the degree of quota utilization (although the latter is surprisingly low for EC imports from Hong Kong). The next two largest suppliers, mainland China and Japan, have significantly lower shares of exports covered by quotas in the US market, and also lower utilization rates (although the rates are still two-thirds to three-fourths). In contrast, the Latin American suppliers have both low shares of exports covered by quotas and relatively low quota utilization rates, while traditional suppliers from the rest of Asia (India, Pakistan, Macao, Singapore) have intermediate to high quota coverage of exports and degrees of quota utilization.

These two sources of leeway in MFA protection—absence of quotas on certain product categories and less than complete utilization of quotas on others—have been both a liberal element in the mechanism and the source of much frustration for textile and apparel interests in importing countries. The fact that imports may rise rapidly in product categories with initially low quota utilization rates, and even more so in categories that have previously been insufficiently sensitive to generate a negotiated quota, lies behind much of the concern with import "surges" that has characterized MFA discussions in the third (1981) and fourth (1986) renewals, and the

---

34. Keesing and Wolf, *Textile Quotas,* p. 86.

Table 6.2   Average quota coverage and utilization: textile and apparel imports into the United States and EC, selected countries, 1982

	United States		European Community	
	Percentage of trade subject to quota[a]	Percentage of quota utilized[b]	Percentage of trade subject to quota	Percentage of quota utilized
Hong Kong	75.7	90.8	94.7	52.6
Taiwan	69.4	94.4	n.a.	n.a.
Korea	76.4	87.3	95.1	61.7
China	51.4	77.7	n.a.	64.2
Japan	53.3	63.1	n.a.	n.a.
Philippines	86.3	45.6	64.6	66.2
India	37.9	80.9	40.8	51.6
Singapore	86.3	66.1	75.6	40.2
Mexico	45.4	33.9	6.4	6.0
Dominican Republic	36.7	78.3	n.a.	n.a.
Macao	75.7	81.4	78.9	66.8
Sri Lanka	74.5	88.3	26.0	41.8
Thailand	71.8	77.3	63.3	74.6
Brazil	12.2	39.8	75.2	43.3
Pakistan	51.1	59.7	36.7	68.5

n.a.   not available.
Source: GATT, *Textiles and Clothing in the World Economy* (Geneva: GATT, 1984), pp. 93–98.
a. Percentage of trade subject to quota: by value.
b. Percentage of quota utilized: simple average across controlled categories.

anger of US producers in particular over the spurt in US imports in the period 1982–84. Yet the allowance of uncontrolled categories and the building in of sufficient quota growth such that over time quota ceilings substantially exceed import levels have been consequences of the original "liberalization" face of the MFA.

The history of the Textiles Surveillance Body has been another manifestation of the underlying internal tension in the MFA between protection and liberalization. If the MFA had been truly a mechanism for promotion of successive liberalization of trade in textiles and apparel, this body would have provided close scrutiny of departures of bilateral agreements from the norms of the MFA. A recent review by a developing-country exporter body concludes that, instead, the TSB has relied heavily on "equivocation" in rendering judgments on violations of the MFA (for example by citing "variations" rather than "departures").[35]

An overall judgment of the merits of the MFA is premature at this point in the analysis, but it is useful to consider some of the principal qualitative implications of the mechanism. In their 1980 study, Keesing and Wolf noted as advantages of the MFA the increased certainty that exporting countries would have market access within the quota bounds and, where quotas are not yet present, that they could expand exports and expect that if quotas were subsequently imposed they would be at levels not below the magnitudes that had then been reached. The authors also noted that by forcing producers to upgrade in order to obtain the highest value per physical unit of quota, the MFA had accelerated the development of product quality and thus entrepreneurship and technical capability in the exporting countries. They also suggested that by displacing some production from established producers such as Hong Kong and Korea to other developing countries, the arrangement had diversified supply to the benefit of less competitive producers. In addition, the MFA had conveyed "quota rents" to exporting countries through the standard use of the bilateral quota agreement rather than special tariffs or quota auctions that would siphon off the rent to the importing country (with the exception of the auction systems of Australia and New Zealand). Against these benefits, Keesing and Wolf stressed the long-run disadvantage to relatively poor developing countries which, in the absence of the regime, could have been expected to take away some share of the market from the big three East Asian suppliers. Given the quota mechanism, the market access of these latecomers is likely to be much more limited. Even the seeming benefit of receipt of the quota rent has its negative aspects, according to the authors, in its encouragement of noncompetitive practices among firms in the supplying countries.[36]

The disadvantages of the mechanism depend, of course, on whether the extent of protection would have been greater or smaller in its absence. There are nonetheless distortions that are inherent to it. One important distortion is that by placing physical limits on imports, the MFA incorporates an incentive for foreign producers to shift from the production of textile fabrics to the processing of apparel products—which have a higher value for a given physical quantity—thereby placing potentially greater pressure on the

---

35. The exporter group also suggests that the structure of the TSB is biased in favor of developed countries by its permanent allocation of three of the eight seats to the United States, the EC, and Japan, facilitating continuity and technical support for these representatives in comparison with the frequently changing representatives from developing countries. UNCTAD, *Manual*, p. 21.

36. Keesing and Wolf, *Textile Quotas*, pp. 122–131.

subsector that is already the more embattled of the two in the industrial countries. Distortions also arise from the use of quotas rather than tariffs. Not only does the quota tend to produce a more rigid restriction of imports, and thus lend itself to a degree of protection that might not be tolerated by the public if its cost were in the more transparent form of a tariff, but the allocation of quotas by supplier country introduces another rigidity in the system that prevents the normal shift of supply to the countries with emerging greater comparative advantage. Not only does this geographical rigidity pose equity problems by disadvantaging the relatively less developed countries, but it causes efficiency costs as well, by failing to locate production in the least-cost supplying countries.

An acute form of geographical misallocation, with distortions in terms of both equity and efficiency, results from the MFA practice of exempting industrial country suppliers from restraints while imposing them on developing countries. For a given absolute level of imports, the efficient means of allocating imports would be to set a global quota and allow all suppliers to compete for entry within it (although as noted in chapter 11, it would tighten total restriction to extend existing quotas to cover countries not now subject to quotas). The realpolitik of textile protection, however, is that both the United States and the EC have the bargaining power of potential retaliation against the other if either were to impose restraints on imports from the other. In contrast, the developing countries are fragmented and in addition have little credible retaliatory power within the sector because their own markets are already protected (especially in apparel) and they would have little incremental protection available to impose. The practice of granting free North-North trade while restraining South-North trade is reinforced by the seeming atmosphere of a gentlemen's club among the industrial country parties, whereby it is tacitly understood that protection is to be raised against the newcomer producers in the developing countries rather than against the industries already under pressure in partner countries of the North.

Tariff versus Quota Protection

In addition to quota protection since the early 1960s, textiles and apparel have long enjoyed high protection from tariffs. As noted above, in the 1930s tariffs were in the range of 50 percent to 60 percent. Table 6.3 shows that tariffs have remained high, especially for apparel, despite successive rounds of tariff liberalization. Thus, in 1962 before the Kennedy Round tariff cuts, nominal US tariffs were 24 percent for fabric, 11.5 percent for yarn and thread, and 25 percent for apparel, compared with an average of only 11.5

Table 6.3 Nominal tariff rates[a] on textiles and apparel

| | Textiles | | | |
	Thread and yarn	Fabrics	Apparel	All manufactures
United States				
1962	11.5	24.0	25.0	11.5
1973[b]	14.5	19.0	27.0	11.5
1987[c]	9.0	11.5	22.5	6.5
European Community				
1962	3.0	17.5	18.5	18.5
1973[b]	8.0	14.5	16.5	9.5
1987[c]	7.0	10.5	13.5	6.5
Japan				
1962	2.5	19.5	25.0	16.0
1973[b]	9.0	12.0	18.0	11.0
1987[c]	7.0	9.5	14.0	6.5

Source: GATT, *Textiles and Clothing,* pp. 67–69.
a. The greater of simple and weighted averages.
b. Pre-Tokyo Round.
c. Post-Tokyo Round.

percent for US manufactures overall. By 1973, after Kennedy Round cuts and before the Tokyo Round, average fabric tariffs had declined somewhat (from 24 percent to 19 percent), but the average for yarn and thread had risen, as had the average for apparel (to 27 percent). Cuts in the Tokyo Round were once again limited for the sector, and after their full implementation in 1987 the average nominal tariff for apparel will still stand at 22.5 percent, although sharper cuts for textile fabrics will bring their average tariff down to 11.5 percent.[37]

The pattern of tariff protection is similar among the three major industrial country areas. Apparel protection is systematically higher than textile

---

37. Note that the averages reported in table 6.3 are, in each case, the higher of: a simple average, and an average weighted by import value. The rationale for this procedure is that the only reason for using an unweighted (simple) average would be to avoid understatement of the tariff by the tendency of imports to be lower in highly protected categories. Thus, if the trade-weighted tariff average is higher, it remains the more relevant measure. Note, however, that if a consistent definition over time is used, the total average for US manufactures did decline, from 11.5 percent in 1962 to 7 percent in 1973 and 5 percent for post-Tokyo Round, using the weighted average definition.

protection. Tariffs have been cut by more in textiles than in apparel over the last two decades. Tariffs on textile fabric are higher than those on the less-processed stage of thread and yarn. Tariffs on apparel and textile fabric have been systematically higher than those on manufactures in general.

Despite these similarities, the table also shows that tariff protection in apparel has fallen further in the EC and Japan than in the United States. Thus, the post-Tokyo Round rates stand at 22.5 percent for the United States, 13.5 percent for the EC, and 14 percent for Japan. Correspondingly, the gap between tariffs on US apparel and on general manufactures is much higher than that in Europe and Japan (with the general tariff on manufactures at 6.5 percent in all three areas).

The tariffs listed in table 6.3 are nominal tariffs. The "effective tariff" rate, which tells the impact of tariff protection on the activity of manufacturing the product in question—and thus examines the effect of tariff protection on value added after removing the influence of intermediate input costs and of protection on intermediate inputs—is much higher. Thus, in 1962 the effective rate of protection on US apparel imports stood at 36 percent and on textile fabric at 50 percent, compared with nominal rates of 25 percent and 24 percent, respectively.[38]

Overall, the trend that emerges is as follows. Tariff protection on US apparel has been high and relatively constant in the range of 25 percent. For the EC and Japan, apparel tariffs have fallen from a range of 20 percent to 25 percent in the 1960s to some 14 percent after the Tokyo Round. For all three areas, tariffs on textile fabric have fallen from the range of 20–25 percent in the 1960s to 10–11 percent after the Tokyo Round, higher than the manufacturing average but by considerably less than in the case of apparel.

While explicit tariff rates are available to demonstrate that tariff protection is relatively high in the textile and (especially) apparel sectors, the protective impact of quota restrictions is much more ambiguous. The entrenched presence of quota protection for more than two decades suggests that this protection is considered important by textile and apparel interests, and by implication, that it is taken seriously as providing a meaningful increment of protection above that offered by tariffs alone. However, it is difficult to estimate the "tariff-equivalent" of quantitative restrictions. While quotas tend to drive up the price to the consumer by restricting supply, and thereby introduce a wedge between the import price and the world price (equal to the tariff-equivalent), comprehensive estimates on these price effects are not available.

Various studies nonetheless provide a basis for gauging the general range

---

38. GATT, *Textiles and Clothing*, p. 67.

of the tariff-equivalent of quota protection. Morkre has examined the price of "quota tickets" in the Hong Kong market. Quota rights are freely traded in Hong Kong, and their value should equal the difference between the price that a Hong Kong producer would charge (at normal profit rates) in the absence of quotas and the price that the products actually command in exports to the United States in the presence of quotas.[39] Morkre has found that in 1980, for nine major clothing products, the average tariff-equivalent of these quota rights amounted to 23 percent for US imports from Hong Kong.[40] Hamilton has estimated a model of tariff-equivalents for Europe and the United States based on data for Hong Kong quota right prices, and has calculated that in 1981–82 the average tariff-equivalent rate for quotas on imports of five major clothing categories into the United States was 19 percent. Moreover, his analysis of production costs in Thailand, Indonesia, and Malaysia concludes that the tariff-equivalent of quotas on exports from these countries was at least as high as in Hong Kong.[41]

In a more aggregate approach, Hickok first notes that as quota restraints were phased in from 1971 to 1984, import prices of clothing rose by 65 percent in relative terms after deflating by the domestic US wholesale price index for textiles and apparel. She then makes alternative estimates of the extent to which imports were reduced by the quotas from levels they would have otherwise reached, and on a basis of the price elasticity of clothing imports (from empirical estimates by Kreinin), she calculates the implicit rise in the price attributable to quota protection. Hickok concludes that the tariff-equivalent of quotas ranged from 20 percent to 50 percent (with the remainder of the 65 percent relative price increase attributable to quality upgrading).[42]

Morici and Megna present an indirect estimate of the tariff-equivalent of voluntary restraints on US imports of apparel.[43] They hypothesize that in

39. Although it might be argued that in the absence of quotas, supply from Hong Kong would move up to higher cost along an upward sloping supply curve, there is little reason to believe that this slope is steep (that is, Hong Kong's supply elasticity is probably relatively high).

40. Morris E. Morkre, *Import Quotas on Textiles: The Welfare Effects of United States Restrictions on Hong Kong*, Bureau of Economics Staff Report (Washington: Federal Trade Commission, August 1984), pp. 10, 16.

41. Carl Hamilton, "Voluntary Export Restraint on Clothing from Asia: Price Effects, Rent Incomes and Trade Barrier Formation" (Stockholm: Institute for International Economic Studies, 1983; processed).

42. Susan Hickok, "The Consumer Cost of US Trade Restraints," *Federal Reserve Bank of New York Quarterly Review*, vol. 10, no. 2 (Summer), p. 6.

43. Peter Morici and Laura L. Megna, *US Economic Policies Affecting Industrial Trade: A Quantitative Assessment* (Washington: National Planning Association, 1983), pp. 22–24, 51.

the absence of restraints, imports at most would have risen by the full increase in US consumption from 1973 to 1978; alternatively, they suggest that if the quotas were removed, foreign suppliers would be able to raise supply in one year by a maximum of the amount they had lost over the previous three years because of quotas. On these bases they estimate that in 1978 imports were in a range of 26 percent to 44 percent below levels they would have reached in the absence of quotas. They calculate that the tariff-equivalent that would accomplish the reduction in imports in the case of lesser impact (26 percent reduction) would amount to 8.8 percent. However, this estimate would seem low even in terms of the authors' approach. Not only is it the lower of their two cases, but it also assumes a high import elasticity (3.66) and therefore obtains the hypothesized reduction with a relatively small required increase in import price.

On the basis of these studies, a reasonable estimate of the tariff-equivalent of voluntary export restraints on US apparel imports would appear to be approximately 20 percent in 1980.[44] This amount is additional to the protection from tariffs. The path of this protection over time may be roughly imputed as follows. After the further tightening of the MFA in 1981, the tariff-equivalent of incremental protection of quotas beyond that of tariffs may have risen to some 25 percent. The 20 percent level would have applied under MFA-II in 1977–81. During the first MFA, the quota regime was less severe, so the tariff-equivalent might be placed at some 15 percent in that period. During the LTA (1962–71), the level may have been at some 5 percent, with an increase to the MFA-I level phased in during 1972–73 as

---

44. This level is chosen primarily on the basis of the Morkre and Hamilton estimates. It might be argued that the prominence of Hong Kong supply in these calculations overstates the estimates, on grounds that supply from other areas might be at higher cost. However, the Hamilton finding that other East Asian suppliers have tariff-equivalents at least as high as Hong Kong, coupled with the large share of the Asian suppliers in US imports (table 2.11, ch. 2), suggests that the Hong Kong-based figure is not an overstatement.

More fundamentally, as long as the East Asian suppliers for whom the tariff-equivalent of quotas (beyond the tariff) is in the range of 20-25 percent do indeed have the supply capacity to expand exports over a wide range at constant cost, it is irrelevant for the calculation of quota protection equivalent that some suppliers may be found (for example, in Latin America) for whom the quota rent is considerably smaller because of higher production costs. In the absence of restraints on the East Asian suppliers, imports would be available at prices lower by the amount of the quota rents in their supply, as they would replace suppliers with higher production cost. In analogy, suppose the price of oil were forced to $60 per barrel by severe quotas on OPEC and other major exporters. Under these circumstances, countries with production costs of $59 per barrel but not restrained by quotas might capture (for example) half of the US oil import market; but it would be incorrect to obtain a "weighted average" tariff-equivalent of the quota based on $1 for half and $50 (for low-cost OPEC supply) for the rest. The correct tariff-rate equivalent would be that based on the low-cost suppliers with ample expansion capacity.

US bilateral agreements preceded the MFA. These levels are the estimates applied in the import model used for simulations in chapter 3 above.

For textile products, the tariff-equivalent of voluntary quotas would appear to be significantly lower than for apparel, just as tariff protection is lower. The simulations of chapter 3 assume that these tariff-equivalents averaged 5 percent increment beyond tariff protection in 1962–73, 10 percent in 1974–81, and 15 percent since 1981, again applying staged increases to reflect the successive tightening of the MFA.

It should be noted that observers who consider the tariff-equivalent of quota protection in textiles and apparel to be lower than the estimates applied here should correspondingly expect the adverse impact of hypothesized liberalization of these quotas to be more modest than calculated in the estimates of chapter 8 and the simulations of chapter 10.

In sum, quota protection for textiles and apparel appears to have been rising over time through the successive tightening of the MFA and its implementing mechanisms. Today the tariff-equivalent of apparel quotas is probably in the range of 25 percent (beyond the tariff), and that on textiles some 15 percent. Moreover, if these magnitudes and trends are accurate, the combined effect of tariff and quota protection would appear to have risen over time for apparel and failed to decline significantly for textiles. Thus, on the basis of table 6.3 and the estimates just discussed, the (multiplicative) impact of both tariff and quota protection would have risen from 31 percent in the early 1960s to 56 percent today for apparel, while that for textile fabric would have changed from 30 percent to 28 percent. In terms of political economy, a plausible explanation of such trends would be that the ongoing pressure to stem a rising import share associated with changing international comparative advantage has led to ever-higher protection in apparel (with the sector's consent to modest tariff liberalization coming only at the price of more meaningful nontariff protection), while in the sector of textiles the success with technological progress obviated the need for increasing total protection (but not to the point that policymakers were prepared to actually reduce total protection significantly).

It is reasonable to ask how the rapid rise of imports into the United States could have occurred in recent years if protection had risen as indicated in the analysis here. The answer is that the regime of tariff and quota protection in textiles and apparel is not an absolute physical limit to imports. A useful analogy is that of a wire-mesh screen that substantially reduces a flow, but that nonetheless permits a greater flow to occur when the pressure increases. The pressure did indeed increase in the 1980s for the United States because of the rising strength of the dollar. Thus, in the period 1982–86 the tariff-equivalent of apparel quotas may have risen by the five percentage points suggested above (while some compensating reduction in tariffs was taking place from the phasing in of the Tokyo Round). This increase in import cost was more than offset by the reduction resulting from the sharp appreciation of the dollar, as examined in chapter 3.

The seeming contradiction between the presence of a regime of physical quotas and the experience of rising imports is explained by the fact that the mechanism for quota implementation provides some room for flexibility. This issue is addressed in chapter 2 and explored with more detailed data in chapter 7. The central point here is that in the first half of the 1980s US imports of textiles and apparel rose rapidly despite protection that was either increasing (apparel) or holding constant (textiles) because other forces in their determination—and the exchange rate in particular—dominated the net outcome for imports.

7

Effectiveness of Protection

Representatives of the US textile and apparel sectors criticize the Multi-Fiber Arrangement (MFA) for being insufficiently protective and call for new legislation to impose tighter import quotas. Critics of the Arrangement from the other side maintain that its costs are high for the economy in general and for the consumer in particular. This chapter examines the extent to which protection has in fact obstructed the growth of imports, and investigates especially the mechanisms through which textile and apparel imports surged in 1983–84 despite MFA restraints.

Protection and Real Import Growth

The evidence suggests that the MFA restricts imports in a manner analogous to that of a wire-mesh screen. It acts as a substantial obstacle that slows the inflow of imports considerably below the rate that would occur in the absence of protection, but it does permit some inflow, and the amount it permits rises when the inward pressure on the flow rises. Thus, because the MFA is a screen rather than a solid wall, there is a significant degree of responsiveness of imports to economic factors such as the exchange rate and the rate of domestic growth, as indicated in chapter 3.

The operational mechanisms that permit this flexibility are as follows. Voluntary quotas under the MFA are country-specific rather than global. Numerous country-product combinations are either uncontrolled or are subject to an observation process in which a "call" for bilateral negotiation is triggered by a sudden rise. Negotiated quotas are frequently less than fully utilized, as noted in chapter 6. Even where explicitly negotiated quotas would otherwise be exhausted, a country may temporarily export more (through swing, carry-forward, and carry-over quota adjustments). Despite these provisions for flexibility, protection under the MFA appears to have had a distinct restrictive impact on the growth of imports.

Table 7.1 Annual growth rates of real US imports of textiles and apparel (percentage)[a]

	SYE[b]	Textile-apparel deflator	Wholesale price deflator
Textiles			
1961–72	16.1[c]	5.9	4.2
1972–77	−9.1	−4.9	−9.3
1977–81	−2.1	4.3	0.4
1981–86	21.9	12.7	12.6
Apparel			
1961–72	18.3[c]	13.8	14.8
1972–77	2.9	11.1	6.7
1977–81	4.7	6.8	1.9
1981–86	12.9	16.4	17.4

Source: Tables 2.4 and 2.6.
a. Calculated from log-linear regressions for each period.
b. Square-yard equivalents.
c. 1964–72.

Table 7.1 reports annual growth rates for US imports of textiles and apparel during the successive phases of the protective regime. Real imports are measured alternatively by physical volume (square-yard equivalents, SYE), dollar value deflated by the domestic textile or apparel price index, and dollar value deflated by the US wholesale price index (chapter 2, tables 2.4 and 2.6). In the first period, 1961–72, protection under the Short Term Arrangement (STA) and Long Term Arrangement (LTA) restricted only cotton textile and apparel products, and the boom in man-made fibers paced a rapid growth of the physical volume of imports (although, especially in the textiles sector, falling prices of synthetic fibers meant a slower growth of deflated values than of square-yard equivalents).

As noted in the previous chapter, by 1972 the United States had negotiated bilateral restraint agreements with the principal developing-country suppliers of man-made fiber products, and the 1973 negotiations launching the MFA formalized and generalized these restrictions. From 1972 to 1977, the period of MFA-I, the rate of import growth dropped sharply, whether measured by SYE or by either of the real value measures. The decline was more severe in textiles. In apparel, growth of imports in SYE also dropped precipitously, while the decline in real value terms was somewhat more moderate (especially if the domestic apparel deflator is used, because apparel prices were falling relative to wholesale prices). The difference between

SYE and real value deceleration reflected a partially offsetting response of upgrading to higher-valued products.

The period of MFA-II, 1977–81, shows similarly low import growth (negative again for textile SYE), unambiguously lower than in 1961–72 and, for apparel, lower in real value terms than under MFA-I. In short, period growth rates show a marked reduction of textile and apparel import growth under MFA-I and MFA-II, suggesting strongly that the protective regime did restrict imports. In an earlier analysis of these periods, Wolf similarly found that, "In all, the United States was able to curb import growth very successfully."[1]

It is in the period of MFA-III, from 1981 to 1986, that US imports of textiles and apparel rose so rapidly that industry critics decried the effectiveness of the Arrangement. Imports surged in particular in 1983 and 1984. For the full period, annual import growth averaged in the range of 12 percent to 17 percent depending on the measure, and was as high as 22 percent for SYE of textiles. As analyzed in chapter 3, the economic forces behind this explosion were the overvalued dollar and the strong US recovery from recession in 1982. The institutional aspects of the import control mechanism that permitted these forces to translate into an import surge are explored below.

Figures 7.1 and 7.2 portray the same history of decelerating import growth after imposition of wider protection under MFA-I and MFA-II, followed by a burst of higher imports during the early 1980s. The figures express imports (under the three different measures) on logarithmic scales of index numbers. The slope of the trend line indicates the growth rate. For textiles, visual inspection shows a relatively steep slope before 1972, followed by a negative slope in 1972–77, a horizontal slope (stagnant imports) in 1977–81, and then a steep upward slope in 1981–86. For apparel, the reversals are far less dramatic, but they follow the same sequence. After a relatively steep upward slope before 1972, the slope (growth rate) declines substantially during MFA-I and MFA-II, but then tilts upward again in the early 1980s.

Overall, the evidence is that the MFA did restrict US imports in the 1970s, but it had sufficient room for flexibility that it could not prevent brisk import growth in the early 1980s when the pressure of an overvalued dollar in particular was too great for the protective apparatus to overcome. Nor can rising import growth under MFA-III be attributed to a liberalization of the regime. As indicated in the previous chapter, the United States either maintained or tightened its implementation of the arrangement in this period.

---

1. Martin Wolf, "Managed Trade: Implications of the Textile Arrangements," in *Trade Policy in the 1980s,* edited by William R. Cline (Washington: Institute for International Economics, 1983), p. 466.

Figure 7.1 Real textile imports, 1960–86

Index 1982=100, log scale

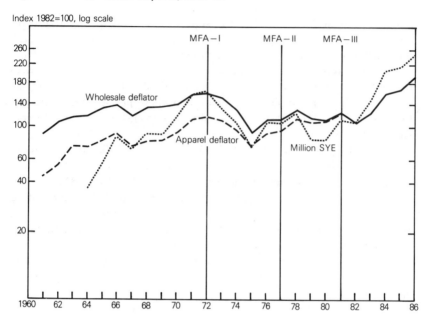

Evidence for the European Community (EC) tends to confirm both of the hypotheses suggested above: that the MFA did restrict import growth, and that dollar overvaluation was a dominant reason for the surge of US imports in the early 1980s. Thus, import data for the EC show not only a deceleration of import growth following the MFA but a continuation of the slowing trend even into the early 1980s, a pattern consistent with the view that the import problem in the later period was specific to the United States because of its exchange rate overvaluation.

Figure 7.3 presents alternative measures of real imports of apparel into the EC (of nine) from sources outside the Organization for Economic Cooperation and Development (OECD), again on a logarithmic scale. The graph shows only mild deceleration after the first MFA in 1973 but a sharp slowdown beginning in 1976, in keeping with the widely held view that the EC only achieved coordination for a major restriction by the second MFA (chapter 6). The slope of the imports curve remains slight through 1978–80, and then turns even flatter during 1981–85. This near cessation of real import growth during the early 1980s is the counterpart of the diversion of developing-country supply to the US market because of the relative ease of selling in that market with an overvalued dollar as opposed

Figure 7.2 Real apparel imports, 1960–86

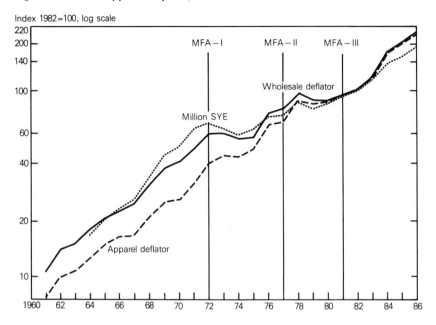

Index 1982=100, log scale

to selling into a European market in the face of relatively undervalued European currencies. Tighter EC enforcement of MFA restrictions during MFA-III may also have played a role in the further slowdown, although in view of the analysis of relative import growth in the United States and Europe during different phases of the dollar cycle under floating rates (table 3.6), it seems likely that the exchange rate played a far greater role than any differential application of further MFA tightening in explaining the differing outcomes for the United States and Europe in the early 1980s.

Upgrading

Because the MFA controls the physical volume of imports rather than their value, it introduces an incentive to upgrade products. In one dimension, this process has occurred from a shift of textiles—which are primarily at the stage of intermediate products such as fabrics—to finished apparel. Indeed, the general shift from lower to higher stages of processing in US apparel imports is striking. Thus, data from the International Trade Commission indicate that while imports of yarn have actually declined from 1.9

Figure 7.3 Real textile and apparel imports[a] into EC-9

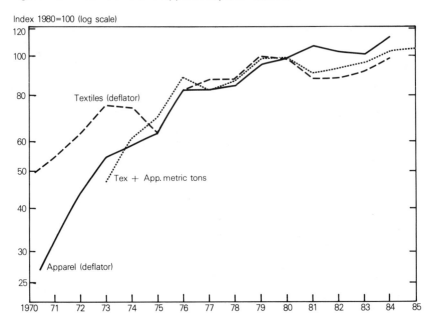

Index 1980=100 (log scale)

a. From non-OECD countries and Japan.

billion SYE in 1972 to 1.25 billion in 1985, those of the next stage of processing, fabric, have risen from 1.7 billion to 2.4 billion; of the subsequent stage, apparel, from 2.2 billion to 5.0 billion; and of made-up textiles (such as carpets) from 0.4 billion to 1.1 billion. The corresponding annual growth rates (− 3.2 percent, 2.8 percent, 6.5 percent, and 8.1 percent) show a clear ascending order by stage of processing.[2]

While controlled suppliers have had an incentive to upgrade by moving up the ladder of processing stages, they have also faced an inducement to upgrade the quality of their exports within each product category. The data in table 7.1 shed light on this process. In the absence of upgrading, real values of imports would grow at rates identical to those of physical volumes. Instead, for apparel, after growing more slowly than physical volume in 1961–72, the real value of imports grew considerably more rapidly in the initial years of the MFA (1972–77), especially on the measure deflating by domestic apparel prices. By the time of MFA-II, this divergence had ended

2. US International Trade Commission, *US Imports of Textiles and Apparel Under the Multifiber Arrangement: Statistical Report Through 1985*, Publication 1863 (Washington: USITC, June 1986), p. A-5.

Figure 7.4   Textile unit values,[a] 1964–85

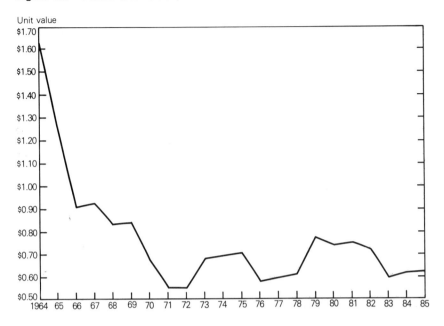

a. MFA category imports.

or become more ambiguous (as real value on the domestic deflator basis grew only modestly more rapidly than physical volume, while on the basis of the wholesale price deflator it grew more slowly). By the period 1981–85, real values once again grew more rapidly than physical volume, but only modestly so. Nonetheless, the principal period of rapid upgrading on the basis of these data was during MFA-I. The patterns for textiles are different. In their case, the principal manifestation of upgrading was in the sudden elimination of the wide gap between high physical volume growth and lower real value growth, during MFA-I again. Moreover, in the rapid import growth of the 1980s, real values of textile imports were growing more slowly than physical volumes.

Figures 7.4 and 7.5 provide direct evidence on the upgrading issue. They display trends in unit values of imports as measured by real value (at 1982 prices, deflating by the overall wholesale price index) divided by number of square yard equivalents.[3] The graph for textiles shows a striking decline

3. The data refer to products covered under the MFA, the bulk of imports. For 1982–85, direct prices per square-yard equivalent (SYE) are calculated from US Department of Commerce, International Trade Administration, *Major Shippers of Cotton, Wool, and*

Figure 7.5 Apparel unit values,[a] 1964–85

Unit value

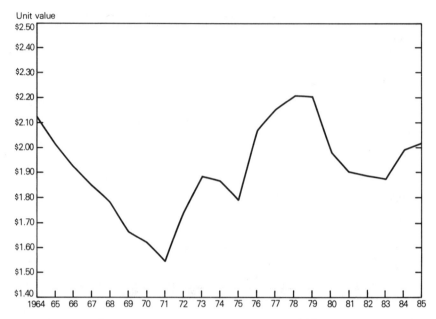

a. MFA category imports.

in unit values until 1972, the first year of US bilateral restraints on Multi-Fiber products. This decline through the 1960s reflects rapid technical change in the production of synthetic fibers. However, during MFA-I the real unit value not only stopped declining but rose by 29 percent from 1972 to 1975. Thereafter the textile unit value fluctuated and showed an overall increase of 42 percent from 1972 to 1979 before resuming a renewed but moderate declining trend in the first half of the 1980s (perhaps as a reflection of eroding oil prices after the 1980 peak). Because of the abrupt end to the pre-MFA trend of declining real prices, the case of textiles suggests at least weak support for the hypothesis of product upgrading upon the advent of the Multi-Fiber Arrangement.

Man-Made Fiber Textiles and Apparel (Washington: Department of Commerce, various issues). For 1980–81 prices per SYE are calculated directly from US International Trade Commission, *The History and Current Status of the Multifiber Arrangement,* Publication 850 (Washington: USITC, January 1978) and *US Imports of Textiles and Apparel Under the Multifiber Arrangement.* For 1964–79, total values are from Department of Commerce *Industrial Outlook* data (ch. 2, tables 2.3 and 2.5), as adjusted downward by the ratio of MFA-covered to total import value in 1980, while SYE are taken from the USITC sources just cited.

For apparel the trends appear to confirm the hypothesis more firmly. Thus, in figure 7.5, real unit values of US apparel imports declined through the 1960s (following textile input prices) but then rose by 22 percent from 1971 to 1973 as US bilaterals took force (and as the economy boomed). After subsiding by 5 percent through the 1975 recession, they then climbed by 23 percent to a peak in 1978 during MFA-II. Thus, during the first two MFAs, product upgrading within apparel appears to have contributed as much as 44 percent to the increase in real import value (the rise in the real unit value from the trough in 1971 to the peak in 1978). Nonetheless, as analyzed above, the growth of the real value of imports did decelerate during the successive MFAs, so that product upgrading only partially offset their restrictive effect on quantities.[4]

The 10 percent drop of real unit values of apparel imports in 1980–83 (figure 7.5) is somewhat of an anomaly. In view of the earlier drop during the 1974–75 recession, it is probably related to the recessions of 1980 and especially 1982. In addition, the general decline in dollar prices in world trade in this period as the dollar rose in strength would have tended to depress real import prices as deflated by US wholesale price indexes (although if this influence were dominant, the rebound by 1984–85 would not have been expected). In any event, after 1983 the upward trend of real unit values of apparel imports had resumed its course, indicating ongoing upgrading. This broader trend for the past 15 years is all the more impressive when it is recognized that real international prices for the intermediate input into apparel—textiles—were either flat (but fluctuating) or gently declining for the period as a whole, as measured by US textile import unit values (figure 7.4), suggesting that rising apparel unit values reflected quality upgrading and not higher input costs.

In sum, there is substantial validity to the view that upgrading has partially offset the restrictive effect of textile and apparel protection. However, for the United States import upgrading was most pronounced in the early phase of the MFA (and the bilaterals that immediately preceded it), 1972–79, and has played a lesser role since then. Moreover, even during the first

---

4. Wolf emphasizes that growth in the real value of developing countries' exports of textiles and apparel to industrial countries slowed as a result of the MFA. He calculates that these annual growth rates declined from 8.2 percent for textiles and 19 percent for apparel in 1970–76 to only 3.1 percent and 4.5 percent, respectively, in 1976–80. Wolf applies GATT data for total developing-country exports of textiles and apparel, as deflated by World Bank indexes for unit values of manufactured exports from industrial to developing countries. Wolf's central point, that product upgrading did not circumvent the restrictive effect of the MFA, is confirmed here. However, he appears to understate the role of product upgrading itself, in part because by choosing 1976 as his base for the MFA (on grounds that it only entered forcefully in the EC by that date), his comparisons miss the sharp upgrading from 1971 to 1976 evident in graph 7.5 for the United States. Martin Wolf, "Managed Trade," pp. 470–71.

MFA, product upgrading was insufficient to prevent the reduction in growth rates of real import values associated with the sharp cutback in physical import growth.

The Import Surge, 1983–84

As shown in table 7.1, protection under the first two MFAs sharply decelerated the growth of US imports of textiles and apparel. This decline occurred in the growth of real value as well as that of physical quantity, despite a significant offset from product upgrading. However, the table also shows an explosion of import growth in the period 1981–86. Much of the recent impetus for increased protection in textiles and apparel has come from this surge. Its economic causes have been examined in chapter 3. However, it is useful to consider further how this rise could have occurred despite the presence of the MFA. A central theme of the demand for new protection has been the argument that imports have increased by more than the MFA envisioned—6 percent per year—and therefore that cutbacks only represent proper enforcement of the protection that the industry believed it already had won.

Tables 2.3 and 2.5 (chapter 2) indicate the rapid rise in nominal imports of textiles and apparel in 1983 and 1984. The current dollar value of textile imports rose by 14.9 percent in 1983, 38.4 percent in 1984, 4.5 percent in 1985, and 16.9 percent in 1986. In apparel, nominal import value rose by 17.6 percent in 1983, 39.8 percent in 1984, 12.2 percent in 1985, and 12.9 percent in 1986. Thus, in both textiles and apparel, although there was a brisk rise in import value in 1983 the true surge in imports was concentrated in 1984, while by 1985–86 import growth had moderated somewhat.

In nominal terms, the value of imports of textiles and apparel rose by 94 percent and 105 percent, respectively, from 1982 to 1986. Moreover, most of this increase was real rather than inflationary. Indeed, under one measure of real imports—physical square-yard equivalents—imports of textiles rose by 170 percent over this period (although measured by either of the two real value concepts, the rise was approximately 94 percent; table 2.4). In apparel, the cumulative increase in imports from 1982 to 1986 was 71 percent in physical volume, and approximately 100 percent under the two alternative real value measures.

In sum, the real value of textile and apparel imports rose by almost 100 percent over the four years 1983–86. If protection under the MFA limited annual import growth to the range of 6 percent or below, how could such increases have occurred?

The Congressional Budget Office (CBO) has analyzed this question. The CBO study first notes that through 1984 the long-term growth of physical volume of imports under the MFA had grown by less than 6 percent annually, not more. If their growth rate had averaged 6 percent annually since 1972, the level of imports in 1984 would have been 23 percent higher than it actually was. However, import growth shifted sharply from slow growth or actual declines in the 1970s to rapid growth in the early 1980s.[5] And, as noted in chapter 2, for the period 1972–86 as a whole, while the physical volume of textile imports grew at only 4.1 percent annually, for apparel the rate was 7.1 percent, moderately above the original 6 percent target of the MFA.

The CBO analysis identified four possible explanations of how imports could have risen so much in 1980–84 despite the MFA restrictions. First, with recession in 1980 and again in 1982, imports could decline for lack of demand even as the scheduled level of quota ceilings continued growing under MFA agreements. The result was a margin of unused quotas that provided scope for a sharp increase once demand recovered. The authors stress that any such rates of increase cannot be sustained, because imports catch up with the quota ceilings. Second, there is flexibility in the administration of quotas that permits importers to "swing" some portion of an underused quota to a product category where the quota is binding, and to shift quotas between years (carry-forward and carry-over). Third, there may have been panic buying by importers in 1984 in anticipation of new import restrictions (although this reason concerns demand, not the effect of restrictions on supply). Fourth, imports could have surged in uncontrolled products or from uncontrolled suppliers. The authors indicate that it is difficult to distinguish imports by uncontrolled products, however, and although their calculations for uncontrolled supplier countries show annual growth of 26 percent compared with 19 percent for controlled countries in 1980–84, the uncontrolled countries accounted for only a small share of imports.[6]

The thrust of the CBO analysis is that the sharp growth of imports in 1980–84 could not continue because the gap between imports and scheduled quotas was closing rapidly, and swing provisions for adjustment give only temporary flexibility rather than long-run increases. This evaluation appears to have been supported by actual experience in 1985. The physical volume of textile imports rose by only 5.1 percent in 1985, after surging by 38.5

---

5. The CBO calculations indicate that while apparel imports grew at 3.3 percent annually in 1972–80, they rose at 13.2 percent annually in 1980–84 (square-yard equivalents). For textiles the contrast was still more vivid: −18.4 percent versus 35.4 percent for yarn, −4.0 percent versus 20.3 percent for fabric, and 0.6 percent versus 41.5 percent for made-up textiles. For all textiles and apparel, physical import growth shifted from −3.0 percent annually in 1972–80 to 20.1 percent annually in 1980–84. Congressional Buget Office, "Protecting the Textile and Apparel Industries," Staff Working Paper (Washington: CBO, September 1985), p. 9.

6. Ibid, pp. 8–12.

percent in 1983 and 53.7 percent in 1984; for apparel, the increase was 8.6 percent in 1985 after a rise of 15.3 percent in 1983 and 20.9 percent in 1984.[7] Although the physical quantity of imports rose more rapidly again in 1986 (with an increase of 20.8 percent in square-yard equivalents for textiles and 13.2 percent for apparel; tables 2.4 and 2.6),[8] the likelihood is that this rise was in response to the extreme overvaluation of the dollar in 1984–85, and perhaps preemptive purchasing ahead of feared tightening in quotas in view of both MFA renewal and the threatened veto override on the Textile and Apparel Trade Enforcement bill, and would again prove temporary.

Further analysis of the import surge after 1982 reveals the following patterns. First, in textiles there was a large and generalized increase in imports, apparently reflecting relatively loose import controls and a backlog of unused quotas in view of the favorable trade performance of this sector in the late 1970s. Second, in apparel increases from the uncontrolled industrial countries and from the minor suppliers far exceeded increases from the major controlled suppliers. Third, even within the major controlled countries, there were relatively large increases in products either loosely controlled by the mechanism of observation for consultation (as opposed to specified quota level) or not controlled. Fourth, within quota-controlled groups, product upgrading was important. Fifth, increases in basic quotas appear to have been small for key suppliers, at least in apparel (for which a special analysis is included below). Sixth, little of the rise appears to have come from adjustments to the basic quotas through flexibility provisions (again based on the cases of apparel examined below). And sixth, despite higher unit values for quota-controlled products, overall the bulk of the increase was primarily in physical quantity; dollar unit values generally advanced only modestly and actually decreased for industrial country suppliers.

Table 7.2 reports US imports of textiles and apparel from principal suppliers in 1982, and their growth to 1984. Most of the post-1982 surge had occurred by the latter year. The most dramatic increase occurred in textiles. Physical quantity rose by 113 percent, while the value of imports rose by 90 percent.[9] The largest proportionate increase occurred in textile imports from the principal industrial country suppliers (132 percent), but import volumes also rose sharply from developing-country suppliers (by

---

7. Tables 2.3 and 2.5.

8. US Department of Commerce, *Major Shippers Report,* 23 December 1986.

9. Because the data in table 7.2 refer to product categories subject to the MFA (and therefore exclude ramie, silk, and noncotton vegetable fiber products), the data on value growth differ from those in tables 2.3 and 2.5.

Table 7.2   US imports of textiles and apparel by major supplier,[a] 1982–84
(million dollars, million SYE, and percentage)

	1982				Percentage rise 1982–84			
	Textiles		Apparel		Textiles		Apparel	
	Value	SYE	Value	SYE	Value	SYE	Value	SYE
Hong Kong	106.8	152.8	1,746.3	689.8	66.0	53.2	26.8	18.1
Taiwan	101.8	190.1	1,408.4	748.1	387.0	240.1	38.4	25.0
Korea	154.2	188.2	1,088.0	575.7	138.5	155.3	38.3	18.8
China	200.6	313.9	589.7	356.7	79.8	73.4	27.1	24.7
Japan	460.5	435.1	231.2	76.3	26.6	39.2	88,1	80.3
Sum of 5	*1,024.0*	*1,280.1*	*5,063.6*	*2,446.7*	*93.8*	*96.2*	*35.3*	*23.3*
India	767.0	59.6	149.1	72.9	63.6	104.6	78.4	79.9
Philippines	6.7	9.9	233.9	161.0	21.1	−23.6	57.0	45.6
Singapore	11.4	22.0	170.9	82.4	−49.9	−44.5	72.6	55.0
Thailand	33.5	63.7	93.3	52.9	49.0	64.7	129.2	101.0
Mexico	20.0	53.5	130.9	55.8	205.8	258.8	55.9	54.1
Sum of 5	*148.5*	*208.7*	*778.2*	*425.0*	*68.8*	*110.1*	*73.0*	*61.3*
Italy	170.8	194.7	137. 7	13.8	81.6	131.7	209.5	302.1
United Kingdom	84.8	36.8	64.5	6.3	54.4	233.5	116.0	176.2
France	72.4	46.5	65.9	6.4	59.2	88.2	94.6	145.3
Germany	61.6	122.5	18.2	2.5	113.2	132.2	148.6	183.4
Canada	51.4	130.7	42.7	7.8	91.0	119.6	51.0	43.3
Sum of 5	*441.0*	*531.3*	*328.9*	*36.8*	*78.2*	*132.1*	*144.2*	*190.6*
Sum of 15	*1,613.5*	*2,020.1*	*6,170.7*	*2,908.5*	*87.3*	*107.1*	*45.9*	*31.0*
Other suppliers	428.7	532.6	939.9	473.8	100.2	137.4	96.4	91.7
World total	*2,042.2*	*2,552.8*	*7,110.7*	*3,382.3*	*90.0*	*113.4*	*52.6*	*39.5*

SYE   square-yard equivalent.
Source: US Department of Commerce, International Trade Administration, *Major Shippers of Cotton, Wool, and Man-Made Fiber Textiles and Apparel,* various issues.
a. MFA categories only.

approximately 100 percent for the top 10). It would appear that it was possible for the doubling of textile imports to occur despite the MFA because the relatively strong earlier performance of US trade in the textiles sector had left a backlog of underused quotas and numerous product categories subject only to loose "consultation" controls rather than quotas.

In apparel, where the trade problem had been chronically more severe, there appears to have been less room for such a surge. The physical volume of apparel imports rose by 39.5 percent from 1982 to 1984, far less than that of textiles. In apparel, the differential tightness of the protective regime in this process is apparent. Thus, in table 7.2 it may be seen that by far the largest increase in the physical volume of apparel imports came from the uncontrolled suppliers—the industrial countries. The top five among them increased their exports to the United States by 191 percent in these two years. The value increase was lower (144 percent), reflecting a declining dollar price as the dollar strengthened. In sharp contrast, the top five controlled developing countries were able to increase their physical export volume by only 23 percent in this period, although by further upgrading they achieved an increase of 35 percent in dollar value. The next five developing countries achieved an intermediate performance, with export volume up 61 percent and value up 73 percent. The more rapid rise in US apparel imports from these countries reflects the fact that, as lesser suppliers, they faced looser controls than the top five developing countries, and within controlled categories had relatively larger amounts of unused quotas. The "lesser supplier" thesis is supported further by the fact that the data for all other suppliers, primarily smaller developing countries, achieved a still higher increase in apparel exports to the United States (92 percent volume, 96 percent value), although not as high as the increase from the totally uncontrolled industrial country suppliers.

An intriguing question is how apparel imports from the large, traditional suppliers managed to increase by 35 percent in value in the face of MFA quotas. Table 7.3 sheds light on this paradox for apparel imports from Korea and China. The first source of such an increase is from products either loosely or not controlled in the base year. These categories dominated the rise of apparel imports from China, where they rose by 94 percent. In contrast, products subject to quotas in 1982 actually declined in volume and rose only slightly in value, as China cut back from substantial overutilization of basic quotas in 1982.

For Korea, the overall rise in apparel imports by value was 30 percent. This rise was achieved by upgrading the quota-controlled items (with a 23 percent rise in unit value), while sharply increasing the physical volume of loosely controlled items (by 42 percent). While upgrading of quota-controlled products occurred in both Korea and China (by around 20 percent in unit value in both cases), the unit value of the loosely controlled products actually declined in both countries. It seems likely that this pattern reflected the natural tendency of dollar prices to decline as the dollar strengthened, except where quota controls placed a premium on upgrading.

The role of quota growth may be seen to have been minor in Korea and China. Basic quotas rose only 2 percent in Korea, and while they rose by 12 percent in China, that nation had to cut back supply in these items to come within quota levels after having exceeded them in 1982. Further

Table 7.3 US imports of apparel,[a] 1982 and 1984: values, volumes, and quota utilization (million dollars and million SYE)

	1982	1984	Percentage change
World			
Value	8,432	13,916	65.0
Quantity	3,382	4,714	39.4
Unit value	2.49	2.95	18.6
Korea			
Quota controlled in 1982			
Value	753	966	28.3
Quantity	335	342	2.1
Unit value	2.25	2.83	25.8
Quota	333	340	2.1
Utilization rate (percentage)	100.6	100.6	0.0
Other			
Value	335	538	60.6
Quantity	241	342	41.6
Unit value	1.39	1.57	12.9
Total			
Value	1,088	1,504	38.2
Quantity	576	684	18.8
Unit value	1.89	2.20	16.3
China			
Quota controlled in 1982			
Value	431	443	2.8
Quantity	246	215	− 12.6
Unit value	1.75	2.06	17.7
Quota	203	228	12.3
Utilization rate (percentage)	121.2	94.3	− 22.2
Other			
Value	158	306	93.9
Quantity	111	230	106.8
Unit value	1.42	1.33	− 6.3
Total			
Value	590	750	27.1
Quantity	357	445	24.7
Unit value	1.65	1.69	2.1

SYE   million square yard equivalent
Source: US Department of Commerce, International Trade Administration, *Major Shippers of Cotton, Wool, and Man-Made Fiber Textiles and Apparel,* various issues; US Department of Commerce, International Trade Administration, "Textile Agreement Performance Report," various issues; and US International Trade Commission, *US Imports of Textiles and Apparel under the Multifiber Arrangement: Statistical Report through 1985.*
a. MFA categories only.

examination of Korea shows that adjustments (swing, carry-over, carry-forward) played virtually no role in import growth. Thus, the ratio of adjusted to basic quotas for quota-controlled items was 100.6 percent in both 1982 and 1984.

The cases of Korea and China also illustrate the policy response of tightening of import quotas after the 1982–84 surge. Thus, in 1982, 71.9 percent of apparel imports from Korea (by square-yard equivalents) were in categories subject to specific quota controls (as opposed to loosely under surveillance); by 1985 this share had risen to 85.4 percent. The corresponding shares under quota controls for China rose from 69.0 percent in 1982 to 86.6 percent in 1985.[10]

Finally, another factor in rapid growth of imports in 1982–84 appears to have been an increase in the share of apparel imports in product categories not covered by the MFA. In the mid-1970s when the MFA began, man-made fibers were the area of explosive growth that industrial countries sought to add to cotton products already under restraints. Foreign suppliers and domestic distributors found a loophole in the MFA in its exclusion of silk, ramie, and other noncotton vegetable fibers, and by the mid-1980s these imports had grown to be substantial. Table 7.4 presents an indirect estimate of their importance, based on comparison of total apparel imports against imports of products in categories covered by the MFA. (A similar comparison for textiles indicates minimal import value in products not covered by the MFA.)[11] MFA coverage has been increasingly incomplete. In 1980, MFA categories accounted for 87.4 percent of the value of apparel imports. By 1985, the share had declined to 75.9 percent. If the MFA-category share of total apparel imports had remained unchanged during the surge period of 1982–84, the value of total apparel imports would have grown by 52.6 percent instead of 64.4 percent.

Most of the elements identified here as important in the import surge of 1982–84 are consistent with the CBO conclusion that it is unlikely that such a rate of expansion will continue in the future. The new MFA negotiated in 1986 adds silk, ramie, and linen to the controlled products (chapter 9). The disproportionate rise in imports from industrial countries should reverse given the decline in the dollar relative to the currencies of these countries. The rapid rise of imports in uncontrolled or loosely controlled categories

---

10. Calculated from US Department of Commerce, "Textile Agreement Performance Report" (Washington: Department of Commerce; processed, various issues).

11. The comparison in table 7.4 is only illustrative, because there are other differences between the series in addition to exclusion of non-MFA categories in the one and inclusion in the other. In particular, the SIC-based import figures are for Standard Industrial Classification industry 23, which includes furs, leather clothing, and certain other items not included in the more narrowly based MFA clothing categories.

Table 7.4   US imports of apparel: categories covered and excluded from MFA, 1980–85 (million dollars and percentages)

	MFA categories	Other	Total	Percentage MFA
1980	5,717	826	6,543	87.4
1981	6,513	1,239	7,752	84.0
1982	7,111	1,321	8,516	84.3
1983	8,241	1,656	10,018	83.3
1984	10,849	3,067	14,001	78.0
1985	11,886	3,770	15,711	75.9

Source: Total, table 2.5. MFA categories: US Department of Commerce, International Trade Administration, *Major Shippers of Cotton, Wool, and Man-Made Fiber Textiles and Apparel*, various issues.

from major developing-country suppliers appears unlikely to continue, given the tightening of the regime to impose quotas on a wider range of categories even by 1984 (and especially by the time of the new bilateral agreements in 1986). To the extent that rising utilization of quotas contributed to the rise (in countries such as Mexico), such increases eventually run their course for the reasons noted by the CBO as rapid exhaustion of slack built up by steady quota growth during earlier years leaves imports constrained by quota ceilings, and flexibility provisions such as interyear quota borrowing must eventually neutralize themselves.

The only component likely to work in the opposite direction in the future is the dollar unit value of imports, which should begin to rise again with the decline in the dollar (especially for imports from industrial countries) and could in addition continue rising through upgrading in quota-controlled items. Rising unit values would increase the dollar value but not the physical quantity of imports and indeed, where the change is purely price rather than quantity, its expected effect would be to reduce the physical volume in response to the higher price.

In short, the explosion of imports from 1982 to 1984 was probably a unique event that is unlikely to occur again in at least the medium term. Import growth subsided substantially in 1985, and although it rose again in 1986, the new rise was far more moderate than the surge of 1984. After a time lag of one to two years from the correction of the dollar beginning in late 1985, and considering that imports in 1986 were probably spurred by anticipatory buying prior to a possible severe increase in protection (as new restrictions were nearly legislated at midyear), the pace of import growth seems likely to decline (as analyzed in chapter 10).

Does the 1983–84 surge mean that protection is ineffective, that MFA restraints are nearly meaningless? If so, should this mechanism be replaced by another, more watertight approach? Taken as a whole, the experience under the MFA since the early 1970s must be interpreted as indicating that the regime did in fact restrict imports. On a global basis, this restraint continued in the 1980s, considering that European imports slowed to a near standstill (chapters 3 and 5) while US imports soared. The principal lesson of the US experience in 1983–84 is not that the MFA fails to restrain imports but that when underlying economic forces (overvalued dollar, recovery from recession) exert strong pressure for higher imports, there may be a temporary flood of imports despite the MFA screen. In the longer term view, it must be reiterated that despite this flood, by the mid-1980s the volume of textile imports was still less than would have occurred if steady annual growth of 6 percent had been maintained as originally envisioned in the MFA (with average growth of 4.1 percent), and for apparel growth had averaged only 1 percent annually above the target rate.

As discussed in chapter 9, recent US bilateral negotiations and the terms of MFA-IV of 1986 do institute mechanisms to reduce further the scope for surging imports even during temporary periods. Although the antisurge provisions go a step further in tightening the MFA, they do not appear to have satisfied representatives of US textile and apparel producers. Their demands are also reviewed in chapter 9. First, however, the costs of protection to consumers and the economy are examined in the following chapter.

8

Costs and Benefits of Protection

The political basis for protection of textiles and apparel is the idea that it will save jobs that otherwise would be lost to competition from imports. Purported net employment effects are questionable, because total employment is determined more by macroeconomic policy than by the impact of trade policies on individual sectors. Nonetheless, there may be protection benefits in the form of avoidance of temporary unemployment associated with sectoral job dislocation. Against any employment benefits, there are economic costs from protection. Its price-raising impact imposes a cost on the consuming public. Its effect of causing resource reallocation toward industries in which the United States is relatively uncompetitive causes a cost of inefficiency in production. The chronic support of protection for the two sectors by many in Congress and, in milder form, by successive administrations suggests that at least in political terms its benefits have typically been judged to outweigh its costs.

It is unlikely, however, that the American public has clearly evaluated the economic cost of this protection and reached the conclusion that the employment benefits warrant the shouldering of this cost. The cost of protection is hidden: consumers are not presented with a clearly identified sales tax designated as a subsidy to the domestic textile and apparel industries. They are not even confronted with an explicit tariff rate because the greater part of protection is in the form of nontariff restraints.

The political appeal of protection is all the greater because of whom it benefits, compared with whom it costs. It benefits domestic producers, who are well organized in associations representing their interests. It also benefits current workers in the two industries, who are also well organized in labor union groups. In contrast, the costs of protection are dispersed among the broad consuming public. There is no corresponding vehicle that organizes all consumers into a bloc that can speak for its interests. And although some representational entities do seek to advocate consumer interests, often they do so with mixed views on trade because of their broader ties with the labor movement on domestic issues. In short, the asymmetry between the political organization of gainers and losers from textile and apparel protection would lead one to expect that protection might be adopted even if the overall costs significantly exceeded the benefits.

This chapter presents quantitative estimates of the benefits and costs of US protection in textiles and apparel. The estimates refer to existing protection; further estimates appear in chapter 9 for the costs of the additional protection sought by industry and labor groups in 1985–86 and rejected by presidential veto, as well as of similar subsequent proposals in early 1987. The analysis here also considers the effects of protection on the distribution of income.

Costs of Protection

Appendix B develops the analytical framework for measuring the costs of protection in textiles and apparel. The methodology considers the economic (welfare) gains that consumers would enjoy if tariff and nontariff protection in the two sectors were eliminated. The driving force in the analysis is the fact that import liberalization would reduce prices paid by consumers. Import prices would decline by the amount by which protection currently boosts prices above the level for world supply. In addition, prices on domestically produced textile and apparel products would decline as well. These domestic substitutes would face lower demand if consumers had the option of buying imports at world prices rather than at the higher prices caused by protection.

Before proceeding to discussion of these effects, it is important to consider two arguments sometimes adduced to counter the view that consumers would pay lower prices if protection were eliminated. One is that because prices of textiles and apparel have risen more slowly than general inflation despite protection, the price-increasing effect of protection must be negligible. The second is that regardless of what happens to protection, retailing middlemen absorb any difference between world price and the competitive domestic price, so that any reduction in protection would merely fatten their profits instead of benefiting consumers.

With respect to the argument concerning inflationary trend, it is correct that the rates for textiles and apparel have been below those for the broad price indexes (chapter 2). At the consumer price level, apparel prices grew at an average of 2.9 percent annually from 1978 to 1985, while consumer prices for manufactures ("commodities less food") generally rose at an annual rate of 7.4 percent. Judged by producer prices, the sector's relative performance is less impressive (annual inflation of 4.3 percent in this period versus 5.9 percent for manufactures), suggesting that most of the favorable consumer price trend has been attributable to moderate inflation in import prices.[1] In any event, for the evaluation of economic effects of protection the relevant question is what prices would have been in the absence of protection. There is every reason to believe that inflation in textiles and apparel would have been even lower in the absence of rising protection.

The argument that retailers absorb any difference between prices of imports and domestic goods so that consumers are neither injured by protection nor would benefit from its elimination is doubtful on grounds of general economic theory. Retailing is a competitive industry, and if import costs declined because of the elimination of protection, retailers could be expected to pass on lower prices to consumers; otherwise, their competitors would undersell them. There is also empirical evidence that indicates that for a range of imported goods, retail prices are lower than for domestic goods of comparable quality, supporting the expectation that retailers do pass on lower prices when they are available. Thus, in a 1978 sample survey involving 1,461 price observations on apparel in four major US cities, imports from Asia and and Latin America were found to be 11.6 percent lower in price than domestic apparel of comparable quality (although imports from Europe, Japan, and Canada were 4.3 percent more expensive than domestic apparel).[2]

Theory and empirical evidence thus both suggest that protection has had the effect of raising US consumer prices of textiles and apparel above levels they otherwise would have attained, even after taking account of their slower inflationary trend than for the economy at large and after consideration of marketing margins. As indicated above, the consumer gain from liberalization would be driven by lower prices on imports directly and on domestically produced goods as their prices declined in sympathetic response.

As shown in appendix B, the consumer gain on imports equals, first, the original volume of imports multiplied by the difference between the original and postliberalization import prices. Second, the consumer gains from the fact that an increased volume of imports enters the country, although the gain on this incremental volume is essentially evaluated at only half of the

---

1. The inflation rates are calculated from Bureau of Labor Statistics data as reported in American Textile Manufacturers Institute, *Textile Hi-lights,* September 1986 and March 1985 (consumer price: apparel less footwear; producer price: apparel); and from US Department of Commerce, *Survey of Current Business,* various issues, and Council of Economic Advisers, *Economic Report of the President 1986* (Washington: CEA, February 1986), p. 318. Note that price indexes for imports themselves are not available, except for unit value indexes which contain a mixture of inflation and quality increases induced by the quota incentive for product upgrading.

2. William R. Cline, "Imports and Consumer Prices: A Survey Analysis," *Journal of Retailing,* vol. 55, no. 1 (Spring 1979), pp. 3–24.

difference between the pre- and post-liberalization import prices (because consumers had revealed before that they were unwilling to purchase the additional volume at the original, higher price). On the domestic product, consumer gains amount to the decline in the domestic price multiplied by the volume of sales (specified, to be conservative, at the smaller volume after liberalization rather than at the larger, preliberalization quantity).

Against these consumer gains, there are losses by producers and the government. The government loses tariff revenue, and domestic producers lose that portion of their "producers' surplus" above their cost of production that is transferred to consumers. There is another gain in the market of the domestic good, however, equal to the saving of excessive resources formerly devoted to inefficient production (measured by that portion of the cost of producing the original volume that exceeded the market clearing supply price after liberalization and competition with the world price). The net welfare gains (but before consideration of any costs of transitional unemployment) are equal to the gross consumer gains, less the transfers away from producers, retailers, and government, plus the efficiency gain in production through resource reallocation.

Table 8.1 presents the estimates of these effects as set forth in appendix B. They refer to the impact of complete elimination of tariff and nontariff protection in textiles and apparel for the base year 1986. The calculations begin with the estimates developed in chapter 6 of the total tariff-equivalent of tariff and quota protection. Elimination of this protection would cause a proportionate decline in import prices by the fraction $T/(1 + T)$ where T is the level of total protection. Thus, elimination of a tariff-equivalent (tariff plus quota) of approximately 50 percent in apparel would cut import prices by approximately one-third; elimination of the lower total protection in textiles would reduce import prices by approximately one-fifth.

The next entry in table 8.1 indicates the response of prices of domestically produced goods to the decline in import prices. On the basis of both theoretical relationships concerning cross-reactions between imports and domestic goods, and previous empirical studies, it is assumed that the price of domestically produced apparel would decline by one-half the proportionate reduction in the import price (the "coefficient of price response" equals one-half). Because imports are a considerably smaller fraction of supply for textiles, domestically produced textiles would experience a smaller price decline in response to that of imported textiles. The coefficient of price response for textiles is selected to be such that the reduction in the quantity of domestic output does not exceed the increase in the quantity of imports (the "coefficient of quantity response" equals -1.0), with a resulting coefficient of price response of 0.14.

The resulting price declines would amount to 19 percent for domestic apparel and 3 percent for domestic textiles. Under the assumption that the

Table 8.1 Consumer and welfare costs of protection, United States, 1986
(percentage and million dollars)

		Textiles	Apparel
T	Total protection tariff equivalent	.28	.53
t	Tariff	.12	.225
$\hat{P}_m$	Percent change in import price from liberalization	−21.9	−34.6
$\hat{P}_d$	Percent change in domestic price	−3.1	−18.9
Z_p	Coefficient of domestic price response to import price change	0.14	0.49
Z_q	Coefficient of domestic quantity response to import quantity change	−1.00	−0.75
$\hat{M}$	Percent change in import volume	29.8	56.7
$\hat{Q}$	Percent change in domestic output volume	−3.1	−18.9
V_{mo}	Base value of imports at wholesale level	5,204	23,367
V_{qo}	Base value of domestic output less exports at wholesale level	50,166	52,221
W_c	Consumer cost of protection from:	2,788	17,556
	A Change in import price	1,072	6,421
	B Consumer surplus on change in imports	203	3,130
	C Change in price on domestic good	1,513	8,005
D	Costs from resource misallocation	24	933
G	Transfers to tariff revenue	488	3,167
C	Transfers to producer surplus	1,513	8,005
W^*	Net welfare cost of protection	811	7,317
N	Employment (1000 workers)	669	1,133
dN	Change in employment (1000 workers)	−20.7	−214.2
c_{nd}	Consumer cost per direct job saved (dollars per job)	134,686	81,973
c_{nt}	Consumer cost per job, direct and indirect (dollars)	52,204	46,052

elasticity (responsiveness) of production supply is unity (as discussed in appendix B), output would also decline by these two proportions, respectively. For their part, imports would rise in quantity by 57 percent for apparel and 30 percent for textiles, considering not only the more familiar price elasticity of demand for imports but also the less commonly included cross-elasticity of import demand with respect to the domestic price (which takes account of feedback from the newly lower price of the domestic substitute).

Given the proportionate changes in quantities and prices of imports and domestic production, it is possible to calculate the consumer benefits and net welfare gains discussed above. First it is necessary to estimate the initial value base on which these effects operate. As discussed in appendix B, the estimates here apply the wholesale values of domestic and imported goods, and therefore obtain a conservative estimate of consumer costs of protection. If instead the retail consumer level were used for the base value, the cost estimates would be approximately twice as large because normal retailing margins are approximately 100 percent above wholesale cost. The approach here assumes that competition in retailing would bid away any temporary rise in profits associated with unchanged rule-of-thumb application of the 100 percent marketing margin to the higher import cost resulting from higher protection. After the effect of new competition, the retailing industry in equilibrium would pass on the absolute increase in cost attributable to protection, but would not add the normal (100 percent) marketing margin to this cost as well; instead, competition would lead them to reduce their percentage markup on protected imports to a rate lower than that on domestic goods. As noted in the appendix, because the scarce evidence available on percentage retailing margins in practice suggests that they are the same on protected imports as on domestic goods rather than lower (and critics contend that the margins on imports are higher than on domestic goods), the estimates here must be viewed as quite conservative.

The wholesale value base for consumption of the domestic good is based on industry production shipments as reported in chapter 2 (table 2.1). The wholesale value base for imports is estimated on the basis of f.o.b. import values (tables 2.3 and 2.5) as increased by c.i.f./f.o.b. ratios and by import tariff rates. The values are for 1986 production and imports and are stated at 1986 prices.

As shown in table 8.1, based on 1986 wholesale values, the elimination of protection would have generated annual consumer gains of $17.6 billion in apparel and $2.8 billion in textiles, a total of $20.3 billion. In both cases, approximately half of the consumer gain from liberalization would come from induced lower prices on domestic goods (with the smaller relative price decline in domestic textiles compared with apparel offset by the larger share of domestic goods in total textile consumption); between 35 percent and 40 percent from lower prices on existing imports; and the remainder from price savings on the increased volume of imports.

After deducting the calculated transfers from producer surplus and government tariff revenue, net welfare gains from complete liberalization amount to $7.3 billion annually in apparel and $811 million in textiles. These gains are relatively high proportions of the gross consumer costs (41 percent in apparel and 29 percent in textiles). The high net welfare costs of protection in the two sectors reflect high protection rates, especially in apparel, in view of the fact that the net welfare cost rises with the square of protection, while consumer cost rises only proportionately to it.[3]

The estimates of consumer costs indicate a major burden on consumers from existing protection in textiles and, especially, apparel. The combined annual cost of $20.3 billion amounts to $238 per household, or 0.72 percent of disposable income per household.[4] It seems highly unlikely that the American public would have voted to enact a special and permanent tax of $238 per household, payable year after year, to subsidize the textile and apparel sectors so that a specific number of jobs can be earmarked for preservation in these industries rather than transferred to other sectors of the economy. Yet this outcome is in effect what the regime of protection for these industries has brought about. Moreover, as developed below, the relative burden of this hidden tax is even greater for a large group of lower income consumers.

As noted above, the conservative value base used for these calculations (wholesale level rather than retail level) may lead to an understatement of these costs of protection by as much as one-half. Thus, US consumers may be paying nearly $40 billion annually for textile and apparel protection (almost $500 per household every year), and the estimate of $20.3 billion should be considered as a minimum statement of this burden.

Employment Effects and Net Cost/Benefit Ratios

Application of the percentage output reduction to the base level of direct sectoral employment gives an estimate of 20,700 jobs lost in textiles and 214,200 in apparel. The relatively small employment effect in textiles is consistent with the analysis of chapter 4 indicating that trade has been only a limited source of employment decline in this sector and that rapid labor productivity growth and slow growth of consumption have played much

---

3. Thus, in appendix B the areas B and D of figure B.1, consumer gains on increased imports and welfare cost of domestic resource misallocation respectively, involve multiplication of the change in price by the change in volume, and the change in volume itself is determined by the change in price applied to a demand elasticity, thereby obtaining the square of the change in price. These two components of consumer cost are net welfare gains, while the remaining components are transfers from foreign suppliers and government (area A) or producers (area C) to consumers, and these transfers depend on the change in protection as applied to original volume (and thus rise only linearly with protection).

4. In 1984 there were 85.4 million households in the United States. In 1985, disposable personal income amounted to $2,801 billion. US Department of Commerce, Bureau of the Census, *Statistical Abstract of the United States, 1985* (Washington: Department of Commerce, 1984), p. 40; Council of Economic Advisers, *Economic Report of the President 1986*, p. 283.

more important roles in the sizable reductions in textile employment (averaging 25,000 jobs annually since 1973). Even in apparel, the estimated reduction of employment by approximately one-fifth as the result of complete import liberalization is more moderate than might be inferred from the policy debate, which often depicts protection as all that prevents imports from virtually eliminating the US industry.

As indicated in table 8.1, the annual consumer cost per direct job preserved by protection amounts to $134,686 in textiles and $81,973 in apparel. These costs are extremely high. Considering that average wages in textiles and apparel are in the range of $12,000 annually, consumers pay nearly seven times as much to sustain apparel job positions through protection as it would cost them to provide permanent vacations at full salary to the workers involved, and for textile jobs the multiple is even higher.

Employment effects of trade policy are sometimes calculated to include as well the impact on indirect jobs in industries supplying intermediate inputs into the sector examined. Input-output analyses indicate that for each direct job in the textile sector itself, there are 1.58 additional indirect jobs from intermediate inputs into the production of textiles; for apparel, the ratio is 0.78 indirect jobs per direct job.[5] If these ratios are applied to the estimates of direct job losses from elimination of protection, total reduction of employment (including direct and indirect) would reach 53,406 jobs from liberalization in textiles and 381,200 jobs from that in apparel. The corresponding consumer costs of protection per total direct and indirect job are then $52,204 annually for textiles and $46,052 annually for apparel.

It is questionable, however, that indirect employment effects should be included in the evaluation of the impact of import liberalization on employment. As production activity shifts from textiles and apparel to other sectors (including services), there will be increased demands for intermediate inputs into the newly expanding sectors. Moreover, the indirect jobs involved are dispersed across a wide variety of sectors, with considerably milder adjustment implications than in the case of the direct jobs in textiles and apparel. The direct employment effects of liberalization, and the consumer cost of protection per direct job preserved in the protected sector itself, would appear to serve as better references for policy determination than the corresponding measures for total employment effects including indirect jobs.

To calculate the employment benefits of protection, it is first necessary to know how long workers displaced from the textile and apparel sectors by liberalization would be unemployed. The opportunity cost to the economy

---

5. Calculated from US Department of Labor, Bureau of Labor Statistics, *The Structure of the U.S. Economy in 1980 and 1985*, Bulletin 1831 (Washington: Department of Labor, 1975), pp. 162, 236–37.

for each job lost may then be calculated as the expected duration of unemployment multiplied by the average wage for the workers in question. That is, the wage reflects the opportunity cost of this labor to the economy, and during the period of unemployment this opportunity cost would be lost.

It is sometimes argued that an additional benefit from protection stems from the fact that in its absence, dislocated workers would eventually have to settle for jobs at wages substantially below their original earnings. While this wage differential is a personal cost to the displaced worker, it is not a cost to the society at large because the new and lower wage obtained by the reemployed worker represents the new opportunity cost of the worker to the economy. Indeed, if the wage after reemployment is significantly lower, use of the original wage to calculate the economic loss during unemployment will overstate the loss to the economy.

A survey of displaced workers carried out by the US Department of Labor in 1984 found that the median number of weeks without work for workers displaced from the apparel industry was 24.8 weeks; for textile mills the median jobless period was 13.3 weeks. The same study found that in apparel, wages in the new jobs were only 2.5 percent lower than those in the jobs lost, and that wages actually rose by 3.3 percent for textile workers.[6]

The average wage for production workers in 1985 was $6.80 per hour in textiles and $5.59 per hour in apparel. Average hours worked per week amounted to 39.7 hours for textiles and 36.4 for apparel.[7] Under the assumption discussed above that lost wages during the period of unemployment represent the opportunity cost to the economy of the temporary unemployment of workers displaced by liberalization, the economic cost per direct job displaced in textiles would amount to $3,590 (13.3 x $6.80 x 39.7); in apparel, the corresponding cost would be $5,046. Multiplied by the direct job losses estimated in table 8.1, these estimates yield a benefit to the economy from avoidance of temporary unemployment of direct workers amounting to $74.3 million in textiles and $1.08 billion in apparel.

A conservative estimate of the net costs of protection would include on the benefit side the corresponding value of avoidance of temporary unemployment in indirect jobs as well, even though as suggested above the limitation of attention to direct jobs in textiles and apparel may be more appropriate. The indirect job benefits of protection may be approximated by applying the average wage, duration of unemployment, and hours per

---

6. US Department of Labor, Bureau of Labor Statistics, *Displaced Workers, 1979–83*, Bulletin 2240 (Washington: Department of Labor, July 1985), pp. 28–29.

7. U.S. Department of Commerce *U.S. Industrial Outlook 1987;* and *Survey of Current Business,* vol. 66, no. 6 (June 1986), p. S-11.

week for manufacturing industry as a whole ($9.53 per hour, 19.2 weeks, and 40.5 hours per week, in 1985).[8] These estimates applied to the calculations of indirect job effects yield costs to the economy of $242 million from liberalization of textiles and $1.24 billion from liberalization of apparel. Combined with the direct employment effects, the estimates indicate total benefits of avoidance of temporary unemployment amounting to $316 million from textile protection and $2.32 billion from apparel protection, or a total of $2.6 billion for the two sectors together.

These employment benefits should be understood as one-time gains, equivalent to a capital value. That is, if imports were liberalized the unemployment costs just estimated would occur once and for all. In contrast, the costs of existing protection are repeated year after year. To compare the two concepts, it is necessary to capitalize the annual stream of protection costs into a single "present value" measure. A conservative present discounted value would be 10 times the annual value. This multiple would represent zero growth of the annual value base, combined with a time discount rate of 10 percent in real terms. In practice, the value base would grow over time along with consumption, while the real discount rate could easily be well below 10 percent (in view of real interest rates of some 5 percent to 7 percent on long-term government bonds). Thus, the true present value of protection costs could be even higher.

On this basis, the annual net welfare costs reported in table 8.1 translate into capitalized values of $8.11 billion for textiles and $73.2 billion for apparel (10 times the net welfare costs shown in the table). The corresponding cost/benefit ratios for protection, with benefits from avoidance of unemployment including both direct and indirect jobs, are $8.11 billion/$316 million = 25.7 in textiles, and $73.2 billion/$2.32 billion = 31.6 in textiles. Thus, the costs of protection exceed its benefits by approximately 30-fold. Elimination of protection in textiles and apparel would appear to have an extremely high rate of return in purely economic terms because the employment benefits of protection (avoidance of transitional unemployment) are only a small fraction of its costs.

Estimates of employment effects in principle could be expanded to include employment in the retail marketing of textiles and apparel. In the model applied here, the total physical quantity of apparel sold rises by 4.5 percent after liberalization (applying the percentage increase in imports and decrease in domestic production to the base level wholesale values, table 8.3). In textiles, the physical volume of sales remains unchanged (the coefficient of quantity response is set at unity, so that the reduction in domestic output

---

8. Ibid., pp. S-11, S-12; Bureau of Labor Statistics, *Employment and Earnings* (January 1986), table 16.

equals the increase in imports). On the basis of physical volume, then, retailing employment might be expected to rise by 4.5 percent in apparel and remain unchanged in textiles. Baughman and Emrich estimate that there are 2 million retailing jobs associated with apparel and 177,000 linked to textiles.[9] On this basis, complete liberalization of apparel could increase retailing employment by 90,000 jobs (4.5 percent of 2 million), enough to offset two-fifths of the loss of direct jobs in apparel production.

The calculation of retail job effects must be interpreted as highly tentative, however. Data on retail employment by product sector are relatively uncertain. In addition, if instead of physical volume, the dollar value of retailing revenue is considered the appropriate base for estimating retail employment effects, and if in addition the assumption that percentage retailing margins vary exactly enough to maintain a constant absolute retail margin for each item as its cost varies with protection, then the estimated retail employment effects could be quite different. On the basis of the competitive model, the analysis here assumes that reduction in wholesale cost either by lower protection (imports) or by lower production price (domestic goods) leaves absolute retailing margins unchanged and, by implication, causes percentage retailing margins to rise. Under these assumptions, retail revenue varies proportionately with the physical volume of sales. It is possible, however, that absolute retailing margins would tend to decline rather than remain unchanged as liberalization reduced the wholesale product price, if retailers tended to retain a fixed percentage markup rather than a constant absolute markup. If so, retailing employment would rise by less (and conceivably could fall) than the physical volume of sales, if retail revenue were one of the determinants of retail employment. In short, it is perhaps best to conclude merely that there might be a modest gain in retailing employment as the consequence of liberalization, rather than to attach a concrete estimate to this effect.

Other Estimates

Table 8.2 reports estimates by other authors of the effects of protection in US textiles and apparel. The study most comparable to the analysis here is that by Hufbauer, Berliner, and Elliott (HBE). These authors also use a model with imperfect substitution between the imported and domestic goods. Their estimates of the tariff-equivalent of total tariff and quota protection are somewhat lower than those here (for example, 39 percent

---

9. Laura Megna Baughman and Thomas Emrich, "Analysis of the Impact of the Textile and Apparel Trade Enforcement Act of 1985" (Washington: International Business and Economic Research Corporation, 1985), appendix C, table C.1.

Table 8.2 Alternative estimates of protection effects
(values in million dollars)

Study, base year	This study 1985	Hufbauer Berliner and Elliott 1984	Hickok 1984	Tarr and Morke 1983
Protection Base	tariffs and quotas	tariffs and quotas	tariffs and quotas	quotas[a] against Hong Kong
Apparel				
Import price increase (percentage)	53	39	17–25	23[b]
Consumer cost	17,556	18,000	8,500–12,000	384–508
Net Welfare cost	7,317	6,000	n.a.	308–488
Jobs created (1,000)	381.2[c]	460	n.a.	9
Consumer cost per job	46,052	39,000	n.a.	n.a.
Textiles				
Import price increase (percentage)	28	21	n.a.	n.a.
Consumer cost	2,788	9,000	n.a.	n.a.
New Welfare cost	811	650	n.a.	n.a.
Jobs created (1,000)	53[c]	180	n.a.	n.a.
Consumer cost per job	52,204	50,000	n.a.	n.a.

n.a.   not applicable.
Source: Table 8.1; Gary Clyde Hufbauer, Diane Berliner, and Kimberly Ann Elliott, *Trade Protection in the United States: 31 Case Studies* (Washington: Institute for International Economics, 1986), pp. 146–49; Susan Hickok, "The Consumer Cost of US Trade Restraints," *Federal Reserve Bank of New York Quarterly Review,* vol. 10, no. 2 (Summer 1985), pp. 1–12; David G. Tarr and Morris E. Morke, *Aggregate Costs to the United States of Tariffs and Quotas on Imports: General Tariff Cuts and Removal of Quotas on Automobiles, Steel, Sugar, and Textiles* (Washington: Federal Trade Commission, 1984), pp. 101–25.
a. For 13 cotton apparel categories.
b. Weighted average.
c. Includes indirect jobs.

versus 53 percent in apparel). However, the authors assume a higher coefficient of domestic price response to the change in the import price: 0.8 for both textiles and apparel. This coefficient is lower in the present study (0.14 for textiles and 0.55 for apparel), giving lower estimates for consumer cost of protection for a given product value base. At the same time, because HBE also apply their calculations at the wholesale level, their estimates of consumer costs—like those of the present study—may be understated (for the reasons outlined above and in appendix B concerning constant absolute as opposed to percentage retailing margins).

The estimates here of the consumer cost of protection are relatively close to those of HBE, who place the annual consumer cost of textile and apparel protection at $27 billion, rather than the $20.3 billion estimated here. Note that the HBE division of the cost between textiles and apparel is much more evenly distributed between the two sectors ($9 billion and $18 billion, respectively) than that found in the estimates here ($2.8 billion and $17.6 billion, respectively). The primary reason is that in the present study, the coefficient of domestic price response for textiles is much lower than in the HBE study, so that consumer savings on induced reductions of domestic product prices are correspondingly lower.

Hufbauer, Berliner, and Elliott find larger employment effects than the present study, by a much wider margin than their also larger consumer cost estimates. They calculate that protection generates 460,000 direct jobs in apparel and 180,000 in textiles, considerably larger than even the total employment estimates here including indirect jobs through interindustry requirements. This divergence stems from the high price-response coefficient assumed in HBE, and thus the relatively large cutback in domestic output.[10] Corresponding to the higher estimates of employment displacement, HBE obtain lower estimates of consumer cost per job ($50,000 in textiles, $39,000 in apparel) than the present study. Despite these differences, the broad implications of the HBE findings and those here are similar.

Another recent study is comparable in approach to that here but is more limited in coverage. Tarr and Morkre examine the consumer and welfare costs of quota protection on imports from Hong Kong in 13 major cotton apparel categories. In the 1980 base year, these imports amounted to $953 million ($1.15 billion at 1963 prices according to the authors' implicit price index). The authors estimate annual consumer cost of protection on this subset of imports at $318 million to $420 million ($384 million to $508 million in 1983 prices), or from 33.4 percent to 44.1 percent of the base import value. They find that the net welfare cost ranges from 80 percent to 96 percent of the consumer cost, a surprisingly high proportion. Considering that total apparel imports in 1985 amounted to $15.7 billion, application of the Tarr-Morkre ratio of consumer cost to base import value would suggest total consumer costs of $5.2 billion to $6.9 billion annually in apparel, with corresponding net welfare costs of $4.2 billion to $6.7 billion.

The method applied by Tarr and Morkre would appear to understate

---

10. See appendix B for a discussion of appropriateness of the price response coefficients used here as opposed to those used by Hufbauer, Berliner, and Elliott.

consumer and welfare costs of protection, because it considers the price-increasing and quantity-restraining effects of protection only on imports. The domestic substitute does not appear in their model; therefore, consumer costs from induced higher prices on the domestic good are absent in their calculations. After consideration of this factor, the Tarr-Morkre results (as expanded) are relatively close to those here.[11]

The third alternative study listed in table 8.2, by Hickok, uses a completely different approach to estimate consumer costs of protection in apparel.[12] The author calculates these costs by identifying an average price increase attributable to protection and applying it to the value of total consumption (both overall and for apparel in particular). She first traces unit values of apparel imports from 1971 to 1984 and finds that they rose by a total of 65 percent in excess of the rise of domestic apparel prices. The author treats any upgrading as equivalent to a price increase because it forces the consumer to purchase higher priced goods by eliminating availability of the low-priced products. She attributes this differential increase to the introduction of quota protection. She concludes that tariffs and quotas together raise the price of imports by 108 percent. This increase translates into an average price increase of 12 percent for all apparel, domestic and imported, according to Hickok.

Next, the author adds the price-raising effect of the forced switching of purchases from imports to domestic goods. For each unit switched, there is a price increase equal to the difference between the domestic and the foreign price—estimated by the difference between the share of imports in total quantity (45 percent, according to Hickok) and their share in total value (25 percent). The author uses a conservative estimate of the magnitude of switching based on the difference in import growth from 1971 to 1984 for apparel as opposed to all manufactures; for a liberal estimate she uses the growth of footwear imports as the benchmark for comparison. The resulting price impact of switching is estimated to add another 5 percent to 13 percent to average apparel prices. Hickok then applies the total price increases (17

---

11. The Tarr-Morkre estimates are in David G. Tarr and Morris E. Morkre, *Aggregate Costs to the United States of Tariffs and Quotas on Imports: General Tariff Cuts and Removal of Quotas on Automobiles, Steel, Sugar, and Textiles* (Washington: Federal Trade Commission, 1984), pp. 102–103. The consumer gains just on imports in the apparel estimates here amount to $9.4 billion (table 8.1). If the Tarr-Morkre estimate (expanded to the full import base) of $5.2 billion to $6.9 billion is increased by the same ratio of consumer costs on domestic goods relative to those on imports as identified here (86 percent: $8.09 billion/$9.45 billion), the implicit consumer cost estimate from the Tarr-Morkre reaches $9.7 billion to $12.8 billion annually for apparel, with the upper end of this range not far from the $17.5 billion estimated here.

12. Susan Hickok, "The Consumer Cost of U.S. Trade Restraints," *Federal Reserve Bank of New York Quarterly Review*, vol. 10, no. 2 (Summer 1985), p. 7.

percent to 25 percent) to an estimated value of total consumption to conclude that the consumer cost of apparel protection in 1984 was between $8.5 billion and $12 billion.

Considering the fundamental differences in Hickok's approach, and in view of the fact that she assumes there are no induced price increases for domestically produced apparel from protection, the upper end of Hickok's range of estimates is relatively close to the $17.6 billion annual consumer cost estimated in the present study.

In sum, among the existing alternative studies, that by Hufbauer, Berliner, and Elliott arrives at estimates of consumer costs of textile and apparel protection that are close to the estimates here. When the other studies are adjusted to take account of induced price effects for domestically produced goods (in the case of Tarr and Morkre) and, more generally, when their different approaches are considered (especially that of Hickok), they also yield cost estimates that are within the same range of magnitudes as those developed in the present study.

Income Distribution Effects

One of the arguments favoring protection of apparel and textiles is that these sectors employ low-wage workers. The implication is that at least in these products, protection achieves a progressive rather than regressive redistribution of income, away from the general public toward a low-income group. The estimates of this chapter permit an examination of the impact of textile and apparel protection on the distribution of income. The discussion here includes redistribution toward foreign suppliers as well.

Table 8.3 presents an allocation of the costs and benefits of protection as developed above into income distributional classes. Each income group is a "quintile," or successive 20 percent grouping of the total of 74.8 million household consuming units (as measured by the Bureau of Labor Statistics).[13] The table first shows the average household income in each quintile; then, the shares of the respective quintiles in total income, total consumption, and the consumption of apparel. Examination of these three shares shows that both total consumption and apparel consumption are income-inelastic: that is, consumption rises more slowly than income. Thus, in the lowest quintile, households receive only 2.9 percent of total income but account for about 10 percent of consumption (both overall and for apparel in particular). The highest quintile accounts for 47.8 percent of income but

---

13. US Department of Labor, Bureau of Labor Statistics, *News*, "Consumer Expenditure Survey Results from 1984," Washington, 22 June 1986; processed.

Table 8.3   Income distributional effects of textile and apparel protection
(by quintile of consumer units)

	Income group					
	Lowest 20 percent	21–40 percent	41–60 percent	61–80 percent	81–100 percent	Total
Income range (dollars)	0–7,582	7,583– 14,232	14,233– 24,179	24,180– 35,623	>35,623	all
Average income (dollars)	3,577	10,828	19,297	30,370	58,639	24,578
Percentage share in						
Income	2.9	8.8	15.7	24.7	47.8	100.0
Expenditure	10.3	12.5	17.2	23.1	37.0	100.0
Apparel expenditure	10.1	11.1	16.3	21.0	41.4	100.0
Effects of protection						
Level (million dollars)						
Consumer cost	−2,057	−2,260	−3,319	−4,276	−8,431	−20,344
Unemployment avoidance	0	110	157	0	0	267
Transfers to producers	0	0	0	0	9,519	9,519
Government transfer	105	319	568	895	1,732	3,621
Net effects	−1,951	−1,831	−2,590	−3,374	2,835	−6,907
As percentage of income						
Consumer cost	−3.84	−1.39	−1.15	−0.94	−0.96	−1.11
Unemployment avoidance	0	0.07	0.05	0	0	0.01
Transfers to producers, retailers	0	0	0	0	1.08	0.52
Government transfer	0.20	0.20	0.20	0.20	0.20	0.20
Net effects	−3.64	−1.13	−0.90	−0.74	0.32	−0.37

Source: Table 8.1 and US Department of Labor, Bureau of Labor Statistics, *News,* "Consumer Expenditure Results for 1984," 22 June 1986; processed.

only 37 percent of total consumption and 41.4 percent of apparel consumption. Compared with other goods, the consumption of apparel is somewhat more elastic with response to income (lags less behind increasing income), but the difference is not large. In broad terms, then, higher apparel prices from protection may be thought of as having a regressive impact similar to that of an excise tax: because apparel consumption is a relatively larger fraction of income at low-income levels, the incidence of higher apparel prices is relatively greater upon low-income households.

A more complete allocation of the costs and benefits of protection must go farther. In addition to consideration of consumer costs, it must incorporate the benefit of unemployment avoidance for direct and indirect workers, as well as the distributional consequences of transfers to producers and government revenue. Part A of table 8.3 allocates these benefits and costs by income distributional group (quintile). The consumer costs of protection in both textiles and apparel (a total of $20.3 billion annually) are distributed across quintiles in proportion to each group's share in total consumption of apparel (in the absence of separate data on textile consumption).

The amounts and quintile allocations of the benefit of unemployment avoidance are as follows. First, these benefits must be converted from their total, once-and-for-all values to annualized rates for comparison to the annual consumer costs and other transfers.[14] This conversion is done by applying the annual discount rate, 10 percent, to the once-and-for-all (capital equivalent) value of the unemployment avoidance benefit. Second, the resulting total annual benefit must be allocated by quintile. In 1985 the average annual wage of direct apparel workers was $10,581; of direct textile workers, $14,038; and of manufacturing workers overall, $20,070 (based on the hourly wages and hours per week discussed above). Multiplication by an average of 1.2 workers per consumer unit yields the average consuming-unit income of these respective groups, with the result that direct apparel workers fall into the second quintile, while the other three categories of workers are classed in the third, or middle, quintile. The amounts of the corresponding benefits allocated are 10 percent of the once-for-all benefits estimated for each respective group in the discussion above of employment benefits.

At this point an important finding may be seen: despite the general impression that apparel and textile workers are in low-income groups, their wage rates place them in the middle- and lower-middle income groups (quintiles 3 and 2). The BLS data indicate that the average income of the poorest 20 percent of consuming units in the United States is only $3,577— far below the $12,700 for households of direct apparel workers and $16,846 for those of direct textile workers. Moreover, much of the employment effect of protection as estimated above occurs in indirect employment in manufacturing sectors other than textiles and apparel, and the average manufacturing wage is even further above the income level of the poorest 20 percent (and even the next 20 percent) in the US income distribution.

---

14. Note that these benefits are the same as calculated above. There is no additional allowance for wage loss by workers in their post-displacement jobs. While in principle incorporation of such losses would be appropriate in this income distributional analysis, because the available evidence indicates little if any such subsequent wage loss on average (as noted above) this further effect is not incorporated here.

Yet it is not really the essentially middle-income locus of the benefits of textile and apparel protection that calls the policy into question on income distributional grounds. Rather, it is the fact that the mechanism is so inefficient—in generating costs far in excess of benefits—that it manages to cause losses even for the broad income quintiles of which the relevant workers are members. That is, consumption losses of households at the same income level as the workers involved substantially exceed, in the aggregate, the benefits to the workers from avoiding unemployment.

To make matters worse from a distributional standpoint, the protection transfers to producers are almost certainly concentrated at the upper end of the income distribution. These transfers tend to raise profits of firms. Because of the extreme concentration of corporation ownership, it is assumed that the entirety of these transfers accrues to the uppermost quintile in the distribution.[15] (The magnitudes of the transfers are the sums of the corresponding estimates for textiles and apparel in table 8.1.)

Finally, the transfer into government revenue from tariffs is allocated across income groups in proportion to their shares in total income. Additional revenue from tariffs reduces the amount of tax revenue the government needs to collect otherwise, and this benefit is distributed to households in proportion to their shares in total income. This assumption is biased somewhat in favor of the conclusion that protection is income-equalizing; in practice, there is some progressivity in the tax system, so that the raising of revenue from foreigners through tariffs tends to alleviate the tax burden of the rich by a larger percentage of income than it does for the poor.

The overall result of this allocation of costs and benefits of protection is that in the bottom four quintiles protection causes net losses. Only the top quintile gains because of the increased profits of producing firms as allocated to the corporate shareholders assumed to belong almost completely to the top quintile. The final, lower right-hand figure in part A of the table shows that the total net income effects of protection are negative in the amount of $6.9 billion annually because the consumer costs exceed the employment, producer, and government benefits by this amount.

These results indicate that protection in textiles and apparel has regressive income distributional consequences. This finding is more clearly evident in part B of the table, which translates the absolute costs and benefits by quintile into percentages of total income in each quintile. As indicated, the consumer cost of protection is 3.8 percent of consumer-unit income in the poorest 20 percent, declining to 1.4 percent in the next 20 percent, and

---

15. Thus, in 1976, just the top 1 percent of persons accounted for 46 percent of ownership of corporate stock in the United States. US Department of Commerce, Bureau of the Census, *Statistical Abstract of the United States, 1985* p. 463.

eventually to 0.96 percent for the richest quintile. Overall, consumer costs amount to 1.1 percent of household income as measured in the BLS sample.

The net costs of textile and apparel protection after taking account of benefits by class are also regressive in their distributional effect. The net impact on the lowest quintile is −3.64 percent of income, while for the highest quintile the net effect is +0.32 percent of income. Even the lower-middle and middle-income quintiles in which the apparel, textile, and indirect workers may be found experience a net negative effect, equal to 1.13 percent of income in the second quintile and 0.90 percent in the third. In short, protection has the ironical effect of redistributing real income away from lower-income and middle-income groups—including those to which the workers in question belong—to the top income group in which the expanded profits may be found. This process is the natural consequence of a policy that redistributes income from the general consuming public to producing and marketing firms and to a selected group of workers.[16]

There is one more group that warrants consideration from a distributional standpoint: foreign producers. As indicated in appendix A and in the discussion of table 8.1, the (rectangle of) consumer costs from higher prices on existing imports under protection (item A in table 8.1) is composed of two parts: transfers to government tariff revenue, and transfers to foreign producers in the form of quota rents. From table 8.1 it may be calculated that foreigners receive quota rents amounting to $3.25 billion in apparel ($6.42 billion consumer gain from lower import prices on existing import volume, less $3.17 billion in government tariff revenue) and $584 million in textiles ($1.07 billion less $488 million). US protection of textiles and apparel thus transfers some $3.8 billion annually from domestic consumers to foreign suppliers in the form of quota rents.[17]

Finally, it should be noted that the regressive distributional impact of protection measured here does not take account of the additional fact that restricted imports probably tend to be purchased disproportionately by low-income groups. As noted above, a large sample survey in the late 1970s

---

16. Note, however, that the net losses of the second and third quintiles do not mean that the workers involved experience losses; on the contrary, they obtain the benefits of unemployment avoidance, but these benefits are too small to outweigh the consumption losses of their cohorts in the same income groups.

17. Some of this amount may be absorbed by domestic firms to the extent that they have greater market power than foreign suppliers. However, the domestic retailing industry for apparel and textiles appears to be highly competitive, whereas the governments of several important foreign supplier countries explicitly administer export quotas in a way that captures their rent. Certainly the practice of allocating export quota tickets within Hong Kong on a historical basis, and the resale of these rights in a secondary market, tends to ensure that quota rent accrues to the supplier country rather than to distributors within the United States. Accordingly, the assumption here is that the quota rent accrues to foreigners.

found imported apparel from developing countries some 12 percent less expensive than domestic apparel of comparable quality. Low-income households are likely to concentrate their purchases on these lower cost supplies, so the consumer costs of protection might appropriately be more heavily allocated to low-income groups rather than distributed in proportion to apparel consumption by class.

In sum, the distributional effects of protection in textiles and apparel appear to be regressive among income groups within the United States and negative for the United States as a whole in the form of allocation of quota rents to foreigners.[18] There is thus little basis for justification of the policy on income distributional grounds.

---

18. Note that it is sometimes argued that US textile and apparel protection has a positive terms of trade effect that redistributes income to the United States by depressing the demand for (and thus the price of) these goods in the world market. See the discussion of estimates by Thomas Bayard, in Martin Wolf, Hans Hinrich Glismann, Joseph Pelzman, and Dean Spinanger, *Costs of Protecting Jobs in Textiles and Clothing* (London: Trade Policy Research Centre, 1984), p. 105. However, as suggested in appendix B, it would seem more likely that the elasticity of foreign supply to the United States is close to infinity (horizontal supply curve), so that while reduction of US demand would reduce the quantity of foreign exports, it would not significantly depress the price. There would appear to be little empirical basis for estimation of a foreign supply curve with less than infinite elasticity. However, considering that the United States already transfers nearly $4 billion abroad annually in quota rents on textiles and apparel, the import price could rise by some 21 percent (on an f.o.b import value base of $19.4 billion) after liberalization and still generate a net improvement for the United States relative to the rest of the world.

9

Recent Pressures for New Restrictions and MFA-IV

In July 1986 the major textile trading countries marked another milestone in the history of the Multi-Fiber Arrangement (MFA). On July 31, the day MFA-III expired, its members agreed to extend the Arrangement for another five years. Rather than liberalizing the regime as developing-country delegations to the MFA negotiations had initially hoped, the terms of the renewal set the stage for another round of tightening.

The ambiance of these negotiations was one of intense pressure for protection in the United States. In the previous year, Congress had passed legislation mandating a sharp cutback in imports of apparel and textiles, but President Ronald Reagan vetoed the measure. The House of Representatives set August 6, 1986, as the date for an override vote, thereby pressuring MFA negotiators to conclude a suitably restrictive renewal by the expiration of MFA-III. The Reagan administration decried the legislative attempt but sought to preempt the override by concluding restrictive new bilateral negotiations and by insisting on provisions for tightening in MFA-IV.

By late 1986 the locus of policy had shifted to the new Uruguay Round of multilateral trade negotiations, and to broader pressure for new trade legislation in the United States. It remained unclear whether textiles and apparel would be discussed seriously within the new round. However, it was widely expected that textile and apparel interests would renew their campaign, with a threefold revival of their hopes. The 1986 elections shifted party control in the Senate; there were growing demands for overall trade legislation as the result of a US trade deficit in excess of $150 billion; and the administration was likely to need some authorizing legislation to pursue negotiations in the new multilateral round. The textile and apparel interests could hope that, as in the past, they would be able to exact some protective price in exchange for this negotiating authority. And by early 1987 the textile and apparel industries had developed a new legislative proposal for additional restrictions on imports. This time they no longer sought an actual rollback, but instead called for a global quota covering all imports, with annual growth limited to 1 percent.

This chapter reviews the recent evolution of trade policy in textiles and apparel in chronological order. It first evaluates the 1985 import-reducing bill. The discussion then traces the negotiations for the new MFA and its terms. After an examination of the role of textiles and apparel in the Uruguay Round launched in September 1986, the analysis concludes with an evaluation of the economic impact of the early 1987 proposal for new restrictions.

The Textile and Apparel Trade Enforcement Act of 1985

In March 1985 Representative Edgar L. Jenkins (D–Ga.) proposed a bill to cut back imports of textiles and apparel (HR 1562); it passed the House in October. The Senate passed a parallel bill (S 680) in November by a vote of 60 to 39, and the House passed the amended version on December 3, 1985 (255–161). President Reagan vetoed the bill on December 17, 1985. The amended bill restricted imports of footwear and copper as well as textiles and apparel.[1]

The bill would have made two basic changes in trade policy. First, it would have replaced the existing system of bilateral negotiations by explicit and comprehensive import licenses. This measure would have ended the myth that textile and apparel quotas are "voluntary." The shift to unilaterally determined import licenses would have ended the rationale for the MFA by overriding its provisions for moderation in restraints and by nullifying its function of providing supplier countries a voice in the design of restraints. Second, for principal suppliers the bill would have rolled back imports to levels based on 6 percent growth since 1980 (hence "enforcement"), while for others it would have set strict growth limits.

The bill (as amended) would have defined three supplier groups: "major producing countries" (Hong Kong, Taiwan, and Korea); "producing countries" (all suppliers with between 1.25 percent and 10 percent of the US import market); and "small producing countries."[2] A benchmark of imports would have been set by applying 6 percent growth from 1980 to 1984, or

1. Edward B. Rappaport, "Textile Imports under the Multi-Fiber Arrangement," (Washington: Congressional Research Service, 26 June 1986), p. 9.

2. For description of the bill's provisions, see ibid.; Jim Berger, "US Textiles and Apparel—Is Protection a Solution?" *Policy Focus,* no.6 (Washington: Overseas Development Council, 1985); and Laura Megna Baughman and Thomas Emrich, *Analysis of the Impact of the Textile and Apparel Trade Enforcement Act of 1985* (Washington: International Business and Economic Research Corporation, June 1985); hereafter referred to as *IBERC Study.*

at the country's actual bilaterally agreed quota in 1984, whichever was smaller. For major producing countries, imports would have to have been cut back to this benchmark and then constrained to grow at no more than 1 percent annually. For producing countries, the bill would have permitted growth from the actual 1984 levels at a rate of only 1 percent annually. For small producing countries, it would have allowed growth of 15 percent in the first year and 6 percent thereafter, but with a ceiling rate of only 1 percent for sensitive categories (defined as having imports equal to 40 percent of US production). Upon reaching 1.25 percent of import supply, a supplier would graduate to "producing country" status.

The bill would have perpetuated the discrimination against developing-country suppliers by exempting Canada and the European Community (but not Japan, Portugal, or Spain) from restraints—although for the first time suppliers from these countries too would need to acquire import licenses. However, it would have favored Mexico and the Caribbean Basin countries by excluding them from the graduation provisions and from tighter restraints for sensitive products. Moreover, in its amended form the bill's three categories placed the harshest cutbacks on only the three largest Asian suppliers, instead of 12 countries (including Brazil) that originally would have faced these absolute reductions. The impact would have been to cut back imports from Hong Kong, Taiwan, and Korea by 59.1 percent in textiles and 18.5 percent in apparel, while virtually freezing at 1984 levels those from China, Japan, Pakistan, Indonesia, India, the Philippines, Thailand, Brazil, and Singapore.[3]

The legislation also would have extended import restrictions to cover ramie, jute, and other fiber products not previously restricted under the MFA, although the final version of the bill continued to exempt silk products. In this area the sponsors achieved their goal indirectly because the US insisted on this wider coverage in the MFA negotiations.

In both houses of Congress the 1985 passage of the bill reflected diverse interests. The votes were not strictly along party lines; thus, in the Senate 25 Republicans voted for the bill, and in the House 75.[4] Regional considerations dominated the voting. Legislators from the South, the center of the textile industry, supported the measure, as did those from shoe- and copper-producing states. But representatives of farm states opposed it on grounds that it would precipitate a trade war in which farm exports would lose out; and representatives from West Coast states that trade heavily with Asia and the Pacific also opposed the bill.[5]

---

3. *New York Times,* 4 December 1985; and *IBERC Study,* table B–1.

4. *Wall Street Journal,* 28 July 1986.

5. *New York Times,* 11 October 1985 and 4 December 1985.

Successful override of the presidential veto would have meant not only a breakdown of the MFA, but also probably the jettisoning of the new Uruguay Round of multilateral trade negotiations. The Reagan administration sought to ensure failure of the override by pursuing a series of tight new bilateral agreements with major textile countries, bargaining "aggressively" in the MFA, and in general taking a more protective stance on a number of trade issues (in a process that may be called "preemptive protection" designed to forestall major restrictive measures by administratively adopting less extreme restraints).

The policy debate preceding the override vote included emphasis on the risk of trade retaliation. The Council of Economic Advisers warned that foreign retaliation could occur against some $50 billion in US exports and that the net effect could be a loss of jobs.[6] The debate also stressed the cost of additional protection. The administration estimated that the 1985 bill would cost American consumers $14 billion annually and the amended version $44 billion over five years.[7] The costs of the bill are examined below.

By the time of the override vote in the House, MFA negotiations had resulted in renewal with more complete coverage, and important bilateral agreements were in place. Nonetheless, the override nearly succeeded. The vote in the House was 276 to 149, even higher than in initial passage and only eight votes short of the necessary two-thirds majority.[8]

Economic Effects of the 1985 Textile Bill

In 1985 opposing sides of the textile bill cited two contradictory studies to support their respective cases. Advocates pointed to calculations by Data Resources, Inc. (DRI), for Burlington Industries that indicated the bill would save 947,000 textile and apparel jobs that otherwise would be lost to imports by 1990, with 1.89 million jobs saved for the economy as a whole.[9] In contrast, opponents cited a study by the International Business and Economic Research Corporation (IBERC) that concluded the bill would save only 71,000 production jobs in textiles and apparel, but would actually reduce employment in retailing by 62,000 jobs and would cost the consumer $3.3 billion in the first year and $11 billion over five years.[10]

---

6. *New York Times*, 6 August 1986.

7. *Journal of Commerce*, 25 June 1985; *Wall Street Journal*, 7 August 1986.

8. *Wall Street Journal*, 7 August 1986.

9. American Textile Manufacturers Institute, Inc., "Textile and Apparel Imports: A National Concern" (Washington, January 1986; processed), p. 3.

10. *IBERC Study*, table C–2.

In its accustomed arbitrational role, the Congressional Budget Office (CBO) examined the two studies.[11] The CBO authors were unable to obtain a copy of the DRI report itself, but examined the consistency of its results as reported by textile groups. They noted that, apparently at the recommendation of those commissioning the study, DRI made the strong assumption that imports would grow at 15 percent annually through 1990. The CBO authors judged growth this high to be improbable and analyzed why rapid growth in 1981–84 was unlikely to continue. (In the protection case, DRI assumed instead that imports would maintain a constant share of the apparel market.) The CBO review also noted that the DRI results implied that domestic consumption would fall by 5 percent over the period; that domestic output would decline during the period; and that the reduction of domestic output would exceed the rise in imports, an outcome considered "implausible."[12]

The CBO analysis then examined the IBERC report, following its underlying methodology but considering the sensitivity of its results to the elasticities and other parameters assumed. The basic implication of this analysis was that the broad range of the IBERC results was appropriate, although the CBO authors questioned inclusion of retail employment effects without symmetrical employment effects in retailing and other secondary activities under the protection scenario.

Both the CBO and IBERC applied a conservative methodology to estimate consumer costs. As in most studies, they used value bases at the wholesale and f.o.b. import level, rather than the larger consumer-retail level. The IBERC study omitted costs associated with higher prices of domestic goods, implicitly assuming that domestic supply was infinitely elastic.

Table 9.1 summarizes alternative estimates of the consumer costs and employment effects of the 1985 bill for Textile and Apparel Trade Enforcement. As may be seen, both the CBO and IBERC provided estimates of the consumer costs of the proposed legislation that were lower than those of the administration: in the range of $3 billion annually, as opposed to the $9 billion estimated by the administration for the amended bill ($44 billion over five years).[13]

The model developed in appendix B and applied in chapter 8 to estimate

---

11. Daniel P. Kaplan and Peter Siegelman, "Protecting the Textile and Apparel Industries," (Congressional Budget Office, Staff Working Paper, Washington, September 1985); hereafter referred to as *CBO Report.* That a neutral opinion was necessary was apparent in such statements as that of Representative Jenkins, who dismissed IBERC as "a registered foreign agent and lobbyist for at least 14 foreign governments." *Washington Post,* 31 August 1985.

12. Kaplan and Siegelman, *CBO Report,* p. 16.

13. *Wall Street Journal,* 7 August 1986.

Table 9.1 Alternative estimates of effects of the 1985 Textile and Apparel Trade Enforcement Bill

		DRI[a]	IBERC[b]	Congressional Budget Office[b] Favor-able	Unfavor-able	Adminis-tration[b]	This study[c]
Consumer costs	T	n.a.	950	341	1,115	n.a.	2,031
(million dollars)	A	n.a.	2,386	699	2,121	n.a.	3,943
	T, A	n.a.	3,336	1,040	3,235	9,000[d]	5,974
Jobs created							
Production	T	n.a.	35,272	34,638	27,861	n.a.	16,528
	A	n.a.	36,141	58,898	22,838	n.a.	52,371
	T, A	947,000	71,413	93,536	50,699	n.a.	68,899
Retailing	T	n.a.	−3,577	n.a.	n.a.	n.a.	n.a.
	A	n.a.	−57,931	n.a.	n.a.	n.a.	n.a.
	T, A	n.a.	−61,508	n.a.	n.a.	n.a.	n.a.
Economy-wide	T	n.a.	n.a.	n.a.	n.a.	n.a.	42,642[e]
	A	n.a.	n.a.	n.a.	n.a.	n.a.	93,220[e]
	T, A	1,890,000	n.a.	n.a.	n.a.	n.a.	135,862[e]
Change in import							
volume	T	n.a.	−36.0	−36.0	−36.0	n.a.	−18.2
(percentage)	A	n.a.	−20.0	−20.0	−20.0	n.a.	−9.2
	T, A	−45[f]	n.a.	n.a.	n.a.	n.a.	n.a.
Change in domestic							
output	T	n.a.	4.7	4.6	3.7	n.a.	2.5
(percentage)	A	n.a.	3.0	4.9	1.9	n.a.	4.6
	T, A	n.a.	n.a.	n.a.	n.a.	n.a.	n.a
Change in import							
price	T	n.a	33.0	15.0	49.0	n.a.	20.9
(percentage)	A	n.a.	16.1	5.3	16.1	n.a.	9.5
	T, A	n.a.	n.a.	n.a.	n.a.	n.a	n.a.
Change in domestic							
price	T	n.a.	0	0.45	7.5	n.a.	2.5
(percentage)	A	n.a.	0	0.48	3.8	n.a.	4.6
	T, A	n.a.	0	n.a.	n.a.	n.a.	n.a.

n.a. not applicable; T textiles; A apparel; T, A combined.
Source: See text.
a. By 1990.
b. First year, original bill.
c. First year, revised bill.
d. Total over five years is $44 billion; amended bill.
e. Direct and indirect jobs.
f. 15 percent growth versus growth at rate of domestic consumption, assumed here to be 2.5 percent annually.

the costs of current protection is reformulated in appendix C to permit examination of proposals for additional import restrictions. Essentially, a postulated decrease in imports is translated into an increase in import price required to achieve the cutback. This import price increase, and the corresponding induced price increase for the domestic substitute, are applied to evaluate consumer and efficiency costs of the new protection proposed.

The model set forth in appendix C is applied here to the protective measures called for by the 1985 bill. The estimates here refer to the final version of the bill, which limited the rollbacks to Hong Kong, Taiwan, and Korea. Based on IBERC's detailed country estimates for the cutbacks originally specified for 12 major suppliers, the modified bill would have cut total textile imports by 18.2 percent and apparel imports by 9.2 percent in the first year. The model of appendix C indicates that cuts of this magnitude would involve import price increases of 20.9 percent for textiles and 9.5 percent for apparel, and price increases of the corresponding domestic goods by 2.5 percent and 4.6 percent, respectively. The resulting estimates indicate total annual consumer cost of $5.97 billion, against employment creation of 68,899 direct jobs and 135,862 total (direct and indirect) jobs—a consumer cost of $43,945 per total job created. These estimates refer to the costs of the first-year rollback only. In addition, there would be further costs associated with the restrictions on future import growth. Moreover, because the value base for the estimates is at the wholesale level, the calculations may understate consumer costs by assuming that retailers do not apply their marketing margins to their cost increments caused by the new protection (as discussed in chapter 8).

In sum, the 1985 bill (as amended) would have raised annual consumer costs from textile and apparel protection by nearly one-third above the existing level of approximately $20 billion annually. Like current protection, it would have been extremely costly to consumers for each job generated. Moreover, it would appear that even the IBERC and CBO cost estimates were conservative and that those introduced into the debate by the Reagan administration more closely captured the true magnitude of the consumer costs involved.

New Bilateral Agreements and Industry Complaints

The Reagan administration concluded key bilateral agreements on the eve of the MFA renewal. While this sequence may have been necessary to avoid a successful veto override, it tended to highlight that to a considerable degree the MFA is an empty shell that somewhat superfluously enwraps the real substance of textile and apparel protection, the bilateral agreements.

Conclusion of the important bilaterals before renewal of the MFA meant in practice that the terms of the new MFA tended to follow those of the bilaterals rather than vice versa as originally envisioned under the conception of the MFA as a moderating influence on concrete restrictions.

The new bilateral agreements of 1986 gave the textile and apparel interests a considerable portion of what they sought under the Enforcement Act. Although it did not roll back imports from the three largest suppliers, it did constrain the future growth of their quotas to the minimalist range of 1 percent annually or less, as sought in the bill for the "producing countries" with sizable market shares. Moreover, the new agreements extended product coverage to ramie and other previously uncovered vegetable fibers.

In early July 1986 the US government concluded a bilateral agreement with Hong Kong. The agreement incorporated silk, linen, and ramie, and it constrained future growth of quotas to 1 percent annually. In mid-July Taiwan accepted a new bilateral agreement that cut back imports by 7 percent from the level reached in the period May 1985 to May 1986, imposed a limit of 0.5 percent annual growth for the future, and extended coverage to nearly all materials including silk blends, linen, and ramie. And in early August the administration concluded a bilateral agreement with Korea that limited its shipments to 0.8 percent annual growth over the next four years and extended coverage to silk blends, linen, and ramie.[14] In practice these bilaterals meant that imports from the three largest suppliers, which accounted for 42.7 percent of the total value of imports of textiles and apparel, would be virtually frozen over the medium term. This freeze would follow a rapid increase in volume terms by a combined total of 28.9 percent in apparel and 135.5 percent in textiles from 1981 to 1985.[15]

The Reagan administration also appears to have tightened the implementation of bilateral restraints. The 108 US product categories under the MFA are divided into three broad groups: textiles, apparel, and woolen textiles and apparel. Before MFA-III, the United States had tended to maintain specific ceilings at three levels: aggregate, group, and individual product. During MFA-III, US authorities tended to move away from aggregate and even group ceilings.[16] Individual products not under specific restraints were

---

14. *Wall Street Journal*, 4 and 5 August 1986; *Journal of Commerce*, 18 July 1986; and *Washington Post*, 15 July 1986.

15. Calculated from US Department of Commerce, International Trade Administration *Major Shippers of Cotton, Wool, and Man-made Fiber Textiles and Apparel* (Washington: Department of Commerce, various issues). Note that these increases refer only to products already covered by the MFA in 1981–85, and thus exclude categories of rapid growth such as ramie.

16. General Agreement on Tariffs and Trade, *Textiles and Clothing in the World Economy* (Geneva: GATT, July 1984), p. 101.

subject to consultation procedures. In December 1983 the United States set indicative triggers for consultations (chapter 6). By 1986 the administration was in addition reimposing the three-tiered restraint levels,[17] and (as noted in chapter 8) had largely replaced consultation categories with specific restraints for major suppliers.

The overall result of the new bilaterals and administrative procedures was that by mid-1986 the wire-mesh screen was drawing tighter. It seemed increasingly unlikely that imports from the major suppliers would in the future be able to grow much more rapidly than the notional overall quota growth rate, as they had in the early 1980s—primarily because few categories remained with consultative provisions rather than outright quotas. Moreover, quota growth itself in the new bilaterals was now under 1 percent annual growth for the major suppliers, far from the 6 percent originally envisioned under the MFA.

Despite the distinct tightening of the protective apparatus, representatives of the US textile and apparel industries attacked the measures as inadequate. Although they conceded that the new bilateral agreements with Hong Kong, Taiwan, and Korea were more restrictive than in the past, they maintained that imports should have been reduced rather than frozen because growth since 1982 had been so large and "disruptive." They also feared that other supplier countries would achieve more liberal bilateral agreements.[18]

Leaders of the textile and apparel industries have long sought legitimation of the idea that the share of imports in the domestic market should be limited to a policy-based ceiling. At the same time, they have called for cutbacks of imports from the major suppliers so that more liberal growth would be possible for smaller and poorer countries.[19] The 1985 bill incorporated these goals, although with an ambitious objective of setting the import market share well below its existing level.

Industry spokesmen have had grievances about the import-restraining mechanisms. They have complained that, for some countries, a unanimous decision of the interagency Committee on the Implementation of Textile Agreements (CITA) is required to impose restraints. CITA includes representatives from the Departments of Commerce, Treasury, State, and Labor, and the US Trade Representative's Office; and industry representatives view the State Department in particular as an obstacle to adoption of restraints.[20] However, a recent study by the General Accounting Office found that the CITA process was generally adequate and indeed was weighted toward

---

17. Based on discussion with government trade experts.

18. *Journal of Commerce,* 8 August 1986; *Washington Post,* 15 July 1986.

19. Edward B. Rappaport, "Textile Imports," p. 8.

20. Jim Berger, "US Textiles and Apparel," p. 7.

protecting the domestic industry; the report recommended that more support be required for statements of market disruption.[21]

The broad industry critique has been that the MFA and the US implementation of protection are riddled with loopholes that permit imports to rise. The most fundamental in the view of the industry spokesmen is that quotas are not set globally (that is, with a single worldwide total permissible in a particular category from all countries covered under the MFA). As a result, imports can rise from countries that do not face specific quotas on a particular item. Other loopholes have included ramie and other vegetable fibers not covered under MFA I through III. Fraud is another class of loophole. Industry representatives have complained that US monitoring agencies have not enforced the MFA aggressively.[22] In the case of Japan, there has been a controversy over transshipment; US negotiators have charged that in 1985, 86 million square yards of fabric were shipped under the Japanese quotas but produced elsewhere (presumably in Hong Kong, Taiwan, and Korea).[23]

The MFA-IV Negotiations

Just as the Reagan administration sought to give the domestic industry half a loaf by virtually freezing, if not rolling back, imports from the three large Asian suppliers in the 1986 bilateral agreements, it pursued several of the industry's complaints in the MFA negotiations. However, it did so at a time of increasing restiveness on the part of the developing countries about the entire MFA mechanism.

Developing-Country Positions

Representatives of the developing countries had experienced a setback during the negotiations of the first renewal of the MFA in 1977, when they found their attempts to coordinate for a liberal outcome foundered in the face of a "massive attack" by the EC in particular.[24] A decade later they appear to have fared little better.

---

21. William Davidson, Charles Feigenoff, and Fariborz Ghadar, *International Competition in Textiles and Apparel: The US Experience* (Washington: National Chamber Foundation, 1986; processed), p. 37.

22. Ibid., p. 5.

23. *Journal of Commerce*, 6 November 1986.

24. United Nations Conference on Trade and Development (UNCTAD), Programme of Cooperation among Developing Countries, Exporters of Textiles and Clothing, *Manual for Textile Negotiators*, vol. 1 (Geneva: UNCTAD, 1983), p. 1.

Developing-country expectations in the negotiations began ambitiously. India in particular pressed for an immediate termination of the MFA so that trade in textiles and clothing would be governed by the rules of the General Agreement on Tariffs and Trade (GATT). Other low-income exporters, including Pakistan and Bangladesh, pursued the same position.[25] This position was more plausible than in the past because of the joint timing of the inauguration of a new round of multilateral trade negotiations and the expiration of the existing MFA. The developing countries could reasonably maintain that textile issues could be handled in the new multilateral trade negotiations (MTN); indeed, they could implicitly threaten to block a new MTN unless it did address textiles. Some observers noted that India, Brazil, and Pakistan appeared to be delaying conclusion of the MFA negotiations until the last moment before expiration in order to exert pressure on the United States and Europe.[26]

Other developing countries appeared less willing to jeopardize the status quo of the MFA. Many analysts note that the position of the big five Asian countries under the mechanism has been relatively comfortable; they have achieved a share of more than 50 percent in exports and their shares could decline under a more liberal regime in the face of growing competition from lower wage newcomers. The leading exporters also enjoy quota rents.[27] At the same time, some of the weaker exporters have appeared to favor the MFA because, paradoxically, they have seen it as an instrument that keeps the major Asian nations from obtaining an even larger share of the world market.[28] Fundamentally, however, the developing countries held few cards in the MFA negotiations because the realistic alternative to a renewal was not free trade but uncontrolled unilateral protection by the industrial countries.

US Position

The ultimate discipline on MFA protection is thus the desire of the leading industrial countries themselves to set limits on the degree of departure from GATT principles of open trade; as informed by each industrial country's recognition that it may have exports diverted to its own market if the rules are not worked out jointly with the others; and as moderated by some influence of domestic consumer costs, by financial and political interests in

---

25. *Journal of Commerce,* 18 July 1986.

26. *Financial Times,* 10 July 1986.

27. Edward B. Rappaport, "Textile Imports," p. 8

28. Gerard Curzon, José de la Torre, Juergan B. Donges, Alasdair I. MacBean, Jean Waelbroeck, and Martin Wolf, *MFA Forever?* (London: Trade Policy Research Centre, 1981), p. 35.

the health of developing economies, and by the seeming historical lesson that unbridled protection can be a prelude to global depression. In previous MFA negotiations, the principal industrial country *demandeur* had been the area then under the greatest pressure of rising imports—in 1972 the United States, and by 1976 the EC. The sharp rise in US imports in the early 1980s and more slack performance of those into the EC meant that this time the United States would be leading the industrial country demands in the negotiations.

To make certain, in his veto message President Reagan stated that he was "directing the Office of the United States Trade Representative to most aggressively renegotiate the MFA on terms no less favorable than present." The US position stressed the following modifications: all natural fibers would be incorporated under MFA coverage; new mechanisms should be provided to stop destabilizing surges of imports; import levels of the largest suppliers would be essentially frozen for some period to make room for growing imports from poorer countries for some period; and flexibility (through carry-over and other provisions) would be reduced in future bilateral agreements.[29]

EC Position

The EC position was more ambivalent. In mid-1985 EC authorities indicated that they favored renewal of the MFA but on terms that would provide for liberalization and an eventual phase-out.[30] At one stage the EC reportedly advocated growth limits of 1 percent per year for imports from the largest suppliers, a range of 4 percent to 7 percent for other classes of developing countries, and free entry for some 25 percent of categories in which quotas had gone largely unfilled. In addition, several Latin American and Near Eastern countries would have been freed from controls or given favored status.[31]

But as the dollar got weaker, protectionist concerns in Europe got stronger. By the second quarter of 1986 it was clear that after a period of relative prosperity, the textile and apparel industries in Europe were again under pressure. Exports to the United States were declining, and the falling dollar intensified import competition from Asian countries that remained tied to the dollar.[32] The EC negotiating position stiffened, and the window to liberalization and phase-out closed.

---

29. Edward B. Rappaport, "Textile Imports," p. 7; *Washington Times,* 1 July 1986.

30. *New York Times,* 23 July 1985.

31. Edward B. Rappaport, "Textile Imports," p. 8.

32. *Journal of Commerce,* 15 July 1986; *Financial Times,* 10 July 1986.

MFA-IV

On July 31, 1986 representatives of 54 countries agreed to renewal of the MFA through July 31, 1991. As in past renewals, the text of the Arrangement remained unchanged, while the important modifications were incorporated through the Protocol of extension and its reference to understandings in the Conclusions adopted by the Textiles Committee of the MFA.[33] The terms of the renewal provide for expanded coverage, antisurge provisions, antifraud measures, greater room for departures from the MFA's provisions for import growth, and for special treatment of imports in certain areas.

The agreement provided that MFA restraints could be extended to cover "textiles made of vegetable fibres, blends of vegetable fibres . . . , and blends containing silk. . . ."[34] Over strong opposition from China, ramie is now to be included under controlled fibers. Silk blends and linen are also now included. However, the language of the Conclusions stops short of declaring that all fibers of any type are subject to restraints, and (mainly to obtain Chinese cooperation) the negotiators left jute and abaca products out of the expanded coverage (although US Trade Representative Clayton K. Yeutter indicated that they would be dealt with through "administrative arrangements").[35] The Conclusions thus specifically exempt "textiles . . . traded in commercially significant quantities prior to 1982, such as bags, sacks, carpetbacking, . . . and carpets typically made from fibres such as jute, coir, sisal, abaca, maguey and henequen."[36]

The renewal provides that in an initial quota freezing the level of imports may be extended for a second year, beyond the one-year period previously provided for prior to expected quota growth (Conclusions, paragraph 8). In addition, for "consistently under-utilized quotas" consideration may be given to removal of the quota, to deal with "real difficulties . . . caused . . . by sharp and substantial increases as a result of significant differences between larger restraint levels . . . and actual imports. . . ." (Conclusions, paragraph 11).[37] These provisions address the US goal of tightening the MFA against import surges.

The renewal provides that where there is a "growing impact of a heavily utilized quota with a very large restraint level" for a supplier accounting for "a very large share of the market of the importing country," the restraint

---

33. GATT, "Extension of Multifibre Arrangement Agreed," Press Release, GATT/ 1390, Geneva, 5 August 1986.

34. Ibid., "Conclusions," paragraph 34.

35. *Journal of Commerce,* 4 August; *Wall Street Journal,* 4 August 1986.

36. *GATT Press Release,* paragraph 24, section iii.

37. Ibid.

may be set according to "any mutually acceptable arrangements"—that is, frozen or actually reduced (Conclusions, paragraph 9). This provision reflects the US goal of restraining the large suppliers more strictly to allow some room for import growth from other developing countries and gives MFA legitimization to the near-freeze imposed on Hong Kong and Korea (Taiwan is not a member of the MFA) in the 1986 bilateral agreements. The same paragraph reiterates that in exceptional cases of market disruption a "lower positive growth rate" may be agreed upon (than the general 6 percent norm of annex B of the original MFA), reaffirming the reasonable departures clause of MFA-II.[38] Thus, the tone of the renewal is one of ample scope for restricting imports at will, especially those from major suppliers. The original MFA target of 6 percent growth in import levels appears all but abandoned.

To deal with fraud, the renewal provides that participants will cooperate and exchange information and that where evidence exists on the true country of origin, the importing country may adjust the charges made against the quotas of the country in question.[39]

At best, only two provisions were oriented toward liberalization. One stipulated that, "Restraints shall not normally be imposed on exports from small suppliers, new entrants and least developed countries" and that where such restraints were necessary treatment should be "significantly more favourable than that accorded to the other groups. . . ." (Conclusions, paragraph 13). This provision was in keeping with the US goal of providing space for lesser developed countries to increase exports. The other provided that "cotton textiles from cotton producing exporting countries should be given special consideration. . . ." (Conclusions, paragraph 13). This clause too would tend to favor nations such as Egypt and Brazil as opposed to the major Far Eastern suppliers.

In sum, the renewal incorporated practically all of the US objectives, most of which amounted to a tightening of the Arrangement. Despite the protective drift of MFA-IV, representatives of the US textiles and apparel industries sharply criticized the new agreement and called for Congress to override the President's veto of the Enforcement Act. They maintained that the renewal would not control import surges and that it left loopholes for rapid growth in other fibers.[40] At the same time, representatives of developing countries criticized the renewal. Spokesmen for China and India in particular opposed its expansion of coverage and charged that this renewal was the most restrictive yet.[41]

---

38. Ibid.

39. Ibid., "Conclusions" paragraph 16.

40. *Journal of Commerce*, 4 August 1986.

41. Ibid., and *Washington Post*, 2 August 1986.

The Multilateral Trade Negotiations

In September 1986 ministers from member nations of the GATT met at Punta del Este, Uruguay, to launch a new round of multilateral trade negotiations. The link between the new MTN and the negotiations for renewal of the MFA was both substantive and tactical. The central substantive issue was, and remains, the extent to which serious negotiations on liberalization of textile and apparel trade would occur in the forthcoming MTN. Tactically, US negotiators faced a delicate balancing act in the discussions of the two respective negotiations in the second and third quarters of 1986. They needed to convince representatives of developing countries that a new MTN would be of sufficient interest to them in key areas including textiles to make their participation worthwhile, rather than focusing exclusively on some of the new areas that the United States had stressed such as trade in services. At the same time, US negotiators could not appear to promise to place too much in the textile field on the negotiating table in the MTN without risking heightened fears among domestic producers and a greater threat that the veto override on the Enforcement Act would pass.

The potential impacts ran in both directions because there was good reason to believe that a successful override would cause the collapse of the MFA. In turn, it was widely believed that failure to renew the MFA would rule out a new round of multilateral trade negotiations.

By late 1986 the tactical hurdles had been overcome; MFA-IV was in place and so was the Uruguay Round. The ministers inaugurating the MTN at least paid lip service to inclusion of textiles in the negotiations. Thus, their declaration stated that the MTN would "aim to formulate modalities that would permit the eventual integration of this sector into GATT on the basis of strengthened GATT rules and disciplines."[42]

Two central challenges would appear to dominate the task of integrating the MFA into the GATT. On the side of the industrial countries, it would be necessary to reach an arrangement that could bridge the gap between the MFA and the provisions of GATT's Article XIX safeguard clause. The MFA by its structure discriminates among supplier countries, most notably between industrial countries, which enjoy free access, and developing countries (and Japan), which face controls. In contrast, GATT's Article XIX calls for nondiscriminatory, most-favored-nation treatment in any temporary protection necessitated by injury from imports. Moreover, Article XIX provides that the protecting country should compensate the restrained

---

42. GATT, "Ministerial Declaration on the Uruguay Round," *GATT Focus,* no. 41 (October 1986).

countries in the form of additional trade concessions, whereas the MFA involves no compensation by industrial countries.

On the side of the developing countries, the crucial change that seems necessary to make the MTN a meaningful forum for textile and apparel negotiations would be a willingness to offer liberalization of their own protection in the sectors. In the past, the principal tendency of the GATT has been toward special and differential treatment of developing countries, under the general presumption that because their external sectors are weak, they not only cannot afford to offer reciprocal liberalization but they also need not do so to ensure effective reciprocity—because they automatically re-spend abroad the foreign exchange they manage to earn. The most concrete expression of this orientation was in the development of the Generalized System of Preferences in the 1970s, which gave tariff-free entry to imports from developing countries (although under seriously circumscribed terms with respect to products and amounts).

The attitude of preferential, nonreciprocal treatment of exports from developing countries remains deeply embedded among their representatives in GATT and other international fora. Thus, in 1983 a group of developing countries engaged in textile negotiations, sponsored by the United Nations Conference on Trade and Development, could declare: "developing countries should bear in mind that the alleged gain of assured access to markets, and assured growth in exports, are in no sense additional benefits for which they have to give anything in return. If GATT has any meaning, access to markets is an assured right for all Contracting Parties. . . . [Developed countries] have been, and will most likely be again, making the allusion that guaranteed access to their markets should be conditional upon improved conditions [of access] to the markets of developing countries which possess competitive textile industries."[43]

The hard fact remains that the principal areas of successful liberalization in the postwar rounds of trade negotiations have been those in which both sides were prepared to make reciprocal concessions. One of the reasons liberalization has proceeded more slowly for imports from developing countries is that these countries have tended not to offer liberalization in return. For at least the last decade, however, policy circles in industrial countries have increasingly pressed for "graduation" of the more successful newly industrializing countries (NICs) to more symmetrical trade treatment. Although the international debt crisis of the early 1980s temporarily set back this trend, it is one that seems likely to persist and resurface, especially with respect to countries that are demonstrating impressive export success.

In short, the second broad prerequisite for meaningful negotiations on textiles and apparel in the MTN would appear to be a new openness of the

---

43. UNCTAD, *Manual for Textile Negotiators,* p. 16.

Table 9.2 Percentage of BTN 4-digit import categories subject to nontariff barriers in developing countries[a]

	Type of Restraint	Fibers and yarns (44)[b]	Fabrics (19)[b]	Made up (25)[b]	Apparel (15)[b]
Argentina	L	9	63	64	100
Brazil	S	50	84	98	100
	LS	95	95	88	100
Colombia	L	100	100	100	100
Hong Kong	—	0	0	0	0
India	L	19	0	0	0
	P	24	47	52	100
Korea	R	11	18	12	40
Macao	—	0	0	0	0
Mexico	L	25	31	52	63
Nigeria	L	25	0	12	13
	P	0	97	52	43
Pakistan	L	89	24	38	7
	P	11	76	62	93
Peru	P	9	0	0	0
Philippines	LS	0	71	0	0
	R	7	0	24	93
Singapore	—	0	0	0	0
Sri Lanka	L	11	74	0	7
Thailand	L	5	5	2	0
Tunisia	L	50	11	20	0
	Q	2	24	4	80
	P	48	37	76	20

— no restraint applies.

L license; LS license suspended; S surcharge; P prohibition, R restriction (type unknown), Q quota.

Source: GATT, *Textiles and Clothing in the World Economy* (Geneva: GATT, 1984), p. 128.

a. Percentages based on weighting category as half when only partially covered.

b. Number of categories in parentheses.

principal developing-country suppliers to the negotiation of liberalization in their own protection, either in the textile and apparel sectors themselves or elsewhere. Textile and apparel protection is substantial for many of them. Table 9.2 reports estimates by GATT of the coverage of textile and apparel trade categories by nontariff barriers in the developing countries. As may be seen, protection in the sectors tends to be generalized, although for some countries the restrictions are less severe for intermediate textile inputs than for final textile and apparel products. In addition, tariffs on these imports are typically high in developing countries. Thus, in the early 1980s average tariff levels in textiles and apparel were in the range of 25–50 percent for Tunisia, Korea, Mexico, Argentina, and the Philippines (in ascending order by tariff rate); 50–75 percent for Thailand, Peru, Nigeria, Taiwan, Sri Lanka, and Colombia; 75–100 percent for Morocco, Brazil, India, and Egypt; and 125 percent for Pakistan.[44]

There are important exceptions to the pattern of high protection in textiles and apparel among developing countries. Hong Kong appears to have virtually free trade in these sectors as well as others. As indicated in table 9.2, restrictions are largely absent in Singapore as well, and nontariff restraints appear to be relatively limited in Thailand. For most supplying countries, however, there is considerable protection to place on the bargaining table.

Bargains within the MTN probably would not need to be strictly reciprocal to suffice for some movement toward liberalization by the industrial countries. The timing of liberalization in particular could be slower for the developing countries. Liberalization of developing-country textile markets presumably would be of more interest to the industrial countries than liberalization in apparel, where the developing countries tend to have natural comparative advantage, so reciprocal liberalization might begin in the textiles sector.

If the MTN seriously negotiates textiles and apparel, it will of course be necessary for the industrial countries to offer liberalization as well. It is by no means clear that any meaningful offers would be forthcoming. Thus, Hong Kong has not in the past enjoyed open access to industrial country markets just because its own textile and apparel protection is minimal.

The possibilities for textile and apparel negotiation within the Uruguay Round are explored further in chapter 11. The central risk, however, is that all parties in the MTN will turn a blind eye to the sector on grounds that it is already covered by MFA-IV. That approach is perhaps the most likely course at present and the least likely to halt the seemingly inexorable trend toward tighter protection in the sector over the past quarter-century.

The Textile and Apparel Trade Bill of 1987

In early 1987 members of Congress from South Carolina proposed the Textile and Apparel Trade Act of 1987 (HR 1154). The bill provided for comprehensive global quotas on imports of textiles, apparel, and footwear, based on actual 1986 volumes. The level of quotas would be constrained to

---

44. GATT, *Textiles and Clothing*, p. 122.

grow at only 1 percent annually in textiles and apparel, with the footwear quota frozen at the 1986 level.[45]

The sponsors of the bill considered it to be a compromise in that the proposal no longer called for an actual rollback but instead accepted as a base the 1986 import level. The new bill adopted a fundamental change by subjecting all sources of imports in the restrictions, including Canada and Europe, a sharp departure from past practice under the MFA in which only imports from developing countries and Japan have been restricted. The shift to a demand for global import quotas reflected the industry's desire to close off the process of geographical diversification to new suppliers. The inclusion of industrial country suppliers indicated not only a concern about import growth from these countries (which account for only about 10 percent of apparel imports but approximately half in textiles) but also a desire to neutralize charges in the previous year's legislative effort that the new protection would be discriminatory against developing countries.[46]

The 1987 bill also sought to deal with the risk of retaliation by providing that suppliers would be provided compensation for the new protection in the form of reductions in the tariff levels applicable to textiles and apparel. Moreover, the advocates of the bill maintained that it could be harmonized with the Multi-Fiber Arrangement because the new legislation would permit the administration to implement existing bilateral agreements and negotiate new ones, subject to the global ceiling.

Opponents of the proposed legislation contended that it was even more restrictive than the 1985 bill because of its more comprehensive nature, that it would cause a collapse of the MFA and of existing bilateral agreements, and that it would bring retaliation. The EC Commissioner for external trade declared that, if adopted, the bill would precipitate certain retaliation by Europe and would induce new restrictions on textile imports into Europe to avoid diversion of trade to its market.[47]

The move to a global quota would radically alter textile and apparel protection. It would eliminate the existing flexibility for total volume increase in the import regime that remains in the form of geographical diversification to uncontrolled countries. It would shift the locus of protection from export restraints to direct import quotas. One crucial decision would be whether to retain earmarked quotas within the total for individual countries at previously negotiated levels, or whether instead to allow all countries to compete for the fixed total. Another would be whether to allocate the import

---

45. *Journal of Commerce,* 4 March 1987.

46. Thus, in testimony the President of the American Textile Manufacturers Institute stressed that the bill did not discriminate among nations. Ibid., p. 6A.

47. *Journal of Commerce,* 5 March 1987; *Financial Times,* 12 March 1987.

quotas on a historical basis to past importers, or instead to auction the quotas (an alternative that could be attractive to legislators as a source of revenue but would be resisted by importers as disruptive to their normal supplier relations). The bill was unspecific on these issues, with the intent that they would be resolved by the administration.

The central issue, however, is whether still tighter import restrictions should be imposed on top of the already highly protective regime for textile and apparel imports. The supporters of the limit of 1 percent growth for imports presented this level as the rate at which the domestic market is growing, and by implication a rate permitting foreign suppliers to retain at least a constant share in the US market in the future. On this basis, the issue would be whether the import share of the market should be frozen at its current level, and at what cost to US consumers and efficiency of US resource allocation.

A limit of 1 percent growth would probably imply a declining share of imports in the US market, however. As indicated in chapters 2 and 10, real consumption of textiles and apparel may be expected to grow at approximately 2 percent annually. Of this amount, 1 percent annual growth occurs merely from expansion of the population. With per capita income rising at some 2 percent annually, and with an income elasticity of demand of 0.5, another 1 percent annual growth in consumption would arise from improving standards of living. As noted in chapters 2 and 10, on some measures past real consumption growth has been significantly higher. The proposed bill would thus imply a gradual reduction in the share of imports in the US market.

One of the more subtle difficulties with the proposed legislation is its likely adverse effect on US exports of textiles and apparel. As analyzed in chapter 3, US textile exports were prospering in the late 1970s, and could be expected to do so again in the late 1980s following the sharp decline of the dollar from its overvalued levels of the early 1980s. But textile exporters would have to expect foreign markets, particularly those in Europe, to close as the result of foreign retaliation against the new US global quota.

The projections of chapter 10 provide a benchmark against which to compare the restrictiveness of a 1 percent limit on annual growth of imports. In that chapter, the trade model developed in chapter 3 is applied to expected future levels of population, income, and real exchange rates to project imports, exports, and domestic production. The projections include a base case of no policy change as well as cases of import liberalization and tighter protection.

As may be seen in table 10.1, in textiles the favorable effect of the dollar's recent decline should be sufficiently powerful that real imports should actually decline over the medium term, rather than increasing further, in the present-policy case. On this basis, a limit of 1 percent annual growth in imports of textiles would appear to have little bite in practice for the next few years. However, as may also be seen in table 10.1, US exports of textiles should expand briskly in response to the correction of the dollar, approximately doubling by 1990. As noted above, any such expansion would have to be ruled out under a new regime of global quotas because of prospective foreign retaliation. Under the present-policy projections of table 10.1, the real trade balance at 1982 prices is expected to shift from a deficit of $2.6 billion in 1986 to a surplus of $197 million by 1995. If instead US exports of textiles are constrained to growth of only 1 percent annually from their 1986 level by foreign retaliation, the trade balance in 1995 would be a deficit of $2.4 billion. In textiles, then, the proposed global quota could be a case of the industry shooting itself in the foot.

In contrast, in apparel the proposed quota would promptly limit imports. Initially the cutback from levels that otherwise would be reached would be modest because for a period of two or three years there should be a pause in import growth as the effects of dollar correction work through to actual trade flows. However, after this adjustment the trend growth rate of apparel imports is estimated at 7 percent annually in real terms (chapter 10). As a result, it would require new price increases each year to suppress import growth to only 1 percent. The cumulative effect of the price increases would be an ever-increasing burden of consumer costs to support the new protective regime.

Table 9.3 sets forth the cost estimates for new apparel protection under the proposed 1987 bill, as obtained from the model of appendix C. The current-policy projections of apparel imports through the year 2000 (chapter 10) are taken as the baseline. Comparison with a corresponding time path of imports under the restriction of 1 percent annual real growth yields the estimates in the table for the percentage reduction in real imports required each year. Thus, in 1995 the proposed bill would cut apparel imports by 25.1 percent from the level they would be expected to reach under current policy as projected in chapter 10.

The price increase (from the baseline price) required to achieve this cutback for each year, and the corresponding induced price increase for domestically produced apparel, are shown in the table. The resulting annual consumer costs, net welfare costs to the economy, direct jobs created, and consumer cost per total employment created (including indirect) also appear in the table. These estimates place the annual consumer cost of the proposed legislation at an average of $1.3 billion in 1987–89, $2.3 billion in 1990–91, and a rapid acceleration thereafter to $5.6 billion in 1992, $8.8 billion in 1993, $12.3 billion in 1994, $16 billion by 1995, and $20 billion by 1996 (all at 1986 prices). The average consumer cost of the bill during the full decade before it would be reviewed would be $7.1 billion annually in 1986 prices.

Table 9.3 Costs of the proposed Textile and Apparel Trade Act of 1987: apparel (percentage, million dollars at 1986 prices, and thousand jobs)

Year	Percentage increase in price		Percentage in imports[a]	Costs (millions dollars)		Employ-ment effect[b]	Consumer cost per job created
	Imports	Domestic		Consumer	Economy		
1987	3.50	1.71	−3.56	1,637	995	19	48,403
1988	1.68	0.82	−1.74	799	480	9	49,825
1989	3.26	1.59	−3.33	1,564	944	18	48,814
1990	4.13	2.01	−4.18	2,004	1,214	22	51,175
1991	5.33	2.59	−5.34	2,615	1,591	28	52,468
1992	11.32	5.42	−10.70	5,593	3,499	59	53,257
1993	17.66	8.34	−15.78	8,801	5,661	89	55,555
1994	24.39	11.35	−20.57	12,259	8,110	119	57,875
1995	31.52	14.45	−25.11	15,996	10,887	149	60,312
1996	39.07	17.64	−29.40	20,037	14,030	179	62,887

Source: See text.
a. Change from baseline projections under present policy; see chapter 10.
b. Direct employment only.
c. Dollars per job at 1986 prices. Includes indirect employment.

The ascending pattern of these costs reflects two forces. First, any specific growth limit for imports placed below their expected trend growth rate will cause growing consumer costs because each year the suppressed level of imports will be further below the natural level imports otherwise would have reached, and the tariff-equivalent of protection (and thus its price-raising effect) will have to rise year after year. Second, in the particular case of 1987–89, the costs of the bill are lower than would otherwise be the case because of the running-in period for adjustment to a lower value of the dollar. In this period apparel imports would be growing relatively slowly even without the proposed new protection. Of course, a corresponding implication is that the initial output and employment gains are also small because of the relatively limited initial bite of the proposed new protection.

Because of these factors, it is probably accurate that, as advocates maintain, the initial consumer costs of the proposed 1987 bill are lower than would have been the case for the 1985 bill (approximately $1.3 billion annually, as opposed to the $6 billion estimated above for the earlier bill). However, within five years the costs of the more recent proposal would soon escalate to the same level as those of the 1985 bill (which, however, is less concrete in regard to future years because of its loophole allowing relatively high growth rates for imports from new suppliers and unrestrained imports from Europe and Canada); and within a decade, the consumer costs newly imposed under the proposed 1987 bill would nearly double the costs of the protective regime already in place.

It should be noted that the welfare costs to the economy (consumer costs and costs of inefficient production, net of transfers to government and producers) closely parallel these consumer costs. Thus, by the mid-1990s the welfare costs would reach two-thirds of consumer costs. In the case of new protection, there is an actual loss of tariff revenue (rather than merely a transfer from consumers to government when new protection is in the form of tariffs) because of the decline in imports from levels otherwise attained. It should also be stressed that the consumer costs per direct and indirect job created are not only high for the proposed new protection ($48,000 per direct and indirect job at the outset) but also rise rapidly over time. Moreover, as argued in chapter 8, the statement of consumer cost per job on a basis that credits protection with indirect as well as direct job effects gives a conservative estimate, considering that in the absence of the new protection the indirect jobs not generated by extra production in textiles and apparel would tend to arise in any event in response to expanding output in alternative sectors to which resources would be rechanneled.

Two alternative estimates of the impact of the 1987 bill have received considerable attention. The first, prepared by the International Business and Economic Research Corporation (IBERC) for the Retail Industry Trade Action Coalition (RITAC), estimates that the bill would cost US consumers $8.1 billion annually in textiles and apparel and another $2.3 billion annually from footwear restrictions. IBERC estimates that costs per job protected would reach $262,000 in textiles and apparel. The second, prepared by ICF Incorporated for the Fiber, Fabric and Apparel Coalition for Trade, (FFACT) concluded in contrast that the bill would increase GNP by $1 billion in 1987 and $1.7 billion in 1988.[48]

The IBERC estimates of consumer costs in the first year are five times as large as estimated here. The difference is wholly accounted for by two factors. First, IBERC calculates that imports will grow so much in 1987 that it would require a 10 percent cutback to reduce them to 1 percent growth; the model applied here projects less import increase in 1987–88 and places the necessary cutback at 3.56 percent (table 9.3). With a smaller forced import reduction, the resulting price increase and consumer cost is smaller. Second, IBERC multiplies wholesale values by two to work at the retail level; the present study conservatively analyzes consumer costs at the

---

48. Laura Megna Baughman, "Analysis of the Impact of the Textile and Apparel Trade Act of 1987" (Washington: IBERC, March 1987; processed); ICF Incorporated, "Analysis of the Employment and Economic Welfare Effects of the Textile and Apparel Trade Act of 1987" (Washington: ICF, May 1987; processed). Also see Burt Solomon, "Our Facts, Their Facts," *National Journal*, 6 June 1987, pp. 1460–61.

wholesale level (as discussed in chapter 8 and appendix B). Over a longer horizon, however, the IBERC estimates are close to those here. IBERC calculates the same $8 billion annual cost over the next 10 years, whereas the analysis here captures the growing consumer cost caused by the ever-widening gap between the import level constrained to 1 percent annual growth and the base case growth of imports under current protection. That is, with a larger and larger gap to be suppressed by protection, the level of protection must rise progressively, and thus so does the price increment and the consumer cost. As noted, the average consumer cost of the 1987 bill is $7.1 billion annually on the basis of the models of this study. IBERC's annual cost of $8.1 billion is close to this estimate.

The ICF study examines only 1987 and 1988. It estimates that consumer costs in 1988 are $2.6 billion. However, it also calculates that the "real employment gain" is $3.3 billion, while producers receive a transfer of $1.7 billion. After taking account of changes in quota rents, the study concludes that the net national gain to the US economy would be $1.7 billion in 1988.

The principal methodological source of the net benefit is ICF's assumption that increased domestic employment in textiles and apparel (194,000 jobs by 1988) would create real economic value equal to $3.3 billion, comprised of $4.2 billion estimated earnings less $900 million "adjustment cost" calculated on the basis of the labor that would otherwise be employed in other activities. The "benefit" of jobs saved in the sectors amounts to $17,000 per job. But as discussed in chapter 8, the actual benefit of such measures is the value of temporary unemployment thereby avoided. This study estimates this benefit at approximately $4,000 per job, based on an average of approximately 13 weeks of unemployment during adjustment in textiles and 25 weeks in apparel. More importantly, the ICF study incorrectly compares a once-and-for-all labor adjustment cost with a recurring (and growing) consumer cost. If the ICF labor benefit is reduced by the proportion $4,000/$17,000 as suggested here, and then converted to a corresponding annual flow value so that appropriate comparison to annual flow concepts of consumer cost is possible, the annual employment benefit even using ICF's estimates would be only $98.8 million ($4.2 billion × [4,000/17,000] × 0.10). This benefit would fall far short of the consumer costs net of producer gains that ICF itself estimates for 1988 ($1.6 billion). It should be added that the ICF estimate of 194,000 jobs created by 1988 would appear to be a serious exaggeration (see table 9.3). Thus, of the two widely publicized studies of the impact of the 1987 bill, that by IBERC would appear much closer to reality than that by ICF.

In sum, the new protection proposed in early 1987 potentially would be extremely costly, even though in the first two or three years its costs (and its sectoral job creation) would be moderated by the pause in import growth to be expected in any event from correction of the overvalued dollar.

10

Long-Term Prospects for Trade and Adjustment

The central trade policy question for textiles and apparel is whether to retain, reduce, or increase the protection against imports that these sectors currently receive. The answer to this question depends on the prospects for the health of these industries, as well as prospective costs to the rest of the nation from alternative protection policies.

A Projection Model

The model developed in appendix A and applied in chapter 3 to explain textile and apparel trade in recent years may be used for projection of future trade, production, and employment in these sectors under alternative policy regimes. The resulting projections provide a basis for evaluating the prospective health of the industry, and the impact of differing policies toward foreign trade.

The basic model structure for the projections of this chapter, and the model parameters, are the same as those set forth in chapter 3 and appendix A, with minor changes. In long-term projections, assumptions about secular growth terms become extremely important. For textiles, in addition to the underlying influences of income growth and exchange rates, it is assumed that in the future US imports from developing countries rise at an annual rate of 1.5 percent annually, while imports from industrial countries decline at 2 percent. These are the same parameters found to give the best results in the simulation of actual experience from 1970 through 1986.

For apparel, the projections here apply a secular growth rate of 2 percent annually to imports from developing countries, slightly higher than the rate estimated for 1986 on the basis of the logistics curve discussed in chapter 3 and appendix A. Note that continued application of that curve to future projections would instead generate zero secular growth within a few years. For apparel imports from industrial countries, a secular growth rate of −3.5

percent annually is applied, the same rate as applied in the simulations for 1970 to 1986.

These assumptions on secular growth mean that the more massive growth rates of apparel imports from developing countries observed in the late 1960s and 1970s are not expected to continue because of the maturation phase of import development from these countries (the transition to the more gentle slope on the "S-shaped" logistics curve). Instead, price effects (through the exchange rate) and income effects (US growth) are expected to be more dominant.

Secular trends are also important for US exports. In textiles, the best fit for 1970–86 was obtained with a secular growth rate of 2 percent, a trend reflecting recovery of US competitiveness through technological change. The projections here retain this annual trend growth in US textile exports, in addition to expansion on the basis of exchange rate change and foreign income growth. In apparel, the best fit for the period 1967–86 was obtained allowing for secular growth in exports at a rate of 2.5 percent. This rate is also retained in the projections through the year 2000.

The secular trend in labor productivity is equally crucial in determining long-term trends in sectoral employment. The rate for apparel is set at 2 percent annually, the average actually experienced from 1961 to 1985 (chapter 4, table 4.1). This rate is lower than the pace during the second half of this period (2.75 percent in 1973–85); however, the most recent years show some deceleration (in 1985 and 1986 the rate averaged only 1.1 percent), and the annual average for the full period since 1960 appears to be a more realistic guide than the 1973–85 rate. In textiles, productivity growth is set at 3.7 percent annually, the rate experienced in 1973–85 (table 4.1). It is unlikely that the exceptionally high rate achieved earlier (4.88 percent in 1961–72) will return, considering that the 1960s were a period of initial mechanization and capital-intensive technical change from a relatively low base.

Underlying product prices for textiles and apparel in the United States and abroad are assumed to remain constant at their 1986 levels, thereby ending their long period of decline in real terms (chapter 2, table 2.7). US population is assumed to grow at 1.02 percent annually. Per capita income is projected to grow at 2 percent annually (giving total GNP growth of 3 percent annually). For the rest of the Organization for Economic Cooperation and Development (OECD), GNP is projected to grow at 2.7 percent annually, a relatively conservative estimate.

Consumption of apparel and textiles is projected to grow on a basis of an income elasticity of 0.5, so that total consumption grows by the rate of population growth plus one-half the rate of per capita income growth. As noted in chapter 2, if alternative Bureau of Labor Statistics data on real apparel consumption are used as the basis for evaluating past trends in consumption, the income elasticity could be much higher. Accordingly, the consumption projections here may be understated. If so, the projections of job losses (under all scenarios) are overstated, and actual adjustment difficulties could be more moderate than projected.

The projections assume that relative to the currencies of industrial countries, the dollar remains at its real level of January 1987. For textile imports from industrial countries, this level represents a real depreciation by 31 percent from its 1985 average; for apparel imports from these countries, the decline is 32 percent.

As indicated in chapter 3, it is more uncertain whether the dollar will depreciate in real terms relative to currencies of developing-country suppliers. In the base case it is assumed that two-thirds of the real appreciation of the dollar from 1980 to 1986 is reversed over a period of three years (1987–89) and that the real rate then holds constant, at a rate still 7 percent higher than in 1980. This assumption reflects the fact that the key newly industrializing countries (NIC) suppliers include Korea, Taiwan, and Hong Kong, countries in strong balance of payments positions. The presence of some much smaller suppliers with weaker external accounts (Philippines, Mexico) is the reason that the real exchange rate is not assumed to return all the way to its 1980 level. The effect of the scenario assumed is that the real value of the dollar relative to the currencies of developing-country suppliers declines by 11.2 percent from 1986 to 1989 for apparel and 18.6 percent for textiles.

The simulation model developed in chapter 3 and appendix A is applied with these parameters and assumptions to project trade, consumption, production, and employment from 1987 through the year 2000. The model is applied to actual 1986 values for the base year (rather than 1986 estimates from the 1970–86 simulations).

The projections include three alternatives for the trade policy regime. The first assumes no change in protection. The second is a gradual liberalization scenario. For textiles, in this projection the tariff-equivalent of nontariff barriers declines by 1.5 percentage points annually, reducing the level from 15 percent to zero over 10 years, while the tariff rate declines from 12 percent to 10 percent over the same period. For apparel, in the liberalization scenario the tariff-equivalent of nontariff barriers also declines 1.5 percentage points annually, falling from 25 percent to zero over 17 years, while the tariff declines from 24 percent to 15 percent over 10 years.

A third policy regime examines the impact of increased protection. In this case, tariffs are left unchanged in both textiles and apparel, but nontariff barriers are increased over a period of three years. The tariff-equivalent of apparel quotas rises from 25 percent to 45 percent, while that for textiles rises from 15 percent to 60 percent. As in the past, quotas are assumed to apply only to developing countries.

The particular values for higher quota protection broadly reflect the protection goals implicit in the textile protection bill (HR 1562) that passed both houses of Congress in 1985 and narrowly failed a veto-override vote in early August 1986. That bill in its original form would have reduced apparel imports by approximately 20 percent and textile imports by 36 percent.[1] The import cutbacks in the protection scenario here are roughly in these ranges. The smaller required increase in the tariff-equivalent of nontariff barriers for apparel than for textiles reflects the larger cutback in textile imports implicit in the recent legislative effort, and the higher share of imports from developing countries (which, unlike industrial country suppliers except for Japan, are subject to quotas): 86 percent for apparel versus 51 percent for textiles.

The following discussion sets forth the results obtained from application of the projection model to the textile and apparel sectors separately. The analysis incorporates the effects of interindustry interaction between the two and examines especially the concern that even though the textile sector might seem to have a sound future on its own, it would be adversely affected by weakness in the apparel sector, one of its principal markets.

Long-Term Prospects for Textiles

Table 10.1 reports the projections under the three policy regimes for textiles. All value data are in millions of dollars at constant 1982 prices and are thus comparable in real terms to the magnitudes estimated in the simulations of the period 1980–86 (chapter 3, tables 3.3 and 3.4) as well as the real value data presented for the period 1960–86 in chapter 2. Data for 1986 in the table refer to actual values.

The projections under present policy indicate a relatively favorable outlook for the textile sector. Domestic production grows by 4.3 percent in 1987, 3.7 percent in 1988, 2.4 percent in 1989, 2.1 percent in 1990–91, and an average of 1.7 percent annually thereafter. For the full 14 years, growth averages 2.1 percent, twice the average from the early 1970s to the present. Maintenance of GNP growth at 3 percent (2.7 percent for non-US OECD) is one reason for this improvement.

Reversal of trade erosion associated with dollar overvaluation is the other reason for improved growth. With the correction of the dollar, real textile

---

1. Daniel P. Kaplan and Peter Siegelman, "Protecting the Textile and Apparel Industries," (Congressional Budget Office, Staff Working Paper, Washington, September 1985), pp. 17–18; hereafter referred to as *CBO Report*). The CBO staff apparently accept these estimates of the reduced quantity of imports, originally prepared by International Business and Economic Research Corporation (IBERC).

Table 10.1 Projections of production, employment, and trade in textiles, 1987–2000 (million 1982 dollars and thousand workers)

Present policy	Production	Employment	Imports	Exports
1986	49,210	669	4,309	1,660
1987	51,308	683	4,117	2,527
1988	53,195	661	3,705	2,936
1989	54,485	653	3,546	3,116
1990	55,656	643	3,584	3,307
1995	60,935	587	4,256	4,453
2000	66,114	532	5,224	5,997
Liberalization case				
1987	51,308	683	4,117	2,527
1988	53,006	659	3,760	2,936
1989	54,089	648	3,655	3,116
1990	55,022	636	3,749	3,307
1995	58,554	564	4,804	4,453
2000	61,448	494	6,125	5,997
Protective case				
1987	51,308	683	4,117	2,527
1988	53,751	668	3,257	2,936
1989	55,492	665	2,792	3,116
1990	57,052	660	2,602	3,307
1995	62,993	607	3,034	4,453
2000	69,190	556	3,640	5,997

Source: See text.

exports rebound by 52 percent in 1987 and another 16 percent in 1988, while real imports decline 4.5 percent in 1987, 10 percent in 1988, and 4.3 percent in 1989 (base case). The later improvement in real imports reflects the fact that US exports are responding to an exchange rate determined by depreciation relative to industrial countries, while approximately half of imports come from developing countries, for which appreciation is delayed. The longer lag structure for imports than for exports also contributes to this difference. As the result of reversal of the dollar's appreciation of recent years, by 1990 the trade account for textiles stands at a virtual balance, and by 1993 and after the sector achieves a trade surplus.

In the base case of present policy, employment in textiles declines significantly. With average output growth of 2.1 percent over the next 15 years and average labor productivity growth of 3.7 percent, the sector's employment declines at an average rate of 1.6 percent annually. By the year 2000, employment declines by 137,000 jobs, or by 20.4 percent from its 1986 base. In contrast, in the previous 14-year period from 1972 to 1986, the sector lost 283,900 jobs, a decline of 29.8 percent.

In the second scenario, that of import liberalization, by the year 2000 both output and employment are only moderately lower (by 6 percent) than in the case of unchanged policy. Reduction of the combined tariff-equivalent of tariffs and quotas from 29 percent to 10 percent provides a reduction of import price by 15 percent (that is, $[.288 - .10]/1.288 = .146)$. With an import elasticity of 1.3, imports rise by approximately 20 percent. However, imports are small relative to output (8.8 percent in 1986) and the resulting impact on domestic output and employment from the direct effect of rising textile imports is correspondingly small. As discussed below, the bulk of the decline in domestic output under liberalization as opposed to the base case is attributable instead to the reduced demand for intermediate textile inputs into the apparel sector as domestic apparel production declines in the face of liberalization.

In the third scenario, that of heightened protection, production in the year 2000 stands only 4.7 percent higher than it would in the base case, and 11 percent higher than in the case of liberalization. The corresponding comparisons for employment are 4.6 percent and 11 percent. This limited gain in output and employment from rather massive new protection stems again from the small relative size of trade compared with output. Even the indirect effects through apparel production do not cause the difference for textiles between the protective and liberalizing scenarios to more than moderate.

In contrast, the proportionate impact of new protection on imports is substantial. In the protective case, by 2000, imports are 30.3 percent below their level in the base case, and 40.6 percent below their level in the liberalization case.

Two broad patterns emerge from the projections through the year 2000. First, textile output should grow satisfactorily, as the consequence of reasonable, steady growth in GNP and correction of the dollar. Production should increase by one-third from 1986 to 2000. However, because of high growth of labor productivity, textile employment should continue to decline at a rate of some 1.6 percent annually, a reduction of one-fifth in textile jobs by the end of the century (although the reduction is significantly smaller than in the preceding 14 years). Second, the performances of output and employment are relatively insensitive to the trade policy regime. Even sharply tighter quota protection would raise output and employment by less than 5 percent by the year 2000, while a phase-down of protection to levels broadly comparable to other sectors would reduce them only by 6 percent. This insensitivity reflects the limited role of imports in the sector, a pattern also reflected by the fact that the trade balance in textiles stands close to zero from the late 1980s until 2000 even under the liberalization scenario, and in the base and protective cases moves into significant surplus by the early 1990s. In the absence of the adverse effect on textile demand from reductions in apparel production under liberalization, the effects of trade policy for textile output and employment would be even smaller.

If the differences of the higher protection scenario from the forecast under present policy are limited for textile production and employment, the same cannot be said for consumer costs or export opportunities of foreign suppliers. As calculated in chapter 9, the additional consumer costs of even a program of new protection less severe than the scenario assumed here are massive ($6 billion annually for the milder 1986 version of the Textile and Apparel Trade Enforcement Act). As for supplier countries, the difference between the outcome under alternative policies is relatively large. Thus, for developing-country suppliers, by the year 2000 exports of textiles to the US market would be 43 percent lower in the protective case than in the case of present policy, and 54 percent lower than in the liberalization case.

Long-Term Prospects for Apparel

The projections for apparel are less favorable than those for textiles with respect to production and trade, but somewhat more favorable in terms of the pace of employment decline in the base case. At the same time, the apparel projections show more sensitivity to the trade policy regime.

Table 10.2 presents the projections for apparel. In the base case of present policy, production rises by 2 percent in 1987 and 2.5 percent in 1988, as the favorable effects of dollar depreciation take hold. Output growth then reaches a plateau at 1.4 percent annually in 1989–91, before falling to 0.6 percent in 1992. Beginning in 1993 the annual growth rate declines by 0.1 percentage point each year, and by the year 2000 output growth has declined to −0.4 percent annually. For the 14-year period as a whole, output grows at an average of 0.7 percent annually, somewhat below the 0.9 percent annual rate experienced in 1972–73 to 1985–86.

The forces determining this output performance are as follows. The pickup in output growth in 1987–88 and the avoidance of lower growth through 1991 is attributable to the improvement in external trade, as discussed below. Otherwise, output is driven by consumption and the long-term trend in trade. Over the long term, consumption grows at 2 percent annually, as the consequence of 1 percent population growth plus an income elasticity

Table 10.2 Projections of production, employment, and trade in apparel, 1987–2000 (million 1982 dollars and thousand workers)

Present policy	Production	Employment	Imports	Exports
1986	49,548	1,133	17,035	1,044
1987	50,545	1,113	17,841	1,520
1988	51,804	1,118	17,686	1,805
1989	52,509	1,111	18,155	1,950
1990	53,244	1,105	18,500	2,106
1995	55,014	1,034	24,879	3,100
2000	54,700	934	35,158	4,562
Liberalization case				
1987	50,545	1,113	17,841	1,520
1988	51,368	1,109	18,666	1,805
1989	51,578	1,091	20,209	1,950
1990	51,728	1,073	21,766	2,106
1995	49,170	937	36,003	3,100
2000	42,872	748	54,609	4,562
Protective case				
1987	50,545	1,113	17,841	1,520
1988	52,408	1,131	16,279	1,805
1989	53,725	1,137	15,420	1,950
1990	55,069	1,142	14,541	2,106
1995	58,151	1,093	19,496	3,100
2000	59,886	1,019	27,477	4,562

Source: See text.

of 0.5 applied to 2 percent annual growth in per capita income. Note that in 1988–90 consumption growth slows down to 1.3 percent annually, in the face of higher average price associated with the impact of dollar depreciation on the price of imports.

With consumption growing at 2 percent, the deviation of output growth from this rate depends on trade. Abstracting from the adjustment to dollar overvaluation, the trend in trade growth is as follows. The income elasticity of import demand is set at 1.7, causing import growth of 5.1 percent with income growth of 3 percent. In addition, secular growth in import supply from developing countries is set at 2 percent annually. After allowing for secularly declining imports of apparel from industrial countries, total import growth is 7.1 percent annually after initial adjustment to dollar correction.

With imports growing more rapidly than consumption, domestic output grows less rapidly. Eventually (by the late 1990s), the import share becomes sufficient so that output begins to decline in absolute terms as increased imports exceed increased consumption.

Trade performance in the base case does improve significantly in 1987–89 as the result of dollar correction. Exports rise by 46 percent in 1987 in quantity terms, followed by an increase of 19 percent in 1988. Thereafter exports grow at 8 percent annually. In imports, the correction is delayed by the dominant role of imports from developing countries and the later real appreciation of the currencies of these countries relative to the dollar, as well as the longer lag structure. Thus, real imports continue to rise in 1987 (by 4.7 percent), but decline by 0.9 percent in 1988 and rise by an average of only 2.2 percent annually in 1989–91 before resuming expansion at their long-term rate of 7.1 percent. The restraining effect of exchange rate correction on import growth in 1987–91 leaves real apparel imports by 1991 lower by 20.8 percent than the level they would have reached otherwise.

The projections on trade and production essentially show a pause in import growth in the near term, followed once again by a rising share of imports in demand. Thus, the trade deficit in apparel as a fraction of domestic consumption (on the basis of the concepts applied in table 10.2) dips from 24.4 percent in 1986 to 23.5 percent by 1988, but then climbs to 35.9 percent by 2000.

The employment projections in the base case indicate a similar pattern corresponding to that of output. The decline in apparel employment is temporarily arrested through 1989, but then resumes. The cumulative decline reaches 17.6 percent by 2000. After the phase of response to dollar correction, the growth rate for employment equals the long-term rate for output (approximately 1.4 percent declining to 0.3 percent by the mid-1990s and −0.5 percent by 2000) minus the rate of labor productivity growth (2 percent). Thus, in the 1990s employment is declining at approximately 1½ percent annually, with the rate of decline at 2.3 percent by the turn of the century.

The employment outlook under the base case must be judged as one of substantial but manageable contraction, and considerably less bleak than suggested by some of the more pessimistic impressions that have characterized the debate on trade policy. Thus, in 1985 the American Textile Manufacturers Institute (ATMI) reported that a study prepared by Data Resources, Inc. (DRI), for Burlington Industries concluded that 947,000 jobs could be lost in the textile and apparel industries by 1990, in addition to 943,000 jobs in other industries as an indirect effect.[2] The assumption

---

2. American Textile Manufacturers Institute, Inc., "Textile and Apparel Imports: A National Concern" (Washington: ATMI, January 1986), p. 3.

behind this estimate was that imports of apparel and textiles would continue growing at 15 percent annually.

It is clear from tables 10.1 and 10.2 that in the base case of no change in policy, employment in the textile and apparel industries is unlikely to decline by anywhere near this number of jobs, on the basis of the model developed here. Employment in the textile sector would decline by 26,000 jobs by 1990, while apparel employment would fall by 28,000, a combined reduction of 54,000 jobs or only 6 percent of the magnitude of the decline reported by the ATMI study. The model here sharply contradicts the notion that real imports of textiles and apparel will grow at 15 percent annually over this period. Instead, correction of an overvalued dollar is expected to cause an actual reduction in the real magnitude of imports by a total of 16.8 percent for textiles, while in apparel the exchange rate correction should limit import growth to a total of only 8.6 percent over the period 1986–90 (tables 10.1 and 10.2). In contrast, the DRI study assumes a total increase of imports by 100 percent over this period.[3] Indeed, even by the year 2000, the estimates of this study show a total decline of employment in textiles by only 137,000 jobs and in apparel by 199,000 jobs, only about one-third of the combined job loss of nearly 1 million jobs in the two sectors by as early as 1990 as projected in the DRI study.[4]

In the second scenario for apparel, the liberalization case, domestic output and employment are less favorable but by no means are they destroyed. The elimination of apparel quotas over 17 years and the reduction of apparel tariffs to an average of 15 percent (over 10 years) limits the cumulative growth of production to 5.5 percent up to its peak in 1991, after which output declines to 8 percent below its 1986 level by the year 2000. Because of ongoing increases in labor productivity, employment declines more and

---

3. It is unclear whether DRI forecasts 15 percent annual growth in textile and apparel imports, or whether the particular study cited by ATMI took this assumption as a point of departure at the suggestion of those commissioning the study. The DRI study is not publicly available, and was not made available to the CBO staff which sought to analyze its conclusions. CBO, *Protecting the Textile and Apparel Industries*, p. 2.

4. In mid-1987, public representations by textile and apparel labor and industry groups were referring frequently to a statement in a study on textile productivity by the Congressional Office of Technology Assessment that, "Unless policy action is taken in the next few years, there is reason to be concerned about the very existence of many parts of the industry." Similarly, the study states that "if penetration of the US apparel markets were to continue at the pace of the past decade (measured in terms of volume), domestic sales of US apparel firms would approach zero by the year 2000." US Congress, Office of Technology Assessment, *The US Textile and Apparel Industry: A Revolution in Progress* (Washington: OTA, April 1987), pp. 3–4. However, the OTA report is primarily an analysis of technology in the industry. It contains no formal economic model of the sectors, and does not make any quantitative projections to support the statements just noted. The director of the study has also objected to the use of the report in press releases by a textile group, FFACT, as "misleading." Burt Solomon, "Our Facts, Their Facts," *National Journal*, 6 June 1987, p. 1460.

by the year 2000 stands at 29.7 percent below its 1986 level. The total loss of sectoral employment is 337,000 jobs, of which 199,000 would be lost in the base case of present policy without liberalization. By 1990, imports in the liberalization case are 13.5 percent above their level in the present-policy case, and by 2000 they are higher by 44 percent.

The liberalization scenario clearly would involve a significant increase in adjustment by the apparel sector. Nonetheless, it is by no means clear that this adjustment would be infeasible. Employment would need to decline at an average annual rate of 2.5 percent. The bulk of this reduction could be accomplished by retirements, which amount to 1.6 percent of the apparel labor force annually; the remainder could come fully out of normal quit rates, which average an additional 2.5 percent of the labor force annually for apparel (chapter 11). Thus, even the 30 percent reduction in apparel employment by 1990 under the liberalization scenario could be accommodated wholly through attrition rather than net displacement of jobs beyond annual natural separations through retirement and quits. The possibilities for adjustment are discussed further in chapter 11.

The third projection scenario explores the impact of an increase in the tariff-equivalent of apparel quotas from 25 percent to 45 percent. In this case, real apparel imports by 1990 are 14.6 percent below their 1986 level and 21.4 percent below the level they otherwise would have reached. This cutback in imports permits larger growth of domestic output, which by the year 2000 stands at 20.9 percent above the 1986 base (average annual growth of 1.4 percent), instead of 9.8 percent in the base case (average annual growth of 0.7 percent). Higher protection raises output by 9.5 percent above its level in the base case by the year 2000. Massive new protection buys an increase in the annual growth of domestic output by 0.7 percent.

Under increased protection, by 2000 employment in the apparel sector stands 9.1 percent above its level in the base case, for a loss of 114,000 jobs instead of 199,000. The cost of this gain of 85,000 sectoral jobs (7.5 percent of the apparel sector's total employment) is a large burden on US consumers, as discussed in chapter 9. Increased protection raises the price of imports and imposes extra costs on consumers. In terms of the projection model, this effect may be seen in the depressing effect of protection on total consumption. By the year 2000, total consumption is 3 percent lower under the protective case than in the base case. As a result, the increase in output is considerably smaller than the reduction in imports ($5.2 billion at 1982 prices versus $7.7 billion, respectively).

Textile-Apparel Interaction

The projections here take account of the interindustry relationship between the textile and apparel sectors. The apparel sector is an important customer of the textile sector in terms of intermediate inputs, and any sharp decline in apparel production would have repercussions on the textile sector.

As discussed in chapter 3, the 1977 input-output table for US industries indicates that in that year the textile sector supplied inputs amounting to 33 percent of the gross output of the apparel industry. Based on 1986 output levels, these interindustry sales also represent about one-third of total production in the textile industry. Thus, although the apparel industry is important to total textile sales, it is not responsible for even a majority of these sales.

It is of interest to examine the impact of apparel trade policy on US textile production. By the year 2000 in the protective scenario, apparel output is larger than in the liberalization case by $14.3 billion (at 1982 prices), or by 31.3 percent. Applying the input-output coefficient of 0.33, protection instead of liberalization for apparel raises textile production by $4.7 billion, or 7.6 percent. The total difference in textile output under protection versus liberalization by the year 2000 is $6.8 billion, or 11 percent of the output under the liberalization case. Thus, three-fourths of the impact of trade policy on textiles comes not from within the consumer market for textiles but indirectly through the effect of protection on apparel output and, in turn, on intermediate use of textiles in apparel production. Even taking this interindustry impact into account, however, the textile sector is only moderately affected by the trade policy choice between protection and liberalization of both sectors.

It may be added that textile output under liberalization could be higher than projected here if there were a concerted effort to obtain reciprocal liberalization of foreign markets in return. Thus, if foreign liberalization increased US textile exports by even 2 percent annually, by 1990 these exports would be higher by 32 percent or $1.89 billion, boosting output and employment by 3 percent.

As for the other direction of input-output linkage between the two sectors, it should be noted that higher protection would impose a higher input cost on apparel by raising the price of textiles. In the protective scenario, the price of imported textiles from developing countries is in a range of 60 percent higher than in the liberalization scenario (with the difference lower at first and greater later, as liberalization takes place). Imports from these countries account for only about 4 percent of textile consumption (rising to over 7 percent), so that the resulting direct impact on price is an increase in the range of 2½ to 4 percent. With textile inputs constituting approximately one-third of apparel output value, the resulting increase in apparel costs is small, in the range of 0.8 percent to 1.3 percent. As noted in chapter 8 in the discussion of protection costs, however, the higher prices of imports would to some extent spill over into higher prices of domestically produced textiles as well, in which case the adverse impact of textile protection on apparel costs would be higher. Indeed, if all textile prices rose by the 60 percent increment for imports from developing countries, the impact would be a 20 percent rise in the cost of production for apparel, a severe burden and one that would considerably undermine the output gains sought for apparel itself through higher protection. The actual outcome for costs of textile inputs into apparel would be somewhere in between these two extremes.

In sum, interindustry relations between textiles and apparel do not substantially alter the conclusions about trade policy based on analysis of each sector separately. Broadly, the choice between liberalization, no policy change, and higher protection would have a moderate effect on the textile sector but a more sizable impact on the apparel sector.

Sensitivity Analysis

Long-term projections are sensitive to changes in growth rates that persist over many years. It is useful to obtain an idea of the effect of some alternative assumptions on the projections here. Because it is in apparel that trade policy has the most impact, the following discussion examines this sector. Moreover, the additional cases examined review only pessimistic alternatives in an attempt to draw some boundary around the magnitude of the potential adjustment problem.

The rate of exogenous increase in developing-country export growth is an important element in the import outlook. On the basis of a past S-curve, the analysis above concluded that this rate had declined from the range of between 10 percent and 20 percent annually in the early and mid-1970s to less than 2 percent by 1986. The projections above freeze this rate at 2 percent through the year 2000. However, if this rate is doubled to 4 percent annual exogenous growth in imports from developing countries—that is, increase in the absence of any change in income, exchange rate, protection, or other variables—thereby raising the underlying growth rate of these imports from 7 percent to 9 percent annually, by the year 2000 total apparel imports would be 30.5 percent higher than in the base case, causing output to be 19.8 percent lower and employment 17.6 percent lower than under the base case assumptions. In this case, employment would decline by 32 percent from 1986 to 2000, instead of 17.6 percent as in the base case.

If developing countries do not appreciate their real exchange rates relative to the dollar from their January 1987 levels, import growth would also be higher, but by a much more modest amount. By the year 2000, total imports of apparel would be 11.7 percent higher than in the base case, causing output to be lower by 4.9 percent and employment lower by 4.5 percent.

The rate of growth of labor productivity is also critical. If apparel productivity continues to grow at the 2.75 percent rate experienced in 1973–85 (instead of slowing to the 2 percent average rate for 1960–85 as assumed in the base case), by the year 2000 apparel employment would be 11 percent lower than in the base case.

These more adverse conditions would make the adjustment to trade liberalization more difficult. If developing-country export growth were at the higher rate of exogenous growth (4 percent annually), then under the liberalization scenario apparel employment would decline by 52.6 percent by the year 2000 instead of 30 percent. Similarly, with no developing-country appreciation, employment under liberalization would fall by 35.4 percent by the year 2000; and with the higher productivity growth rate (2.75 percent), the decline in employment under liberalization would be 36.9 percent.

To recapitulate, the dimension of the apparel adjustment task may be summarized as follows. With no change in trade policy, the central estimate is that apparel employment will decline by approximately 18 percent by the year 2000. Liberalization eliminating quotas and cutting the tariff (to 15 percent) would increase this cutback to 30 percent. If pessimistic assumptions (from the standpoint of apparel employment) are made about exogenous growth of developing-country exports (4 percent annually instead of 2 percent), NIC exchange rate (no appreciation), or labor productivity growth (2.75 percent instead of 2 percent), the outlook for apparel employment would be a decline by the year 2000 by 21–32 percent under current trade policy and by 35–53 percent under trade liberalization.

The outer limit of employment reduction through attrition would be a rate of 4.1 percent annually (1.6 percent retirement plus 2.5 percent quit rate; chapter 11). At this rate, apparel employment could decline by 43 percent by the year 2000 through attrition alone. This reduction is comfortably in excess of the cutback foreseen in the base case even with trade liberalization. Under some of the unfavorable alternative assumptions, however, total attrition would fall short of the needed labor adjustment under liberalization.

As in other public policy areas, it can be extremely costly to base the main trade policy strategy on the principle of avoiding even the chance of the worst possible case. (Thus, fiscal policies designed to maintain high employment at all costs run the risk of unacceptable inflation; monetary policies geared toward avoiding any risk whatsoever of inflation risk severe recession; a program of total self-sufficiency in oil would be enormously costly.) Moreover, the parameters of the projection model and the assumptions of variable behavior are selected in the base case to be the most consistent with actual past experience. The closeness of the fit of the model estimates to actual data for 1970–86 (chapter 3) provides some assurance that these parameters and assumptions are a reliable basis for future planning.

The central evaluation of the forecasts here thus remains that of the base case (and its three trade policy options). It should be kept in mind, however, that there are more pessimistic parameter assumptions under which natural labor force attrition would fall short of covering the needed decline in employment under a policy of trade liberalization. However, even at the more unfavorable end of the range of pessimistic alternatives (higher developing-country exogenous export growth), attrition could still accommodate approximately four-fifths of the employment decline under trade liberalization.

11

Conclusion and Policy Implications

Trade policy in textiles and apparel stands at an important crossroads. Angered by the rapid increase in imports in recent years, representatives of the domestic US industry are intent on tightening restrictions, including through mechanisms (especially global quotas) that would probably destroy and certainly supersede the Multi-Fiber Arrangement (MFA). The Reagan administration has opted instead for the more familiar path of another renewal of the MFA, while tightening restraints not only through the new provisions of the latest MFA but also through implementing procedures in its bilateral agreements such as the replacement of surveillance categories by specific product and aggregate quotas.

While the recent thrust of actual policy and, especially, industry pressure for policy change has been in the direction of increasingly severe restrictions, now is paradoxically a relevant time to consider instead a move toward liberalization of the trade regime in these two sectors. The Uruguay Round of trade negotiations provides a vehicle for reciprocal bargaining with principal developing-country suppliers of textiles and apparel. The consumer cost of protection of the sectors is mounting to remarkable levels and shows every sign of escalating with no end in sight if still more severe restrictions are imposed in the future in the attempt to continue to block the natural trade patterns that would otherwise arise from evolving comparative advantage.

This chapter draws upon the findings of this study to evaluate the principal options for trade policy in the textile and apparel sectors over the next 15 years. The discussion seeks to identify a strategy that achieves balanced attention to the need to moderate the adjustment burden for existing workers in the industries, on the one hand, and the goals of reducing excess cost imposed on consumers and providing export opportunities for both the United States and developing countries, on the other.

247

Policy Significance of Principal Findings

The quantitative estimates of this study provide a concrete basis for evaluating the future policy options. The analysis here indicates that although consumers and especially the poor have paid a high cost for protection, it has not brought the industrial revival to internationally competitive levels that was the original implicit bargain in public acceptance of protection, especially in apparel. The simulations demonstrate the important role of macroeconomic forces, especially the strong dollar in the early 1980s, and indicate that a deceleration of import growth from its rapid rate of recent years is likely as the result of the decline of the dollar. The projections of the quantitative model indicate much greater capacity for survival of the industries without new protection than predicted by its advocates, and they provide specific estimates of the impact of alternative trade policies.

Protection and Adjustment

The textile and apparel industries have received special protection under international arrangements since the early 1960s in cotton products. In the early 1970s that protection widened to include man-made fibers and woolen products as well as cotton products and spread globally in a formal Multi-Fiber Arrangement. From the beginning, the rationale for protection was that it would permit the domestic industry to adjust. Yet instead of the eventual liberalization implicit in that premise, protection has systematically increased in the sectors.

In the absence of a fundamental change of strategy, ever-increasing protection would appear to be the inevitable consequence of the past and present approach. As more developing countries achieve quality production and can take advantage of abundant labor, the natural evolution of comparative advantage will be toward rising imports from them. Apparel in particular is labor intensive and difficult to mechanize. This fundamental dynamic has generated an increase in the tariff-equivalent of total protection in apparel from approximately 30 percent in the early 1960s to some 55 percent today (chapter 6).

In apparel, there is little evidence that adjustment behind protective barriers has strengthened the industry to provide the basis for eventual competitiveness. Labor productivity growth in the industry has lagged behind that of general manufacturing (chapter 4). Nor has the industry adjusted very rapidly through the process of downsizing. Real output grew through the 1970s and has reached a plateau but not fallen substantially in more recent years. The total number of workers in apparel has declined by only 19 percent since its peak in 1973—far less than the reduction of employment in some other industries adjusting to imports, such as steel and footwear. The cutback in US apparel employment is also much smaller than in Germany (55 percent below peak), France (39 percent), the United Kingdom (52 percent), and the Netherlands (88 percent reduction; table 5.2). In apparel, protection for the purpose of orderly adjustment either through increased productivity or employment reduction is a failed policy and should be acknowledged as such. Instead, apparel protection should be viewed as a social policy that sustains employment and profits in a particular sector, and its sectoral benefits should be weighed against the costs to the broader economy.

The record of adjustment behind protective barriers is more favorable in textiles. Largely because technological change has permitted a considerable shift from labor- to capital-intensive production ("factor reversal"), over the past two decades the textile sector has staged an impressive comeback. Its labor productivity has grown considerably more rapidly than that of general US manufacturing. At the same time, adjustment has also taken place in the form of labor downsizing, as employment in textiles has declined by 32 percent from its peak in 1973. Mechanization and technological change meant that by 1979–80 the textiles sector had achieved a small trade surplus. Moreover, import penetration in textiles has remained low, at less than 10 percent of domestic consumption.

Role of the Dollar

For both textiles and apparel, the overvaluation of the dollar was a major factor in the surge in imports in the first half of the 1980s. From 1982 to 1986, real imports rose by approximately 100 percent in both textiles and apparel. The protective screen of quotas under the MFA had proved to be a clear depressant for imports in the 1970s, but nonetheless it was sufficiently permeable that when the economic pressure behind imports intensified their actual flow did increase sharply.

The simulation analysis of chapter 3 indicates that if the dollar had not risen by some 40 percent above its equilibrium level in the early 1980s, by 1986 the level of real imports would have been approximately 21 percent lower in textiles and 20 percent lower in apparel. In the absence of dollar overvaluation, the textile sector would have been in trade surplus in 1982–85 instead of in deficit (on the basis of the simulation calculations). The sector thus appears to be internationally competitive at an appropriate exchange rate.

Projections of trade under the base case of no policy change indicate a sharp improvement in the trade balance of the textile sector by the late 1980s as the result of depreciation of the dollar, even if the dollar declines no farther than the level reached in January 1987. Weighted by textile and apparel trade with the five largest industrial countries, the real exchange rate of the dollar had declined by 32 percent from its average in 1985 to January 1987, thereby reversing the overvaluation of the dollar experienced in the first half of the 1980s. (The decline of some 30 percent from the higher base was equivalent to the earlier rise of 40 percent from a lower base.)

For apparel, the outcome for future trade projections depends importantly on whether the developing-country suppliers follow the industrial countries in allowing their exchange rates to appreciate relative to the dollar. As of early 1987 this reversal still had not occurred. With 1980 as a base of 100, the index of the dollar's real value relative to currencies of developing-country suppliers had risen to 123 by 1985 but retreated only to 117 by January 1987. On the basis of past experience, nonetheless, the real exchange rates of these countries relative to the dollar would be expected eventually to move similarly to those of the other industrial countries (table 3.1).

A direct policy implication of this analysis is that US trade officials would appropriately concern themselves with currency discussions with officials of the newly industrialized countries (NICs), particularly those in Eastern Asia, to help ensure that their exchange rates are not at inappropriate levels that have the adverse effect of putting severe pressure on US apparel (as well as other) imports. On the basis of its large current account surplus, Taiwan in particular would appear to be a logical candidate for exchange rate appreciation, and a similar but perhaps less obvious case may be made for Hong Kong and Korea. The initial evidence by early 1987 suggests that at least Taiwan has indeed begun to respond to such pressures. By then the New Taiwan dollar was appreciating at a rapid rate.[1]

If the NICs do appreciate—and a return of perhaps two-thirds of the distance between the 1980 and 1985 rates would seem warranted in view of the balance of payments strength of the principal NIC suppliers—import pressure in apparel should be considerably alleviated. Over the longer term, however, it is likely that it would be necessary to maintain at least the current level of protection if the public's goal is to avoid reduction of employment in this sector. Indeed, the evolution of comparative advantage would suggest that ever rising levels of protection could be required for this objective. Thus, in apparel the essential issue is how much the public is prepared to pay for the maintenance of a particular sector's employment.

---

1. From 1985 to 1986 the New Taiwan dollar appreciated relative to the US dollar by 4.0 percent. From the 1986 average to the first week in February 1987 the rate appreciated another 8.3 percent. Central Bank of China, *Financial Statistics, Taiwan District, Republic of China* (Taipei: May 1987), and *Wall Street Journal*, 6 February 1987.

Costs of Protection

Already the cost borne by the rest of the economy for protection of the apparel and textile sectors is extremely high. Consumers pay an estimated $17.6 billion annually for apparel protection and $2.8 billion for protection in textiles (table 8.1). The reason is that the restriction of import supply drives up the price of imports and, to a lesser extent, of substitute goods produced domestically. These costs amount to approximately $50,000 per job (direct and indirect) created by protection in both sectors, far above the wage received by the workers. Consumers would benefit by an arrangement to pay for retirement at full wages of the workers whose jobs are created by protection, as an alternative to import restrictions. Moreover, these cost estimates are highly conservative. They assume that retailers do not apply their normal percentage marketing margins to the cost increase resulting from protection, but instead only pass on to consumers the absolute amount of the extra cost. The estimate of cost per job may also be understated by including in the employment estimates the indirect jobs associated with intermediate inputs into textiles and apparel.

Further calculations to take account of the facts that much of the consumer cost is a transfer to producers and therefore not a net welfare loss to the economy, and that there are adjustment costs in the alternative case of liberalization, do not fundamentally alter the finding that protection is costly. Thus, after redistributive transfers are netted out and labor adjustment costs are deducted, the net cost of existing protection in textiles and apparel still amounts to $8.1 billion annually. Net costs after exclusion of transfers to producers are high because quota rents accrue to foreign producers instead of the US government, and because the additional production induced by protection takes place under inefficient conditions and is thus much more costly than obtaining the same supply through importing at the world price.

Protection of textiles and apparel is often interpreted as an equitable measure because it secures low-income workers. While it is true that workers in these sectors, and especially apparel, have wages below the average for US manufacturing, their incomes are nonetheless high enough to place them in the second and third quintiles of the US income distribution (the 20–40 percent and 40–60 percent brackets). At the same time, owners of stock in textile and apparel corporations and retailing firms are concentrated at the upper end of the income distribution. The effect of protection is to redistribute income away from the general consuming public to the textile and apparel workers in the middle brackets and the owners of capital in the sectors in the top bracket.

It is largely unrecognized that textile and apparel protection imposes an especially high cost on low-income families. This protection reduces the income of the poorest 20 percent of households by nearly 4 percent. Over the rest of the income distribution, textile and apparel protection reduces the incomes of the next three quintiles (20–80 percent) by approximately 1 percent, and raises the income of the top bracket (80–100 percent) by 0.3 percent (table 8.3). Ironically, even the brackets of which the textile and apparel workers are members lose out on balance, because the losses from higher textile and apparel costs to other families in these income brackets substantially exceed the gains to the textile and apparel workers (as the consequence of the underlying inefficiency of the mechanism of protection). In sum, protection in these sectors has perverse income distributional consequences, rather than furthering social equity as many people would appear to believe.

So far, the high cost of protection in these industries has exercised only mild limitations on the advance of restrictive measures. The executive branch has rejected proposals for far tighter protection, in part because of recognition of such costs, but even so it has adopted measures (recently, in the MFA renegotiation of 1986 and revised implementing procedures) that go a substantial distance toward increasing protection.

For their part, many in Congress appear to place little weight on the costs of protection in the sector. In August 1986 a House vote to override the President's veto of a bill to roll back textile and apparel imports failed to pass by only eight votes. The estimates of chapter 9 indicate that this bill (the Textile and Apparel Trade Enforcement Act) would have added another $6 billion to annual consumer costs; calculations by the administration placed the figure even higher at $9 billion.

In early 1987 another legislative proposal called for global import quotas limiting the growth of textile and apparel imports to 1 percent annually. Although the consumer costs of this new proposal would be lower than under the 1985 bill in the initial years (an average of $1.3 billion annually in 1987–89 and $2.3 billion in 1990–91), the costs would escalate rapidly to extremely high levels in the 1990s ($5.6 billion by 1992, $12.3 billion by 1994, and $20 billion by 1996, at 1986 prices). For the full decade, the average consumer cost of the 1987 bill would be $7.1 billion annually (at 1986 prices).

Trade Policy Issues

The high costs of protection to consumers and the economy as a whole, the regressive effects on the distribution of income, and the real threat that the costs will rise even higher as protection escalates to halt the natural progression of comparative advantage in a labor-intensive industry are the principal reasons for considering a policy reversal in the direction of liberalization at this time. There are additional reasons from the standpoint of overall trade policy.

In recent years the United States has moved in the direction of protection in a number of sectors. Overvaluation of the dollar and a resulting trade deficit of some $170 billion by 1986 have meant intensifying political pressure for protection. The textiles and apparel sectors are a hallmark for trade policy. The Multi-Fiber Arrangement has protected the sectors for more than a decade, following the Long Term Arrangement in cotton textiles that stretches the period of protection to more than two decades (and as many as three, if special protection is dated from Japanese voluntary restraints in the late 1950s). Decisions taken in the textile and apparel sectors will inevitably have implications for the basic trade policy stance on a wider range of industries, even as the seeming legitimacy to protection already given by the longevity of the MFA has no doubt contributed to increasingly cartel-like protective arrangements in other sectors such as steel.

The stakes in protection as opposed to open trade are high in textiles and apparel alone. They are even higher for trade policy across the whole range of industries. It is well known that heightened protection in the 1930s contributed to global depression. It is less well known that the vast bulk of evidence on the process of economic growth points in the direction of more favorable results under more open trade regimes, as illustrated by the contrast between the growth experiences of some of the East Asian NICs and those of some protection-oriented Latin American countries. The same principles apply to industrial countries. Protection tends to divert resources to inefficient uses and thus to reduce the rate of growth for a given rate of capital accumulation and population growth. To the extent that a shift in textile and apparel trade policy toward tighter protection served to legitimate a broader shift across many industries in the same direction, the long-term consequences would almost surely be lower economic growth.

Future Strategy

These considerations suggest that it is time to design a long-term program for eventual liberalization of trade in the textile and apparel sectors, rather than adopt still tighter protection for them. Such a program should seek to terminate an important distortion under the current protective regime: the constant incentive—provided by an inflated domestic price—for the sectors to devote still more resources to production rather than scaling back by phasing out the most inefficient product lines and firms. The alternative of higher protection would simply aggravate further this misleading price signal.

An important feature of a longer term program for liberalization would be its clear willingness to accept downsizing of the domestic industries. At the same time, for equity purposes such a program should seek to moderate any displacement burden for existing workers.

An additional element of a long-term strategy should be the pursuit of reciprocal liberalization in foreign supplying countries. There is little evidence that the trade problems of textiles and apparel are caused by "unfair trade" in the sense of foreign subsidies or dumping by foreign firms. Broadly, the natural comparative advantage of the developing countries in labor-intensive apparel in particular means that their exports do not need such artificial stimulants to succeed in the markets of industrial countries. And while there is some incidence of fraud (for example, in the transshipment of some Far Eastern supply through Japan to qualify for its more liberal access to the US market), it should be recognized that such distortions are like smuggling in the face of a prohibitive tariff: they tend to be the natural consequence of a larger and larger wedge between the domestic price and the competitive international price.

The reciprocity that would appropriately be sought in a long-term program of liberalization would not be primarily elimination of such "unfair trade practices," although where present they should be addressed. Instead, it is the more traditional arena of reciprocal liberalization of restrictive regimes on each country's imports that would provide considerable scope for reciprocity. With the notable exception of Hong Kong, most of the principal foreign suppliers of textiles and apparel maintain relatively high import restrictions of their own on textiles and apparel. It would be appropriate for a program of liberalization in industrial countries to seek at least eventual corresponding import liberalization in the supplying countries (and more rapid liberalization by those in strong external sector positions). Such liberalization would be especially significant for exports of textiles from the United States and other industrial countries, considering that in this sector capital-intensive technical change has placed the industrial countries in a relatively favorable competitive position.

Can Domestic Industry Survive?

A central question must be considered in any program for long-term trade liberalization: Can the textile and apparel industries survive in the face of reduced protection, or would even gradual liberalization devastate the industries and their employment? Various elements of the analysis in preceding chapters shed light on this question. As already indicated, there is evidence that the textile sector is relatively competitive at the right exchange rate, and a large part of the necessary exchange rate correction had already taken place by early 1987. The underlying health of the textile and apparel sectors is more vigorous than commonly perceived. Thus, in chapter 2 it is shown that profit rates are relatively high in apparel, in part because of low wages. The analysis of chapter 5 indicates that the relative economic productivity of US textiles and apparel stands up fairly well against that of other countries, including some important NICs, when measured by the ratio of physical labor productivity as adjusted by the corresponding ratio of wages. Essentially, higher output per worker in the United States tends to offset much of the foreign advantage from lower wages. Moreover, when measured appropriately, import penetration is less than 10 percent of US consumption in textiles and one-third or less in apparel, rather than one-half or more as sometimes argued in policy debates (chapter 2).

Chapter 10 presents a specific set of simulations of future trade, production, and employment in the two industries under alternative policy regimes. The base case of unchanged protection yields results that show considerable resilience in the two industries. After a two-year lag, the beneficial effects of dollar depreciation show up in lessening import pressure. By the year 2000, nonetheless, employment in textiles is 20 percent below its 1986 level, and in apparel 18 percent lower. Productivity growth means that in both sectors employment declines even though production rises significantly under present policy. In comparison, during the preceding 14-year period textile employment declined by 30 percent and apparel employment by 17 percent. Sensitivity analysis for apparel (the sector more vulnerable to imports) examines the impact of more pessimistic assumptions by ruling out exchange rate appreciation by the NICs, doubling the annual rate of spontaneous increase in developing-country supply, or assuming higher labor productivity growth. Even in these cases, the reduction of apparel employment from 1986 to the year 2000 is limited to a range of 20 percent to 30 percent.

The analysis of chapter 10 also examines the impact of trade liberalization on the two sectors. The calculations specify a gradual elimination of quotas by the year 2000 and reduction of tariffs to 10 percent for textiles and 15 percent for apparel. Compared with the base case, the scenario for liberalization decreases textile employment by the year 2000 by only 6 percent, but reduces apparel employment by an extra 15 percent, bringing the total reductions in employment by the year 2000 to 25 percent in textiles and 30 percent in apparel.

These calculations for the impact of gradual liberalization in the future indicate that the industries would be far from obliterated. As expected, the adverse impact of liberalization would be proportionately greater in apparel than in textiles, where import penetration is low. In this regard, it is important to note the implications of the calculations for a major argument that has been used by advocates of protection of the textile sector. Many argue that although textiles as an individual sector is relatively competitive internationally, the sector could not withstand a broad program of textile-apparel liberalization because textiles depend importantly on demand from the domestic apparel industry and that sector would be irreparably damaged by liberalization. The projections of chapter 10 confirm that the greater part of the impact of liberalization on textiles comes from the indirect effect on textile inputs into apparel. Three-fourths of the impact of liberalization on textiles comes from this interindustry effect on textile inputs into apparel, as liberalization reduces apparel production. The central point, however, is that even after taking account of this interindustry demand, the impact of the liberalization program on the textile sector is modest—a reduction of output by only 6 percent from the baseline under unchanged trade policy (for the year 2000).

The main thrust of these calculations is the finding that even with major liberalization, the declines in apparel and especially textile employment would be within manageable bounds. The reductions would mean that the United States would approximately catch up with the adjustment through employment reduction that has already taken place in Europe and Japan, and (viewed from a domestic perspective) with that already experienced by some other major sectors within US industry that have faced severe import competition (such as steel). Importantly, as set forth below, these magnitudes of employment cutbacks can be accommodated by a relatively temperate program of gradual adjustment that limits job reductions to the rate of natural attrition from retirement.

Protection for People or Positions?

A fundamental question, of course, is whether it is desirable to phase out any jobs at all in the textile and apparel sectors. They are, after all, the two largest sources of manufacturing employment in the United States. As discussed in chapter 4, however, there is little basis in public policy for establishing a target number of jobs in the abstract for a particular industry. Policy should protect people, not positions. Named people deserve some assurance that national trade policy will not abruptly impose on them individually an intolerable adjustment burden. Abstract job positions in particular industries warrant no such privilege. A central feature of any long-term program of liberalization and adjustment should be that new entrants who join the sector after the adoption of the program should be ineligible for special adjustment benefits. Otherwise the process of incorrect signals would be compounded: still more workers would be attracted to the sector, adding further adjustment cost or consumer cost if protection is retained as the result. Indeed, this has been the case over the past 25 years.

A premise of the approach here is that protection reshuffles employment among sectors but does not increase its aggregate level. Macroeconomic policy is the principal determinant of overall employment. In fact, by introducing inefficiency into the allocation of resources, sectoral protection is likely to reduce the total number of jobs in the economy rather than increase it.

The view that no guaranteed number of jobs in the textile and apparel sectors should be pursued as a matter of national policy will disturb those who fear the "deindustrialization" of the United States. A special concern about the preservation of manufacturing jobs as somehow superior to service-sector jobs is central to such concerns. However, textile and especially apparel jobs do not pay significantly more than the average service-sector job. Moreover, the baby-boom demographics of the 1970s that swelled the ranks of the labor force are projected to reverse to a period in the next two decades of relatively slow growth in the labor force and probably a relative tightening of the availability of lower skilled workers. Under these circumstances it is questionable to adopt as a national objective the maintenance of a target number of abstract job positions in the textile and apparel sectors, whereas it is eminently sensible for policy to pay attention to the effects of liberalization on existing, named workers in the sectors.

Some parties clearly have incentives to preserve positions rather than protect people. Firms in the sectors stand to earn higher profits under a regime of extended protection. Labor unions may expect larger membership through the retention of more workers in the organized textile and apparel sectors than with a greater transfer of these workers to the unorganized service sectors. Elected representatives of states where textile and apparel jobs are concentrated stand to reap greater short-term political benefits from programs that preserve sectoral positions rather than liberalize trade even with adjustment benefits. However, as a matter of national policy, it would appear that the overall balance of costs and benefits would favor a program that seeks gradual liberalization, increased efficiency, and cushioned labor adjustment rather than the preservation of 2 million jobs specifically earmarked for the textile and apparel sectors at all costs.

The findings of the study as enumerated here, and the principles of future policy design as just set forth, provide a basis for the outlines of a program for liberalization and adjustment in the textile and apparel sectors as set forth below. The specific modalities suggested here are less important than the strategy they represent, and other plans might serve equally well or better. However, the case for gradual liberalization is sufficiently controversial that concrete illustration of how it might be implemented is warranted.

A Program of Gradual Liberalization

The objective of phased-in liberalization would be to eliminate special protection by the year 2000, leaving only tariff protection in textiles and apparel. The target levels of tariffs at the end of this period would be 10 percent for textiles and 15 percent for apparel. These levels would continue to afford a degree of unusual protection to the two sectors because they are considerably above the averages for US manufacturing; however, these rates would involve lower costs for consumers than the current tariffs, particularly in apparel (where the average rate is 22.5 percent).

Special protection in the sectors currently takes the form of quotas. The transition to elimination of special protection would involve the early conversion of quotas to "tariff rate quotas." A tariff rate quota is an additional tariff that is imposed when the imports in question exceed a specific volume (the "quota" base). However, unlike a quota it does not specifically limit the physical volume of imports to the quota trigger level, but relies instead on the tariff surcharge to hold imports to this level.

Under the program for gradual liberalization, all existing bilateral agreements specifying quota levels would be transformed into arrangements whereby the imports would be subject to a tariff surcharge for amounts exceeding the quota volume. This surcharge would be set at 25 percent for apparel and 15 percent for textiles—the current tariff-equivalent rates estimated in this study for the effect of quota restrictions in excess of the tariff rates. On the basis of the tariff rates reported in chapter 6 (table 6.3), the tariff rate quota would bring the total tariff to approximately 25 percent in textiles and 50 percent in apparel. For those product categories currently not covered by quotas for a particular supplying country, there would be no tariff rate quota. And those countries currently not facing quotas at all (Europe, Canada, and many low-income countries in Africa) would also be exempt from the tariff rate quotas.

The initial conversion of quotas to tariff rate quotas would in principle leave protection unchanged. The surcharge imposed under the tariff rate quota is estimated to leave the increase in price of the imported good at the same level that now results from the tariff-equivalent of existing quotas.[2] Consumers would face the same price and demand the same volume of imports. The conversion to tariff rate quotas would leave the allocation of existing quota rents unchanged, as there would be no new tariff (or auction) to absorb these rents from foreign suppliers. However, at the margin, any expansion of imports beyond the specified quota threshold for the tariff quota would involve a transfer of the rent to the US government.

---

2. It might be objected that foreign suppliers would "average" the surcharge on the above-threshold units with the absence of any surcharge on all units below the threshold, thereby so diluting the impact of the surcharge as to render it ineffective. However, the decision to ship an additional unit above the threshold would always face the full force of the surcharge for that unit, and this impact would be unlikely to be perceived as minimal in terms of this decision at the margin. The sphere of marginal tax rates is perhaps a more familiar arena in which there is ample evidence that behavior at the margin is affected by marginal, not average, prices.

The basic strategy would then be to phase down the restrictive effect of the tariff rate quota over time. In terms of the surcharge, a timetable would provide for a reduction of the extra tariff by 1½ percent per year. At the end of a decade the tariff surcharge on textiles would disappear. The tariff surcharge on apparel would disappear in 17 years, or by 2004. The longer phase-out for apparel is consistent with the diagnosis that the textile sector is already internationally competitive at an equilibrium exchange rate but that apparel faces more serious adjustment through downsizing.

It would be appropriate to address the concern of domestic producers and workers that imports might surge beyond the tariff quota threshold despite the heavy surcharge. For this purpose, a second-tier surcharge of 10 percent would be imposed on major suppliers (defined as suppliers providing more than 5 percent of total US imports of textiles or apparel, respectively) that increased the volume of their exports to the US market by more than 5 percent in a given year. This higher tier would bring the surcharge on the tariff rate quota to 35 percent for apparel and 25 percent for textiles. The timetable for phase-out would still be reduction by 1½ percent annually, but in this case it would require an additional six years for elimination of the surcharge.

If in subsequent years the volume of imports from the country in question fell behind a growth path of 5 percent from the base year, the second tier of tariff surcharge would terminate, leaving only the basic surcharge, which itself would be following a descending timetable. The second tier would place total protection at approximately 35 percent for textiles and 60 percent for apparel. The policy position would implicitly be that these levels were the extremes to which the public was prepared to go to provide temporary shelter for the two industries. Higher levels would involve not only more severe consumer and efficiency costs but would be more likely to invite smuggling and fraud.

Except for the basic and penalty surcharge tiers, there would be no other differentiation of the tariff rate quota by country or product. It would be undesirable to invite domestic political pressure for lower surcharges for some suppliers and higher for others. (On the lower end, of course, differentiation would exist in the sense that countries not currently subject to a quota in the product category in question would have no surcharge.) The uniformity of the surcharges would adhere to the most-favored-nation principle as well (except for the second-tier surcharge, in one direction, and surcharge-free entry for countries not currently subject to quotas, in the other).

The volume threshold that would trigger the tariff rate quota would grow over time. In the case of the four major Asian suppliers (Hong Kong, Korea, Taiwan, and China), the volume at which the tariff rate quota began would rise by 1 percent yearly. For other suppliers with less than 5 percent of market share in US imports of textiles or apparel, the volume threshold for the tariff quota would grow at 6 percent. For recent-entry and low-income suppliers, defined as countries with less than 1 percent of the market in question and with per capita incomes qualifying them for assistance from the International Development Association (IDA, the concessional lending window of the World Bank), the volume threshold for the tariff rate quota would grow at 15 percent annually. In all cases, however, tariff rate quotas would apply only to those categories in which bilaterally agreed quota restraints existed in 1987 or for which subsequent bilateral negotiations established new tariff quotas. Other country-category contributions would remain unrestricted by special protection.

The presence of a tariff rate quota on some suppliers but not others would raise the question of compatibility with The General Agreement on Tariffs and Trade (GATT), which stresses the most-favored-nation (MFN) principle of identical tariffs facing all suppliers. Some would argue that while in the past the GATT has admittedly been forced to countenance violation of MFN in regard to selective application of quotas (particularly "voluntary" quotas), it would be a serious further retrogression for it to do so in the area of tariffs. This view would appear excessively concerned with form rather than substance. Because the program outlined here would be far superior to the existing MFA in terms of movement back to GATT principles, it would be a fundamental strategic mistake to allow rigid adherence to such past GATT distinctions as this one (between "acceptable" non-MFN treatment for voluntary quotas and "unacceptable" similar treatment using tariffs) to block the program, or even to push it from the best design to a less favorable one.

Any revenue generated by the tariff rate quotas would be channeled to a program of adjustment assistance. This program would focus on retraining, relocation, and employment services for displaced workers. These funds would be additional to general US employment programs, and if necessary could be supplemented by funding from broader US programs of adjustment assistance for workers affected by imports. However, because the textile and apparel sectors are so large and their regime of protection so unique, all such funds would be coordinated under an Integrated Adjustment Program for Textiles and Apparel (IAPTA).

Upon the adoption of the strategy outlined here, there would be a national registration of all employees that had worked in the textile and apparel industries for at least two years. Only workers thus registered would in the future be eligible for benefits under the IAPTA, in the event that they suffered job loss. The concept here would be to protect people: those specific individuals already working in the sectors. The restriction of eligibility would be a strong signal to other workers that they entered the textile and apparel industries at their own risk. This signal would help offset the opposing price signal attracting excessive labor into the sectors resulting from the continuing protection of the industries.

The Integrated Adjustment Program for Textiles and Apparel would not provide adjustment funds to firms (with the exception of financial credit as an incentive to firms that provide advance notification of plant closings, as noted below). Adjustment through revitalization based on new investments would have to come from the firms' own profit and credit sources. European experience with subsidies to firms suggests that they have little lasting impact. There are also issues of equity in public policy; because the owners of firms tend to be in the upper income brackets, as holders of the bulk of stock shares, they have little claim on public funds on equity grounds. In contrast, it would be appropriate for some of the adjustment assistance funds to be directed toward communities in which concentrated job displacements occurred (as discussed below).

The presence of a firm timetable for the phase-out of special protection would provide an environment of investment certainty for the sectors. Firms would have a good idea of the prospective time path of textile and apparel prices, and those investments that would ultimately be profitable at international prices would still be undertaken. Other investments not meeting this criterion should not be pursued in any event.

In addition, US firms could enjoy benefits from increased export opportunities. It would be appropriate to undertake multilateral negotiations (probably within the Uruguay Round) to seek liberalization of textiles and apparel by the major NICs. Indeed, despite the possible adverse implications for the most-favored-nation principle of the GATT, it would seem desirable to set as a condition for phase-down of the tariff rate quota surcharge facing a particular supplier country that the country itself undertake gradual liberalization of its own textile and apparel imports. This approach would establish an open trade club in the two sectors, with the price of admission being a commitment to liberalize home markets. Although Hong Kong and a few other countries would easily qualify because of low existing protection, other key suppliers such as Korea and Taiwan would need to make major liberalization changes to become eligible for membership in this club. (However, for low-income countries eligible for concessional assistance from the International Development Association, it would be appropriate to waive this obligation of sectoral reciprocity; similarly, NICs with severe debt-servicing difficulties would reasonably warrant a delayed timetable for its adoption.)

International negotiations would also be desirable to encourage the other industrial countries to launch a program of gradual liberalization similar to that proposed here. With a balanced phase-down of protection across all industrial countries, there would be no problem of intensification of pressure on US imports as the consequence of diversion of foreign supply from the markets of nonliberalizing industrial countries to that of the United States.

The discussion near the end of this chapter on an Arrangement for Open Trade in Textiles and Apparel (AOTTA) sets forth a concrete strategy for achieving both supplying-country reciprocity and parallel liberalization by the European Community.

Adjustment Through Attrition

The program outlined here is one of gradual liberalization. It is similar in broad terms to the liberalization scenario analyzed in the projection model of chapter 10. It is informative to consider the employment effects analyzed in those projections to determine the pace at which employment in the textile and apparel industries would have to decline under the program of gradual liberalization.

In chapter 10 it is calculated that, in the base case in which there is significant reversal of the real depreciation of NIC exchange rates and the exogenous outward shift of NIC supply proceeds at 2 percent annually (in addition to income and exchange rate effects), employment in textiles under the liberalization scenario would decline from 669,000 workers in 1986 to 501,000 by the year 2000, or by 25.1 percent, and in apparel employment would decline from 1,133,000 workers to 796,000 over the same period, or by 29.7 percent.

Worker adjustment would be the least painful under conditions in which the pace of job decline did not exceed the rate of natural attrition of employment through retirement. The rate of job reduction could also be considered relatively mild if it proceeded no faster than the sum of two sources of exit from the industry: retirement and normal quit rates.

Table 11.1 presents data on the age structure of workers in the textile and apparel sectors in the United States. As indicated, 35.3 percent of workers in yarn, thread, and fabric mills are 45 or more years old; 33.2 percent are in this age group in other textile mills; and 36.7 percent are in this group in apparel and other finished products. By intrabracket interpolation, and aggregating the two textile sectors, it may be calculated that workers 50 or more years old account for 25.7 percent of textile employment and 27.4 percent of employment in apparel.

The liberalization program outlined above would achieve elimination of special protection over a 15-year period (or somewhat longer, in the case of apparel). Thus, at the end of this process any worker currently of age 50 or more would be 65 years or older, a normal retirement age. Attrition through retirement could thus reduce the work force by the end of this period by 25.7 percent in textiles and 27.4 percent in apparel, if there were no new

Table 11.1   Age and sex composition of textile and apparel employment, 1980 (thousand; percentage in parentheses)

Age (years)	Yarn, thread, fabric mills		Other textile mills		Apparel and other finished products	
Male						
16–44	204.8	(64.7)	121.1	(67.1)	183.4	(64.9)
45–54	54.8	(17.3)	30.3	(16.8)	45.9	(16.2)
55–59	28.8	(9.1)	14.5	(8.0)	23.1	(8.2)
60–64	19.6	(6.2)	9.6	(5.3)	17.0	(6.0)
>65	8.3	(2.6)	4.9	(2.7)	13.3	(4.7)
Total	316.3	(100.0)	180.4	(100.0)	282.7	(100.0)
Female						
16–44	168.9	(64.6)	125.0	(66.4)	639.4	(62.8)
45–54	49.0	(18.7)	34.0	(18.1)	196.3	(19.3)
55–59	23.2	(8.9)	15.5	(8.2)	92.0	(9.0)
60–64	14.8	(5.7)	9.5	(5.1)	60.8	(6.0)
>65	5.7	(2.2)	4.1	(2.2)	29.1	(2.9)
Total	261.6	(100.0)	188.1	(100.0)	1,017.6	(100.0)
Total						
16–44	373.7	(64.7)	246.1	(66.8)	822.8	(63.3)
45–54	103.8	(18.0)	64.3	(17.4)	242.2	(18.6)
55–59	52.0	(9.0)	30.0	(8.1)	115.1	(8.9)
60–64	34.4	(6.0)	19.1	(5.2)	77.8	(6.0)
Total	577.9	(100.0)	368.5	(100.0)	1,300.3	(100.0)

Source: US Department of Commerce, Bureau of the Census, *1980 Census of Population: Detailed Population Characteristics, United States Summary*, Washington, pp. 1–392, 1–194.

entrants. These magnitudes are almost exactly equal to the employment reduction calculated for textiles under the liberalization scenario and only slightly short of the reductions projected for apparel under liberalization.

Normal quit rates may be added to retirement for a measure of the outer limits of job reduction through attrition. In 1981 (the year with the most recent data), 1.8 percent of workers in textile mills quit their jobs; in apparel, the rate was 2.5 percent.[3] The rate of retirements comes to 2 percent annually

---

3. US Department of Labor, Bureau of Labor Statistics, *Employment and Earnings* (March 1982), table D-2.

in textiles and 2.2 percent annually in apparel. If these rates are added to the quit rates, worker exits through retirement or voluntary departure sum to 3.8 percent annually in textiles and 4.8 percent annually in apparel. At this rate, the total reduction of employment in the two sectors through attrition (in the absence of new entrants) would reach 42.8 percent of the labor force in 15 years in textiles and 50.5 percent in apparel. Even for apparel, this potential employment reduction through retirement and normal quits would comfortably exceed the cutback projected under trade liberalization under base-case assumptions (50.5 percent versus 29.7 percent). And even in the more unlikely cases calculated under pessimistic assumptions for sensitivity analysis, apparel retirements and natural quits would cover the great bulk of prospective job reductions. In these less likely cases, employment cutbacks range from 35 percent to 53 percent of the apparel labor force, in the presence of import liberalization.

The employment effects estimated here are conservative in that they omit increased output and employment from additional US exports under a strategy in which foreign liberalization accompanies that by the United States. As noted in chapter 10, if the growth rate of US textile exports increased by just 2 percentage points annually as the result of reciprocal liberalization abroad, by the year 2000 textile production and employment would be 3 percent higher than otherwise. The resulting gain of 15,000 jobs would offset 50 percent of the job loss otherwise associated with trade liberalization in textiles. (A similar calculation for apparel would be less meaningful, in view of the labor-intensive nature of the sector and the lower likelihood that the United States could achieve comparative advantage even with foreign liberalization.)

In short, a program of gradual liberalization would be unlikely to displace workers from textiles and apparel faster than they would retire or quit voluntarily. As long as the number of new employees entering the sectors was limited, liberalization would not eliminate positions in the sectors more rapidly than the natural decline in the sectoral labor force. The program of registration of workers as of 1987 would act as a clear signal to new entrants that these two sectors were risky.

Despite the tailoring of employment reduction to rates compatible with normal attrition, there would inevitably be some job losses under the program of liberalization. Individual firms could fail and release all of their workers, in contrast to a smoothly distributed reduction of uniform proportions in the employment levels of all firms. The IAPTA would be in place precisely to deal with the cases of such workers. If experience indicated that the incidence of displacement was greater than provided for under the funding from the tariff quota surcharges and from general programs coordinated under the IAPTA, it could then be appropriate to earmark some portion of the basic tariff collections on apparel and textiles for labor adjustment purposes, even though the result would be to divert some fiscal revenue from general purpose availability. The comparisons of potential attrition rates with the calculations of prospective employment reduction suggest that any such needs would be limited, however.

Deindustrialization, Collapse Threshold, and Footwear Lessons

Advocates of new protection for textiles and apparel maintain that, without additional restrictions, the industry could largely disappear. An analogy supporters of new protection often cite is the case of the footwear industry.[4]

The projections of this study do not confirm the view that radical deindustrialization is in store for textiles and apparel in the absence of new protection. The model of chapter 3, which closely tracks actual trends in output, employment, and trade over the past 15 years, is the basis for calculations in chapter 10 that project that by the year 2000, real production will rise by 34 percent in textiles and 10 percent in apparel with no change in trade policy. Thus, production rises despite declining employment associated with productivity gains. Even in the scenario of gradual trade liberalization, textile production rises by 27 percent by the year 2000, and although apparel production does fall, its reduction is by only 8 percent (tables 10.1 and 10.2).

Actual past experience in textiles and apparel also cannot be characterized as deindustrialization. While it is true that the real value of output has held virtually constant since 1977 in textiles and risen only modestly in apparel (table 2.1), there has been no collapse of output to a fraction of former levels that would warrant the description of deindustrialization.

Reformulation of the deindustrialization diagnosis in relative terms would seem inappropriate at the level of an individual sector; it is hardly plausible to expect every individual product sector to maintain its share in gross national product—otherwise there would be no high-growth sectors. Relative deindustrialization is a more meaningful concept at the aggregate level; but past experience has not shown deindustrialization on this basis either.

Some representatives of the textile and apparel sectors emphasize, in contrast to the projections here, that a serious discontinuity may be antici- pated in the industry; that, as imports reach a certain high level, domestic production may be expected to collapse. This view appears to consider purchasing patterns to have critical threshold tendencies in which, once the market has shifted to a high level of imports, the entire structure of sourcing will then rapidly move away from domestic production. Industry represen-

---

4. See for example the statement of John Gregg, Chairman of the Fiber, Fabric and Apparel Coalition for Trade, in *Journal of Commerce*, 6 March 1987, p. 15A.

tatives argue, moreover, that once the domestic collapse has occurred, the United States will be vulnerable to predatory pricing practices by foreign suppliers who will then be in a position to impose sharp price increases.[5]

Concern about foreign monopoly practice would seem unfounded, considering the large number of developing countries capable of producing textiles and apparel. Even in products in which the number of suppliers is more limited, such as coffee and cocoa, past experience has shown that cartel-like efforts to impose a high, monopolistic price have usually been unsuccessful.

The thesis of a threshold of collapse, for its part, is difficult to assess. The economic logic calling for some saturation point after which still higher imports cause the domestic industry to collapse would seem tenuous. Some supporters of protection cite analogies from other economic areas (for example, in the racial mixture of schools or neighborhoods), but there is little basis for carrying these analogies to the mixture between imports and domestic production.

Supporters of the view of an import threshold causing domestic production collapse, and of the more general position that, in the absence of new protection, the domestic textile and apparel industries will largely disappear, tend to invoke the case of the footwear industry in support of these diagnoses. The stylized facts of the sector are typically summarized as follows. Footwear, like apparel, is labor intensive. Except for a brief period in the late 1970s, footwear has not had protection. Today (in the stylized facts) the domestic industry retains only 20 percent of the footwear market.[6] The argument concludes that, in the absence of more protection, and certainly if there were a liberalization of imports, textiles and apparel would turn out like footwear.

It is clear that footwear is not an appropriate analogy for the case of the textile sector. As analyzed in chapters 2 and 4, the US textile industry has become highly mechanized and capital intensive; and, as found in chapters 3 and 10, the sector can be expected to perform well in international trade at the proper exchange rate.

For apparel, the footwear comparison is more relevant. Both are indeed labor intensive, and thus subject to pressure from the natural comparative advantage of developing countries where labor is relatively abundant. In other dimensions, however, there are important differences between apparel and footwear. For example, the advantage of a country such as Brazil from

---

5. These views were expressed by Art Gundersheim of the Amalgamated Clothing and Textile Workers Union and Seth Bodner of the National Knit and Sportswear Association at a study group meeting at the Institute for International Economics, 18 February 1987.

6. The market share cited by John Gregg, *Journal of Commerce*, 6 March 1987.

availability of hides for leather inputs has no counterpart in the apparel industry; indeed, for many fabrics (such as denim) the US industry is sufficiently competitive that US apparel may have an advantage over foreign suppliers with respect to intermediate inputs.

Moreover, the stylized facts about footwear are somewhat misleading. In economically meaningful terms, the penetration of footwear imports into the US market is lower than 80 percent. Penetration estimates based on physical volume (number of pairs of shoes) are misleading because a significant portion of imported footwear is in low-priced, low-quality lines. Thus, in 1986 domestic production amounted to 244 million pairs, imports 951 million pairs, and exports 14 million pairs, giving an import penetration ratio (market share) of 80.5 percent on a basis of number of pairs. However, the import value at the f.o.b. level amounted to $6.3 billion, domestic production at the wholesale level $3.79 billion, and exports $119 million.[7] After allowing a generous 20 percent increment for import value from the f.o.b. level to the wholesale level (for the c.i.f./f.o.b. ratio and tariffs), the footwear import penetration ratio on a value basis amounted to 63.2 percent. Domestic footwear production has not disappeared but instead still retains almost 40 percent of the economically meaningful market (as expressed in terms of value, rather than number of pairs).

It is true that the footwear industry has experienced a sharp downsizing. From 1972 to 1986, domestic production value in real terms declined by 42.6 percent and employment by 52.9 percent, while real import value rose by 220 percent. (For apparel, in contrast, real production rose 17.4 percent and employment fell only 17.2 percent, even though real import value rose more sharply from a relatively smaller base, by 391 percent.)[8] It is unlikely that the apparel sector would experience such output and employment cutbacks even if its import penetration did, over time, reach the level attained in footwear.

The value-based import penetration ratio in footwear rose rapidly during the early 1980s (from only 35.9 percent in 1980), almost certainly spurred by the severe overvaluation of the dollar. The level of 63 percent reached by 1986 is thus probably a plateau from which further increase is unlikely to be rapid or substantial. As a benchmark for the "footwear model," then, it is useful to consider a rise of apparel import penetration to a level of two-thirds by the year 2000.

The projections of chapter 10 indicate that in the year 2000, under present policy the import penetration ratio for apparel (in meaningful, value terms)

---

7. US Department of Commerce, *U.S. Industrial Outlook 1987* (Washington: US Department of Commerce, 1987), p. 43-6.

8. Ibid., pp. 43-6 and 43-10; and Chap. 2, tables 2.1 and 2.5.

will have reached 50 percent;[9] these projections thus reject the notion that the market share of apparel imports would reach footwear proportions in the absence of new protection. Under the liberalization scenario, however, the apparel import penetration ratio would reach 64.8 percent by the year 2000, so that the footwear model may not be inappropriate in gauging the import effects of gradual liberalization. Indeed, the projections under liberalization in this study cannot be faulted as too optimistic by those who cite the footwear example because the estimates here give future import penetration that is close to the two-thirds benchmark that characterizes footwear.

There remains a critical difference between the two sectors even under the liberalization scenario, however. As discussed above, even under the liberalization case, the level of real domestic production in apparel would decline by only 8 percent by the year 2000, and the reduction of employment by 30 percent could be fully accommodated by natural rates of retirement and voluntary quits. The reductions in footwear output and employment over the past 15-year period, in contrast, were proportionately more severe (as noted above: cuts of 42.6 percent in production and 52.9 percent in employment). The principal reason for this difference is that the base-period import penetration ratio in footwear (19.8 percent in 1972) was considerably lower than the 1986 ratio for apparel (31.1 percent), so that the rise in imports relative to the base level of production was much higher in footwear over the past 14 years than is projected to occur in apparel over the next 14, even under the liberalization scenario, and even though the end result in both cases is estimated as an import penetration ratio of over 60 percent.[10]

---

9. The import penetration ratios for the year 2000 are calculated from table 10.2, after expanding the constant dollar f.o.b import value in that table to allow for the higher foreign price in dollars following dollar depreciation from the 1986 base (11.2 percent times an 80 percent pass-through), and after conversion from the f.o.b to the wholesale level (including the c.i.f/f.o.b ratio and the tariff).

10. Consumption and labor productivity patterns for apparel in 1986–2000 are relatively close to those of footwear in 1972–86. Under liberalization, apparel consumption is projected to rise by 39.9 percent, versus 38 percent for the footwear experience; labor productivity should rise by 31.1 percent for apparel, versus 21.9 percent for footwear. These variables thus do not explain the milder employment and output effects projected for apparel under liberalization than occurred in footwear despite a similar end result of import penetration ratios at nearly two-thirds. Instead, the divergence stems from the fact that, beginning from a lower import penetration base (19.8 percent in 1972 versus 31.1 percent for apparel in 1986), footwear experienced a larger rise in imports as a fraction of production (from 25 percent in 1972 to 200 percent in 1986, a rise of 175 percentage points) than is projected for apparel under liberalization (from 45 percent to 166 percent, a rise of 121 percentage points). In addition (but less important), there is a somewhat larger rise in exports as a fraction of output (from 2.1 percent to 10 percent) in apparel than occurred in footwear (from 0.3 percent to 3.1 percent).

In summary, while apparel import penetration would indeed approach the footwear benchmark of nearly two-thirds by the year 2000 under the liberalization scenario, real apparel production would decline by only 8 percent and, as analyzed above, the reduction in employment would remain within magnitudes that would not exceed attrition through retirement and normal quits. These output and employment changes would be much milder than those experienced in the footwear sector over the past 14 years, despite a similar prospective outcome for import penetration because, with the import base already higher in apparel than in the case of footwear 14 years ago, the proportionate rise in imports and (especially) the proportionate cutback in production would be less severe. Moreover, if imports are not liberalized, the prospective level of import penetration by the year 2000 is far below that of footwear today.

Alternative Policy Options

Policymakers face three basic options for trade policy in the textile and apparel sectors. The first is to continue on the past course, renewing the Multi-Fiber Arrangement perpetually. The second is to adopt a clear program of gradual liberalization. Elimination of protection instantaneously is politically out of the question, so any plan for liberalization would almost certainly have to be phased in over a period of years. The program set forth above is one such plan. The third policy option would be to increase protection systematically and substantially. The discussion below reviews these options.

Dimensions of Program Design

It is first useful to consider the components of any textile and apparel trade regime. A program of trade protection or liberalization involves decisions on design in several dimensions. They include the following: tariffs versus quotas versus tariff rate quotas; auction quotas versus allocated (typically, historical) quotas; most-favored-nation (MFN) versus non-MFN treatment; financing for adjustment or absence thereof; limitation of adjustment programs to workers versus inclusion of firms; requirement of reciprocal liberalization by developing countries (either in textiles and apparel specifically or more broadly) versus nonreciprocity; multilateral regime versus bilateral arrangements. Several of these dimensions concern the choice among alternative instruments in plans for gradual liberalization, but others are equally relevant to policies of increased protection.

Special protection in the postwar period has typically been through quotas rather than tariffs or tariff rate quotas (although in textiles and especially apparel, tariffs have also been unusually high). This choice has in part reflected the preference of protected sectors and labor groups for a seemingly certain outcome as opposed to the possible increase of imports beyond target levels despite the higher price resulting from a higher tariff. Moreover, at the institutional level, provisions of the General Agreement on Tariffs and Trade (Article XIX) have required that increases in previously negotiated ("bound") tariffs be offset by compensation to the supplier countries in the form of additional liberalization of other products. Partly as a result, the voluntary export quota has emerged as the de facto form of preferred protection. It circumvents the compensation requirement of the GATT while allowing the controlled exporting country to capture some or all of the scarcity rent generated by the restriction (whereas with higher tariffs these rents would go to the government of the importing country). The MFA adopts the export quota approach with an extra degree of formality in explicitly recognizing bilateral negotiations on their levels (essentially, the orderly marketing agreement [OMA] variant of export restraints rather than the "voluntary" variety [VER]).

Most economists prefer a tariff over a quota of equal protective effect, on grounds that the tariff is more transparent to the public, creates less distortion in relative supply costs (by having an equal incidence on alternative suppliers subject to protection), and is less rigid (and thus not subject to generating protection far higher than expected). Economists and importing groups would generally prefer a liberalization plan that converted existing protection to tariffs, and then gradually phased down the tariffs.

Domestic producers and labor groups tend to oppose such an approach, from the fear that the tariffs thus imposed will turn out to be insufficiently high to generate the same quantitative outcome in restricting imports. For their part, foreign suppliers are at least ambiguous as between tariffs and negotiated export quotas, and probably prefer the latter, because with the export quotas they are likely to receive some or all of the scarcity rent, and in addition they too obtain assured trade volumes. The coincidence of interest between domestic producers and foreign suppliers on the convenience of quotas as opposed to tariffs is one reason for the longevity of the MFA. The interests of negotiators may be added because the problem of Article XIX compensation would confront them if they shifted from the MFA's quota regime to a system of comparable tariffs.

The tariff rate quota is an alternative instrument that combines aspects of the tariff and the quota. Its protective effect need not differ from that of a quota or a tariff. The market-clearing price is the one set "at the margin," inclusive of the tariff rate quota surcharge. The same price can result from a quota, a tariff, or a tariff rate quota.[11]

---

11. A quota may be considered as a tariff-quota with an infinite tariff surcharge at the point of the quota threshold. The fixed quantity thereby permitted to enter will

The program proposed above opts for the tariff rate quota. The presence of an abrupt and steep break in the price of the good at the quota threshold of the tariff surcharge should provide substantial assurance to producers and labor groups that the quantity imported will settle at the targeted amount, especially in view of the provision for a second tier of still higher tariff surcharge if actual imports begin to exceed the intended levels. Yet the tariff rate quota does not transfer the scarcity rent away from suppliers because no special tariff applies for the volume of imports up to the quota-threshold level. (As in the case of voluntary export quotas, of course, if the supplying country provided for no specific allocation of the limited surcharge-free exports among its exporting firms, and if those firms competed intensely among themselves, the rents could be transferred to the importers.) For this reason, moreover, suppliers of textiles and apparel would have no basis for invoking GATT Article XIX against a tariff rate quota because by definition the instrument would not be imposing on them a tariff on the amount of imports that supposedly were to take place under the bilaterally negotiated MFA provisions. (More fundamentally, suppliers would not seek to block such an instrument if it were clear that it was to be put in place as an integral part of a program of gradual liberalization, particularly considering that no supplying country would be made worse off than before in light of the country-specific conversion of existing quotas to tariff rate quotas.)

The tariff rate quota does place a cap on the height of protection at the margin, whereas a quantitative quota does not. But the principal reason the program above selects this instrument is its facility for gradual liberalization over time. If outright conversion of quotas to tariff rate quotas, as suggested here, is ruled out as politically infeasible (perhaps on the side of suppliers as well as domestic producers), that leaves the quota (auctioned or historical) as the only alternative to the tariff rate quota. The mechanism for gradual liberalization is then forced into the mode of successive escalation of the physical quota base to the point where it is so large that it is no longer binding. Quota growth would have to be set at some rate well above market growth (perhaps some 10 percent annually) to accomplish eventual elimination of the binding effect of the quota. This process would appear to invite supplier "targeting" to ensure continual full use of quotas and could actually stimulate more development of foreign supply than would occur under a comparable program of tariff surcharges phased down over time. In practice, however, it is far more likely that political forces would seize

---

set a market-clearing price based on the intersection of the demand curve with this specific quantity of supply. The excess of this price above the world price (exclusive of tariff) is the total tariff-equivalent of the quota. A tariff-rate may be designed such that the same tariff-equivalent of total protection faces the domestic market. Note that the only difference is that the infinite tariff-surcharge on the simple quota contains "water in the tariff"—an excess of the "tariff" above the amount required to constrain imports to the specific level intended.

on the rate of quota growth as a key objective for control and would press for reduction of this rate to a level that would be too low to accomplish elimination of the quota's binding effect even over a long period. Certainly the history of the supposed 6 percent growth target for quotas under the MFA, with its erosion and replacement by "departures," would suggest a high likelihood of this outcome.

The principal alternative mechanism of gradual liberalization using quotas as such would be instead to declare arbitrarily that on certain future dates specific subsectors would revert from quota-controlled to uncontrolled status. The percentage of products so liberalized could then rise over time. While such a program could conceivably be related to relevant criteria such as the import penetration (or its change) for each category, the likely result would be considerable disparities among products as the consequence of the knife-edge division between controlled and uncontrolled.

In contrast, the tariff rate quota lends itself naturally to gradual reduction of protection. It has two dimensions for variation: the volume base for the threshold at which the additional tariff enters force, and the magnitude of that surcharge. Gradual liberalization may be applied in both dimensions. The volume threshold may be successively increased, but at moderate rates (and thus more slowly than the rates that might be required to make the quota nonbinding by a specific future date). And the size of the over-threshold excess tariff may be scheduled to decline according to a timetable. Overall, the tariff rate quota would appear superior to either the quota or the tariff as a feasible and not economically inefficient means of achieving transition from high to lower protection.

It is possible that domestic industry and labor groups would reject the tariff rate quota, on grounds that it provides no assurance that imports will in fact be constrained to the trigger quota level. In this case, it would be worth considering the alternative of the auction quota as a mechanism for gradual liberalization. In early 1987 this instrument was generating considerable debate among policymakers and industry groups,[12] and it is discussed separately below. At this point it is relevant to note, however, that the alternative form of an import quota—allocated on the basis of historical business shares—has serious inequities and inefficiencies, as it locks in the positions of existing importers.[13]

In the dimension of MFN versus non-MFN treatment, at some point a program of textile liberalization would have to come to terms with the

---

12. *Wall Street Journal*, 6 February 1987.

13. Note that the current regime based on *export* quotas means instead that the decision between historical versus auction allocation quotas devolves to the governments of the exporting countries (which in most cases lean toward the historical basis).

question of whether the industrial countries should continue to enjoy unrestrained market access while the regime of special protection is directed only at developing countries. If tariff rate quotas were to replace quotas, GATT practice would once again pose an obstacle because of the premise of MFN treatment in tariff protection under the GATT. In practice the feasible approach would appear to be to seek eventual MFN treatment through the phase-out of the regime of special protection against developing countries (for example, through the program suggested above) rather than through new imposition of mutual restraints among the industrial countries. Note, however, that a program of global quotas (such as might result either from a new policy departure toward much tighter restriction or, ironically, from a program of liberalization using the auction quota) would tend to invite inclusion of industrial as well as developing countries in the global restraint.

Within liberalization schemes, the choice between programs with funding for adjustment and those without is a function of equity, fiscal feasibility, and philosophy. A persistent obstacle to financial support for trade adjustment in the United States has been the view that there is nothing special about displacement from imports as opposed to technical or other economic change. This view would appear to ignore the fact that, in the policy decision of liberalizing trade, the public as a whole benefits at the expense of selected groups that must adjust, and there is a case for providing some compensation to these groups. At the practical level, purist insistence that trade-affected workers are not special has tended to generate not the bracing breezes of laissez faire but continued protection instead.

The principal reasons for limiting adjustment assistance to workers rather than including firms have been noted above. Considerations of income-distributional equity (shareholders versus the general public) and the dynamics of accustomed dependence on subsidies suggest that firms had best be left to fare on their own. In contrast, there is a substantial case for making adjustment assistance funding available to communities where there is a concentration of workers displaced by the trade policy. There are adverse spillover effects for these communities (declining tax base, decreased demand for local services, possibly declining real estate values). Any inclination of legislators to protect positions instead of people probably stems from their concern about the community effects of sectoral reallocation of labor.

Although the Reagan administration has sharply curtailed funding for Trade Adjustment Assistance (TAA), in late 1986 a special task force appointed by Secretary of Labor William E. Brock recommended a program of approximately $1 billion annually in assistance to dislocated workers. The program, to be funded by deductions from paychecks and by payroll taxes paid by employers, would focus on training, counseling, basic education, and job placement. The task force recommended that TAA be absorbed into the new program.[14] The Reagan administration has followed up on the proposal and incorporated funding of $980 million for worker adjustment assistance in its budget request for 1988.[15] If such a program were adopted, it would be appropriate for the Integrated Program of Textile and Apparel Adjustment suggested here to be implemented as a sectoral program under its auspices.

A major issue for adjustment assistance is whether firms should be required to provide advance notice of plant closings. The Secretary of Labor's task force on adjustment concluded in late 1986 that advance notice is "an essential component of a successful adjustment program." The physical presence of an open plant in the last weeks or months before closing is important, as it serves as a base for the development of placement and adjustment services prior to the dispersal of the work force. However, members of the task force were unable to agree on whether advance notice should be mandatory.[16] By July of 1987, the issue had become an important area of contention in the Senate's version of the omnibus trade bill.[17]

While there seems little doubt that advance notice of plant closing can assist worker adjustment, the central question is whether it should be a mandatory requirement for firms. Many firms fear that workers will slacken efforts after notification (although the Secretary of Labor's task force found little evidence of adverse labor effects). There is also concern that advance notice could dry up financing for a struggling business, and by definition if the terms of notice exceed the period of time a firm normally would take for closing once a decision had been made, mandatory notification would cause extra losses for the firm. At a broader level, there is ample evidence that rigidity in the obligations to employees has been a factor discouraging employment in Europe and contributing to its high unemployment rate. There is considerable risk in moving in the direction of greater employment rigidity in the United States.

A compromise could be the establishment within the adjustment assistance program of financial credit that would be available only to those firms that did give advance notice of plant closings, but with no mandatory requirement of notification. This "carrot" would be an exception to the general principle of limiting adjustment assistance to workers, on grounds that in this instance assistance to the firms would be the inducement to an action by the firm

---

14. Secretary of Labor's Task Force on Economic Adjustment and Worker Dislocation, *Economic Adjustment and Worker Dislocation in a Competitive Society* (Washington: Government Printing Office, December 1986); *New York Times,* 11 December 1986.

15. Executive Office of the President, Office of Management and Budget, *Budget of the United States Government: Fiscal Year 1988* (Washington: OMB, 1987), p. I-P3.

16. Secretary of Labor's Task Force, pp. 22–23.

17. *Journal of Commerce,* 9 July 1987.

that would provide a considerable benefit to the worker. The credit would be at rates sufficiently above government borrowing costs that there would be no ultimate loss of government revenue. Within the annual budgeting allocation for adjustment assistance, however, it would be appropriate to limit the credit available to firms to a modest share on grounds of the logic for supporting labor adjustment but not the owners of capital (as discussed above).

In the dimension of developing-country reciprocity, the discussion above suggests that the prospects for acquiescence of industrial country producer and labor groups in the process of gradual liberalization will be more favorable if there is a counterpart of import liberalization in the apparel and especially textile sectors in the markets of newly industrialized countries. As discussed in chapter 9, ample protection exists in these countries, and most have been slow to go beyond the somewhat outdated formulations of the 1960s and 1970s whereby tariff preferences and nonreciprocity were considered practically to be economic rights of developing countries. Such a position is at best warranted for countries with per capita income sufficiently low to qualify for international transfers in other areas (for example, eligible for low-interest loans from IDA), although there remains a case for delayed phase-in of liberalization by the NICs. As argued in chapter 6, to a large degree even unilateral liberalization of protection from its high levels in many developing countries would spur their development, and it makes sense to combine this reform with negotiated liberalization in industrial countries through reciprocal bargaining.[18]

In the final dimension cited above, multilateral versus bilateral regimes, the logical evolution for textiles and apparel is continuation in the multilateral mode. The original intent of the MFA was to act as a transitory vehicle toward eventual liberalization, and a program such as that proposed here fits naturally into the multilateral structure of the MFA. Indeed, in the absence of a multilateral move to a program of phased liberalization, it would be difficult for the United States to adopt such a plan. Unchanged

---

18. It might be objected that the suggestion of reciprocity here runs counter to the general trade-negotiating principle that reciprocity should be achieved in a balance of overall concessions but not enforced at the sectoral level. However, because apparel in particular is likely to be a product sector with natural comparative advantage for developing countries (with their abundant labor), it is a logical sector for reciprocal concessions to be offered by these countries. Indeed, if the developing country is unprepared to offer reciprocity even in a sector of its comparative advantage, the usual injunction against sectoral reciprocity becomes a smokescreen for offering no reciprocity at all. Sectoral reciprocity would be more likely to go astray if invoked in products in which industrial countries more clearly had comparative advantage (such as chemicals), considering that the developing country might wish to pursue infant-industry development over some period of time (a phase long since past in the traditional product areas of textiles and apparel).

protection in Europe in the face of gradually lower protection in the United States would concentrate an undue share of the adjustment on US firms and workers.

Auction Quotas

The program of gradual liberalization proposed above opts for tariff rate quotas as the mechanism for phasing in lower protection. If this instrument is unacceptable to industry and labor groups, and the vehicle of import quotas is employed instead, the auction quota warrants consideration as the mechanism for gradual liberalization.[19]

Under the auction quota, rights to import would be sold to the highest bidder. This process would tend to transfer the quota rents from foreign suppliers to the US Treasury, especially if the quotas were redefined on a consolidated rather than country-specific basis. Moreover, it would establish a market price for the quota rent, making its tariff-equivalent transparent. Under a program of gradual liberalization, the magnitude of the quota would be increased sufficiently rapidly over time that within a specified period the market value of the import right in the auction would fall to zero. Special protection in the sector would then be eliminated.

There are advantages and disadvantages of the auction quota approach. The following discussion seeks to summarize them, with special reference to a program of gradual liberalization in textile and apparel trade.

A major advantage of the auction quota is that it could raise substantial revenue that, in turn, could be used to finance adjustment programs. Thus, in apparel, 1986 imports from non-OECD countries amounted to $14.7 billion, while textile imports from these countries stood at $2.2 billion. Of these totals, $10.5 billion in apparel and $2.1 billion in textiles were covered by quotas,[20] with the sizable difference in apparel attributed to the absence of controls on some products from some countries. If the tariff-equivalent rates of quota protection discussed in chapters 3 and 6 are applied to these trade values (25 percent in apparel and 15 percent in textiles), a rough estimate would be that the auction quota could raise $2.6 billion in apparel

---

19. See C. Fred Bergsten, Jeffrey J. Schott, Wendy Takacs, and Kimberly Ann Elliott, *Auction Quotas and US Trade Policy*, POLICY ANALYSES IN INTERNATIONAL ECONOMICS 19 (Washington: Institute for International Economics, September 1987).

20. US Department of Commerce, International Trade Administration, *Major Shippers of Cotton, Wood, and Man-Made Fiber Textile and Apparel* (Washington: Department of Commerce, November 1986).

and $315 million in textiles, for a total of nearly $3 billion annually.[21] Clearly, if this sum or even one-half of it were devoted to programs of labor adjustment, the process of import liberalization could potentially be greatly facilitated.

In contrast, such revenues under the program suggested above would be far lower. If the tariff rate quota successfully held imports to the quota-threshold level as designed, there would be no revenue at all. Adjustment assistance funding would have to come solely from general funds for this purpose, such as the $1 billion program suggested by Secretary Brock. It is informative, nonetheless, to consider the amount of additional funding that could be available for adjustment assistance if imports moderately exceeded the quota-threshold levels and did generate some surcharge revenues.

As a purely illustrative estimate, suppose that in actual implementation imports of apparel and textiles from previously quota-controlled countries and products exceeded the tariff rate quota trigger points by 10 percent in a given year, or by $1.05 billion in apparel and $210 million in textiles on the basis of 1986 import levels. Application of the 25 percent surcharge to these overquota imports in apparel and 15 percent in textiles would generate $262 million from apparel and $32 million from textiles, for a total of approximately $300 million annually. Although only one-tenth of the revenue under the auction quota approach, this amount could make an important contribution to the financing of labor adjustment. More specifically, in the calculations reviewed above for the liberalization scenario, a total of 512,000 textile and apparel jobs would be lost over 14 years (of which 336,000 would be lost even without liberalization). The average reduction annually would be 36,600 jobs. Making the extreme assumption that none of this reduction came from retirement (virtually the opposite of the finding on the potential of adjustment through attrition as examined above), and assuming a period of two years of adjustment benefits, the illustrative revenue of $300 million annually from the tariff rate quota surcharge would be sufficient to provide $4,000 annually per worker in adjustment assistance. Considering that the figure of $4,000 per worker was suggested for retraining, relocation, and rehiring services by the studies reviewed in chapter 4, and in view of the fact that a large portion of the employment loss could be absorbed by the ranks of the retiring who would not need adjustment assistance, the

---

21. The Congressional Budget Office places the estimate for the two sectors at $1.9 billion, with the difference attributable to its assumption that not all quotas are binding and that the tariff-equivalent is only 20 percent for apparel and 7 percent for textiles. However, the more conservative figure is still large in terms of potential revenue for adjustment assistance. Steven Parker, "Revenue Estimate for Auctioning Existing Import Quota" (Washington: Congressional Budget Office, 27 February 1987; processed).

revenue potential of the tariff rate quota mechanism proposed above could well be sufficient for the bulk of the adjustment financing needs. (Correspondingly, the auction quota alternative could generate a considerable excess of revenue above the actual requirements.)

Another possible advantage of the auction quota is that it might satisfy insistence of industry and labor groups on adequate protection, whereas they might either fully reject the tariff rate quota alternative or demand that the tariff surcharge be set at such a prohibitive rate that the effect would be to raise protection. It must be recognized, however, that opposition of these groups may be expected to be intense for any program of planned liberalization over time, whether its instrument is the tariff rate quota or the auction quota.

On the side of disadvantages, the revenue potential of the auction quota is a two-edged sword. Critics of the mechanism are concerned that this new source of fiscal revenue would be so tempting that US authorities would cling to existing protection rather than preside over its gradual elimination (and thereby disappearance of the revenue). From the international standpoint, the transfer of quota rents from foreign suppliers to the US Treasury would raise the issue of compensation. A major reason why the voluntary export restraint is tolerated by foreign suppliers is that they obtain a large share of the quota rents; under auctioned import quotas, they might press their GATT rights to compensation for the protection. A clear commitment to use auction quotas solely as a temporary mechanism during a program of strictly enforced gradual liberalization would seem essential as the response to such demands.

The most serious danger of the auction quota is that it might actually increase protection. To be assured of raising revenue, the auction quota probably would have to be implemented on an "internationally consolidated" basis, in which existing quotas from all covered countries were pooled. That is, there would be one import quota (in a particular product category) for all such suppliers that the government would auction off. If instead individual bilateral quotas were retained, each of the foreign governments could hold its own auction and preempt the rent from the quota, leaving little to be raised through the second auction at the level of the importing country. Moreover, the political dynamics of trade pressure could easily cause internationally consolidated quotas to transform into "global" quotas restricting not only countries already subject to restraints but all others as well (or at least all except the industrial countries). Legislators and industry and labor groups could argue that with quotas now imposed by the United States on imports rather than by individual countries on their exports, it no longer made sense to have some countries exempt from the quotas just because they had not yet begun large-scale exporting (although a general exception for industrial country suppliers would seem more likely to persist on grounds of political relations and general trade retaliatory capacity).

If the quotas did become "global" (even exempting industrial country suppliers), as opposed to "internationally consolidated," the consequence could be an increase in protection. In the MFA (as well as some other instances of protection, such as the 1977–81 restrictions on footwear) one of the most important escape valves for liberal treatment in practice has been the fact that the quotas are bilateral rather than global. This feature has meant that numerous countries for which there are not yet specifically negotiated quotas on individual textile and apparel items may expand their production and exports of those items, at least until the point where there is a call in importing countries for negotiations to limit further growth.

Retailers add the complaint that an auction quota would introduce uncertainty into the procurement process and would invite monopolization by powerful groups capable of buying up a commanding share of the quota. These fears are probably exaggerated, and may mask a different concern— that the auction could extract that portion of the scarcity rent currently retained by retailing groups. Nonetheless, it would appear likely that some disruption to normal supplier-retailer relations would result from an auction quota. There are differences between transactions in the "customer market" or "fix-price sector," on the one hand, and the "auction market" or "flex-price sector," on the other.[22] In the customer market, pricing on the part of both parties takes a longer term view than the maximization of immediate profit, with an eye to maintaining a good relationship over time. In light of this institutional behavior, it could well be true that under an auction system certain groups could buy up access to supply that otherwise would be channeled more broadly to traditional customers (because of the reluctance of suppliers correspondingly to sell to the highest bidder of the moment in view of longer-term relationships).

Some analysts are concerned, furthermore, that by shifting protection from the foreign voluntary export restraint to the US-imposed import quota, the auction quota would tend to generate sector-specific legislation within Congress, identifying appropriate levels for quotas. That is, the very presence of a mechanism for assigning quotas unilaterally could be an invitation to members of Congress to set the levels themselves, at amounts lower than the original voluntary export quotas in the aggregate. One of the reasons for the high Smoot-Hawley tariffs of the 1930s was the log-rolling process within Congress in which various groups would support each other's requests for such sector-specific protection. A factor contributing to postwar

---

22. Arthur M. Okun, *Prices and Quantities: A Macroeconomic Analysis* (Washington: Brookings Institution, 1981).

liberalization has been the insulation of tariffs from sector-specific legislation through foreign negotiations.

In view of these considerations, it would seem prudent to use auction quotas as the mechanism for liberalization only under certain strict conditions.[23] The most important is that all parties would agree at the outset that auction quotas would be imposed solely as an inseparable part of a concrete program for liberalization over time. This firm commitment to liberalization would discipline revenue appetites, probably allay foreign demands for compensation, preempt the opportunity for congressional log-rolling in setting tight quotas, and reject at the outset the imposition of quota levels with growth rates so slow that liberalization would never arrive. An international agreement undertaking a known timetable of liberalization would provide a highly useful means of ensuring that the auction quotas did not become divorced from the liberalization commitment.

A second condition on the auction quota would be that its initial levels incorporate only existing country-product quotas (international consolidation) rather than imposing global quantitative limits newly restricting countries and products formerly unrestricted. This safeguard would involve some idiosyncracies, such as treating sweaters from Tanzania as well as from Italy as not subject to the quotas allocated, because neither country is under quotas today. Importers would not need a quota right to import from such sources (or other country-product combinations where quotas did not exist previously). If there were a large surge in imports thus exempted from the auctioned quotas, in practice bilateral consultations would probably lead to moving the country product from outside to inside the quota restraint, with some corresponding increase in the total of quotas to be auctioned.

A third feature that could help ensure against trade disruption would be to reserve initially for purchase at the going price perhaps one-half of the quotas for importers on a historical basis, while auctioning the remainder. Over time the share auctioned would rise as importers gained experience in coping with the new regime.

An Alternative Liberalization Plan

The considerations discussed above on the design of a future trade regime for textiles and apparel, and the examination of auction quotas in particular, are relevant in the evaluation of future programs other than that proposed above. In the category of gradual liberalization, an important proposal has been suggested by Hufbauer and Schott (HS).[24]

---

23. As developed more fully in Bergsten, Schott, Takacs, and Elliott, *Auction Quotas*.

24. Gary Clyde Hufbauer and Jeffrey J. Schott, *Trading for Growth: the Next Round of*

The HS proposal also envisions gradual liberalization over 15 years. However, it relies on auctioned quotas rather than on the tariff rate quota. The authors propose that each industrial country establish a global import quota for the major textile and apparel categories at the level of imports in the base year (in their study, at the end of MFA-III in mid-1986). These global quotas would then be increased annually by 6 percent. National quotas for specific supplier countries would be reduced by 10 percent annually. The corresponding amounts of imports would be shifted from national-specific origin to a pool of quotas available for distribution on a global basis that, in addition, would incorporate the annual 6 percent growth increment in the global total. This pool of floating quotas would be auctioned off to the highest bidders.

Over time, national quotas would disappear, while the global quota would rise to magnitudes so large as to be no longer the binding constraint on imports. The price of the auction rights would fall to zero. In the meantime, however, revenues raised from the quota auction would be applied to adjustment assistance programs. The authors calculate that some $10 billion over six years would be raised for this purpose, enough to finance 2.4 percent annual reduction in employment at an extremely liberal allowance of $35,000 per worker transferred. The authors see the package as balanced; it would not impose too abrupt a change on supplying countries (which would only gradually lose their national quotas), while at the same time it would provide at least temporarily an additional degree of protection for industrial country producers in the form of a global quota.

The Hufbauer and Schott proposal has much to recommend it. The mechanism would raise considerable revenue for adjustment assistance, given its reliance on the auction quota. However, it is subject to some significant drawbacks. Perhaps the most serious is its provision that there would be immediate global quotas. As noted above, the present absence in the MFA of a global quota is probably the largest single source of flexibility for import expansion in the regime. Geographical diversification has been a constant theme of response by foreign countries to the MFA restrictions. Their proposal would also appear to impose for the first time quota restraints against imports from industrial countries. This process could well lead to trade repression that would at least erode, and possibly exceed, the trade creation under the program as a whole. The proposal also turns on the merits of the auction quota. As noted above, there are grounds for concern about this mechanism. The principal appeal of this option would thus appear to be as a vehicle for liberalization in the case that producer and

---

Trade Negotiations, POLICY ANALYSES IN INTERNATIONAL ECONOMICS 11 (Washington: Institute for International Economics, September 1985).

labor interests were adamantly opposed to the tariff rate quota option but amenable to their alternative based on auctioned quotas.

Continuation of Past Policy

By default, the easiest policy option would be to let textile and apparel protection run its course for yet another round of the MFA, followed by still another. The current, fourth renewal provides for continuation of the past approach for another five years.

In some regards, there could be worse outcomes from the standpoint of an open international trading regime than mere perpetuation of the MFA regime along past lines. While protective, the regime has been a semipermeable screen rather than an absolute wall against imports. It has slowed but not stopped import growth. Its structure tends to generate new sources of supply internationally as importers seek to establish suppliers in as yet uncontrolled country-product combinations, thereby possibly disseminating growth. (Note, however, that the argument is also made that without their historic quotas the big four Far Eastern suppliers would not be able to hold onto their market shares against competition from lower wage countries, as quotas available to such countries—or at least the certainty for new investment in the case of uncontrolled countries—would be greater in the absence of large quotas earmarked for the East Asian NICs.)

The principal drawback of the policy option of "more of the same" is that the likely result will be successive tightening of import protection, albeit on a lower profile and more gradually than in some of the directly protective policy options. Chapter 9 enumerates the trend toward tightening of the regime in 1986, both in the provisions of MFA-IV and in the implementation of principal US bilateral agreements. The MFA of the late 1980s is thus unlikely to be as porous as that of the first half of this decade. With US consumer costs of textile and apparel protection already in the range of $20 billion annually, the prospect of upward-ratcheting protection under the mantle of the MFA should be of concern to policymakers.

Major New Restrictions

The third broad policy alternative is to adopt substantial new protection against textiles and apparel. Chapter 9 reviews and analyzes the principal recent efforts in this direction, the Textile and Apparel Trade Enforcement Act narrowly defeated on presidential veto override in 1986, and the successor Textile and Apparel Trade Act of 1987 proposed early the following year. After the 1986 defeat, the groups seeking tighter import restriction concentrated their efforts in the direction of proposing global quotas, with growth in the quotas calibrated to avoid a rise in the share of imports in the domestic market.[25] The replacement of the previous year's attempt to roll back imports from major suppliers by a large amount with a new thrust of essentially clamping down more comprehensively on imports at current levels appeared to reflect the belief of groups seeking restrictions that the latter, seemingly milder position would stand a better chance of adoption.

The costs of sharp new restrictions involved in the 1985–86 and 1987 initiatives are analyzed in chapter 9. The potential effects of such measures in increasing domestic employment are considered in chapter 10, where simulations indicate a surprisingly small impact on textile employment but larger effects for apparel. The principal point about such proposals is that they would intensify the economic costs and distortions already built up under the regime of protection of the MFA. Whether that intensification should be adopted as a matter of public policy turns again primarily on the primacy in the public eye of artificially creating or maintaining jobs specifically in the textile and apparel sectors. For the numerous reasons set forth at various places in this study, and which will not be repeated here, sharply increased protection would appear to be highly counterproductive for the economy as a whole.

It should be added that the new orientation in 1987 toward demands for global quotas is a potentially deceptive and dangerous approach. Calls for sharp rollbacks are transparent and may be evaluated in straightforward terms of benefits and costs of higher protection. The alternative plea for global quotas superficially would appear less restrictive—it would only seem to codify the existing level of imports and then control its growth. There are two principal points to recognize about this alternative. First, it would remove the main source of flexibility in the MFA—the scope for geographical diversification. Second, it would raise difficult problems among the industrial countries because if US imports from Europe for the first time were to be subject to quotas controlled from a recent base, there would no doubt be European retaliation setting similar quotas against US exports. Ironically, adoption of quotas at the present time could lock in artificially high US imports from, and low exports to, Europe because the base levels would be taken from the worst point in the phase of trade deterioration following the overvaluation of the dollar. The broader problem, however, would be the likelihood of future trade repression as the open trade area among industrial countries disappeared in textiles and apparel without an offsetting extension of more liberal trade to developing-country suppliers.

---

25. Bruce Stokes, "Trade Report: Setting the Stage," *National Journal*, 17 January 1987, p. 124.

An Arrangement for Open Trade in Textiles and Apparel (AOTTA)

The analysis of this study suggests that the ideal policy option is the program for gradual liberalization set forth above. Inevitably, this choice incorporates a value judgment that the net benefits to the economy as a whole should be pursued, rather than the specific gains of firms and workers currently in the textile and apparel sectors. In addition to dealing with the political issue of whether textile trade policy will be set by sectoral or national interests, however, it will be necessary to address the questions of foreign reciprocity and parallel liberalization by the European Community (EC) if the liberalization option is to have a realistic chance of adoption.

One strategy for accomplishing both of these objectives would be the development of an open trade club in textiles and apparel that would require reciprocity for admission on the part of the NICs but with their reciprocal liberalization available only to the industrial countries that themselves provided liberalization.

Consider first the stakes in NIC reciprocity. From tables 10.1 and 10.2, it may be seen that the liberalization option would increase US imports of textiles and apparel by $827 million in 1988 and by $16.42 billion by the year 2000 (at constant 1982 prices) above the levels they would otherwise reach under present policy. In terms of annual growth, for the full period through the year 2000 textile imports would grow at 1.4 percent annually without liberalization and at 2.6 percent annually with it, while apparel imports would grow at 5.3 percent annually under present policy and 8.1 percent annually under liberalization. The increase attributable to liberalization would be 1.2 percent annually for textiles and 2.8 percent annually for apparel, or 2.5 percent annually for both sectors combined.

In broad terms, then, on an import base of $22.1 billion in textiles and apparel (tables 2.3 and 2.5), there would be annual increments of approximately $560 million (2.5 percent) attributable to the liberalization program, growing over time with the size of the import base. The cumulative effect of these increments would generate the $16.42 billion increase in imports attributable to liberalization by the year 2000, just noted.

The implications of seeking reciprocal liberalization from NICs may be illustrated with the cases of Korea and Taiwan. The two countries together account for 31.4 percent of US imports of textiles and apparel (tables 2.3, 2.5, and 2.11). Thus, if they were expected to liberalize their markets sufficiently to increase their own imports from the United States by amounts equal to increased US imports from them as the result of US textile and apparel liberalization, their increases in imports would amount to $260 million in 1988 and $5.16 billion by the year 2000 (31.4 percent of $827 million and $16.4 billion, respectively). This increase is approximately one-fourth above the total imports they would otherwise purchase from the

United States at the turn of the century (assuming 4 percent real growth in the trade base).[26] A considerable portion of this reciprocal trade increase could arise in the textile and (to a much lesser extent) apparel sectors themselves. Thus, the ratio of imports of textiles and apparel to exports is 66 percent in free-trade Hong Kong but only 8 percent in protected Korea (table 5.4). If Korea and Taiwan increased their textile and apparel imports by amounts equal to one-third of their export levels (leaving the import-export ratios still well below Hong Kong's level), and if the US share in this increase matched the Korea-Taiwan share in US textile and apparel imports, US textile and apparel exports to the two countries in the year 2000 would be $5.9 billion higher than otherwise, fully covering the reciprocity objective.[27]

These calculations are purely illustrative, since there would be many other factors to take into account in a more meaningful model of potential reciprocity effects (including, importantly, the fact that the flavor of bilateral matching in the above illustration is less appropriate than reciprocity on a multilateral basis, and the need to take account of changing trade shares). It seems likely in particular that the volume of reciprocal import increase by the NICs that would arise in the textile and apparel sectors themselves would fall short of the volume of increased US imports from liberalization of the sector, so that additional liberalization in other sectors might be necessary by the NICs (and the United States could appropriately place this consideration on the bargaining table more generally within the Uruguay Round). Moreover, other developing-country suppliers would be in a much less adequate position than Korea and especially Taiwan to offer immediate reciprocity because of the more typical weakness in balance of payments. Despite these qualifications, these illustrations do suggest substantial scope for reciprocal trade gains from US liberalization of textiles and apparel.

Additional evidence that underscores the potential for reciprocity is the surprisingly large share of world imports of textiles that the developing countries purchase despite their widespread protection—30.8 percent (table 6.1). The presence of this sizable base of imports reinforces the view that liberalization by the NICs could provide meaningful reciprocity for that granted by industrial countries.

An Arrangement for Open Trade in Textiles and Apparel could begin

---

26. US exports to Korea and Taiwan amounted to $10.95 billion in 1986. US Department of Commerce, *Survey of Current Business*, vol. 67, no. 3 (March 1987), p. 45.

27. That is, in the year 2000 total US imports of textiles and apparel would be $56.8 billion in the liberalization case (in 1982 prices; tables 10.1, 10.2). Applying the 1980 Korea-Taiwan share of 31.4 percent, they would provide $17.8 billion of this total. If the increment of US exports set equal to one-third of the Korea-Taiwan export base is applied to this estimate, US exports in the sector would rise by $5.9 billion.

from this premise of broadly balanced reciprocity, with NIC liberalization in their own textile and apparel sectors in the first instance but also possible liberalization in other sectors as the balance to US textile and apparel liberalization. Countries such as Korea and Taiwan would be expected to offer this reciprocity as the price of admission to the US liberalization offered within the AOTTA. Developing countries with weaker balance of payments positions could enter with commitments to liberalize their own trade over a longer time schedule.

The second challenge in the liberalization strategy would be to bring Europe along. It is highly unlikely that US political forces would permit liberalization unless there were a parallel reduction in European restrictions on imports, on grounds of the risk that otherwise NIC supply would be diverted to the US market.

An initial observation on the problem of parallel EC liberalization would be that fears of inundation by imports from such diversion may be overstated. The projections of chapter 10 assume that foreign supply is "infinitely elastic," and as such there is an unlimited availability of imports from the developing countries regardless of what Europe does about its own protection. In such a model, projected US imports of textiles and apparel would be unchanged by European liberalization as opposed to the lack thereof.

A major risk to liberalization efforts is that at each point in time the international regime is negotiated on the basis of what is acceptable to the area least willing to liberalize. The original MFA set restrictions driven by the hard-pressed US position; MFA-II and MFA-III tightened in accordance with EC demands as Europe was then under pressure; and tightening under MFA-IV in 1986 reflected US demands in view of its rapidly increasing imports. Thus, even if US policymakers decided in favor of an AOTTA, it could be blocked by European unwillingness to liberalize.

A strategy that could deal with this risk would be to limit the benefits of reciprocal liberalization by the NICs within the AOTTA to those countries that were members by virtue of their own liberalization. If the EC were unprepared to liberalize textile and apparel imports, it would remain outside the arrangement. The liberalization of textile and apparel imports (as well as other product sectors) in the NICs designed to provide the reciprocity for US liberalization of the two sectors would not be accorded to Europe unless the EC also decided to join the AOTTA and liberalize its own textile and apparel sectors. As illustrated above, the trade stakes in reciprocal trade could be quite substantial, and policymakers in Europe could well be prepared to reconsider any initial opposition to participation (and liberalization) in light of the new export opportunities they could miss.

In short, the open trade club approach could accomplish two objectives simultaneously: ensuring reciprocal liberalization by suppliers of textiles and apparel, and prompting parallel liberalization by Europe. It could, of course, raise questions about departure from MFN principles; but its central purpose would be liberalization of textile and apparel trade, and because the current regime of trade in these sectors is so diametrically opposed to the basic GATT principles (including MFN treatment) anyway, the AOTTA approach would be an improvement in moving toward the underlying objectives of GATT principles. Moreover, there has been a growing trend toward conditional trading arrangements, in which only those countries that agree to provide liberalization of their own markets are granted entry. The Tokyo Round of trade negotiations in the late 1970s moved in this direction with its codes on subsidies, government procurement, and free trade in aircraft. The central issue in the compatibility of such arrangements with open trade objectives is whether the resulting trade creation exceeds the trade diversion. In the case of AOTTA, it almost certainly would.

A final word about trade policy strategy under this approach is in order. The AOTTA approach would have a strong element of sectoral reciprocity. As the United States (and, one hopes, Europe and Japan) liberalized textiles and apparel, it would seek in the first instance liberalization of textile and apparel markets in supplier countries. As noted above, the reciprocity would not be strictly sectoral; in some cases, supplier countries might have to offer liberalization in other sectors as well to provide a balanced outcome, and in other cases it would make sense for liberalization in other sectors to serve as sufficient reciprocity when liberalization in textiles and apparel in the supplier country was impossible politically. Nonetheless, an AOTTA would begin from a starting point of sectoral reciprocity.

In general, sectoral reciprocity is a doubtful strategy for world trade. It tends to ignore the principle of comparative advantage, under which one trading partner specializes in one good and the other in another good. It inhibits trade negotiations by ruling out the trading off of concessions in other sectors against requests for liberalization in the sector in question. And, as formulated by some in recent US trade policy discussions, it could prove to be a basis for retaliation against other countries that do not liberalize their markets in a particular product, even when the home country maintains barriers of its own in other products ("aggressive reciprocity").[28] Such retaliation can easily provoke counterretaliation and a generalized increase in protection.

There is, nonetheless, an important feature of the textile and apparel sectors that makes them more appropriate than most for sectoral reciprocity: the countries that would be asked to offer reciprocity for US liberalization should already have a strong competitive position (that is, relatively strong

---

28. William R. Cline, *"Reciprocity": A New Approach to World Trade Policy?* (Washington: Institute for International Economics, POLICY ANALYSES IN INTERNATIONAL ECONOMICS 2, September 1982).

comparative advantage) in these sectors. The greatest potential for mischief under the sectoral reciprocity concept arises when a powerful trading country such as the United States insists that a trading partner offer reciprocal liberalization in a sector in which the powerful country has comparative advantage, while refusing to offer liberalization in other sectors in which the powerful nation has comparative disadvantage. This pattern has characterized most of the US discussion of the reciprocity-retaliation approach; its adherents typically seek to force liberalization of foreign markets in products in which the United States has comparative advantage (such as telecommunications) while remaining silent about any reciprocal liberalization by the United States in areas of comparative disadvantage (such as apparel and steel).

In the case of the AOTTA, the United States would be proposing just the opposite. US liberalization would open up the apparel sector in which the United States has comparative disadvantage. It seems only fair that the least the US negotiators could request in return is that the suppliers of apparel, who enjoy comparative advantage in the sector, do the same.

The textiles sector is somewhat different because capital intensity and technology make it closer to a case of outright US comparative advantage. However, "factor reversal" is possible in the sector and some developing countries are also competitive in textiles on the basis of labor-intensive technologies. The joint inclusion of both textiles and apparel in an AOTTA would tend to give "the sector" a balance of comparative advantage on both sides that would typically be absent in a narrower sector. Industrial countries would have comparative advantage in textiles and developing countries in apparel.

Beyond the AOTTA strategy for achieving reciprocity and liberalization by Europe (and Japan), it is useful to keep in mind a further consideration. The principles of comparative advantage and the basic economics of international trade suggest that it is to a country's own benefit to liberalize its imports even if its trading partners do not. The presence of an annual consumer cost of some $20 billion or more (and net welfare costs of nearly half this size) suggests that it would behoove the United States to move toward liberalization in the textile and apparel sectors even if the degree of foreign reciprocity that US negotiators could achieve would be less than complete.

Implementation

The steps for implementation of the program suggested here could include the following.

The new Uruguay Round of trade negotiations is the natural forum to pursue the aspect of reciprocal trade bargaining discussed above, either for the specific development of the AOTTA or more generally. In this forum, the principal developing-country suppliers could reasonably seek a policy reorientation on the part of the industrial countries along the lines suggested here. Industrial country representatives in turn could pursue commitments by the developing countries to liberalize their own markets gradually, with priority on the textiles sector, considering that the industrial countries have relatively good prospects for international competitiveness in this sector. It is important that the Uruguay Round not shunt aside the textile and apparel sectors on grounds that they have already been taken care of by MFA-IV.

The next step in implementation would be to develop a serious effort for planning for the future of the MFA upon termination of MFA-IV. In the past, negotiators have waited until the last minute and then adopted a replication of the previous MFA with some fine tuning, typically in the area of closing loopholes. This time trade officials would instead explicitly establish a calendar that would permit serious reevaluation of the MFA. In particular, it would be desirable to set a ministerial meeting for July 1989, after the third full year of MFA-IV (and judiciously after the US presidential election of 1988), to establish a timetable for serious negotiations on fundamental reform of the MFA regime by the time of the expiration of its current round. Change of the MFA along the lines set forth here would be sufficiently fundamental that a period of two years could well be required for its adoption. If the negotiations went well, there is no reason that an early termination of MFA-IV could not be declared. Moreover, these negotiations and decisions would be naturally linked to emerging results in the Uruguay Round.

This seemingly lengthy process has to recommend it the fact that it will take some time for the intense pressure on US textile and apparel imports resulting from the overvalued dollar to abate and for the overall protectionist pressures in the United States associated with the massive trade deficit to reverse.

For the immediate future, the principal challenge for policymakers will be to avoid being swept along by strong pressures for increased restrictions. Moreover, in this period it will be important that tactical retreats by officials avowedly favoring open trade not turn into a source of major new protective measures in the name of preemptive action. In 1986 the measures of the Reagan administration on textile and apparel trade came dangerously close to this outcome.

The near-term political challenge includes the presidential campaign of 1988. As discussed in chapter 6, several presidents have made pledges during campaigns that have committed them to new restrictions on textile and apparel imports. In his 1960 campaign, John F. Kennedy promised to seek a multilateral arrangement on textiles, setting the stage for the Short

Term Arrangement in 1961 and the Long Term Arrangement in 1962. In the 1968 campaign, Richard M. Nixon pledged extended coverage of protection to man-made fibers, providing the groundwork for the MFA. And in the 1980 campaign, Ronald Reagan sent a letter to Senator Strom Thurmond (R–SC) pledging to strengthen the MFA at the time of its expiration in 1981, and this pledge was a major influence in subsequent tightening under the Reagan administration (including the move to more automatic mechanisms for implementing quotas). There will be a strong temptation for the candidates in the 1988 election (including in the primaries) to make similar pledges. At the same time, there could be political risk in such commitments, as they could be interpreted as identification with a special interest group (which appears to have been a factor in the 1984 election in the public's perception of Walter Mondale's commitment to the labor unions after their early endorsement of him). Indeed, a campaign clearly articulating the reasons for favoring increased US competitiveness but rejecting protection could well be more successful even on purely political grounds than one embracing the calls of various groups for further restricting US imports.

12

Textile and Apparel Negotiations in the Uruguay Round: An Evaluation of Proposals

The Uruguay Round of multilateral trade negotiations is scheduled to conclude by the end of 1990. The round has the potential to achieve important trade liberalization, especially in new areas not previously covered by the GATT (General Agreement on Tariffs and Trade). However, differences must be overcome in at least two crucial areas—textiles and apparel, and agriculture—if the negotiations are to succeed. A breakdown in either area could cause a collapse of the entire round.

In textiles and apparel, the challenge is to provide a means of liberalizing trade over time and reintegrating the sector into normal GATT treatment, and away from the current regime of bilateral quotas under the fourth Multi-Fiber Arrangement (MFA–IV). Developing countries are insisting on such an outcome in textiles and apparel if they are to cooperate with liberalization in other areas, especially new fields of particular importance to the United States, namely, trade in services, intellectual property rights, and investment practices.

US negotiators thus find themselves in a position in which they must make meaningful liberalization offers on textiles and apparel if they want the Uruguay Round to succeed. At the same time, they need to take into account the complaints of domestic textile and apparel producers that even the existing MFA mechanism, let alone a more liberalized arrangement, provides insufficient certainty about levels of imports and is susceptible to large import surges in product categories, or from countries, that are unrestricted. Indeed, representatives supportive of textile interests have again introduced in Congress proposed legislation (discussed below) that would severely tighten protection.

Under the fast-track procedure for ratification of Uruguay Round agreements, both houses of Congress must approve or reject the overall results of the round by a simple majority. In the past, textile and apparel producers and labor groups have been able to marshal congressional majorities of close to two-thirds in support of their proposals to tighten protection. Their ability to do so would be considerably less certain if the issue were the much broader question of Uruguay Round agreements, because legislators would have to consider the interests of a much wider set of constituents; US negotiators must nonetheless face the risk that textile and apparel interests could block fast-track passage of the agreement.

This chapter examines the proposals that US negotiators have submitted in pursuit of these two objectives: liberalization of trade in textiles and apparel to secure developing-country cooperation, on the one hand, and the addressing of concerns of domestic textile and apparel producers, on the other. The analysis also considers proposals offered by Japan, the European Community, and Switzerland, as well as the proposed Textiles, Apparel, and Footwear Trade Act of 1990. The emphasis is on the economic logic and implications of each alternative approach, with particular attention to the costs of protection to US consumers.

The Proposals

In early February 1990, both the United States and Japan submitted proposals for textile and apparel trade liberalization. The European Community had already proposed an approach in July 1989. The discussion below first describes the proposals and then presents a model-based analysis of their implications.

United States

The Office of the US Trade Representative (USTR) has proposed three options in the Uruguay Round negotiations.[1] All three call for complete elimination of quotas on textile and apparel imports by the year 2001. The broad structure of the US proposals is a trade-off in which the US government offers domestic producers greater certainty over the period 1991–2000 in exchange for outright elimination of the quota regime thereafter.

Global Quotas

Under the first option, textile and apparel trade would shift from its current regime under MFA–IV, according to which quotas are bilaterally negotiated

---

1. "Communication from the United States," 5 February 1990 and 5 March 1990, reproduced in appendix D.

with exporting developing countries, to a structure of global quotas setting annual ceilings for total imports regardless of the country of origin. Under this proposal, for the first time, European and other industrial countries previously exempt from quotas under a gentlemen's agreement (although not by explicit MFA provisions) would become subject to quota restrictions, as would developing countries not currently under controls, including many in Africa. For each product category, the global quota would grow at a specified annual rate that would rise over time. At the end of 10 years, all quotas would disappear.

KEY FEATURES   Important features of the global quota proposal include the following.

First, for any product category the total global quota would be composed of country-specific ceilings for those countries now subject to quotas, plus a global "basket" component (appendix D, figure D.1), for which all countries, including those possessing country-specific quotas, could compete. In practice, this distinction would mean that countries such as Korea, whose exports are presently controlled by quotas, would receive more favorable treatment than others. Not only would they be assured of their base-year quotas, but they could also compete for a share of the global basket. In contrast, a country such as France, whose exports are not now controlled, would have no assurance that its base-year export volume would be secured in the future under the new regime, and at the same time it could lose out to competition from Korea and others within the global basket. If countries besides the United States also adopted the global quota approach, US exporters similarly for the first time would face the need to compete within a global quota limitation.

Second, the basis for the global quota would be actual trade in the base year, not the aggregate of existing country quotas plus trade for uncovered countries. As noted in appendix D, the average of exports to the United States during 1987–89 would be the basis for the new initial quota level, although there would be some "uplift" (percentage expansion) at the outset to ensure against an actual reduction from existing trade levels. In practice, this specification means that quotas currently unused would be lost.

On the basis of GATT data on quota utilization in 1982, and on actual trade levels in 1987, for the top 15 suppliers of textile and apparel imports to the United States the aggregate level of quotas exceeded actual imports from covered countries by 30 percent.[2] An approximate estimate might thus

---

2. Calculated from data in chapter 6, p. 160; Organization for Economic Cooperation and Development (OECD), *Foreign Trade by Commodities, Vol. II, Imports, 1987* (Paris: OECD, 1988), pp. 192–94, 237–39.

be that actual imports are only 80 percent of the existing sum of quotas plus actual imports for uncovered countries and products.[3] Over the transitional decade, the use of actual trade as the base rather than the initial quota level is thus equivalent to cutting the average annual quota growth rate by about 2 percentage points.[4]

Third, over time the quota regime would shift toward general-source rather than country-specific quotas. Each year, one-tenth of the original country quotas would be transferred from the country-specific component to the basket component within the global quota. As a result, the composition of supply would shift gradually toward countries with strong underlying competitiveness and away from less efficient suppliers that have maintained market share solely through their historical possession of country quotas. This phased shift to general rather than country-specific quotas and the imposition of global quotas are also the central features of a proposal for textile liberalization suggested previously by Hufbauer and Schott.[5]

Fourth, there would be some simplification, consolidation, and elimination of quota categories. For example, the 140 categories under present US implementation of the MFA might be reduced to 100 through the aggregation of some categories and elimination of quotas in some others in which US

---

3. On the basis of physical data for 1989, the share of quotas currently unused may be even larger. Apparel imports subject to quotas stood at 3.60 billion square-meter equivalents (SME), only 67.0 percent of the 5.37-billion-SME quota total. The "fill rates" were even lower for other broad categories: miscellaneous textiles, 61.9 percent; yarn, 48.2 percent; and fabric, 46.3 percent. American Textile Manufacturers Institute, *Trade Winds,* vol. 2, no. 3, 17 January 1990, p. 7. The unused quota share by value would tend to be lower, however, if countries typically fill more completely their quotas in categories with high values per square meter.

4. However, this growth rate correspondence between the actual trade base and existing quotas assumes a complete flexibility in quota transfer among countries, currently absent but eventually achieved in the USTR proposal through reallocation to the global basket. Suppose the quota level were 125 and the import level 100 (with a quota utilization rate of 80 percent). Annual growth of imports at 7 percent (for example) and of quotas at 5 percent would then yield approximately the same levels for imports and quotas at the end of a decade (197 and 204, respectively). However, in the absence of progressive reallocation to a global basket, or an alternative mechanism permitting trading of quotas among countries, the utilization rate would be likely to remain unchanged. Actual imports at the end of the decade would then be considerably lower under a formulation adopting the lower growth rate as applied to the actual quota base rather than the higher rate applied to the trade base.

5. Gary Clyde Hufbauer and Jeffrey J. Schott, *Trading for Growth: The Next Round of Trade Negotiations* (Washington: Institute for International Economics, September 1985), p. 57. In chapter 11 (p. 281) I criticize the Hufbauer-Schott proposal on grounds that it would tend to increase protection at least temporarily by imposing quotas on countries not previously subject to them.

production is considered to be more competitive (typically in textile rather than apparel categories).[6]

Fifth, there would be a gradation of quota growth rates across products in accordance with their differing sensitivity to imports, with more sensitive products held to a lower rate of quota growth. The illustration in the US communiqué (appendix D, figure D.2) suggests that there would be a basic, or minimum, growth rate x for all products. Product categories with "very high" import sensitivity would have their initial quota growth rate set at x percent annually. For products with "high" sensitivity the rate would be $x + 1$ percent (in the communiqué's example), and for categories with only "moderate" sensitivity the rate would be $x + 2$ percent.

Sixth, the growth rate for quotas would rise over time. Again in the illustration presented in the US communiqué, the rates just cited would apply for the first three years of the transitional decade; for the second three years they would all rise by 1 percentage point; for the next two years by a further percentage point; and for the final two years by an additional percentage point. Thus, in 2000–01 the growth rates would range from $x + 3$ percent to $x + 5$ percent.

Seventh, free trade area partners would be exempt from global quotas. For imports to the United States, this provision would include Canada and Israel and might in the future include Mexico.

Eighth, the US proposal offers the possibility of special treatment for imports manufactured from raw materials originating in the United States. Goods covered under item 807-A of the Tariff Schedules of the United States, which limits duties to the value added abroad on products manufactured using raw materials (fabric) produced in the United States, could be exempted from the global quota.[7] This provision could be important in the future, as these imports have been growing relatively rapidly; however, at present they remain modest, at only 12.6 percent of US apparel imports and 1.4 percent of textiles.[8]

---

6. The low quota fill rates in yarn and fabrics, cited above, suggest the ability of the textiles sector to dispense with quota protection immediately in at least some categories.

7. Note that this provision could benefit US textile producers at the expense of domestic producers of apparel.

8. These figures are for all item 807 imports, of which the bulk are covered under 807-A. Calculated from US Department of Commerce, *Major Shippers Report,* December 1989. Note that apparel 807 imports rose from 630 million square-yard equivalents (SYE) in 1987 to 916 million SYE in 1989, or by 46.6 percent.

UNRESOLVED QUESTIONS   Beyond these specifics, the global quota proposal leaves several crucial questions open.

First, what would be the basic, or minimum, quota growth rate? If this rate were set too low, the result would be a rising severity of protection over time. Consumers would face increasing protection costs during the 10-year transition period. Moreover, the gap between the actual level of imports and the magnitude that would occur in the absence of quotas would be so great by the tenth year that producers would face the prospect of a large and abrupt rise in import competition in 2002, when quotas would be scheduled for abolition. Under such circumstances, there would be intense pressure from domestic producers and labor to postpone the elimination of quotas. In contrast, if the rate were set too high, quota growth could cause dislocation of domestic employment in the sector.

Second, how would global quotas be allocated? The country-specific component presumably would continue to be allocated among firms as in the past, by the government of the exporting country. But the global basket component by definition would not be reserved for any particular supplier countries. In principle, an efficient and equitable means of allocation would be for the importing-country government to auction these global basket quota rights.[9] However, retailers have typically rejected proposals for auctioned quotas on grounds that they would face severe uncertainty and disruption in established supplier channels. These concerns may be summarized by what might be called the "deep pockets" factor. The fear is that some actor with enormous resources would bid for a large portion of the quota tickets and leave the traditional market participants (the major retail houses) suddenly cut off from supply.[10]

The alternative of allocating the basket component among importers on the basis of their historical market shares also raises serious questions. In this case existing importers would enjoy a windfall gain, as they could now obtain the "quota rent," the difference between the high domestic market price and the price at which foreign countries competing against each other in the global basket would be willing to sell.

Still another alternative allocation mechanism would be a first-come, first-served approach. Within the global basket, any importer could import from any country up to the point where the ceiling volume for the textile category in question had been reached. But this process could become chaotic.

---

9. This is the option proposed by Hufbauer and Schott, *Trading for Growth*, p. 57.

10. Arguments for and against the auction quota are reviewed in C. Fred Bergsten, Kimberly Ann Elliott, Jeffrey J. Schott, and Wendy E. Takacs, *Auction Quotas and United States Trade Policy* (Washington: Institute for International Economics, September 1987). The authors favor auction quotas where protection is necessary, and advocate the channeling of revenue to labor adjustment in the protected industry.

Importers would rush to fill orders early in the year. As the year wore on and cumulative imports began to approach the quota ceiling, importers would face a greater and greater probability that their shipments would be blocked (presumably at considerable additional storage and other costs).

In short, under the global basket approach the progressive redistribution of country quotas would mean that, increasingly, quotas could not be allocated by the supplying countries, yet the options for allocation of quotas by the importing country all appear to have drawbacks. In May 1990 the chief US textile negotiator suggested that existing country quotas might be kept intact rather than cut by 10 percent each year.[11] Although this variant could allay importers' fears of disturbance in supply channels, and could appease existing exporters intent on retaining quotas, it would sharply curtail global efficiency gains.

Third, would there be any compensation to exporters for the loss of market share? Former quota holders would lose quota rents as their quotas were cut back by 10 percent annually, and the benefit of these quota rents has been part of the implicit bargain for their historical acceptance of MFA protection. They would need to be persuaded that their ultimate gains from dismantling protection exceeded their quota-rent losses during the transition.

Exporters not previously subject to quotas could lose market share as well. Although their losses would not be the classic welfare loss of a rent, because the reduction in their resources devoted to export production would be equal to their sales losses, they could nonetheless object, on grounds of the traditional GATT criterion of reciprocity, to the cutback in their exports. Moreover, this class of exporters would not be securing future market liberalization in exchange for their losses, because they already enjoy quota-free market access.

Global Tariff Rate Quotas

The second option proposed by the United States is a global tariff rate quota system. A tariff rate quota uses the price mechanism rather than an absolute embargo to limit imports to a specific quantity. Specifically, it sets a quantitative threshold at which a penalty tariff surcharge begins to apply to imports, rather than absolutely prohibiting the entry of imports beyond the threshold level. Correspondingly, a program of import liberalization based on the tariff rate quota would end the absolute prohibition of imports above the quota level and replace it with a duty surcharge that would be phased down over time.

---

11. *Journal of Commerce,* 11 May 1990.

KEY FEATURES The central features of the USTR tariff rate quota proposal are as follows.

First, the tariff rate quota would be global rather than country-specific. For example, if the United States set a global threshold for sweaters at 2 million dozen, any sweaters imported above this level would pay the basic, existing tariff plus a tariff surcharge. As long as the total number of sweaters imported fell short of 2 million dozen, there would be no surcharge. As in the case of the absolute global quota, the move to a global threshold for a tariff surcharge would risk increasing rather than decreasing protection, because it would bring under protection for the first time European and other suppliers not now covered by MFA restrictions.

Second, as in the absolute global quota approach, for countries currently under controls there would be an initial set of country thresholds that would essentially guarantee those countries surcharge-free entry. If such a country exceeded its base-year threshold ("quota"), it would have to pay the tariff surcharge on the excess if the aggregate global threshold had been reached (but otherwise it would not). Note that, as in the case of the absolute global quota, the conferring of assured country-specific quotas to countries currently under control (in this case, a threshold level exempt from any surcharge) would give them an advantage over countries currently not controlled (which would have no such assured base threshold).

Third, more generally the tariff rate quota scheme would be analogous to the absolute global quota scheme. In particular, it would have the same feature of gradual reallocation of the country-specific thresholds into a global basket.

Fourth, there would be special treatment for nations in which the state is the principal or only exporter. The concern here is that such countries tend not to respond to price signals, and might be prepared to continue selling even in the face of a tariff surcharge that would be prohibitive for suppliers operating under normal profit and loss incentives.

ADVANTAGES AND DISADVANTAGES There are two major advantages of the tariff rate quota approach over that of absolute global quotas. The first is that the use of a surcharge penalty instead of an absolute prohibition to enforce the quantitative ceiling provides greater flexibility in the system and thereby helps ensure that excess consumer costs (and inefficiencies in production allocation) do not reach exorbitant levels. Conceptually, an absolute quota is the equivalent of a tariff rate quota with the surcharge tariff set at infinity. Infinity is a high price and can mean extreme distortions.

The second advantage of the tariff rate quota is that it lends itself more naturally to a phaseout of protection. Under a tariff rate quota system, phaseout would come about through the implementation of a firm timetable for gradual reduction of the penalty surcharge. There is abundant international experience with tariff liberalization according to set timetables, and thus precedent for a schedule of phasedown in the penalty tariff surcharge. In contrast, under an absolute quota system the phaseout would have to come about by the adoption of a relatively high quota growth rate that would make the quota completely nonbinding by the end of the transition period. Otherwise, the system would be left with a gap between the uncontrolled level of imports and the controlled level at the end of the transition phase, and the sudden elimination of quotas could cause adjustment difficulties.

In principle, a firm international commitment could be entered into with respect to quota growth rates at a pace that would exactly replicate the effects of a corresponding timetable for phaseout of a tariff rate quota surcharge. However, past experience with quantitative restrictions has been less than reassuring in this regard. The MFA itself originally set 6 percent as the growth rate for quotas, but in subsequent renegotiations the mechanism increasingly facilitated "departures" permitting lower growth rates in bilaterally negotiated quotas (although actual import volumes tended to rise at rates comparable to or above the 6 percent benchmark after taking account of uncontrolled suppliers and categories). In contrast, countries have almost uniformly adhered to promised timetables for reducing tariffs.

The main drawback of the tariff rate quota, as typically enunciated by producer representatives, is that there would be no assurance that the surcharge would be sufficient to halt imports at the threshold level. Although the USTR proposal does not go into detail on the surcharge, one solution would be to apply an additional, second-tier surcharge if imports of the category in question exceeded the target threshold by more than, say, 5 percent.

The principal concern of importers about a tariff rate quota is that the surcharge might be set too high and somehow raise import prices. This concern is inappropriate if the alternative is an absolute quota system, because for such a system the implicit above-threshold surcharge is infinity. There is simply no way that a tariff rate quota could be more restrictive, and cause higher import and consumer prices, than an absolute quota set at the same threshold.

Part of the misgiving of importing entities may stem from confusion about the nature of the tariff rate quota. Some may be under the impression that the tariff surcharge would apply even to the original volume of imports—that is, to all imports including those below the quota threshold. That is not the case. Under the tariff rate quota, the basic tariff up to the quota-threshold of import volume would not rise. The alternative approach of "tariffication," or conversion of the quota into an equivalent outright tariff applicable for any amounts, would indeed involve raising the basic tariff and might increase protection of existing imports if the rate were set too high; tariffication, however, is not among the options proposed by the United States.

One difficulty for the tariff rate quota option is identification of the appropriate size of the surcharge. The objective is to set the surcharge at just the correct amount so that initially imports equal the targeted threshold level. Although a "high" surcharge would not reduce imports below the threshold level (because the surcharge would not apply at those import levels), a "low" surcharge could leave imports at levels above the targeted threshold level (i.e., the level corresponding to the quota in an absolute quota approach).

On the basis of the price of quota tickets in Hong Kong and other East Asian nations, I have estimated that an appropriate tariff rate quota surcharge for imports into the United States would be 25 percent in apparel; as the degree of protection has been less in textiles, the appropriate rate in that subsector would be perhaps 15 percent (chapter 6, pp. 162–67). It would be possible, but difficult, to identify appropriate individual surcharge rates by product category, for example through detailed surveys of quota-ticket prices in East Asian and other textile-exporting countries.

Perhaps the simplest alternative would be to base the surcharge on a historical benchmark that all would agree to have been restrictive, namely, the Smoot-Hawley tariffs of the 1930s. These rates are still present in US tariff law as the "column 2" rates applicable to countries not eligible for most-favored-nation treatment and the benefits of tariff reductions negotiated in the various postwar rounds (primarily the countries of what until recently was called the socialist bloc). The Smoot-Hawley tariffs are in the range of 50 percent for textiles and 70 percent for apparel.[12] These ranges correspond to surcharges of 34 percent and 39 percent, respectively, and are thus considerably higher than the 15 percent and 25 percent surcharges I have suggested for textiles and apparel, respectively.[13]

---

12. For textiles, the US tariff code (chapter 50) contains 807 entries with *ad valorem* column 2 tariffs. Their simple average is 52.3 percent. The average for the lowest quartile is 19 percent, and that for the highest quartile is 84.7 percent. For apparel (chapter 61), the 393 categories with *ad valorem* column 2 tariffs have an average tariff of 70 percent; the first-quartile average is 43.6 percent and the fourth-quartile average 90 percent. Calculated from US International Trade Commission, *Harmonized Tariff Schedule of the United States (1990)* (Washington: USITC, Publication 2232, 1990).

13. With the basic tariff rate at 22½ percent for apparel, a column 2 total tariff of 70 percent would correspond to a surcharge of 39 percent ($1.225 \times 1.39 = 1.7$). For textiles, the basic tariff is 12 percent, so that the total column 2 tariff of 50 percent implies a 34 percent surcharge ($1.12 \times 1.34 = 1.5$).

Although the column 2 rates are high, because of the asymmetry described above (whereby high surcharges do not affect imports below the quota and are by definition lower than the "infinite surcharge" imposed above an absolute quota), they would not cause jeopardy to importers or consumers so long as the thresholds were at least as high as the alternative absolute quotas would be. The higher the surcharge, of course, the more substantial its annual decrease would be under the timetable of phaseout over a specific period of time such as a decade.

A closely related question for implementation of the tariff rate quota is whether the base-year level of the quota-threshold would also rise over time in the liberalization phase, or whether liberalization would be carried out entirely through the phasedown of the surcharge. This question is not addressed in the USTR proposal. If the surcharge were set properly, the latter alternative would be appropriate. However, if the surcharge were set higher than the level sufficient to hold imports to the base-year threshold level, for at least the early years the tariff rate quota would tend to depress imports from levels they would otherwise reach with more normal quota growth (for example, what might have been expected under the MFA, or under the absolute global quota option). In this case it would be necessary to provide for growth in the underlying quota-threshold to avoid a tightening of protection.

Another issue for the tariff rate quota as proposed by the USTR is the allocation problem. In this case, what is being allocated is the quota-right to import at the basic tariff rate, without the surcharge. For countries already controlled, these rights would presumably continue to be allocated in the same way that quotas were allocated under the previous system. However, the presence of a global basket in the USTR approach raises the question of allocation, just as it does in the absolute quota alternative. Simply ignoring the allocation issue would lead, again, to the "calendar stampede" phenomenon in which all suppliers seek to concentrate shipments early in the year before the year's surcharge-exempt global volume threshold has been reached. Essentially, the same allocational issues are present with the global tariff rate quota as with the absolute global quota, as discussed above.

In my own preferred option for liberalization (presented in chapter 11, pp. 257–62), which likewise involves conversion from absolute to tariff rate quotas, allocation would present no problem. Tariff rate quotas would apply only to those countries currently covered by quotas (and for those countries, only the product categories already subject to quotas). There would be no reduction in these quota thresholds over time, hence no transfer to a global basket. Allocation of the surcharge-exempt import tickets would thus remain identical to allocation of bilateral quotas today.

Overall, the tariff rate quota option has important advantages over the absolute quota option, although in both cases globalization raises the risk

of increased protection. Considerably greater effort at education and expo-
sition would be required to convey the advantages of the tariff rate quota
alternative, to the public as well as to importers, domestic producers, and
foreign exporters.[14]

Phasedown Through Growth in Existing MFA Quotas

The third option, mentioned briefly and in general terms in the US
communiqué, is liberalization working within the MFA framework. By this
it is presumably meant that existing MFA quotas could be enlarged during
a transition period and then eliminated. The proposal was worded in such
a way as clearly to imply that the US negotiators did not prefer this option
(see appendix D).

Two reasons would appear to explain the lack of official US enthusiasm
for the MFA option: it could fail to liberalize trade, and it would not provide
the certainty domestic textile and apparel producers seek through a globalization of restrictions. The past history of the MFA does suggest that
strong skepticism is warranted about the possibility of liberalization through
this mechanism. Protection of cotton textiles began in the 1960s under the
Short Term and then the Long Term Arrangement, and was extended in
1974 to man-made fibers under the MFA. Each of the three subsequent
renewals of the MFA has facilitated the tightening of bilateral quotas.

The MFA framework does have important structural features limiting
protection, however: by tradition, under a gentlemen's agreement (though
not by letter), it exempts the industrial countries from protection (with the
partial exception of Japan). Approximately one-eighth of US apparel imports,
and half of US textile imports, come from industrial countries, so this feature
provides some built-in assurance of open trade. The MFA also provides a
"moving loophole" whereby countries not yet covered can become sites for
new export production until the resulting pressure induces a bilaterally
negotiated quota.[15]

The other side of this coin is that the MFA tends to promote inefficiency
in the global allocation of production. The pattern of country quotas under
the MFA creates an artificial incentive to open up new capacity in uncontrolled countries, including not only the industrial countries but, in more

---

14. The potential for erroneous headlines such as "US boosts textile tariffs to Smoot-
Hawley levels" illustrates the educational challenge.

15. Importers note, however, that the scope for this process has been successively
narrowed as more and more countries have come under controls, and this feature of
the MFA may provide little flexibility in the future.

extreme cases, countries (such as the United Arab Emirates) that would appear to have no basis for comparative advantage in the absence of their unrestricted status. The history of the MFA has been that production is displaced to such areas until eventually the importing country negotiates a bilateral quota with the new supplier, inducing producers to move on to still other uncontrolled areas.

The central risk of the MFA option is that of an "MFA forever," with constantly tightening bilateral quotas and ever-increasing distortions in the international allocation of production. The key solution to this problem, if the MFA is to be used as the liberalizing mechanism, is to negotiate in the Uruguay Round a strictly binding floor rate of expansion for all quotas. The MFA has notionally provided for a 6 percent annual quota growth rate, but the provisions permitting departures have increasingly led to agreements such as those negotiated by the United States with Korea, Taiwan, and Hong Kong in recent years, which provide expansion at rates of less than 1 percent or even outright contraction in quota levels.

The MFA option could provide a vehicle for meaningful liberalization only if countries pledged to achieve actual quota growth of at least 6 percent (and, as will be analyzed below, more appropriately somewhere in the range of 7 percent to 10 percent) annually. The simplest and perhaps most effective approach would be to state explicitly that there will be no departures from the floor rate of expansion, and to establish an explicit rate of, say, 7 percent for annual quota growth.

US and other negotiators have additional objectives that might necessitate one qualification: the aggregate of country quotas would have to grow at the floor rate of 6 percent to 7 percent, but individual-country quota growth could vary around this average. The United States in particular has sought to redistribute quota growth away from the traditional large East Asian suppliers toward other developing countries, including the least developed countries. The concern is that otherwise the large suppliers might achieve a privileged share of the world market that they could not sustain on a competitive basis, as their labor costs rise with development.

Beyond an unambiguous commitment to increase aggregate quotas for controlled countries by a floor rate annually, it would be necessary under the MFA option to state explicitly that, by a certain date, MFA protection (and its system of bilaterally negotiated quotas) would end and textile and apparel trade would once again revert to treatment according to standard GATT principles. The US global quota option sets the year 2002 as the deadline. The same target should apply if the MFA alternative is used as the transition mechanism.

Representatives of US textile and apparel producers tend to criticize the MFA as "nonprotection." They cite the rapid rates of import expansion that were possible in the early 1980s because of loopholes in the mechanism. However, US implementation of the MFA tightened substantially in the mid-1980s. Thus, whereas the Carter administration had shifted from absolute quotas to mere "surveillance" for many product categories and countries, by the mid-1980s the Reagan administration was reinstating absolute quotas and superimposing broad category ceilings on top of more detailed product ceilings (chapter 9, pp. 214–15). Moreover, the renewal of the MFA in 1986 brought formerly uncontrolled natural fibers (such as ramie) under restrictions. The principal remaining "loophole" is the absence of complete country coverage and the scope for the emergence of production in new, uncontrolled countries. This situation explains the absolute priority that producer representatives place on shifting to a global quota regime (as in their proposed 1990 legislation, analyzed below). But closing the geographical escape valve could make protection considerably more restrictive unless the global quota growth rate is set high, as analyzed below.

Japan

The Japanese proposal (appendix D) calls for complete termination of the MFA on 31 July 1991, the date on which it is now scheduled to expire unless renewed. There would follow a transition period through 1999, after which textile and apparel trade would be governed strictly by the standard provisions of the GATT.

During the transition period, quotas could continue to be applied only to products that meet certain objective criteria. The communiqué cites in particular the level of import penetration (ratio of imports to domestic consumption of the product), the growth rate of total imports of the product, and the growth rate of imports of the product from a single country. The importing country would have to submit data to a "multilateral surveillance body" for confirmation that the product meets the criteria for special treatment.

As in the US global quota proposal, products granted special protection in the Japanese proposal would be subject to rising quota growth rates over time, as would the amount of quotas that could be shifted from one category to another. The trigger point for eligibility (e.g., attainment of a certain import penetration ratio) would also rise over time. The proposal provides that the special restrictions would not be applied against least developed countries, countries newly entering the market, or small suppliers. It stipulates that protection would be limited only to "the necessary products" (i.e., those meeting the criteria), not group aggregates. For the sake of equity, the special restrictions would not be applied to a country's exports if another country enjoyed unrestricted access and provided a larger amount of supply of the good than the country in question.

The proposal provides that if the importing country and the exporting country do not reach agreement, the importing country may impose a quota unilaterally. This clause is somewhat out of character with the liberalizing nature of the proposal, even though unilateral restrictions may be (and in a small minority of cases are) imposed under the existing MFA.

In essence the Japanese proposal seeks to impose discipline of the type found in GATT Article XIX on safeguards: there should be criteria of injury rather than complete latitude to restrict. However, other key elements of Article XIX are missing, such as compensatory measures and most-favored-nation treatment.

There are questions as to how workable the Japanese proposal would be. In practice, seemingly objective criteria can become controversial. The measurement of import penetration is a major example.[16] An equally difficult obstacle is that firms in the textile and apparel sector have long been accustomed to receiving protection without having to demonstrate injury, and there would be resistance to the sudden introduction of required criteria for protection, especially criteria administered by an international body.[17]

European Community

The proposal of the European Community (appendix D) is framed in more general terms than those of the United States and Japan. Importantly, it makes no specific mention of a firm date by which all textile and apparel special protection would be phased out (in contrast to the target dates of 2002 and 1999 in the US and the Japanese proposals, respectively). The EC proposal stresses the need for reciprocity in the developing countries, and it specifically criticizes the application of infant-industry protection on grounds that the textile industry by now is mature in most countries.

The EC communiqué takes note of the two basic means of liberalization: reducing existing restrictions, and converting them to other forms (such as

---

16. Thus, producer advocates of protection have stated that apparel import penetration in 1986 was 50 percent. My own estimates placed the figure at 31 percent on a value basis and 38 percent on a square-yard-equivalent basis. Part of the divergence stems from the absence of direct data on final consumption and the need to estimate on the basis of assumed markups from import and domestic wholesale values. See chapter 2, pp. 47–49.

17. Some would add that the greater facility of the Japanese system in applying intangible obstacles to trade would mean that the "objective criteria" conditions would fall primarily on the United States and the European importing countries.

tariffs) for progressive reduction. It does not propose a specific modality, however. Its principal emphasis is on the application of safeguard protection during the transitional period. If a market is "disruptive," there should be consultations; if these fail to lead to restraints (including through bilateral agreements), the importing country "should be able, for a limited period, to restrict those textile imports causing the disruption. . . ."

The strategic approach of the EC proposal is that safeguard restraints in the transitional period would be strictly limited, and after the transition would be replaced by safeguard measures under the new general safeguard provisions of the GATT to be negotiated in the Uruguay Round. The EC proposal also emphasizes tariff harmonization in the sectors, as its own tariffs in textiles and apparel are much closer to average industrial tariffs than are those in the United States, where the gap is more than 10 percentage points.

In broad terms, the EC proposal gives importing countries much discretionary leeway and provides fewer concrete guidelines as to how protection would be reduced during the transition period than do the US and the Japanese proposals. Nonetheless, EC (and perhaps developing-country) representatives appear to regard the EC proposal as considerably more liberal than that of the United States. In particular, EC representatives argue that the move to a global quota regime in the US proposal would be a step backward, involving new protection (against countries not previously controlled), and that it therefore violates the pledge at the Punta del Este meeting that launched the Uruguay Round to move toward "progressive" liberalization of textiles and reintegration of the sector into the GATT.

Switzerland: *Chacun à Son Gout*

In mid-1989 the Swiss also submitted a proposal. It provides that once there has been a multilateral determination as to the target date by which all special restrictions in textiles and apparel would be phased out, each importing country would be free to choose its own modality of liberalization. The proposal includes two basic options: the enlargement of existing quotas (or outright elimination where they are nonbinding), and gradual conversion into nondiscriminatory restrictions, such as global quotas, tariffication, or tariff rate quotas, with successive reduction of the converted form of protection.

The Swiss approach is particularly significant because it provides a certain legitimacy to what could well be a failure of the United States and the European Community to reach a meeting of minds on the proper approach to liberalization. There are limits to the approach of permitting each country to choose its own liberalization technique, however. A major reason why the MFA emerged in the first place was that US firms felt that Europe was unduly restricting imports and diverting them to the US market, and that some international mechanism was needed to discipline the process. Ironically, by the time the MFA was first renewed, in 1977, it was Europe that was the main proponent of tighter protection (chapter 6, 148–51). The lesson of this cycle was that there needed to be a perceived symmetry in the degree of openness in each area's practices; otherwise the less protected area would militate for tighter protection, in an upward ratcheting process.

Reactions to the Proposals

By April 1990, negotiations on textile and apparel liberalization were in a contentious phase. The US negotiators were still addressing differences at home, in particular between producer and importer groups. European and developing-country representatives had reportedly reacted negatively to the US global quota proposal and paid little heed to the tariff rate quota proposal.[18] It remained to be seen which direction the negotiations would take.

One reason for the European criticism of the global quota approach was that the Community enjoys a surplus in textiles and apparel trade with the United States. In 1988 EC members exported $1.6 billion in textiles to the United States and imported only $838 million in US textiles; in apparel, the corresponding trade flows were $1.7 billion and $197 million.[19] A shift to global quotas imposing new restraints on the exports of industrial countries would tend to fall more heavily on the Community than on the United States.

A more fundamental critique, and one more germane for the developing countries, was that unless the global quota mechanism were specified at relatively high rates of quota growth, it could indeed violate the Punta del Este commitment by introducing a phase of tightening rather than declining protection.

The adverse reaction to the US proposal raises the issue of whether the Swiss approach, whereby each country would adopt its own liberalizing

---

18. By May, the European Community had publicly rejected the US proposal for global quotas. The Community argued that there could be a spillover effect on the developing countries, as new US quotas against EC exports would make EC markets less tolerant of imports from developing countries. *Financial Times,* 22 May 1990.

19. OECD, *Foreign Trade by Commodities, Series C,* 1988, Volume 2 (Paris: OECD, 1990), pp. 61, 237.

measures, might be adopted as a compromise. Yet there have been indications of strong opposition to this approach from the European Community and the developing countries.

Effects of Alternative US Proposals

The decade prior to elimination of quotas under the USTR proposals could see additional costs imposed on consumers if permitted import growth rates are low. The model of apparel and textile trade and production presented in the original edition of this study (appendix A in both editions) may be used to evaluate these potential costs and other economic aspects of the alternative proposals.

The Projection Model

As an initial guide to the adequacy of the model, it is useful to review its performance in predicting what actually happened to output and trade for the 1987–89 period. Table 12.1 shows the growth of US textile and apparel trade from 1978 through 1989. Table 12.2 then compares actual trends in 1987–89 against those projected by the model.[20]

As table 12.2 shows, the projected values of production turned out to be close to actual values for this period. The projections underestimated the rise in imports in 1987 but thereafter closely tracked the actual trend. In particular, the projections accurately captured the abrupt slowdown in imports (from their sharp rise in the early 1980s) that was in store as the result of depreciation of the dollar. After rising by a total of 101 percent from 1980 to 1986, the number of square-yard equivalents of apparel imports increased by only 4.3 percent in 1987, and actually declined by 1.4 percent in 1988. Imports did rise again in 1989 to volumes about 10 percent higher than projected by the model, but the contrast with the earlier period remained sharp and in broad terms was accurately captured by the model projections.[21]

---

20. The projected values in my original study (appendix A) were in constant 1982 dollars. The corresponding figures shown here have been converted to 1987 dollars based on the apparel shipments price deflator used in US Department of Commerce, *US Industrial Outlook*, 1989 and 1990, or the Bureau of Labor Statistics import price deflator.

21. US International Trade Commission, *US Imports of Textiles and Apparel under the Multifiber Arrangement: Statistical Report through 1988* (Washington: USITC, June 1989), USITC publication 2000, referred to hereafter as ITC, *US Imports 1988*. The corresponding figures for textiles were 251 percent, 0.4 percent, and −9.2 percent.

Table 12.1 US trade in apparel and textiles by value and volume 1978–89,[a] (millions of dollars except where noted)

Year	Apparel			Textiles		
	Imports		Exports	Imports		Exports
	Value	Volume	(value)	Value	Volume	(value)
1978	6,108	2,905	677	2,400	2,835	2,225
1979	6,291	2,671	931	2,399	1,967	3,189
1980	6,849	2,884	1,202	2,676	2,000	3,632
1981	8,008	3,136	1,232	3,250	2,639	3,619
1982	8,703	3,382	953	3,000	2,553	2,784
1983	10,292	3,875	818	3,460	3,832	2,368
1984	14,513	4,707	807	4,874	5,500	2,382
1985	16,056	5,117	755	5,274	5,677	2,366
1986	18,554	5,867	900	6,151	7,008	2,570
1987	21,960	6,126	1,132	6,918	7,029	2,900
1988	22,877	5,969	1,575	6,748	6,405	3,651
1989	26,026	6,729	2,087	6,417	7,129	3,897

a. Values are for Standard International Trade Classifications (SITC) 84 (apparel) and 65 (textiles). Imports are stated on a c.i.f. (cost plus insurance and freight) basis, exports on an f.a.s. (free alongside ship) basis. Import volumes are in millions of square-yard equivalents.

Sources: American Textile Manufacturers Institute, *Textile Hi-Lights*, March 1990, 24–26; US Bureau of the Census.

The projections in the first edition assumed that over the period 1987–89 the real value of the dollar would decline by 11.2 percent against the currencies of developing-country suppliers weighted by apparel import shares, and by 18.6 percent weighting by textile import shares among countries (a reversal by two-thirds of the dollar's real appreciation in the 1980s; chapter 10, p. 233). In fact, the real value of the dollar did fall from 1986 to 1989: by 18.7 percent against the Korean won, 18.3 percent against the New Taiwan dollar, and 9.4 percent against the Hong Kong dollar.[22] As the currencies of other developing countries typically did not appreciate as much against the US dollar, overall the dollar's decline was probably in

22. Calculated from International Monetary Fund, *International Financial Statistics*, January 1990; Central Bank of China (Taiwan), *Financial Statistics*, December 1989; and Data Resources, Inc., data bank. Note that Korea, Taiwan, and Hong Kong accounted for 17.1 percent, 18.5 percent, and 23.2 percent of US apparel imports in 1983, respectively, and 7.5 percent, 6.9 percent, and 4.9 percent of US textile imports. See chapter 2, p. 58.

Table 12.2 Predicted and actual output and trade performance in apparel and textiles, 1987–89 (1986 = 100)

		1987	1988	1989
Apparel				
Production (constant prices)	P	102.0	104.6	106.0
	A	101.3	101.7	104.7
Imports				
Constant prices	P	104.7	103.8	106.6
Millions of SYE	A	104.4	101.8	114.7
Constant prices[a]	A	108.5	108.3	118.0
Exports				
Constant prices	P	145.6	172.9	186.8
Constant prices[b]	A	122.5	165.7	211.8
Textiles				
Production (constant prices)	P	104.3	108.1	110.7
	A	102.7	104.4	106.2
Imports				
Constant prices	P	95.5	86.0	82.3
Millions of SYE	A	100.3	91.4	101.7
Constant prices[a]	A	103.1	98.9	92.5
Exports				
Constant prices	P	152.2	176.9	187.7
Constant prices[b]	A	111.7	137.3	142.1

P = predicted; A = actual; SYE = square-yard-equivalents.

a. Deflated by the Bureau of Labor Statistics index of apparel (SITC 84) or textile (SITC 65) import prices in *Monthly Labor Review*, April 1988 and March 1990.

b. Deflated by US Department of Commerce, SIC 22 and 23 shipments price indexes.

Sources: chapter 10, 235–38; table 1; US Department of Commerce, *US Industrial Outlook* 1988, 1989, 1990.

approximately the same range as had been anticipated in the study for apparel (although somewhat less than anticipated for textiles). The slowdown in US apparel imports was also attributable in part to the negotiation of more restrictive bilateral import quotas, especially for the four major East Asian suppliers. A more detailed analysis would be required to distinguish between the exchange rate and trade policy effects.

The earlier projections also accurately predicted the strong surge in US apparel exports, which rose by a total of 112 percent from 1986 to 1989 (at constant 1985 prices); this percentage increase was even higher than forecast. In short, the 1987 model appears to have performed sufficiently well during the 1987–89 period to provide a useful basis for consideration of the outlook for the 1990s, and the effect of global quotas during that period.[23]

Effects of Global Quotas

Consumer Costs

Beyond the period 1987–89, I projected in the first edition that real apparel imports would rise by only 1.9 percent in 1990 and 2.2 percent in 1991 as the consequence of lagged effects of anticipated real dollar depreciation in the period 1987–89 (especially against the currencies of the East Asian newly industrializing countries). The model projections indicated that following this initial adjustment apparel imports would resume a relatively brisk, steady growth rate of approximately 7 percent annually in real terms. (The projected rates of growth and the corresponding import volumes for the period 1992–2000 are presented in the first column of the upper two sections of table 12.3.) This baseline projection assumed that protection would remain unchanged at an average tariff-equivalent of 53 percent (composed of two multiplicative components: the 22½ percent average tariff and the estimated 25 percent tariff-equivalent of quotas). The baseline projections have the important implication that *any growth rate of global quotas for apparel of less than 7 percent annually would represent a tightening of protection from current levels.*

Because of its importance, the baseline for import growth warrants further discussion. In the apparel model, imports depend on the relative price of imports and domestic products, the growth of domestic income, and special

---

23. The analysis that follows applies the 1987 model as updated to a 1989 data base. For 1989, US domestic production in apparel is set at $69.505 billion, imports at $25.219 billion, exports at $2.602 billion, and employment at 1,090,000 jobs. Output, exports, and employment data are from US Department of Commerce, *US Industrial Outlook 1990* (Washington: US Department of Commerce, 1990), p. 35-1. Imports are estimated by applying the ratio of Standard Industrial Classification category 23 imports (on a free-on-board, or f.o.b., basis) from this source for 1988 to the final Standard International Trade Classification (SITC) category 84 imports (at cost plus insurance and freight, or c.i.f.) for 1989 (table 12.1). The model disaggregates imports between OECD and developing-country sources. Based on data for 1987 and 1988 (from OECD, *Foreign Trade by Commodities, Series C*, 1987, and US Department of Commerce, *Highlights of US Export and Import Trade*, FT990, December 1988), the share from OECD (industrial) countries is set at 12 percent for 1989.

Table 12.3 US imports and consumer costs in apparel under alternative global quota growth rates, 1992–2000

	Base-line					Global quota growth path					
Year		A	B	C	D	E	F	G	H	I	J
Import growth rates (percentages)											
1992	6.6	0	1	2	3	4	5	6	7	8	9
1993	6.6	0	1	2	3	4	5	6	7	8	9
1994	6.7	0	1	2	3	4	5	6	7	8	9
1995	6.7	1	2	3	4	5	6	7	8	9	10
1996	6.7	1	2	3	4	5	6	7	8	9	10
1997	6.8	1	2	3	4	5	6	7	8	9	10
1998	6.8	2	3	4	5	6	7	8	9	10	11
1999	6.8	2	3	4	5	6	7	8	9	10	11
2000	6.9	3	4	5	6	7	8	9	10	11	12
Import volume (billions of 1989 dollars)											
1992	27.9	26.2	26.5	26.7	27.0	27.3	27.5	27.8	28.0	28.3	28.6
1993	29.8	26.2	26.7	27.3	27.8	28.4	28.9	29.5	30.0	30.6	31.1
1994	31.8	26.2	27.0	27.8	28.6	29.5	30.3	31.2	32.1	33.0	33.9
1995	33.9	26.5	27.5	28.7	29.8	31.0	32.2	33.4	34.7	36.0	37.3
1996	36.2	26.7	28.1	29.5	31.0	32.5	34.1	35.7	37.5	39.2	41.1
1997	38.6	27.0	28.7	30.4	32.2	34.1	36.1	38.2	40.5	42.8	45.2
1998	41.3	27.5	29.5	31.6	33.8	36.2	38.7	41.3	44.1	47.0	50.2
1999	44.1	28.1	30.4	32.9	35.6	38.4	41.4	44.6	48.1	51.7	55.7
2000	47.1	28.9	31.6	34.5	37.7	41.0	44.7	48.6	52.9	57.4	62.4
Change in import price from baseline (percentages)											
1992	0.0	6.2	5.2	4.3	3.3	2.4	1.4	0.5	−0.4	−1.3	−2.1
1993	0.0	12.9	10.8	8.7	6.7	4.8	2.9	1.1	−0.7	−2.4	−4.1
1994	0.0	20.0	16.7	13.4	10.3	7.3	4.5	1.7	−1.0	−3.6	−6.1
1995	0.0	26.4	21.7	17.3	13.0	9.0	5.1	1.4	−2.1	−5.5	−8.8
1996	0.0	33.2	27.1	21.3	15.9	10.7	5.8	1.2	−3.2	−7.4	−11.3
1997	0.0	40.4	32.7	25.5	18.8	12.5	6.5	1.0	−4.3	−9.2	−13.8
1998	0.0	46.7	37.4	28.7	20.7	13.3	6.4	−0.1	−6.1	−11.7	−16.9
1999	0.0	53.3	42.2	32.1	22.7	14.1	6.2	−1.1	−7.8	−14.0	−19.8
2000	0.0	58.7	45.9	34.3	23.7	14.0	5.2	−2.9	−10.3	−17.1	−23.3

	Base-	Global quota growth path									
Year	line	A	B	C	D	E	F	G	H	I	J

Consumer costs[a] (billions of 1989 dollars)

Year	Base-line	A	B	C	D	E	F	G	H	I	J
1992	26.1	4.4	3.7	3.0	2.3	1.7	1.0	0.4	−0.3	−0.9	−1.5
1993	27.2	9.1	7.7	6.3	4.9	3.5	2.1	0.8	−0.5	−1.9	−3.2
1994	28.3	14.2	11.9	9.8	7.6	5.5	3.4	1.3	−0.8	−2.8	−4.9
1995	29.5	18.9	15.8	12.8	9.9	6.9	4.0	1.1	−1.7	−4.6	−7.4
1996	30.7	24.1	20.1	16.1	12.3	8.5	4.7	1.0	−2.7	−6.5	−10.2
1997	32.1	29.6	24.6	19.7	14.9	10.2	5.5	0.8	−3.8	−8.5	−13.1
1998	33.5	34.9	28.7	22.8	17.0	11.2	5.6	−0.1	−5.7	−11.4	−17.1
1999	35.0	40.5	33.2	26.1	19.2	12.4	5.7	−1.0	−7.8	−14.6	−21.5
2000	36.6	45.7	37.1	28.8	20.7	12.8	4.9	−2.9	−10.8	−18.9	−27.3

a. Baseline consumer costs are given in the "Baseline" column. Changes from baseline are given for cases A through J.

terms for trends in supply from industrial and developing countries.[24] In the absence of any price change, a steady 3 percent growth in US GNP would cause 5.1 percent annual growth in import volume. Inclusion of the trend growth terms brings the weighted-average annual import growth rate to 6.7 percent.[25]

Apparel import growth at a rate of approximately 7 percent in the absence of any further tightening or loosening of protection is also consistent with the past history of import growth. From 1964 through 1988 the physical volume of apparel imports grew at an average annual rate of 8.9 percent; for the period 1974 through 1988 the average rate was 8.5 percent.[26] As noted above the growth of physical import volume for apparel slowed sharply after 1986. Overvaluation of the dollar contributed to acceleration

24. As discussed in chapter 2, for the developing countries an S-shaped "logistics" curve was estimated, with rapid initial growth and eventual deceleration to 2 percent annually (the trend element for the projections). For imports from industrial countries the trend component is −2½ percent annually.

25. With an income elasticity of 1.7 for supply from developing countries (appendix A, table A.1). Note that apparel import growth is slightly lower than the original 7.1 percent rate discussed in chapter 3 (p. 238) because the 1989 base share of industrial-country supply (which grows slowly) is somewhat larger than originally projected.

26. Calculated by regression of the natural logarithm of square-yard equivalents on time. From chapter 2, p. 42, and ITC, US Imports 1988, p. A-5.

of import growth in the period 1983–86; otherwise the trend in the 1980s would likely have been lower than from 1964 through 1980 as the consequence of maturation of key developing-country suppliers. The 7 percent benchmark used here is consistent with some deceleration in apparel import volume growth from the 1964–88 average, but a rebound from the slow growth during 1986–89.

The first column of table 12.3 (final section) shows the baseline consumer costs of protection through the 1990s as well.[27] These costs stand at $22.4 billion in the base year 1989 (not shown) and rise steadily to $36.6 billion by the year 2000. Even in the absence of changes in protection, consumer costs rise as the size of the market increases. The corresponding net welfare costs after deducting transfers to the government (tariff revenue) and to domestic producers amount to $10.3 billion in 1989 and $18.3 billion by the year 2000.

The division of consumer costs between tariff and nontariff protection is approximately equal. Thus, in the absence of quotas, consumer costs due to apparel tariffs in 1989 would have been only $12.5 billion, or about half of total consumer costs. Because net welfare costs to the country rise with the square of the total tariff-equivalent (whereas total consumer costs rise approximately in proportion to the total protection rate), the net welfare costs would have been much smaller in 1989 if the only protection had been from tariffs ($1.7 billion versus $10.3 billion).

The remaining columns of table 12.3 present a menu of alternative growth paths of quotas and their estimated impact on import volumes and consumer costs during the 1992–2000 period. In each case there is an accelerating import quota growth rate, as postulated in the USTR proposal. The growth rate for the initial three years ranges from 0 percent in the most restrictive case (path A) to 9 percent in the least restrictive (path J). The growth rate for the second three years is 1 percentage point higher than in the first three years; for the next two years the rate rises by another percentage point, and for the final year by yet another point. The top portion of the table shows the resulting alternative time paths of quota growth rates. Note that the quotas are now global, so that the rates of growth refer to total apparel import volumes.[28]

The other three sections of table 12.3 develop the consumer costs that correspond to this menu of alternative global quota growth paths. The

---

27. The methodology for calculating baseline consumer costs is shown in appendix B, p. 355. The consumer costs of additional protection are estimated using the methodology of appendix C, p. 369.

28. Moreover, they are from prospective actual import levels in the base year 1991, rather than from quota levels including unused quotas.

second section reports the target import volumes corresponding to quota growth paths A through J; the third section shows the price increase in imports that would be required to suppress imports from baseline levels to meet the quantitative targets in question; and the fourth section indicates the increase in consumer cost above the baseline level.

In the case of an initial quota growth rate of 1 percent annually, rising to 4 percent by 2000–01 (path B), in 1996 it would be necessary for import prices to rise by 27.1 percent above the baseline level to compress imports to the targeted level. The corresponding tariff-equivalents of total protection range as high as 143 percent (path A, year 2000).[29] In contrast, for path J with quota growth set at 9 percent initially and rising eventually to 12 percent, the increase in import availability permits a reduction in price from the baseline level by 23 percent by the year 2000, leaving the tariff-equivalent of total protection at only 17 percent[30]—below the level of the tariff alone (22½ percent).   The consumer costs of protection depend on both the imposed increase in import prices resulting from higher protection, and the induced rise in prices of domestic production (estimated at approximately half the proportionate import price increase). The final section of the table reports the increase in consumer costs above baseline levels for each of the alternative time paths for global quota growth. In the cases on the far right-hand side of the table, the consumer costs are less than in the base case (incremental costs are negative), because the quota growth rates exceed the baseline 7 percent.

The central finding of table 12.3 is that if the growth path of a global quota scheme is set at a relatively low level, the result could be a large escalation in the consumer costs of apparel protection above those associated with current levels of protection. For example, suppose that quota growth were limited to 2 percent in the first three years, 3 percent in the second three years, 4 percent in the next two years, and 5 percent in the last year (path C). At the halfway point of the period (1996), the consumer costs from apparel protection would have risen by $16.1 billion from their baseline level of $30.7 billion (in 1989 dollars), for a total of $46.8 billion. Yet in the 1987 textile bill, producers sought to limit global quota growth to an even lower rate of 1 percent annually,[31] and in April 1990 this proposal reemerged in Congress (as discussed below).

The menu of quota growth rate estimates in table 12.3 must be interpreted

---

29. The total tariff-equivalent of protection equals that in the baseline (53 percent) amplified by the required additional percentage price increase ($1.53 \times 1.587 = 2.43$, or a 143 percent increase from the unprotected price).

30. That is, $1.53 \times (1 - 0.233)$.

31. The consumer costs of the 1987 bill are examined in chapter 9, pp. 224–30.

Table 12.4 Impact of the USTR global quota proposal on US consumer costs, 1992–2000 (millions of 1989 dollars)

Year	Change from constant-protection baseline under initial minimum growth rate:[a]							
	0	1	2	3	4	5	6	7
1992	3.8	3.1	2.5	1.8	1.1	0.5	−0.1	−0.8
1993	7.9	6.5	5.2	3.8	2.4	1.1	−0.3	−1.6
1994	12.4	10.2	8.1	5.9	3.8	1.7	−0.4	−2.4
1995	16.5	13.4	10.4	7.5	4.6	1.7	−1.1	−4.0
1996	20.9	17.0	13.1	9.3	5.5	1.7	−2.0	−5.7
1997	25.7	20.7	15.9	11.1	6.4	1.8	−2.9	−7.5
1998	30.0	24.0	18.1	12.4	6.7	1.1	−4.6	−10.3
1999	34.7	27.5	20.6	13.8	7.0	0.3	−6.4	−13.2
2000	38.9	30.5	22.3	14.4	6.5	−1.4	−9.3	−17.4

a. The growth rate is that for products with "very high" sensitivity. It is assumed that 40 percent of base-year import value is in products with "very high" sensitivity, 40 percent in products with "high" sensitivity, and 20 percent in products with "moderate" sensitivity.

further to obtain estimates of the impact of the USTR global quota proposal. The proposal calls for a blend of three separate growth rates for products with "very high," "high," and "moderate" sensitivities. Table 12.4 presents the incremental consumer costs (above baseline) for each alternative minimum quota growth rate x according to the USTR illustration (appendix D, figure D.2). It is assumed that 40 percent of products (by value) are treated as having "very high" sensitivity, 40 percent "high," and 20 percent "moderate" sensitivity.[32] The table thus shows, for example, that when $x = 3$ (so that the three product categories have quota growth paths corresponding to paths D, E, and F, respectively, in table 12.3), the increase in consumer costs over those in the baseline scenario at the midpoint year 1996 amounts to $9.3 billion annually (in 1989 prices).[33]

32. This breakdown is arbitrary. It diverges from a strict allocation by thirds only because of the political likelihood that domestic producers would seek to compress the "moderate" classification to as low a share as possible.

33. It should be kept in mind that the growth rates listed at the head of table 12.4 are minimum growth rates, and that for each path the average growth rate is approximately 2 percentage points higher. Thus, in the case where $x = 6$, the table shows declining consumer costs over time even though the basic constant-protection import growth rate is 7 percent, because average import growth for this case is approximately 8 percent.

The case in which $x = 5$ is of special interest. Here the average growth rate over all three categories and over the full period 1992–2000 is 6.9 percent,[34] or almost identical to the baseline growth rate. Yet even in this scenario there is some excess consumer cost above the baseline case, reaching a peak of $1.8 billion in 1989 prices in 1997 (table 12.4). The reason is that imports are compressed below baseline by a cumulative 3 percent after the first three years; they then parallel the baseline but remain below it over the next three years (when their growth rate, 6.8 percent, is almost identical to that of the baseline); above-baseline growth only begins to narrow the gap by 1998. Essentially, a low initial growth rate incurs costs that outweigh the cost reduction from a faster rate of growth late in the period.

Inspection of table 12.4 suggests that a minimum initial growth rate of approximately $x = 5\frac{1}{4}$ percent would be required for the USTR package to avoid an increase in consumer costs above baseline trends at unchanged levels of protection.[35] That rate would correspond to an average annual growth rate for all apparel imports of 7.2 percent. Again the required overall average growth rate would have to be somewhat higher than the baseline average (6.7 percent) because of the greater impact of slow growth early in the period.

The Exit Problem

If the USTR proposal were implemented at $x = 5\frac{1}{4}$ percent (and average annual growth were 7.2 percent), consumers would not experience additional damage beyond what they could expect given unchanged levels of protection. However, in the year 2000 the apparel market would be no closer to liberalization than today: the tariff-equivalent of total protection would still stand at 53 percent. Higher quota growth rates are required to leave the market prepared to make a smooth transition to complete quota elimination. Otherwise, the impact of quota abolition would be comparable to that of immediate elimination today, at least in terms of prospective proportionate import response (although by being forewarned the domestic industry would presumably be better prepared).

Table 12.3 may be used to examine the pace of quota growth required to provide a smooth exit from quotas by the year 2001. Under the highest

---

34. That is, the average growth rates for cases F, G, and H in table 12.3, respectively, are 6.1 percent, 7.1 percent, and 8.1 percent. With weights of 0.4, 0.4, and 0.2, the overall average for the case where $x = 5$ is 6.9 percent.

35. The reduced incremental consumer costs at $x = 6$ are about three times the increased costs at $x = 5$ (without the refinement of time discounting), so incremental consumer costs would be zero at about one-fourth of the way between the two.

quota growth case considered (path J), imports grow at 9 percent annually, the rate rising to 12 percent by the year 2000. In that case, as noted previously, the total tariff-equivalent of tariff and quota protection would be down to only 17 percent by the year 2000, or less than the present tariff (22½ percent). In path I, the tariff-equivalent protection of quotas would be down to 3.5 percent by the year 2000, and total tariff-equivalent protection (including tariffs) down to 26.8 percent.[36] As may be seen in table 12.3, the size of the import price reductions from baseline is widening at a pace of about 3 percent annually under path I by the year 2000. By implication, quotas could be completely eliminated by the year 2001 under path I without a surge in imports. Indeed, thereafter the long-term growth rate of 7 percent would again apply, so that import growth would actually fall.

Average annual growth of total quotas in path I in table 12.3 amounts to 9.1 percent. From another perspective, this scenario corresponds to a minimum growth rate $x = 7.2$ percent (based on table 12.4). Thus, *to ensure a smooth transition to complete elimination of quotas by the year 2001, it would be necessary to set the minimum growth rate in the USTR proposal at* x = *7 percent, and to achieve an overall annual average quota growth rate of 9 percent during the period 1992–2001 (and 11 percent by the final two years).* Otherwise there would remain a substantial gap between the quota-free level of imports and the actual level at the end of the period, and a corresponding surge in imports would occur upon the elimination of quotas.

It may be noted that the 9 percent benchmark for smooth transition out of quota protection by the year 2001 may be biased downward by the model's assumption of a low import growth rate for supply from the OECD countries. As noted, because of the adverse time trend, this supply rises at a rate of only 0.58 percent annually even though US apparel consumption rises by approximately 2 percent annually. If OECD supply (estimated at 12 percent of US apparel imports in the base year 1989) should grow faster during the 1990s, developing-country supply would require greater suppression for total imports to grow at any specified rate, and a gap between actual and quota-free imports greater than otherwise estimated would remain. Nonetheless, a range of 9 percent to 10 percent for annual quota growth (paths I and J) would seem likely to bracket the actual path required for the protective effect of quotas to disappear by the end of the period.[37]

---

36. That is, $(1.53 \times [1 - 0.171]) \div 1.225 = 1.035$.

37. In commentary on an early draft of this study, an expert from the American Textile Manufacturers Institute judged that "At a 10 percent annual growth rate, imports would triple their current level and claim virtually all of the US textile and apparel market by the year 2002 . . . [at a loss of] wages of $200 billion. . . ." (personal communication, 20 March 1990). However, the simulations in case J with 10 percent

The Nature of a Bargain

The essential question for achieving an agreement satisfactory to both importing and producing groups is whether quota growth rates in these ranges are acceptable to all parties. Although producer groups might be expected to resist quota growth rates in the range of 7 percent to 11 percent, they might nonetheless be prepared to consider such rates in return for removal of the uncertainty that led to import growth rates reaching as high as 37 percent in 1984.[38] For importers, the risk would be that increased protection due to imposition of global quotas on countries not currently restricted could outweigh the effects of liberalization.

One possible assurance to importing interests could arise from a specific commitment in US law that by the year 2002 there would be no quantitative restrictions on apparel (and textile) imports. Once such a commitment was made, revised legislation would be required to reverse it. Repeal would require a two-thirds majority to override a presidential veto, unless the President in office at the time agreed with those requesting repeal or extension.

A potential bargain may be formulated in terms of the "expected present value" of consumer costs. Consider table 12.3. By the year 2000, the baseline estimate of consumer costs from apparel protection at unchanged protection amounts to $36.6 billion (in 1989 dollars). Elimination of all quotas thereafter would sharply reduce these costs, to approximately $14 billion annually— the amount associated with persistence of only the 22½ percent tariff on apparel.[39] If a longer period were considered (such as 20 years), it could be in consumers' interest to accept higher costs in the first 10 years in exchange for lower costs later. In such a calculation, it would be necessary to take account of the political reality that the entire commitment might come undone at the end of the first 10 years, and that quotas might remain in place after all. So some probability of less than 100 percent should be

---

average quota growth show domestic apparel production in the year 2000 only 11.6 percent below the 1989 level, and apparel employment still at 813,000 workers. Imports would claim 57 percent, not 100 percent, of the domestic market. In textiles, where the role of imports is smaller, the impact would be even more limited. It should be kept in mind that despite average import growth in apparel of nearly 9 percent annually over the past quarter century (as noted above), in 1989 domestic apparel production stood at its highest level ever (at an index of 110.8, where 1977 production equals 100). Council of Economic Advisers, *Economic Report of the President 1990* (Washington: CEA, 1990), p. 350.

38. Chapter 2, p. 42. This rate was in terms of constant-price values. In terms of square-yard equivalents, the rate for 1984 was 21.5 percent (table 12.1).

39. Based on interpolation between cases I and J for the year 2000 (table 12.3).

Table 12.5 Impact of alternative global quota growth paths on US apparel employment, 1992–2000 (thousands of jobs)

Year	Baseline (6.7)	A (0–3)	B (1–4)	C (2–5)	D (3–6)	E (4–7)	F (5–8)	G (6–9)	H (7–10)	I (8–11)	J (9–12)
					Change from baseline under growth path:[a]						
1992	1,065	32	27	22	17	12	7	3	−2	−7	−11
1993	1,051	65	54	44	34	25	15	6	−4	−13	−22
1994	1,036	97	82	66	51	37	22	9	−5	−18	−32
1995	1,020	125	104	83	63	44	25	7	−11	−28	−45
1996	1,003	152	126	100	75	51	28	6	−16	−37	−58
1997	985	179	147	117	87	59	31	5	−21	−46	−69
1998	967	201	164	128	94	61	30	0	−29	−57	−84
1999	947	222	179	139	101	64	29	−5	−37	−68	−98
2000	927	237	190	145	102	62	23	−13	−48	−82	−114

a. The numbers in parentheses represent the range in annual quota growth rates for each path.

assigned to maintenance of the bargain, with the remaining probability assigned to a scenario of keeping the quotas in place after the tenth year.

In such an approach, the higher the probability attached to the honoring of the original commitment to eliminate quotas at the end of the first decade, the lower the annual quota growth rate could be during the first decade with the consumer still ending up better off over a 20-year horizon (with consumption appropriately time-discounted). Consumers might thus still come out ahead if they accepted a somewhat lower quota growth rate (and higher costs) during the first decade than in the baseline case of unchanged protection, because the expected present value of consumer costs for the whole 20-year period would be lower as the consequence of the expected value of eliminating quotas at the end of the decade.

Employment Effects of Global Quotas

Table 12.5 reports the impact of alternative global quota growth rates on US apparel employment. The baseline for unchanged protection shows employment declining by a rate of 1.3 percent annually at the beginning of the period, and by 2.4 percent in the year 2000. With domestic consumption rising at only 2 percent annually, the 6.7 percent annual rise in imports means that the rate of domestic production growth will be low (and eventually slightly negative). Rising labor productivity (at 2 percent annually) means that the resulting requirements for labor decline over time.

The table shows that a restrictive program of global quotas could increase employment over baseline trends. Thus, under quota growth path A (rising from 0 percent import growth in 1992–94 to 3 percent in 2000–01), there would be an additional 237,000 jobs in the year 2000 above the baseline projection, or an increase of 25.6 percent from baseline. This increase would come at an incremental consumer cost of $45.7 billion annually by the year 2000 (table 12.3), or at an annual cost of $193,000 per direct job created (in 1989 dollars).

In contrast, the employment effects of an aggressive program of import liberalization are shown by path J in table 12.5. Here, imports grow at an annual rate of 9 percent in 1992–94, the rate rising to 12 percent by 2000–01. Total job losses beyond baseline amount to 114,000 by the year 2000. This outcome would mean that total job losses over the period would reach 23.7 percent of total employment in the industry, instead of 13.0 percent as in the base case of unchanged protection. The additional 10.7 percentage points of employment cutback would permit a reduction of consumer costs by $27.3 billion annually by the year 2000, for a consumer savings of $239,000 per job eliminated.

The large consumer benefits suggest considerable opportunity for a mutually beneficial bargain between consumers and apparel workers that could provide for generous funding of adjustment programs. It may be seen in path J (table 12.5) that the maximum increment in job displacement (beyond baseline) from liberalization among alternatives considered here amounts to an average of about 20,000 workers every two years. Suppose special adjustment funds (in addition to unemployment benefits) were set at $10,000 annually for a period of two years for each displaced worker. The resulting annual adjustment transfer would amount to only $200 million. With imports initially in the range of $30 billion and rising (on an f.o.b. basis), these funds could be fully covered by a special "worker adjustment" fee of ⅔ percent. Consumers would benefit vastly from accepting an increase in apparel tariffs by ⅔ percentage point in exchange for assured growth in total imports (i.e., the global quota) by a schedule beginning at 9 percent and reaching 12 percent annually by the year 2000 (path J).[40]

Quota Revenues

A final consideration affecting the global quota proposal concerns its potential for raising revenue. Each year one-tenth of existing quotas would be

---

40. The costs would be even lower if only workers certified as already employed at the beginning of the liberalization program were eligible for assistance. For a fuller discussion, see chapter 11.

Table 12.6 Potential quota revenue under alternative global quota growth paths, 1992–2000 (billions of 1989 dollars)

	Potential revenue under growth path:[a]									
Year	A (0–3)	B (1–4)	C (2–5)	D (3–6)	E (4–7)	F (5–8)	G (6–9)	H (7–10)	I (8–11)	J (9–12)
1992	0.67	0.65	0.62	0.60	0.58	0.55	0.53	0.58	0.55	0.52
1993	1.71	1.63	1.54	1.45	1.36	1.26	1.16	1.21	1.08	0.95
1994	3.13	2.96	2.77	2.58	2.37	2.14	1.90	1.90	1.59	1.26
1995	4.85	4.57	4.26	3.91	3.54	3.12	2.67	2.51	1.91	1.25
1996	6.92	6.52	6.06	5.53	4.94	4.27	3.53	3.11	2.05	0.89
1997	9.35	8.83	8.20	7.46	6.60	5.61	4.48	3.66	1.98	0.10
1998	12.07	11.41	10.59	9.59	8.38	6.95	5.28	3.83	1.25	0.00
1999	15.17	14.39	13.36	12.05	10.42	8.45	6.08	3.76	0.00	0.00
2000	18.59	17.66	16.37	14.67	12.50	9.79	6.47	2.82	0.00	0.00

a. The numbers in parentheses represent the range in annual quota growth rates for each path.

reallocated to a global basket, and the logical means of allocating this basket would be by auction. Table 12.6 shows the potential quota revenue under the global quota approach for each alternative quota growth time profile (corresponding to the same paths examined in table 12.3).[41]

It is evident from the table that quota revenue could be very large, especially under restrictive quota growth programs (such as path A). Even under the most liberalizing schedule (path J), until the last four years of the transition period quota revenue would far exceed the range of $200 million suggested here as the amount of annual adjustment assistance for additional workers displaced beyond baseline.

---

41. The calculations apply the methodology of appendix B, p. 355, for the baseline quota rents and appendix C, p. 369, for the quota rents arising from additional protection. The quota rent equals total consumer cost less the components associated with tariff collections by the government (G), higher prices on domestic products (C), and loss of consumer surplus on imports forgone (B), referring to the diagram areas in the appendices cited.

Revenue rises from 10 percent of quota rents in the first year to 90 percent by the year 2000. It is assumed here that countries not now subject to quotas are granted quotas at their base trade levels, and only gradually lose these quotas to the global basket. If such countries were to possess no initial quota, but quotas corresponding to their base trade levels were immediately placed in the global basket, the quota revenues from the program would be somewhat larger in the initial years than shown in the table. On the other hand, the estimates here make no allowance for exemption of some currently controlled products; this factor would tend to reduce quota revenues.

Path G is of special interest, as it reflects potential quota revenue under the path closest to an unchanged level of total protection (that is, average annual quota growth of about 7 percent, approximately the rate of import growth projected in the absence of change in total protection).[42] Revenue in the first year is $530 million, indicating that total quota rents in 1992 are an expected $5.3 billion (as one-tenth would be captured in the first year of the program). Revenue rises steadily to $6.47 billion by the year 2000, as quotas progressively shift to the global basket and the baseline volume of the apparel market rises.

The large quota rents generated under the US proposal illuminate one reason it is likely to be opposed by foreign producers, who currently enjoy the bulk of these rents. Producers would have to be convinced that the eventual benefits of free access outweighed the loss of a rising portion of their quota rents. They would also have to be convinced that the program will in fact lead to eventual liberalization. One reason they would be skeptical about the outcome is that Congress could come to regard the quota revenues as a permanent source of income, contributing to reduction of the US fiscal deficit. This contribution could become a source of additional future opposition to liberalization.

Costs of Global Tariff Rate Quotas

The apparel projection model may also be applied to estimate the consumer costs associated with the strategy of global tariff rate quotas. In this case there are two influences that determine the outcome: the initial level of the tariff surcharge, and the rate of expansion of the threshold level at which the surcharge becomes applicable. The threshold, for its part, is comparable in concept to the physical volume of quotas under the absolute global quota proposal, and the same menu of quota growth paths as used in the global quota case may be investigated.

The model is estimated by first calculating the level of imports under the assumption that marginal importers pay the total tariff-equivalent including the surcharge; then comparing that level of imports against the physical threshold level for the surcharge; and then identifying the larger of these two values as the projected level of imports. For example, suppose that the surcharge is initially 40 percent, so that total protection including the underlying tariff begins at 71.5 percent (second half of table 12.7). In the absence of the exemption granted by the threshold, such a tariff-equivalent

---

42. As may be seen in table 12.3, cumulative additional consumer costs beyond baseline are the closest to zero for growth path G.

Table 12.7 US apparel imports and consumer costs under alternative tariff rate quotas, 1992–2000 (billions of 1989 dollars)

Year	A (0–3)	B (1–4)	C (2–5)	D (3–6)	E (4–7)	F (5–8)	G (6–9)	H (7–10)	I (8–11)	J (9–12)
					Threshold growth path[a]					

Initial surcharge = 25 percent

Imports

Year	A	B	C	D	E	F	G	H	I	J
1992	27.9	27.9	27.9	27.9	27.9	27.9	27.9	28.0	28.3	28.6
1993	30.6	30.6	30.6	30.6	30.6	30.6	30.6	30.6	30.6	31.1
1994	33.5	33.5	33.5	33.5	33.5	33.5	33.5	33.5	33.5	33.9
1995	36.8	36.8	36.8	36.8	36.8	36.8	36.8	36.8	36.8	37.3
1996	40.5	40.5	40.5	40.5	40.5	40.5	40.5	40.5	40.5	41.1
1997	44.5	44.5	44.5	44.5	44.5	44.5	44.5	44.5	44.5	45.2
1998	49.1	49.1	49.1	49.1	49.1	49.1	49.1	49.1	49.1	50.2
1999	54.2	54.2	54.2	54.2	54.2	54.2	54.2	54.2	54.2	55.7
2000	59.9	59.9	59.9	59.9	59.9	59.9	59.9	59.9	59.9	62.4

Consumer costs (change from baseline)

Year	A	B	C	D	E	F	G	H	I	J
1992	0.0	0.0	0.0	0.0	0.0	0.0	0.0	−0.3	−0.9	−1.5
1993	−1.9	−1.9	−1.9	−1.9	−1.9	−1.9	−1.9	−1.9	−1.9	−3.2
1994	−4.0	−4.0	−4.0	−4.0	−4.0	−4.0	−4.0	−4.0	−4.0	−4.9
1995	−6.3	−6.3	−6.3	−6.3	−6.3	−6.3	−6.3	−6.3	−6.3	−7.4
1996	−9.0	−9.0	−9.0	−9.0	−9.0	−9.0	−9.0	−9.0	−9.0	−10.2
1997	−11.9	−11.9	−11.9	−11.9	−11.9	−11.9	−11.9	−11.9	−11.9	−13.1
1998	−15.2	−15.2	−15.2	−15.2	−15.2	−15.2	−15.2	−15.2	−15.2	−17.1
1999	−18.9	−18.9	−18.9	−18.9	−18.9	−18.9	−18.9	−18.9	−18.9	−21.5
2000	−23.1	−23.1	−23.1	−23.1	−23.1	−23.1	−23.1	−23.1	−23.1	−27.3

would suppress 1992 apparel imports to $23.5 billion. But the threshold in path C (for example) indicates that $26.7 billion may be imported exempt of the surcharge. In this case, then, it is the threshold, not the tariff surcharge, that determines the volume of imports.

In contrast, after the surcharge has been phased down over a number of years, it is more likely to be the surcharge itself rather than the threshold that sets the level of imports. Again consider threshold path C and an initial surcharge of 40 percent, which is phased down by 4 percentage points per

	Threshold growth path[a]									
Year	A (0–3)	B (1–4)	C (2–5)	D (3–6)	E (4–7)	F (5–8)	G (6–9)	H (7–10)	I (8–11)	J (9–12)

Initial surcharge = 40 percent

Imports

Year	A	B	C	D	E	F	G	H	I	J
1992	26.2	26.5	26.7	27.0	27.3	27.5	27.8	28.0	28.5	28.6
1993	26.2	26.7	27.3	27.8	28.4	28.9	29.5	30.0	30.6	31.1
1994	28.7	28.7	28.7	28.7	29.5	30.3	31.2	32.1	33.0	33.9
1995	31.9	31.9	31.9	31.9	31.9	32.2	33.4	34.7	36.0	37.3
1996	35.4	35.4	35.4	35.4	35.4	35.4	35.7	37.5	39.2	41.1
1997	39.5	39.5	39.5	39.5	39.5	39.5	39.5	40.5	42.8	45.2
1998	44.2	44.2	44.2	44.2	44.2	44.2	44.2	44.2	47.0	50.2
1999	49.5	49.5	49.5	49.5	49.5	49.5	49.5	49.5	51.7	55.7
2000	55.6	55.6	55.6	55.6	55.6	55.6	55.6	55.6	55.6	62.4

Consumer costs (change from baseline)

Year	A	B	C	D	E	F	G	H	I	J
1992	4.4	3.7	3.0	2.3	1.7	1.0	0.4	−0.3	−0.9	−1.5
1993	9.1	7.7	6.3	4.9	3.5	2.1	0.8	−0.5	−1.9	−3.2
1994	7.5	7.5	7.5	7.5	5.5	3.4	1.3	−0.8	−2.8	−4.9
1995	4.8	4.8	4.8	4.8	4.8	4.0	1.1	−1.7	−4.6	−7.4
1996	1.7	1.7	1.7	1.7	1.7	1.7	1.0	−2.7	−6.5	−10.2
1997	−1.8	−1.8	−1.8	−1.8	−1.8	−1.8	−1.8	−3.8	−8.5	−13.1
1998	−5.8	−5.8	−5.8	−5.8	−5.8	−5.8	−5.8	−5.8	−11.4	−17.1
1999	−10.4	−10.4	−10.4	−10.4	−10.4	−10.4	−10.4	−10.4	−14.6	−21.5
2000	−15.6	−15.6	−15.6	−15.6	−15.6	−15.6	−15.6	−15.6	−15.6	−27.3

Note: Above the jagged line in each panel, import volume is determined by the threshold; below the line, import volume is determined by the tariff and surcharge.

a. The numbers in parentheses represent the range in annual quota growth rates for each path.

year. By 1996 the surcharge has been cut to 20 percent, giving total protection of 47 percent including the 22½ percent underlying tariff (1.225 × 1.20 = 1.47). By this period, the tariff and surcharge would be sufficiently moderate that imports would reach $35.4 billion. As this magnitude exceeds the amount of the threshold under path C ($29.5 billion in 1996), it is the larger volume that enters (and indeed the government collects some revenue from the surcharge on the excess volume over the threshold).

More generally, when the initial surcharge is relatively high and the threshold growth rate high, the threshold will tend to determine the import volume. When the initial surcharge is relatively low and the threshold growth path low, the surcharge will tend to set the import volume. With the projected level of imports known (for each year, the greater of the threshold level or the level set by the surcharge), the consumer costs may be calculated according to the same method as set forth above for the global quota approach.

Table 12.7 shows the results of these calculations. In the first part of each of the two cases considered, import volumes are shown for alternative implementations of the program (A through J). In the top half of table 12.7, the tariff surcharge is set initially at 25 percent and declines steadily to zero by the year 2001. It turns out that in this approach the volume of imports the public would be willing to buy, even with the surcharge included in the price, is almost always slightly higher than the volume set by all the threshold paths except the highest path J. This result is represented by the jagged line in the top section of table 12.7: import volumes above and to the right of this line are set by the threshold and are thus identical to the corresponding volumes in table 12.3. Those below the line are set by the tariff surcharge when it yields higher imports than the threshold path; they are thus greater than in table 12.3. For the case of the initial 25 percent surcharge, consumer costs under the tariff rate quota approach (second section of table 12.7) are almost always lower than under the absolute global quota alternatives considered here; the two are identical in the highest quota growth case J (again the numbers above the jagged line are identical to the corresponding values in table 12.3).

In contrast, when the initial surcharge is set at 40 percent and thus higher than the current level of protection, the consumer costs of the tariff rate quota approach are identical to those of the absolute global quota approach for any given path, until enough time has passed for the tariff surcharge to become more moderate and thus generate more imports than the absolute global quota approach. Thus, in the lower half of table 12.7, about half of the cases are above the jagged line, where the surcharge is so high that imports expand only up to the threshold volume where the surcharge takes effect.

A crucial aspect of the tariff rate quota strategy shown in table 12.7 is that, by the end of the transition period, it leaves the sector with no special protection above the basic tariff, because by definition the surcharge terminates. This end result occurs regardless of the initial level of the surcharge and whatever the transition path for the threshold triggering the surcharge. In a word, the tariff rate quota is a guaranteed path to elimination of special protection, so long as the timetable is not altered. Although the same is true in principle of the absolute global quota regime, with low global quota growth rates there is a large gap between imports in the last year of the transition and in the following year when quotas are abolished. Under such conditions, elimination of quotas on schedule is politically unlikely. In contrast, the tariff rate quota mechanism ensures a smooth transition at the end of the period.

Comparison of tables 12.3 and 12.7 thus shows that, even with a high initial surcharge, the global tariff rate quota regime imposes considerably lower consumer costs than do absolute global quotas. Consider path C, where absolute global quotas grow at 2 percent rising to 5 percent, with the same path for the 40 percent surcharge threshold in the case of the tariff rate quota. Under the absolute global quota option, total consumer costs in excess of baseline over the period 1992–2000 (discounting at 2 percent annually) amount to $130.9 billion (at 1989 prices). In contrast, consumer costs are less than baseline under tariff rate quotas for the same path (a discounted total of − $6.7 billion), even for the high-surcharge case. The sharp contrast illustrates that the key ingredient of liberalization in the tariff rate quota approach is the progressive reduction of the surcharge over time. Thus, path C in table 12.7 imposes lower consumer costs over the full period than the baseline, despite the relatively low growth rate in the threshold.

Costs of Transition Through MFA Quota Expansion

If the rates of quota growth are set lower than the expected rate of growth of apparel imports at unchanged levels of protection (i.e., below 7 percent), the option of MFA quota expansion will be less costly to consumers than global quotas, because only a subset of supply will be subject to the restrictions. Nonetheless, a large portion of apparel imports is already controlled by MFA quotas (as noted above), so that the difference between the two alternatives is not enormous.

The US Department of Commerce indicates that of the 5.28 billion square-meter equivalents (SME) of apparel imported in 1988, 4.24 billion SME came from MFA–controlled sources. Deducting the 244 million SME imported from OECD countries, there were an estimated 795 million SME imported from developing countries not controlled by the MFA.[43] Among developing-country suppliers, then, 15.8 percent of supply was free from MFA restrictions. Within the OECD, imports from Japan, Turkey, and

---

43. US Department of Commerce, *Major Shippers Report,* 14 December 1989. Note that these data are in square meters rather than square yards as in table 12.1. In addition, there are minor divergences between the totals in this source and the Census Bureau volume data in that table.

Yugoslavia were subject to bilateral MFA quotas.[44] These three countries accounted for one-fourth of OECD supply of US apparel imports in 1987.[45] Thus, the apparel import base subject to MFA restrictions amounts to 83.2 percent of developing-country supply and 25 percent of OECD supply.[46]

It is possible to quantify the effects of a liberalization program based strictly on increasing the magnitudes of quotas on currently restricted products while avoiding imposition of any new quotas. This may be done by applying specified quota growth rates to this base of MFA–controlled supply while retaining baseline (i.e., unchanged protection) growth rates for imports from OECD sources (0.58 percent annually) and noncontrolled developing-country sources (7.37 percent annually).[47]

As may be seen by comparing tables 12.3 and 12.8, limitation of alternative quota growth paths to currently controlled MFA suppliers permits a substantial reduction in the consumer costs relative to those under strict global quotas, when quota growth levels are set at rates below the baseline. Thus, for example, if imports are allowed to rise by only 2 percent initially and 5 percent by the year 2000 (path C), annual consumer costs by the year 1996 above and beyond baseline levels amount to $16.1 billion under global quotas (table 12.3) but only $13.8 billion, when the quotas are limited to suppliers currently restricted, under the MFA–growth option (table 12.8). However, this outcome depends on avoidance of any new restrictions under the MFA. A less disciplined MFA permitting imposition of new quotas as in the past would tend to generate higher consumer costs, closer to those of the global quota option.[48]

---

44. ITC, *US Imports 1988,* p. A-1.

45. OECD, *Foreign Trade By Communities 1987* (Paris: OECD, 1988), p. 237, and US Department of Commerce, *Major Shippers Report,* 14 December 1989.

46. The 1989 trade base estimates used here place OECD supply at $3.03 billion and developing-country supply at $22.19 billion (f.o.b.).

47. Chapter 10, p. 238, and detailed model results.

48. Note that comparison of the MFA expansion and global quota alternatives is not meaningful for quota growth rates above the level of approximately 7 percent. The MFA option assumes noncontrolled imports grow at baseline levels, and a global quota alternative with 10 percent average growth (for example) would ironically generate more import growth than an MFA expansion option with 10 percent quota growth. In the latter case about one-fourth of supply would still be growing at the baseline level of approximately 7 percent. In practice, the 10 percent global quota growth case really implies quota growth for MFA–controlled suppliers at approximately 11½ percent after taking account of slower-growing (baseline) imports from the OECD and noncontrolled developing-country supply.

Table 12.8   Impact of alternative MFA apparel quota paths on US consumer costs, 1992–2000 (billions of 1989 dollars)

Year	Baseline consumer costs	Change from baseline under growth path:[a]						
		A (0–3)	B (1–4)	C (2–5)	D (3–6)	E (4–7)	F (5–8)	G (6–9)
1992	26.1	3.6	3.1	2.6	2.1	1.6	1.1	0.6
1993	27.2	7.5	6.4	5.4	4.3	3.3	2.2	1.2
1994	28.3	11.6	10.0	8.3	6.7	5.1	3.5	1.8
1995	29.5	15.5	13.2	11.0	8.7	6.5	4.2	2.0
1996	30.7	19.6	16.7	13.8	10.9	8.0	5.1	2.2
1997	32.1	24.1	20.5	16.9	13.3	9.6	6.0	2.4
1998	33.5	28.2	23.9	19.5	15.2	10.8	6.4	2.0
1999	35.0	32.7	27.5	22.4	17.2	12.0	6.8	1.5
2000	36.6	36.8	30.8	24.8	18.7	12.7	6.6	0.4

a. The numbers in parentheses represent the range in annual quota growth rates for each path.

The Textile Subsector

The textile industry differs sharply from that of apparel. Textile production is much easier to mechanize, and productivity gains from high capital investment in textiles over the past two decades have essentially made the US textile industry internationally competitive—as long as the sector is not handicapped by an overly strong dollar (see chapters 2 through 4).

The extent and costs of protection in textiles have been substantially lower than in apparel. I have estimated that, in 1986, US consumer costs from protection in textiles amounted to only $2.8 billion annually, compared with $17.6 billion in apparel. My estimate of the tariff-equivalent of nontariff protection in textiles is 15 percent rather than 25 percent as in apparel. Import penetration was only 10 percent of consumption for textiles in 1986, versus 31 percent in apparel (chapter 2, p. 49; chapter 6, pp. 164–67; chapter 8, p. 191). Approximately half of US textile imports are from the industrial countries, and therefore largely exempt from MFA quota restrictions.[49]

The magnitudes of imports themselves are suggestive of the difference between the two sectors: in 1989, US textile imports stood at only $6.4

49. For 1987, members of the OECD accounted for 46.9 percent of US imports in SITC category 65 (textile yarns, fabrics, and made-up articles). OECD, *Foreign Trade by Commodities, Series C, 1987, Imports* (Paris: OECD, 1989), p. 192.

billion, versus $26.0 billion in apparel (table 12.1), even though domestic production in the two sectors was approximately equal. Similarly, the textile sector has a much stronger relative performance in exports: the ratio of exports to imports in 1989 was 60.7 percent for textiles versus only 8.0 percent in apparel.

Baseline projections for the textile subsector, applying a model of trade and domestic production similar to that for apparel, indicate that in the period 1987–90 textile imports could actually be expected to decline, because of effects of real depreciation of the dollar (chapter 10, p. 235). As indicated in table 12.2, real imports did drop in 1988, although their level by 1989 had not declined as much as predicted.

For the period 1990–2000, the model predicted relatively moderate growth of textile imports in the base case of unchanged protection: an average of 3.8 percent annually. In principle, any rate of global quota growth (or growth of imports under an alternative approach) in excess of this level would provide some degree of liberalization. In contrast, as discussed above, any total import growth rate for apparel below 7 percent would tend to increase the degree of protection.

For policy purposes, it would be inappropriate to set a lower global quota growth rate for textiles than for apparel when by all measures the textiles subsector is the more competitive of the two. The analysis here does not examine the options for the textiles subsector in detail, in part because the stakes for consumers are smaller (costs of protection are only about one-sixth the magnitude of those in apparel, as noted). Instead, the qualitative conclusion is that whatever the transitional path chosen toward reintegration of apparel into GATT practices, the corresponding path for the textiles subsector should be at least as liberalizing, because the domestic textiles subsector is more competitive and needs less protection. In particular, the 7 percent import growth benchmark for apparel would appear to be an appropriate standard for textiles as well.

Policy Implications

On the basis of the above analysis, the following options would appear to be the most appropriate, with the first two considerably more attractive as means of gradual liberalization than the second two. Table 12.10 presents a summary evaluation of the negotiating options.

Historical-Base Tariff Rate Quotas

The best approach to gradual liberalization of the sectors would still appear to be that recommended in the first edition of this study (chapter 11, pp.

257–62): conversion of *existing* quotas into tariff rate quotas, with phasedown of the above-threshold surcharges and their elimination by 2002 (chapter 11, pp. 257–62). This approach may be called the "historical-base tariff rate quota" strategy, as it would start from the existing protection base, that is, those countries and products currently subject to quotas. There would be an absolute standstill precluding new protection on suppliers and products not already in the historical protection base. Thus, in contrast to the global tariff rate quota option proposed by the USTR, there would be no extension of tariff rate quotas to other countries.

The initial surcharge on imports above the quota threshold would be 25 percent for apparel and 15 percent for textiles, as discussed above. Alternatively, column 2 tariffs (Smoot-Hawley) could be applied in place of the basic tariff to above-threshold imports. For example, with a column 2 tariff of 70 percent and an underlying basic tariff of 22½ percent, the surcharge would amount to 39 percent ($1.70 \div 1.225 = 1.39$). Because the column 2 tariffs could reach as high as 90 percent (as noted above), it would be particularly important in this case to ensure that the threshold levels escalate annually by at least the 7 percent rate associated with baseline import growth at unchanged protection.[50]

This approach would ensure that during the next decade there would be a progressive liberalization of textile and apparel trade. In particular, there would be no risk of an increase in protection through the imposition of absolute quotas or tariff rate quotas on countries not now subject to them.

MFA Quota Expansion

A second-best strategy would be to liberalize within the MFA. Under this approach, it would be imperative to set a minimum growth rate of 7 percent for MFA quotas (slightly more liberal than the 6 percent floor originally incorporated in MFA language but successively eroded in renewals and actual implementation), and to establish a target average growth rate of 9 percent (a pace that would be liberalizing as analyzed above). However, where countries do not fully use their existing quotas, the minimum could be adjusted accordingly.[51] The MFA would have to be amended in its next

---

50. In contrast, if the surcharge begins at the existing level of nontariff barrier protection (25 percent) and declines steadily over time, the pace of threshold growth is largely irrelevant, as analyzed above.

51. For example, if a country's quota is 100 and the country is currently using only 80, the quota growth rate could be set at zero for three years before shifting to the target of 8 percent annually without violating the target average growth rate of 8 percent for actual trade.

revision to include strong language against "departures." There would also need to be a clear commitment to eliminate MFA protection by, say, 2002.

In the absence of firm floor quota growth rates in the range of 7 percent, and a firm commitment to termination of the MFA, the MFA option is not a liberalizing alternative but one of retrogression toward higher protection. At least for apparel, comparative advantage tends not to be on the side of the industrial countries, because of the subsector's high labor intensity, and progressively tighter quotas would have to be anticipated as the political response to the natural tendency otherwise for the market share of imports to rise over time. Past experience, and especially that of the United States since 1986, has confirmed the tendency of the MFA to grow more restrictive over time.

Constrained Global Tariff Rate Quotas

An alternative second-best strategy would be a constrained version of the global tariff rate quota. By subjecting currently uncontrolled countries to restriction, this option could be more restrictive than the MFA–growth approach. However, because of its feature of assured smooth transition out of special protection, the tariff rate quota could also be as liberalizing as the MFA-growth approach, and it could be more liberalizing than an MFA alternative with low quota growth. Similarly, the global tariff rate quota approach would provide greater assurance of transition out of protection than the global quota approach, and would offer greater flexibility and less likelihood of extreme costs.

A revised and disciplined version of the global tariff rate quota proposal would run much less risk of having a net protective effect than the USTR formulation. The first "constraint" to be added to the proposal would be to exempt industrial countries and the least developed countries from global quotas. The fact is that the industrial countries provide only a small portion of apparel imports to the US market. Thus, in 1987 imports from all OECD member countries accounted for only 12.8 percent of total US apparel imports by value.[52] The fraction was much higher for textiles (46.9 percent), but the US import sensitivity problem is essentially an apparel problem, as discussed above.

If it is accepted that the primary "need" for protection concerns apparel, not textiles, then it makes little sense to impose tariff rate quotas (or absolute quotas) on Europe in particular. The reason is that pursuance of this strategy is likely to undermine cooperation between the European Community and

---

52. OECD, *Foreign Trade by Commodities, Imports, Vol. II, 1987* (Paris: OECD, 1988), pp. 192, 237. The data refer to SITC categories 84 for apparel and 65 for textiles.

the United States in Uruguay Round bargaining more generally. Viewed in another way, it seems unlikely that the United States would be well advised to give up much if anything in other crucial areas of negotiations in the Round (including on agriculture) to secure EC acquiescence in a new US program of global textile quotas applying to the Community.

Similarly, given that a major objective of the US proposals is to bring along the developing countries in an overall Uruguay Round negotiation, it would seem important symbolically to exempt the least developed countries from the global tariff rate quota as well. These countries account for a minimal share of US apparel imports (only 2.4 percent in 1987).[53] Nor does it seem likely that there would be a rush of new investment to create an artificial export base in these countries over the next decade if there were a clear commitment to eliminate the regime of quota protection by the year 2001. Exemption of the least developed countries would be important symbolically to obtain developing-country support of the entire approach.[54] However, the middle-income developing countries would have to be content with the prospect of complete elimination of quotas by the end of the decade, and the assurance of adequate quota growth in the interim.

The central mechanism for liberalization under the constrained global tariff rate quota would be progressive elimination of the tariff surcharge over the transitional decade. However, in addition there would be a second "constraint" to ensure against a protective implementation: the threshold for application of the tariff surcharge would rise over time. The pace of its increase could be determined as in the USTR formula (a minimum growth rate x, increased over time and faster for less sensitive products). Once again, either estimated tariff-rate equivalents of existing protection or column 2 tariffs could be used as the basis for determining the initial surcharge. If a high initial surcharge were adopted (as in the column 2 approach), threshold growth in the range of 7 percent average (minimum rate $x = 5$ percent) would be crucial to ensure against an increase in protection.

Other features of the global tariff rate quota would be the same as in the global quota approach summarized below. Base-year trade levels would be the basis for the threshold at which the surcharge would apply. Similarly, one-tenth of the initial country-specific threshold "quotas" (i.e. surcharge-exempt entitlements) would be reallocated to a global basket annually.

---

53. Based on US imports in SITC category 84 from the 42 countries designated by the United Nations as "least developed." United Nations Conference on Trade and Development, *Trade and Development Report 1989*, p. 143; OECD, *Trade by Commodities 1987*, pp. 237–39.

54. A possible alternative would be to grant the least developed countries duty-free entry under an exceptional extension of the Generalized System of Preferences to textiles and apparel, but leave them subject to the global quota regime.

Constrained Global Quotas

An alternative option could be more feasible in political terms, yet still broadly consistent with progressive liberalization of trade in textiles and apparel. This approach would be a constrained global absolute quota strategy. Once again the country coverage would be constrained to exclude the industrial and the least developed countries, for the reasons just discussed.

The second, and perhaps even more important, constraint would be a floor quota growth rate consistent with gradual liberalization. As analyzed above, in terms of the USTR formula the minimum quota growth rate x would need to be at least 5¼ percent (average growth rate 7¼ percent) in order for the transition mechanism to avoid tightening protection rather than gradually loosening it. As discussed above, setting the actual trade base as the point of departure rather than existing quotas would mean that, in terms of the original quota base, the corresponding minimum and average annual growth rates would amount to 3 percent and 5 percent, respectively, over the 10-year period.

As noted above, there are some considerations that suggest that actual import growth would exceed the rates set for the constrained global quota. The USTR proposal would exempt from quotas products covered under item 807-A of the Tariff Schedules of the United States, that is, those manufactured abroad using US fabric as inputs. The proposal also states that controls would be removed from some undefined portion of currently restricted categories. There is furthermore some marginal consumer benefit contained in the new opportunity to purchase more from tightly constrained suppliers (such as Indonesia) under the global basket approach. However, these factors would seem unlikely to be equivalent to more than a percentage point or so increase in the growth rate of the quotas. The minimum growth rate proposed here—5 percent for x, 7 percent average—would just barely replicate import growth under *unchanged* protection. The extra measure of liberalization from these three factors would still leave the prospective liberalization well below the expansion rate of some 9 percent to 10 percent annually that would be required to leave quota protection redundant at the end of the decade. In other words, the industry would still face going "cold turkey" to at least some degree at the end of 10 years, unless the minimum and average quota growth rates were set at higher levels.

It would be essential for US law to state explicitly the minimum quota growth rate to be accepted under the constrained global quota approach, and in addition to require the elimination of these quotas after 10 years. Otherwise the mechanism would be highly susceptible to pressures for subsequent tightening and a reneging on the essential bargain that trades the medium-term certainty of more generalized quotas for the longer-term goal of quota elimination.

The USTR proposal of reallocating one-tenth of country-specific quotas to a global basket each year would be desirable. Allocation of the remaining country-specific quotas would, as in the past, be left in the hands of the exporting country. For the globally untied basket, quota allocation would appropriately be by auction in the importing country. Because this "floating" basket would begin as only a small portion of total imports, there would be time for all parties to become accustomed to the auction process, and a large initial disruption of supplier networks would be avoided.

Another desirable feature would be to permit trading of country quotas. The trading of emission rights under recent US environmental legislation sets a useful precedent for using the market to introduce greater flexibility into systems that rely on regulated quantitative targets. Intercountry quota trading would reduce price distortions. Also, a market in quota rights would provide a measure of whether protection was in fact declining over time: failure of prices of quota rights to decline would be a signal that faster quota growth was required to pursue progressive liberalization.

Retrogressive Options

The options proposed by the USTR risk transformation into alternatives that in fact would restrict textile and apparel trade further over the next decade rather than provide for a progressive transition toward liberalization. That outcome would almost certainly occur if a global quota option were adopted with quota growth rates in the range of, say, 1 percent to 4 percent annually. Increased protection would also be the likely result if prospective quota growth were simply left undefined, as the pressures on the USTR in implementation would be to set low growth rates. Similarly, MFA renewal without a firm floor growth rate would be likely to lead to progressively higher protection, for the reasons discussed above.

Producer representatives have called for much more restrictive options and have revived their proposal of global quotas with only 1 percent annual growth (as analyzed below). If their arguments were to prevail, it would be best for all concerned to be candid about the trade-restricting nature of the arrangement, rather than to present the policy as a transition to liberalization. It is simply implausible that a period of severely tightening protection, even with quota growth rates of 2 percent to 4 percent (for example) rather than 1 percent, could be followed by a sudden plunge into complete quota elimination. The United States' negotiating partners in the Uruguay Round would be the first to discern this essential contradiction.

Protective Legislation

In April 1990, Representative Marilyn Lloyd (D-TN) introduced in Congress the Textile, Apparel, and Footwear Trade Act of 1990 (H.R. 4496). The bill closely resembles similar legislation introduced in 1987, which passed the House of Representatives by a majority of almost two-thirds. After the Senate passed the bill in 1988, Congress failed to override the President's veto late that year. The crucial provision of both the earlier proposal and the new 1990 bill was that textile and apparel imports would be subject to global quotas, with quota growth limited to 1 percent annually.[55]

Table 12.9 presents calculations based on the apparel model showing the impact of adoption of the global quota with 1 percent annual quota growth. The table first repeats the baseline paths for imports, consumer costs, and apparel employment. It then presents the changes from the baseline that would result from adoption of a 1 percent global quota growth regime beginning in 1990. By the year 2000, the volume of imports would be 40.3 percent lower than in the baseline case. Evaluated at constant 1989 prices, imports would stand $19.0 billion below the $47.1 billion level they would otherwise reach.

Consumer costs under the proposal would escalate from an additional $510 million in the first year to $4.96 billion by 1992 and would reach $48.5 billion above baseline by the year 2000.[56] Although the restrictive regime would increase employment—by as much as 252,000 workers by the year 2000—the extra jobs would be created only at extremely high cost to consumers. In the first year the consumer costs per additional job would stand at $128,000; by the year 2000 the cost per job would reach $192,000 (at 1989 prices). Moreover, these costs per job do not take account of likely employment reductions in the retailing sector caused by reduced availability and higher prices of clothing.[57] Comparison of tables 12.3 and 12.9 indicates

---

55. Like the Senate version of the 1987 bill, the Lloyd bill provided for a pilot program to auction 20 percent of quotas. It also authorized compensation to exporting countries through liberalization in other products or a limited reduction in textile tariffs; exempted Canada and Israel from quotas because of free trade pacts; excluded textiles and apparel from tariff cuts in the Uruguay Round; and provided for quota protection in footwear.

56. The modest consumer costs in 1990–91 stem from the model's projection of relatively slow import growth under unchanged protection in these years, as the lagged effects of earlier exchange rate change.

57. At the same time, however, the job estimates refer only to direct employment and do not include indirect jobs generated in intermediate input activities. Inclusion of indirect employment would not alter the qualitative conclusion of extremely high consumer costs per job. Model estimates for 1986 indicated that, in apparel, consumer

that the 1990 textile bill would impose consumer costs almost identical to those of path A, the lowest global quota growth path considered in this study, with zero initial annual growth rising to 3 percent by the year 2000.

Summary and Policy Conclusions

The Uruguay Round of multilateral trade negotiations offers a unique historical opportunity to return international trade in textiles and apparel to the normal rules of the GATT, from the current regime of quota controls under the Multi-Fiber Arrangement. US negotiators have suggested two approaches for a 10-year transition: absolute global quotas and global tariff rate quotas. They have acknowledged that the MFA framework could provide a third basis for transition back to GATT rules. Table 12.10 summarizes the advantages and disadvantages of these and the other approaches examined here, with the alternative strategies listed in order of desirability.

The principal findings of this study are the following:

☐ The US proposal to establish global quotas on textiles and apparel during 1992–2001 and abolish quotas thereafter would restrict trade and increase the consumer costs of protection during the transitional decade unless the quota growth rate achieved an average of at least 7 percent annually—the projected rate of apparel import growth in the absence of change in the level of current (tariff-equivalent) protection.

☐ For the textiles subsector, baseline import growth is somewhat lower (about 4 percent). However, by virtually all measures (import penetration, export performance, productivity growth, mechanization) US textiles are more competitive internationally than US apparel, and so it would be inappropriate to set lower quota growth rates for textiles than the benchmark adopted for apparel.

☐ To provide a smooth transition out of protection in 2002, the average annual quota growth rate for apparel would need to be at least 9 percent. Otherwise a substantial gap would remain at the end of the period between actual imports and the quota-free level.

---

costs per total employment change (direct and indirect jobs), excluding in retailing, amounted to 56 percent of the figure for direct jobs only. (chapter 8, p. 191). On this basis, consumer costs per total employment (direct and indirect) created under the proposed legislation would stand at $71,400 per job in 1990, rising to $108,000 by 2000 (at 1989 prices).

Table 12.9 Impact of the 1990 textile quota bill on US apparel imports, consumer costs, and employment, 1990–2000 (billions of 1989 dollars except where noted)

Year	Baseline Imports	Baseline Consumer costs	Baseline Employment (thousands of jobs)	Change from baseline under proposed bill Imports	Change from baseline under proposed bill Consumer costs	Change from baseline under proposed bill Employment (thousands of jobs)	Consumer costs per job created (thousands of 1989 dollars)
1990	25.7	24.6	1,084	−0.20	0.51	4	128
1991	26.2	25.1	1,078	−0.49	1.24	9	131
1992	27.9	26.1	1,065	−1.95	4.96	37	135
1993	29.8	27.2	1,051	−3.54	8.98	64	140
1994	31.8	28.3	1,036	−5.27	13.33	91	146
1995	33.9	29.5	1,020	−7.13	18.05	119	152
1996	36.2	30.7	1,003	−9.15	23.16	146	158
1997	38.6	32.1	985	−11.33	28.71	173	166
1998	41.3	33.5	967	−13.69	34.74	200	174
1999	44.1	35.0	947	−16.24	41.31	226	182
2000	47.1	36.6	927	−18.99	48.48	252	192

□ Low global quota growth rates would impose high consumer costs. For example, average annual growth of only 3 percent (path C in table 12.3) would raise the expected annual US consumer costs of protection in apparel in the midpoint year 1996 from a baseline $30.7 billion (at 1989 prices) under current levels of protection to $46.8 billion.

□ Insistence on a global absolute quota regime (or a global tariff rate quota regime) could jeopardize the Uruguay Round by causing conflict with the European Community and the developing countries. In any move toward globalization, the industrial countries should remain exempt as at present; so should the least developed countries. These groups account for only a small portion of US apparel imports (about 13 percent and 2½ percent, respectively). A wave of artificial new apparel export investment in these areas is unlikely if the pledge to abolish quotas at the end of the decade is credible.

□ The reallocation of one-tenth of initial country-specific quotas to a global basket each year is a favorable feature, if a global quota approach is adopted. Production would be more rationally allocated internationally than if quotas were continued on a strictly historical basis. The most appropriate means of distribution of the floating global basket component of quotas would be by importing-country government auction. As the phase-in would be gradual, all parties including importers would have time to adjust, and disruption to established supply networks should be limited.

□ Quota revenues could be large by the later years when the bulk of quotas would be in the global basket subject to auctioning. With low rates of quota growth (e.g., paths A through D, table 12.6), revenue could reach the range of $10 billion to $15 billion annually by the late 1990s (at 1989 prices). Even with quotas growing at an average of about 8 percent per year (path H, table 12.6), revenue would reach some $3½ billion annually in the second half of the 1990s. Quota growth averaging some 10 percent per year (path J, table 12.6) would limit revenue to about $1 billion annually and eliminate revenue before the end of the transition period by eliminating the protective effect of quotas. The potential for quota revenue through tight protection poses the danger that fiscal convenience could militate against open trade policy.

□ A program of restrictive global quotas could generate employment, but only at a very high consumer cost per job created. For example, global quotas growing initially at 2 percent and rising to 5 percent by the end of the decade would create some 145,000 direct jobs in apparel beyond baseline levels by the year 2000, but at an annual consumer cost of

$199,000 per job (tables 12.3 and 12.5). Similarly, large consumer gains could be achieved for each job displaced under a program of liberalization. Correspondingly, there is ample scope for consumer compensation to disemployed workers. A fee of only ⅔ percent on imports would suffice to provide two years of adjustment assistance (at $10,000 annually per worker) to workers displaced by a liberalization program, yet would absorb only a small fraction of the consumer gains from liberalization.

☐ The global tariff rate quota option is more liberalizing, and less costly to consumers, than the absolute global quota option (except at high quota growth rates for the absolute quota option). If the initial tariff surcharge is set equal to the current tariff-equivalent of quotas (estimated at 25 percent) and steadily phased down over the decade, the effect of the global tariff rate quota is approximately the same as in the highest quota growth path considered under the absolute global quota option (i.e., an average of 10 percent quota growth annually). Most important, the tariff rate quota option provides for a smooth transition to standard GATT discipline at the end of the decade, when by definition the surcharge disappears and no quotas remain. The tariff rate quota also provides greater flexibility; an absolute quota, in contrast, is like a tariff rate quota with a surcharge of infinity above the trigger threshold.

☐ Even a tariff rate quota regime with an intentionally high initial surcharge (such as 40 percent) could result in lower consumer costs and a more assured phaseout than absolute global quotas. In this case, however, it would be essential to ensure that the physical threshold triggering the surcharge grows at a moderate rather than a low rate. In general, with a high initial surcharge the level of imports is determined by the physical threshold in the early years, and by the surcharge only in the later years when the size of the surcharge has been phased down.

☐ If absolute quotas (rather than tariff rate quotas) are deemed essential to provide greater certainty to domestic producers, consumer costs would be substantially reduced by limiting quotas to those countries and categories currently restricted under the MFA. For any given growth path of quotas, application solely to the existing MFA base rather than on a global basis permits a sizable reduction in consumer costs. For example, if the quota growth path begins at 2 percent annually and rises to 5 percent by the year 2000 (path C, table 12.3), the global quota approach generates additional consumer costs (beyond baseline) amounting to $16.1 billion annually by 1996. The same program limited to countries and products already subject to MFA quotas imposes an additional consumer cost of $13.8 billion in the same year (tables 12.3 and 12.8).

Overall, the order of preference for alternative strategies based on the analysis of this essay is as follows (table 12.10):

☐ The most desirable strategy would be to convert *existing* country and category quotas to tariff rate quotas. At the quota threshold, additional imports could be purchased with payment of a tariff surcharge, instead of being totally prohibited by the quota as at present. Currently uncontrolled countries and products would not be subject to the tariff rate quota. The initial surcharge would need to be an estimated 25 percent for apparel and 15 percent for textiles to leave import levels unchanged from present. Alternatively, the column 2 (Smoot-Hawley) tariffs could be used to construct the above-threshold surcharge (this would result in surcharges averaging 39 percent for apparel and 34 percent for textiles). Liberalization over the decade would occur through annual increases in the threshold level (especially important if the column 2 tariffs were employed) and through annual reductions in the tariff surcharge. Scheduled tariff cuts have a well-established record as an effective means of liberalization. Annual threshold increases would ideally be at least 5 percent.

☐ Of the three US proposals (absolute global quotas, global tariff rate quotas, and MFA quota expansion), the last two are more favorable than the first, but both are less favorable than the option just described. Either the global tariff rate quota or the MFA quota expansion option could be the more liberalizing, depending on the details of implementation. If the initial surcharge is set at the tariff-equivalent of the existing quota, then the tariff rate quota provides faster liberalization and lower consumer costs. Even with a high initial surcharge (such as 40 percent), the global tariff rate quota would be preferable to MFA quota expansion at low quota growth rates (this can be seen by comparing table 12.7 with table 12.8).

☐ If the global tariff rate quota is chosen, it would be highly desirable to constrain the option to exempt the industrial countries and the least developed countries. Moreover, there should be a clear minimum growth rate of the threshold level for the tariff surcharge, especially if the initial surcharge is high.

☐ If the MFA quota expansion option is chosen, it should provide an unambiguous floor of 7 percent annually for MFA quota growth, with a target of 9 percent average growth. There should also be a binding commitment to terminate the quota regime at the end of a decade.

Table 12.10 Policy options for liberalization of textile and apparel trade, ranked by preference

Preference	Option	Key features
1	Historical-base tariff rate quotas	Conversion of *existing* absolute quotas to tariff rate quotas. Phaseout of surcharge on imports in excess of threshold over 10 years. Initial surcharge of 25 percent for apparel, 15 percent for textiles (alternatively, column 2–based surcharge). Threshold for surcharge to rise by 7 percent annually if surcharge is set above 25 percent for apparel, 15 percent for textiles.
2 or 3	Constrained global tariff rate quotas	Exclusion of industrial countries and least developed countries from tariff rate quotas; global tariff rate quota system for all others. For each category, global threshold based on base-year trade. Global threshold to rise by minimum of 5 percent annually, average of 7 percent over 10 years. Surcharge set and phased out as in option 1.
2 or 3	MFA quota expansion	Expansion of all present MFA quotas by minimum of 7 percent annually, target average of 9 percent. Elimination of quotas after 10 years. Minimum growth rate to apply to any new quotas negotiated.

4	Constrained global quotas	Exclusion of industrial countries and least developed countries; global quotas for all others. Quotas to rise by minimum of 5 percent annually, average of 7 percent over 10 years following USTR escalation and sensitivity formula. One-tenth of base-year quota to be reallocated to global basket each year. Quotas in global basket auctioned by importing country. Actual trade used as basis for initial global quota and country quotas. Minimum growth rates set in law. Law to provide for elimination of quotas by year 2002.
Undesirable[a]	Low-growth global quotas	Global quotas restricting all suppliers. Average quota growth rates below 7 percent annually.
Undesirable	Ill-defined global quotas	Global quota with quota growth "at discretion of USTR" or otherwise open-ended (susceptible to restrictive implementation).
Undesirable	MFA forever	Continuation of MFA as in past, with use of "departures" to restrict quota growth to low rates.
Undesirable	Textile bill of 1990 (H.R. 4496)	Global quotas with quota growth limited to 1 percent annually.

a. Options listed as "Undesirable" would increase rather than decrease existing levels of protection.

□ The least favorable option among the US proposals is the absolute global quota. If this option is adopted, it would again be important to constrain the option to exempt the industrial and the least developed countries, and to ensure average quota growth of at least 7 percent annually. The USTR formula relating quota growth to time period and product sensitivity could be applied, with the minimum x value set at 5 percent (yielding average quota growth of 7 percent annually).

□ In interpreting quota growth rates, it is important to recognize that at present the aggregate of country quotas plus actual imports from uncontrolled countries and categories stands some 20 percent above the actual level of total imports. Accordingly, formulation of quota growth from the actual trade base (as in the options discussed here) translates into annual growth rates from the existing base of quotas that are about 2 percentage points lower. That is, average quota growth measured from the initial quota base rather than the trade base could be as low as 5 percent annually without causing protection and its costs to rise.

□ Finally, among policies under consideration within the United States, the most damaging would be the proposed textile legislation, earlier vetoed but resubmitted in Congress in 1990 as H.R. 4496, to impose global quotas and limit their growth to 1 percent annually. This legislation would increase consumer costs by some $5 billion annually by 1992, $23 billion by 1996, and $48 billion by the year 2000 (at 1989 prices), equivalent to well over $100,000 annually per job created in the early years and eventually reaching close to $200,000 per job (table 12.9). Total consumer costs of tariff and quota protection would rise from $22.4 billion in 1989 to $85.1 billion annually in the year 2000.

□ The European Community's proposal for trade liberalization lacks a firm timetable for elimination of quota protection. It is formulated in terms of interim safeguard protection and eventual integration of textiles and apparel into the general safeguard treatment to be negotiated in the GATT. The proposal stresses reciprocity by the developing countries. It would be possible to implement the EC approach in a more liberalizing manner than the US proposals, but the reverse is also true.

□ The Japanese proposal emphasizes concrete criteria of injury that domestic products must meet to obtain continued protection. However, seemingly unambiguous standards such as import penetration can be difficult to measure in practice.

Appendices

Appendix A   A Model of Production, Employment, and Trade in Textiles and Apparel

This appendix sets forth the model applied in chapter 3 to examine the influences determining trade in recent years, and in chapter 10 to project trade, output, and employment through the year 2000 under alternative policy regimes. The price of imports from countries in the Organization for Economic Cooperation and Development (OECD) is:

(1) $P_t^{M1} = P_{t-1}^{M1} [1 + \dot{T}_{1t}][1 - a(0.4\dot{E}_{1t} + 0.6\dot{E}_{1t-1})][c1_t/c1_{t-1}]$,

where the overdot refers to proportionate change; the subscript t refers to the year; T *equals* unity *plus* the tariff; E_{1t} is the real exchange rate (foreign currency per dollar, deflating by wholesale prices) in year t, weighted by shares in US textile (or apparel) imports; E_{1t-1} is the same rate in the prior year; a is the pass-through ratio relating import price changes to real exchange rate changes; and $c1_t$ is the real price of the product in the foreign market. For purposes of the simulation of past experience, in the absence of data on real foreign prices it is assumed that they move identically with the domestic US real price facing the consumer (product shipments price index for textiles or apparel, as deflated by the consumer price index). Similarly, for imports from developing countries, the price is:

(2) $P_t^{M2} = P_{t-1}^{M2} [1 + \dot{T}_{2t}][1 - a(0.4\dot{E}_{2t} + 0.6\dot{E}_{2t-1})][c2_t/c2_{t-1}]$,

where variables are as before except that the protection variable T_{2t} includes the tariff equivalent of quota protection, which applies to developing countries but not to OECD countries (with the partial exception of Japan).

The price facing domestic purchasers is then a weighted average of the two import prices and the domestic price:

(3) $P_t = P_{t-1}^c [W_t^d (P_t^d/P_{t-1}^d) + W_t^{M1}(P_{t-1}^{M1}/P_{t-2}^{M1}) + W_t^{M2}(P_{t-1}^{M2}/P_{t-2}^{M2})]$,

where P_t^d is the real price of domestic output (deflated by the consumer price index), and the weights W^d, W^{M1}, and W^{M2} are shares of domestic

347

output, imports from the OECD, and imports from developing countries, (as calculated below). The time operators on import prices are lagged one year because, as set forth below, imports are calculated to respond to import prices with a one-year lag (and thus with a mixture of one- and two-year lags with respect to the exchange rate). Accordingly, the effective import price facing the consumer in the current year is based on the import price in the prior year.

Consumption is then calculated as:

(4) $C_t = C_{t-1} [1 + g_t^{pop}][1 + e_y\, g_t^y][1 + e_p(P_t^c/P_{t-1}^c - 1)]$
$\cdot [1 + e_c(Y_t/\hat{Y}_t - Y_{t-1}/\hat{Y}_{t-1})],$

where g_t^{pop} is the rate of population growth, g_t^y is the rate of growth of per capita income, e_y is the income elasticity of per capita demand with respect to per capita income, e_p is the price elasticity of demand, e_c is the cyclical elasticity of demand, Y_t is real GNP, and $\hat{Y}_t$ is the trend value of real GNP based on steady growth.

For textiles, the consumption according to equation (4) refers to all uses of textiles except as inputs into the apparel sector. The latter component of textile demand is estimated as:

(4a) $C_t^{TA} = kQ_t^A$

where C_t^{TA} is the output of textiles channeled into production of apparel, k is the corresponding inter-industry coefficient (0.331, chapter 3), and Q_t^A is output of apparel in year t. Total consumption of textiles is then:

(4b) $C_t^T = C_t^{TA} + C_t^{TO},$

where C_t^{TO} is "other" textile consumption as calculated by equation (4).

Imports from the OECD, expressed in terms of constant real values of 1982 prices (tables 2.3 and 2.5), are:

(5) $M1_t = M1_{t-1} [1 + \lambda_1 \{(P_{t-1}^{M1}/P_{t-2}^{M1}) - 1\}][1 + \lambda_2 \{(Y_t/Y_{t-1}) - 1\}]$
$\cdot [1 + \lambda_3 \{(Y/\hat{Y}) - (Y_{t-1}/\hat{Y}_{t-1})\}][1 + S_{1t}],$

where λ_1 is the price elasticity of demand for imports, λ_2 is the income elasticity of import demand, λ_3 is the cyclical elasticity of import demand, and S_{1t} is a proportionate growth factor reflecting long-term (secular) trend in market share. The secular term is designed to capture such influences as changes in taste, the evolution of international distribution systems, and changing transportation costs. Its estimation is discussed below.

Imports from non-OECD countries are estimated as in equation (5), but with M_2 as the import variables, P^{M2} as the price variable, and S_{2t} as the secular growth variable. The price, income, and cyclical elasticities of import demand are also permitted to vary between OECD and non-OECD products.

Exports are estimated as:

(6) $X_t = X_{t-1} [1 + E_1\{(Y_t^{RO}/Y_{t-1}^{RO}) - 1\}]$
    $\cdot [1 + E_2 b\{0.4(R_t^U/R_{t-1}^U - 1) + 0.6(R_{t-1}^U/R_{t-2}^U - 1)\}]$
    $\cdot [1 + E_3\{(Y_t^{RO}/\hat{Y}_{t-1}^{RO}) - (Y_{t-1}^{RO}/\hat{Y}_{t-1}^{RO})\}][1 + S^E],$

where E_1 is the income elasticity of export demand, Y^{RO} is real GNP in the rest of the OECD (excluding the United States), E_2 is the price elasticity of exports, R^U is the real, trade-weighted exchange rate for the dollar (foreign real currency per real dollar, deflating by wholesale price indexes), and b is the pass-through ratio from real exchange rate changes to US export prices abroad.

The market share weights for equation (3) are calculated as:

(7a) $W_t^d + [Q_{t-1} - X_{t-1}]/C_{t-1};$

(7b) $W_t^{M1} = M1_{t-1}/C_{t-1};$ and

(7c) $W_t^{M2} = M2_{t-1}/C_{t-1},$

where Q is domestic output. The shares are based on the previous year's estimates because the current year values of simulated output and imports are endogenously determined. (That is, the model is recursive, solving for values one year at a time in light of the previous year's estimates).

Domestic output is determined as the residual between domestic consumption and exports, on one hand, and imports on the other hand:

(8) $Q_t = C_t + X_t - M1_t - M2_t.$

The secular growth term for apparel imports from OECD countries is set at a constant rate of -2.5 percent annually, based on the best fit for 1970–86. For textiles, secular import growth is set at 1.5 percent for imports from developing countries and -2 percent for imports from industrial countries.

For apparel imports from non-OECD countries, the secular trend must capture a more complicated process of rapid initial growth followed by eventual moderation. As discussed in chapter 3, this pattern is that of a logistics curve—in S-shaped curve, first rising slowly, then rapidly, then tapering off to a plateau. This curve may be estimated by specifying the percentage change of the import penetration ratio as a constant rate plus a negative function of the penetration ratio itself:

$\dot{m}_t = 0.28045 - 1.6514\, m_t$; $\bar{R}^2 = 0.822$
      (17.7)   (-8.7)

where m_t is defined as $M2_t/C_t$ and the overdot indicates proportionate change, estimated for 1967 to 1983 (t–statistics in parentheses). Thus, in the beginning of this period the import penetration ratio from non-OECD countries is rising at over 25 percent annually, but by the end of the period (when $M2_t/C_t$ has risen to approximately 16 percent) the import penetration ratio is rising at only about 2 percent annually.

The secular growth term in equation (5) is, in the first instance, merely the percentage growth rate calculated in the logistics regression for imports from non-OECD sources ($\dot{m}_t$). Unless adjusted, however, this growth rate when superimposed on the growth already calculated on the basis of the other factors in equation (5) tends to overstate imports—because the import penetration ratio is itself the outcome of the various factors including income elasticity of imports as applied to income growth. Iterative experimentation with the secular growth factor indicates that the best fit is given by applying a fractional term of 0.85 to the regression estimate; thus, in equation (5) the term S is estimated as 0.85 $\dot{m}_t$.

A further word on the secular trend variable is warranted. As noted above, this variable seeks to capture such phenomena as changing tastes and the shift toward developing-country supply as US retail firms expand their international networks and develop foreign sources producing to their own specifications. In addition, the fitted secular variable to some extent represents outward shifting supply in developing countries. In one sense, this influence might already be captured in the price variable. Secular shift in the supply curve would be expected to drive down the price of imports and show the resulting impact on import volume through the standard price response. In the present case, as indicated above there are no data series available directly on the imported good itself; import price variation is imputed from changes in exchange rates and in protection levels, while it is assumed that the real foreign-currency price of the import moves identically to the real price of the domestic US good. The secular trend variable may well be registering in addition the price impact of long-term outward shifting supply from developing countries, because this component of price change will tend to be missed in the price variable used in the model (which does not reflect sector-specific price changes in the supplying country). More generally, a time trend has been found important in the explanation of US imports overall, as imports have risen over time more rapidly than can be explained by income and price effects—although there is evidence that the time trend effect has diminished in importance in recent years.[1]

The final variable calculated in the simulation model is sectoral employment. The calculation is:

$$(9) \quad N_t = Q_t/h_t,$$

---

1. Barry Bosworth, "Discussion of 'The Persistence of the US Trade Deficit' by Paul R. Krugman and Richard E. Baldwin," *Brookings Papers on Economic Activity* (Washington: Brookings Institution, forthcoming).

in normal years, or (if the alternative estimate is larger)

(9a) $[0.75(Q_{t-1}/h_{t-1}) + 0.25(Q_t/h_t)]$,

in years of output decline, where N_t is sectoral employment and h_t is the trend value of output per worker (based on the period 1970–84). This formulation allows for the process of labor-hoarding during recession, when redundant labor is retained to avoid frictional costs of firing and rehiring once output revives.

Table A.1 presents the parameters used for the simulation model in the applications of chapter 3, which examines actual experience in 1970–86 and the impact of dollar overvaluation and slow growth in the early 1980s. The notes to the table identify changes made in its application to projections through the year 2000, in chapter 10.

The income elasticity of 0.5 for domestic consumption is based on the Houthakker-Taylor estimate cited in chapter 3. The cyclical consumption elasticities are set at 1.5, reflecting the higher short-run demand elasticity for clothing estimated by the same authors. For apparel, the price elasticity of total demand of -0.9 is based on estimates by Clopper Almon.[2] For textiles, the price elasticity is set at a lower level (-0.4), although not as low as the estimate by Almon in the same study (-0.133).

The pass-through ratio for changes in the exchange rate as translated into import price increases is set at 0.8 for both textiles and for apparel, in view of observed responsiveness of imports during periods of exchange rate variation. The price elasticity of demand for textile imports (-1.3) is based on estimates by Buckler and Almon as reported in Stern, Francis, and Schumacher.[3] The higher price elasticity of demand for apparel imports (-1.5 for imports from developing countries and -2.5 for imports from OECD sources) is intermediate in a range of estimates by several authors.[4] It is plausible that the elasticity would be higher for apparel, a finished consumer good (that in some respects is a durable good), than for textiles,

---

2. Clopper Almon Jr., Margaret B. Buckler, Lawrence M. Horwitz, Thomas C. Reimbold, *1985: Interindustry Forecasts of the American Economy* (Lexington, Mass., Toronto, London: Lexington Books, 1974), Table 2.2, p. 37.

3. Robert M. Stern, Jonathan Francis, and Bruce Schumacher, *Price Elasticities in International Trade: An Annotated Bibliography* (Macmillan Canada and Maclean-Hunter Press/London and Basingstoke, 1976) p. 141.

4. Almon and Buckler estimate an elasticity of -3.77; Robert Stone, et al., estimates -1.24. Ibid., p. 141, 342. Robert M. Stern reports a range of -0.52 to -3.92 in Robert M. Stern "Comments on Data, Elasticities, and Other Key Parameters," Seminar Discussion Paper no. 134. Paper presented at the Conference on General Equilibrium Trade Policy Modelling, Columbia University, April 5–6, 1984. Hufbauer, et al., estimate an elasticity of -2.0 in Gary Clyde Hufbauer, Diane T. Berliner, Kimberly Ann Elliott, *Trade Protection in the United States: 31 Case Studies* (Washington: Institute for International Economics, 1986), p. 135.

Table A.1 Parameters for textile and apparel simulation models

	Parameter	Value Textiles	Value Apparel
Consumption			
e_y	Income elasticity of demand	0.5	0.5
e_c	Cyclical demand elasticity	1.5	1.5
e_p	Price elasticity of demand	−0.4	−0.9
Imports			
a	Exchange rate pass-through	0.8	0.8
λ_1	Price elasticity of import demand		
	from developed countries	−1.3	−2.5
	from developing countries	−1.3	−1.5
λ_2	Income elasticity of import demand:		
	from developed countries	1.2	1.0
	from developing countries	1.2	1.7
S	Secular growth rate of imports		
S_1	from developed countries	−0.02	−0.025
S_2	from developing countries	0.015	S-curve
λ_3	Cyclical import demand elasticity		
	from developed countries	2.0	2.0
	from developing countries	2.0	1.5
Exports			
b	Exchange rate pass-through	0.8	1.0
E_1	Elasticity for ROECD[a] income	1.5	2.0
E_2	Price elasticity of export demand	−3.0	−2.5
E_3	Cyclical elasticity for ROECD income	3.0	3.0
S^E	Secular growth rate of exports	0.02	0.025
Employment			
r	Labor productivity growth rate	.037	.0275

Note: in projection model, parameters are unchanged except that for apparel imports from developing countries the secular growth rate is fixed at 2 percent annually, and apparel labor productivity growth is set at 2 percent annually.
a. ROECD is non-US OECD.

of which a good portion represents intermediate inputs into industrial production. The distinction between OECD and non-OECD imports, with a higher price elasticity for the former, is the consequence of experimentation to obtain the best fit for the period 1970–86, and also reflects the view among industry experts that the impact of exchange rate changes in the

1980s has been greater on apparel imports from other industrial countries than from the developing countries.[5]

The income elasticity of import demand is set at 1.2 for textiles. The literature contains few estimates of this elasticity for textiles and apparel. However, the aggregate elasticity of 1.46 estimated by Hayes and Stone for US imports suggests the use of an elasticity greater than unity, while the fact that only a portion of textiles is in the form of finished consumer goods suggests a lower elasticity than the general average.[6] For apparel, the sharp difference in the trend for imports from developing countries versus OECD suppliers warrants a higher income elasticity for the former, set here at 1.7 (somewhat above the general Haynes-Stone level), than for the latter (set here at 1.0). Haynes and Stone also estimate the cyclical income elasticity of US import demand at 2.0, the value applied here to both textiles and apparel for OECD goods, and to textiles from developing countries. For apparel from developing countries, a cyclical income elasticity of 1.5 accords better with the behavior of imports from 1970 to 1986.

For exports, the experience of the early 1980s reveals a strong reaction to the real exchange rate. On this basis, the pass-through ratio assumed for exchange rates is placed at a relatively high level, 0.8 for textiles and 1.0 for apparel. Similarly, the price elasticity of demand for exports is specified at relatively high levels of -2.5 for apparel and -3.0 for textiles. The income elasticity of non-US OECD demand for US exports is based on the secular income elasticity for foreign demand for general US exports as estimated by Haynes and Stone (1.5), with an increment for apparel in view of its brisk underlying rate of increase (from a low base) after taking account

---

5. It would be possible to incorporate into the model an additional cross-price elasticity for US imports from developing countries with respect to the price of imports from the OECD, and a corresponding cross-price elasticity for imports from the OECD with respect to the price of developing-country supply. The combined impact of a cross- and direct-price elasticity would tend to show a greater sensitivity of imports from a single region in response to a price change for that region alone. The formulation here omits the interregional competition, and implicitly the separate price elasticities for apparel imports from the OECD and from developing countries are specified to indicate the response from both regions when each changes price by an amount identical to that of the other. The principal implication of the model specification in this regard is that the projections of future imports would tend to understate the share of developing countries and overstate that of OECD suppliers, to the extent that exchange rate appreciation in the developing countries lags behind that of Europe and Japan. However, there would be no reason for the projections of overall imports to be biased. In any event, because developing countries account for nearly 90 percent of apparel imports, further refinements on the share of OECD suppliers would have little impact on the developing country and total estimates in this sector.

6. Stephen E. Haynes and Joe A. Stone, "Secular and Cylical Responses of U.S. Trade to Income: An Evaluation of Traditional Models," *Review of Economics and Statistics*, vol. 55, no. 1 (February 1983), pp. 83–97.

of exchange rate effects. The cyclical elasticity for textile and apparel exports, 3.0, also reflects the observed greater volatility of these flows than their counterparts on the import side. The secular growth rates are selected to obtain the best fit given application of the other parameters.

The selection of the parameters for the simulation models applies a mixture of adoption of corresponding econometric estimates in the existing literature and direct selection of values deemed reasonable on general grounds. In principle it would be desirable to obtain the estimates from new econometric estimation as applied to the data under examination. In practice statistical regressions tended to yield uneven results, with cases of extreme values for some parameters and frequently insignificant values for others, and with fluctuations in values depending on specification of the equation estimated. The final approach of blending existing estimates with plausible hypothesized values drew in addition upon experimentation with ranges of the parameters to ensure a relatively good fit of simulated to actual trade and production performance.

Appendix B   Calculation of Consumer and Welfare Costs

Protection imposes costs on consumers by raising the price of imports and, by sympathetic response, of domestic goods. A substantial portion of these consumer costs is merely a transfer away from consumers to domestic producers and to the government in its tariff revenue. However, because protection causes the reallocation of domestic productive resources into products in which the economy is relatively inefficient, the producer and government gains do not offset fully the consumer costs, especially if the protective mechanism is a quota that does not capture revenue for the government (but instead permits "quota rents" to accrue to foreign suppliers). The difference between consumer costs and producer-government gains is the net welfare cost to the economy.

The consumer cost of protection may be measured by the increase in consumer benefits that would result from elimination of protection. This increase is the change in "consumer surplus," a concept representing the difference between what consumers have to pay for the good and the maximum they would be willing to pay.

Figure B.1 presents a diagram of the two relevant markets: that for the domestic good and that for the import. If the two products (for example, domestically-produced apparel and imported apparel) were homogeneous, they could be consolidated into a single supply-demand diagram by simply adding their quantities together and specifying a single price that must apply to both. In reality, substitution between the two is not perfect, and varying price differentials between them can exist. Thus, the imperfect-substitute approach of figure B.1 is the more appropriate treatment.[1]

---

1. For similar approaches applying the imperfect substitute model and incorporating feedback of an induced, second-round shift in the import demand curve, see Gary Clyde Hufbauer, Diane T. Berliner, and Kimberly Ann Elliott, *Trade Protection in the United States: 31 Case Studies* (Washington: Institute for International Economics, 1986), pp. 31–42; and Donald J. Rousslang and John W. Suomela, "Calculating the Consumer and Net Welfare Costs of Import Relief" (Washington: International Trade Commission, July 1985; processed).

Figure B.1 Supply and demand for domestic and imported products

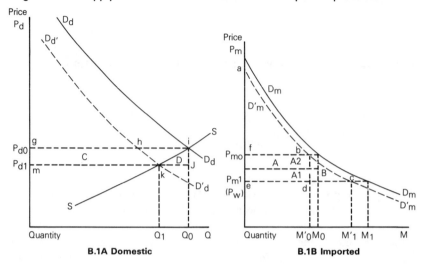

B.1A Domestic

B.1B Imported

In diagram B1-B, the demand curve for imports $(D_m D_m)$ shows that consumers purchase higher quantities of imports (M) at lower import prices (P_M), assuming no change in the price of the competing domestic good. The world price of the import is P_w (also designated as P_{M1}), and supply is assumed to be available in unlimited amounts at this price (infinite supply elasticity). This price is specified at the wholesale level for c.i.f. import values. Under protection, the price facing importers is the world price plus the protective effect of the tariff and the quota, $P_w + T$ (also designated as P_{MO}). In the market for the home good, shown in diagram B1-A, domestic demand is shown by curve $D_d D_d$, which shows the quantities purchased at alternative prices assuming the competing import price is held constant. The domestic supply curve, SS, shows the amounts that domestic producers will provide at alternative prices. Under protection, the initial equilibrium in the two markets is at import quantity of M_0 and domestic output quantity of Q_0. Note that the corresponding equilibrium prices (P_{MO} for imports and P_{DO} for the domestic good) are related but not necessarily equal, because the goods are not perfect substitutes.

If protection were eliminated, equilibrium in the import market would occur at the intersection of the foreign supply curve (which is a horizontal line at world price level P_w) with the import demand curve, or at import quantity M_1. There would be repercussions in the market for the domestic substitute, because with a lower price of imports and a shift of their purchases to imported goods, consumers would demand lower quantities of the domestic good at each alternative price. As a result, the domestic demand curve would shift downward, to $D'_d D'_d$. The new equilibrium in the domestic product market would occur at the new intersection with the supply curve, at quantity Q_1 and price P_{D1}. That is, as liberalization increases the quantity of imports from M_0 toward M_1, it decreases the quantity produced and sold for the domestic good, from Q_0 to Q_1, because of the lower demand for the domestic product, the lower price it can now command, and thus the lower quantity domestic firms are willing to produce.

The decline in the price of the domestic substitute has a feedback effect on consumers' demand for imports. At any given price, a lower quantity of imports will be demanded than before because the price of the domestic substitute has declined. The import demand curve thus moves inward to $D'_m D'_m$, and the final equilibrium level of imports is at the intersection of the international price line with the new import demand curve, at import quantity M'_1.

Consumer surplus is the area under the demand curve and above the equilibrium market price. This area is the sum of each successive unit sold multiplied by the maximum price that unit would command if it were the last one available, less the actual price for which it sold. In the import market, consumer surplus at the original price (including protection) evaluated under the final demand curve $(D'_m D'_m)$ is the area enclosed by points abf.[2] After liberalization, consumer surplus on imports rises to the area ace. The difference, composed of a rectangle A and a near-triangle B, is the increase in consumer surplus in import consumption from liberalization.

Liberalization increases consumer surplus in the domestic product market as well, by driving down the price there. Thus, given the new demand curve $D'_d D'_d$ consumer surplus at the new lower price is larger than it would have been at the old price by the area C (enclosed by $ghkm$), which is approximately equal to the price change times the new quantity demanded.

---

2. In comparing pre- and post-liberalization consumer surplus, it is necessary to use the final demand curves in both the import and domestic markets (that is, $D'_m D'_m$ and $D'_d D'_d$ rather than $D_m D_m$ and $D_d D_d$). Otherwise the consumer surplus would appear to decrease by the area between the original and final demand curves and above the original prices—a nonsense result that could imply consumers had been hurt by lower prices. In technical terms, the use of the ex post demand curves to evaluate the welfare effects of the price changes amounts to an "index number problem," in which value changes must be measured using either base or terminal period quantity weights. The procedure here applies quantity weights based on the terminal demand curves (for example, M'_1 rather than M_1), and may be thought of as analogous to a Paasche (terminal quantity weight) price index. The direction of bias in this approach is to understate welfare gains to consumers, because the corresponding (Laspeyres) base-period weighting approach would apply the ex ante demand curves and would generate larger changes in consumer surplus.

In sum, the consumer welfare gain (W_c) from import liberalization is:

(1) $W_c = A + B + C;$

where

(2) $A = [P_{M0} - P_{M1}]M_0;$

(3) $B = 0.5[M_1 - M_0][P_{M0} - P_{M1}];$ and

(4) $C \cong [P_{D0} - P_{D1}]Q_1;$

(where $\cong$ refers to approximate equality).

A simple supply-demand consistency model relating the import and domestic markets may be used to estimate these welfare effects. First, in the import market, the quantity of the import demanded depends on the price of the import itself as well as the price of the domestic substitute. With prices and quantities defined such that if in the base period one unit of constant quality of the imported good has a price of unity, and one unit of constant quality of the domestic good also has a price of unity, then the following system applies.

(5) $M = M_0 P_M^a P_D^b,$

where M is import volume, M_0 is import volume in the base year, P_M is the import price, and P_D is the price of the domestic good. The exponent a is the price elasticity of import demand with respect to the import price, and b is the cross-elasticity of import demand with respect to the price of the domestic good. (Note that in functions of this type—"log-linear"—the exponent of an independent variable is also the elasticity of the dependent variable with respect to that independent variable.) For imports, supply is assumed to be infinitely elastic, so that the demand equation alone is sufficient to determine the equilibrium level.

In the domestic goods market, on the side of demand:

(6) $Q_D = Q_0 P_D^c P_M^d,$

where Q_D is the quantity of the domestic good demanded, Q_0 is the equilibrium quantity of the domestic good in the base period, c is the price elasticity of domestic good demand with respect to the price of the good itself, and d is the cross elasticity of demand for the domestic good with respect to the price of the import.

On the side of domestic supply,

(7) $Q_S = Q_0 P_D^e,$

where e is the elasticity of supply.

Because domestic supply and demand must be equal, equations (6) and (7) may be set equal to each other. The domestic price may then be solved for in the resulting equation, as:

(8) $P_D = P_M^{[d/(e-c)]}$

The final exponent, $[d/(e-c)]$, is of economic significance in that it tells the elasticity of the domestic price with respect to the import price. If the "coefficient of price response" is defined as the ratio of the percentage change in the domestic price to the given percentage change in the import price, this coefficient will equal this exponent (for small changes).

Equations (1) through (8) may be used to evaluate the welfare effects of import liberalization (and, correspondingly, the costs of existing protection). The initial prices P_{M0} and P_{D0} both equal unity. The post-liberalization import price equals:

(9) $P_{M1} = [1/(1 + T)] P_{M0}$,

where T is the total tariff-equivalent of tariff and quota protection. Equation (8) is then applied to obtain the corresponding value of P_{D1}. Equation (7) is then applied to obtain the new quantity of domestic output.

At this point estimates for the following variables in equations (1) through (4) are available: P_{M0}, P_{M1}, M_0, P_{D0}, P_{D1}, and Q_1. In addition, it is necessary to estimate M_0' and M_1'. These variables represent the import quantities consumed at the original and final import prices with the domestic good's price changed to its new, lower level, or:

(10) $M_0' = M_0 P_{M0}^a P_{D1}^b$

and

(11) $M_1' = M_0 P_{M1}^a P_{D1}^b$

With these values, the estimates are complete for calculating consumer cost of protection, W_c, using equations (1) through (4).

There are some offsetting losses that must be counted against the consumer gains to reach net welfare changes at the national level. Part of the consumers' savings on purchases of imports are transfers away from the government as it loses tariff revenue. Moreover, in the domestic-good market, the consumer gain C is merely a transfer away from what otherwise would be producer surplus (revenue to producers in excess of their cost as reflected by the supply curve). On the other hand, there is an additional benefit from the production side in the form of released real resources which previously had been inefficiently employed. Thus, the previous amount of output beyond Q_1 was being produced with cost shown by the segment ki of the supply curve; but this cost exceeded the free-trade value of output by area ijk (D), considering that at free trade the output price is only P_{D1}.

The gain in production efficiency through reallocation of resources, area D, may be estimated as follows:

(12) $D = 0.5[P_{D0} - P_{D1}][Q_0 - Q_1]$.

The government tariff revenue (G) that is lost equals:

(13) $\quad G = tP_{MOf}\, M_0'$

where as before the initial import quantity is evaluated at the adjusted import demand curve after feedback from the domestic market, M_0', and where the relevant price is the original f.o.b. (free on board) import price, P_{MOf}. That is, ad valorem tariffs are applied to f.o.b. import values, equal to the c.i.f. price less insurance and freight charges. The f.o.b. price may be expressed as $P_{MOf} = P_{MO}/[(1 + i)(1 + t)]$ where i is the ratio of c.i.f. to f.o.b. cost and t is the tariff rate. (Note that P_{MOf} exceeds the free trade world price by the amount of the quota rent obtained by foreign producers under protection.) Equation (13) becomes:

(14) $\quad G = tP_{MO}M_0'/[(1 + i)(1 + t)]$.

In terms of figure B.1, the gross consumer gains from lower prices on the original volume of imports, area A, may be divided into two components. The first, A_1, equals the tariff rate times the f.o.b. value of initial imports (adjusted for the shift in the import demand curve), or value G (equation [14]). The second, A_2, equals the remainder of the total protection tariff-equivalent T, multiplied by this original import value. This second component is the quota rent currently obtained by foreign producers, whose supply price is higher than the world price under free trade because they are able to capture the scarcity rent of import quotas. If the market structures of importing and retailing were monopolistic or oligopolistic, in contrast, US firms would be able to capture some or all of this rent. However, these industries are not concentrated and appear highly competitive, so that the bulk of the quota rent probably accrues to foreign suppliers.

Total net welfare gains to the economy (W^*) equal consumer gains less the transfer from producer surplus on the domestic good, plus efficiency gains from resource reallocation, less government tariff revenue loss. Thus:

(15) $\quad W^* = [A + B + C] - C + D - G = A + B + D - G$.

It should be noted, however, that this net welfare effect is the static gain, and makes no allowance for any transitional costs of unemployed resources. The welfare cost estimate also is from the US standpoint; it does not incorporate efficiency losses at the global level associated with the excessive allocation of resources to production in those countries with relatively high-cost production caused by restrictions imposed on lower cost suppliers. Nor does the welfare cost include any estimate of the loss of consumer surplus associated with the reduced product options in consumption as the upgrading process forced by protection limits the availability of lower quality, lower priced imports (which tend to be especially important for low-income consumers).

The model applies empirically based values for the import elasticity *(a)*, as discussed in appendix A (with the estimate for apparel an import-weighted average of the individual elasticities for imports from developing and industrial countries). In addition, the model requires the following elasticities: the cross-elasticity of import demand with respect to the domestic good's price *(b)*; the direct price elasticity of demand for the domestic good with respect to its own price *(c)*; the cross-elasticity of demand for the domestic good with respect to the price of the import *(d)*; and the elasticity of domestic output supply *(e)*.

Following Hufbauer, Berliner, and Elliott, the analysis here assumes a supply elasticity of unity. It is sometimes argued that protection does not raise prices of domestic goods because the domestic supply curve is horizontal or infinitely elastic, rather than upward-sloping with a finite elasticity. Indeed, the supply elasticity assumption has been singled out in the debate among analysts of protection as a reason why alternative estimates prepared by the two sides in the policy debate tend to differ.[3]

The principal reason why this study rejects an infinite elasticity for domestic supply is that it is not compatible with the observed persistence of production in the face of declining real prices. A horizontal supply curve means not only that the domestic price does not increase as domestic volume rises in response to new protection, but also that domestic output falls immediately to zero when there is an infinitesimal reduction in the product price in the marketplace. The declining trends in real prices discussed in chapter 2, and the downward pressure of imports on domestic prices as acknowledged by all sides of the policy debate, mean that if in fact domestic supply of textiles and apparel had been infinitely elastic, the production levels in these sectors would have virtually disappeared in recent years. Instead, production has held up relatively well. A supply elasticity of unity as adopted by Hufbauer, Berliner, and Elliot is still a relatively high parameter value, and seems unlikely to bias, either upward or downward, the estimated costs of protection.

Empirical estimates of the cross elasticities of demand and of the direct elasticity for the domestically produced good as a subcategory of total demand are rare. There are relationships among them that should provide a benchmark for reasonable values, however. On the basis of consumption theory, Rousslang and Suomela provide two alternative approaches to estimate the cross elasticity of import demand with respect to the domestic price:[4]

(16) $\quad b = [e_{DT} - c][V_{q0}/V_{m0}]$,

---

3. Burt Solomon, "Our Facts, Their Facts," *National Journal*, no. 23 (6 June 1987), pp. 1457–61.
4. Rousslang and Suomela, "Calculating the Consumer and Net Welfare Costs," pp. 86–88.

where e_{DT} is the price elasticity of total demand (imported plus domestic goods) and V_{q0}, V_{m0} are the base period values of domestic and imported goods respectively; and

(17) $\quad b = -S + c,$

where S is the elasticity of substitution in demand between the domestic and the imported good; that is, the percentage change in the ratio of import quantity to domestic good quantity for a 1 percent change in the ratio of the import price to the domestic good price.

Equations (16) and (17) must be equal (both equal b) and may be written as equal to each other; and, rearranging and solving for c:

(18) $\quad c = [S + e_{DT}(V_{q0}/V_{m0})]/[1 + (V_{q0}/V_{m0})].$

The elasticity of substitution, S, is estimated as -2.5 on the basis of various past statistical estimates.[5] Those estimates refer to substitution between alternative foreign supplying countries in the composition of imports. The additional assumption made here is that the elasticity of substitution between the domestic good and the imported good is equal to that between alternative foreign sources of the import. (For example, men's suits from the United States and Hong Kong are assumed to be as equally close substitutes as men's suits from Hong Kong and Italy.)

The elasticity of total demand with respect to the overall price of both imports and domestic goods, e_{DT}, is more commonly available from econometric estimates, and values for textiles and apparel are discussed in appendix A. The right hand side elements of equation (18) are thus known, and the direct price elasticity of demand for the domestic good, c, may be estimated.

With the estimate for c in hand, b may be estimated from either equation (16) or (17).

As noted above, the coefficient of price response, Z_p, is equal to the following expression involving the elasticities:

(19) $\quad Z_p = d/[e - c].$

Accordingly, if a particular value is assumed for the coefficient of price response, the cross elasticity of domestic demand with respect to the import price, d, may be estimated from (19) given the unitary elasticity assumed for supply e and the estimate in equation (18) for c:

(19') $\quad d = Z_p[e - c].$

---

5. See William R. Cline, Noboru Kawanabe, T. Kronsjo, and Thomas Williams, *Trade Negotiations in the Tokyo Round: A Quantitative Analysis* (Washington: Brookings Institution, 1978), pp. 60–62.

Some general principles may guide the value chosen for the price-response coefficient, Z_p. First, the greater "product differentiation," the further below unity Z_p should be. If the imported and domestic goods were perfect substitutes, coefficient Z_p would equal unity (their prices would always be identical and, by definition, move together). Second, the smaller the magnitude of imports relative to the domestic good in the total market, the lower one would expect the domestic price response coefficient to be. In the limiting case, if imports are negligible in size, one would expect a de minimis response of the domestic price even if the import price change were large.

The consideration of product differentiation suggests that for apparel the coefficient of domestic price response be significantly below unity. At the same time, in apparel the market share of imports is substantial (approximately 30 percent), suggesting a sizable value for Z_p. The central assumption here is that this coefficient equals 0.5 for apparel.[6]

For textiles, products such as yarn and fabrics would tend to have higher homogeneity between imports and domestic goods than in apparel, although for household textiles such as draperies and carpets product differentiation is probably as great as in apparel. The dominant factor for textiles, however, is the small market share for imports, approximately 10 percent; this consideration suggests that the textile domestic price response coefficient should be smaller than that for apparel. Indeed, as discussed below, if the

---

6. Hufbauer, Berliner, and Elliott assume instead that the coefficient equals 0.8. Note that their direct estimate of the parameter, from their underlying elasticities, is an unacceptably high value (1.9, implying domestic prices move by twice the percentage change in the import price), so they impose 0.8 as a ceiling. (Compare their equation (3) for this coefficient—the same as equation (19) here—with their actual estimate). However, while the assumption might suggest that the coefficient of 0.5 used here is too low, an alternative approach indicates that if anything it is too high. The Rousslang-Suomela study shows that, analogously to estimates in equations (16) and (17) for the cross-elasticity of import demand with respect to the domestic price (b), consumption theory also provides relationships for estimating the cross-elasticity of demand for the domestic good with respect to the import price:
(a) $d = [e_{DT} - a][V_{mo}/V_{qo}]$ and
(b) $d = (-S + a)$.
Equations (a) and (b) may simply be averaged to estimate d directly, while as before equation (18) provides the value of c. When the resulting values of these two parameters are applied to equation (19), the estimated value for the coefficient of domestic price response, Z_p, is 0.20 for apparel. This direct estimate would appear to understate the actual responsiveness of the domestic price, and if applied in the model would probably bias downward the estimates of welfare cost and domestic output reduction. The assumed value of Z_p used as the central case here has the advantage of being virtually half-way between the HBE value and the magnitude that may be estimated directly using the Rousslang-Suomela relationships. Hufbauer, Berliner, and Elliott, *Trade Protection*, pp. 34, 146–48; and Rousslang and Suomela, "Calculating the Consumer and Net Welfare Costs," pp. 86–88.

price response coefficient for domestic textiles is greater than approximately 0.13, the implausible result occurs that the reduction in quantity of the domestic good in response to liberalization exceeds the increase in the quantity of the imported good.

Actual trends in import and domestic-good prices can provide a hint of the appropriateness of the assumption for the domestic price response coefficient, but only a hint in the absence of a formal econometric model. The price-response relationship of equation (8) refers to the induced change in the domestic price when domestic demand shifts along an unchanged domestic supply curve in response to a shift in the supply price of imports. Actual price movements observed in practice may contain numerous other effects. Thus, if the domestic supply curve is shifting backward because of higher labor or input costs, the domestic price will be rising even in the absence of an import price increase.

Given this caveat, it is informative to consider price movements in recent years.[7] From 1980 until 1983, apparel import prices as measured by unit values rose by a total of 7.1 percent, while domestic consumer prices ("apparel excluding footwear") rose by 7.7 percent. In this period the relationship suggested a higher value for Z_p than 0.5, although the extraneous influence of a domestic supply shift (as just discussed) may have dominated. From 1983 to 1985, however, the price increases were consistent with the price response coefficient used here: a 9.4 percent increase for the import price, compared with an increase of 4.1 percent for the domestic consumer price. (Refinements would need to take account of import upgrading, on the one hand, and the fact that imports constitute a significant part of the total domestic consumer price being observed, on the other.)

For textiles, price trends diverged sharply in 1980–83, when import unit values declined by 9.2 percent (as industrial country suppliers depreciated relative to the dollar) but domestic producer prices ("selected textile mill products") rose by 11.2 percent. In the period 1983–85 the respective changes were +6.3 percent and +2.8 percent. The opposing trends in the earlier period provide support to the view that the domestic price response coefficient should be considerably lower for textiles than for apparel.

Table B.1 lists the elasticities used in the basic model of consumer and welfare effects of liberalization. For apparel, the unknown elasticities b, c, and d are calculated (as set forth above) under the assumption that the elasticity of domestic price with respect to the import price, $d/(e-c)$, is equal to 0.50 (also the value for the coefficient of domestic price response, Z_p, for small changes; the actual ex post Z_p is slightly larger). As applied to the

---

7. Import unit values are from the series discussed in chapter 7. Domestic prices are from the Bureau of Labor Statistics as reported in American Textile Manufacturers Institute, Inc., *Textile Hi-lights* (March 1985), pp. 18–19, and (October 1986), p.6.

Table B.1 Elasticity estimates

		Textiles	Apparel
a	Import elasticity of demand	-1.3	-1.6
b	Cross-elasticity of import demand with respect to price of domestic good	1.90	1.10
c	Direct price elasticity of demand for domestic good	-0.60	-1.40
d	Cross-elasticity of demand for domestic good with respect to import price	0.205	1.18
e	Elasticity of domestic supply	1.0	1.0
e_{DT}	Price elasticity of total demand domestic and imported goods	-0.4	-0.9
Z_p	Coefficient of price response	0.128[a]	0.50[b]
Z_q	Coefficient of quantity response	-1.00	-0.85

Source: see text.
a. Ex ante for small changes. Ex post: 0.14.
b. Ex ante for small changes. Ex post: 0.55.

base year data for apparel and with complete liberalization of protection, the resulting coefficient of domestic quantity response is -0.85. That is, the reduction in the quantity of the domestic good equals 0.85 times the increase in the quantity of the imported good.

For textiles this method generates a quantity response coefficient that exceeds unity unless the coefficient of domestic price response is approximately 0.13 or lower. The essential reason is that imports are such a small fraction of total supply that if the domestic price falls by a sizable fraction of the import price decline, the resulting reduction in domestic output swamps the physical increase in the imported good even though that increase is large in proportionate terms. Thus, for textiles the value for unknown elasticities b and c are found as before. However, the value for cross elasticity d is chosen by iterative approximation so that the coefficient of quantity response is no greater than the maximum acceptable value, unity (in absolute value). That is, an increase of a given physical quantity of imports should cause no more than an identical decrease in the quantity of the domestic good. The resulting value of d is 0.205, which yields a coefficient of price response of 0.128—in keeping with the above analysis suggesting that this coefficient should be lower for textiles than for apparel (0.5).

It should be stressed that the method used here applies values at the wholesale rather than retail consumer level. Because retailing margins are typically approximately 100 percent above cost, there is some possibility that the estimates substantially underestimate consumer costs of protection. The logic for use of the wholesale value is that in a competitive retailing industry, any change in protection costs should leave the retail margin unchanged in absolute terms and correspondingly altered in percentage terms. Thus, higher protection will be passed on by retailers as a rise in the final price by the same absolute amount as the increase in protection cost at the border, without applying the normal retailing percentage markup to this protection cost. If instead retailers sought to pass along to consumers not only the higher absolute protection cost but in addition their normal marketing percentage margin as applied to this added cost, their profits would rise, attracting new entrants into the industry that would bid down this extra layer of retailing profit.

Nonetheless, estimation at the wholesale level may understate consumer costs of protection. The reason is that the sparse evidence available on retail margins suggests that they are the same on protected imports as on domestic goods (and critics of the industry charge that the markups are higher on imports than on domestic goods, although with little empirical support).[8] Yet if retailers did not apply their normal percentage markups to the protection cost component of imports, their overall percentage margin would be expected to be much lower on protected imports than on domestic goods. Thus, in the case of apparel with a tariff-equivalent of total protection in the range of 50 percent, an imported good costing the retailer 100 would have protection cost of 33 and imported product cost of 67 at the world price. If the retailer applied a normal 100 percent markup only to the world price but not to the protection cost component, the retail consumer price would be 167 (67 world price, plus 67 retail markup, plus 33 protection cost). The overall retail margin would be only 67 percent above product cost including protection, far below the 100 percent normal margin on domestic goods.[9]

In sum, the approach here is highly conservative in its estimation of consumer costs of protection, because it assumes that protection raises the

---

8. US House of Representatives, Committee on Ways and Means, *Library of Congress Study on Imports and Consumer Prices* (Washington: US Government Printing Office, 1977).

9. This is the margin found by the International Trade Commission in its detailed study of the footwear industry pursuant to injury investigation. US International Trade Commission, *Footwear: Report to the President on Investigation No. TA-201-7* (Washington: ITC, February 1976), p. A-117. Retail margins for apparel are similar to those for footwear.

price by the same absolute amount at the retail level as it does at the wholesale level, and that retailers reduce their percentage markups as higher protection raises their purchasing costs. But because in fact retail percentage margins appear to be the same on protected imports as on domestic goods, in reality retailers may apply some or all of their normal percentage markup to the protection cost component of the import as well. If so, then consumer costs of protection are as much as twice as high as estimated here.

Chapter 8 applies the methodology set forth here to estimate the consumer and net welfare costs of US protection in textiles and apparel, and examines corresponding effects on production and employment.

Appendix C   Prospective Costs of New Protection

Chapter 9 reviews a legislative proposal of early 1987 that called for global quotas limiting growth of imports to 1 percent annually. This appendix sets forth the reformulation of the cost of protection model presented in appendix B that is used for the cost projections reported in chapter 9.

Figure C.1 shows the impact of new protection on consumer costs. In the figure, initial imports are at M_0, the expected level at a future year under current protection. The imposition of the 1 percent growth limit cuts back permissible imports from M_0 to M_1'. This effect may be captured by a corresponding rise in the price of imports from P_{M0} to P_{M1}, which at the initial price of the domestic substitute causes the quantity demanded to contract to imports of M_1 but after adjustment to the induced price rise for

Figure C.1   Supply and demand for domestic and imported products

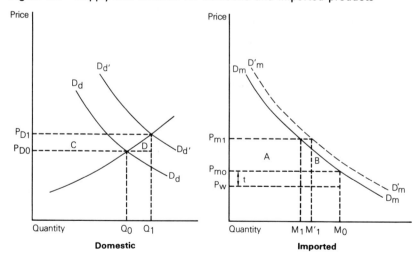

the domestic good (and the outward shift of the import demand curve from $D_m D_m$ to D'_m) leaves the quantity of imports demanded at M'_1, the quota-constrained level. On imports, consumer costs of the new protection equal the loss of consumer surplus. This loss (conservatively estimated at the original import demand curve) equals areas A (the change in import price multiplied by the newly lower import volume before outward adjustment from feedback from a higher domestic price, M_1) plus area B (one-half of the change in price as applied to the magnitude by which imports decline along the original demand curve, $M_0 - M_1$). On domestic goods, the consumer loss equals the rise in domestic price as applied (conservatively) to the original, lower quantity of domestic goods, or area C. To obtain national welfare effects, it is necessary to add the loss of government tariff revenue caused by the shrinkage of imports (tariff rate t as multiplied by the quantity of reduced imports, $M_0 - M'_1$), as well as the efficiency loss from additional allocation of resources with cost greater than the market value of output at the original price (area D).

The model developed in appendix B is used to calculate these effects. First, however, it is necessary to determine the price increase for imports that is required to generate the cutback of import volume corresponding to the newly constrained quota level.

From appendix B, we have:

(1) $\quad M = M_0 P_M^a P_D^b$,

(where all variables are as described in appendix B). If it is required that imports after new protection be restricted to the ratio "k" of the level they would otherwise reach, that is,

(2) $\quad k = M'_1/M_0$,

then considering that the initial prices are all defined as unity, and that the term M_0 divides out in the ratio of equation (2), we have:

(3) $\quad k = P_{M1}^a P_{D1}^b$,

where the price subscript "1" denotes the postprotection level.

From appendix B, $P_D = P_M^{(d/(e-c))}$. Thus, equation (3) may be written as:

(4) $\quad k = P_{M1}^{\{a + (bd/(e-c))\}}$

Solving for the new import price required to suppress imports to the target quota level,

(5) $\quad P_{M1} = EXP[\ln k /(a + \frac{bd}{e-c})]$,

where EXP is the exponential function (natural logarithm base to the power within the brackets).

The lower import level before feedback from higher domestic price, M_1, is:

(6) $M_1 = M_0 P_{M1}^a P_{D0}^b.$

The consumer loss in area A is:

(7) $A = [P_{M1} - P_{M0}]M_1.$

The loss in area B is:

(8) $B = 0.5[P_{M1} - P_{M0}][M_0 - M_1].$

Domestic output responds to the higher domestic price according to the supply curve,

(9) $Q_1 = Q_0 P_{D1}^e$

The consumer loss on higher domestic price is:

(10) $C = [P_{D1} - P_{D0}]Q_0.$

The efficiency loss from inefficient allocation of resources to more domestic output is:

(11) $D = 0.5[P_{D1} - P_{D0}][Q_1 - Q_0].$

Government tariff revenue loss is:

(12) $G = t[M_0 - M_1'].$

Consumer cost of the new protection is then:

(13) $W_c = A + B + C,$

while welfare cost to the economy is:

(14) $W^* = A + B + D + G,$

and the number of domestic jobs created in the textile or apparel sector is:

(15) $N = N_0([Q_1/Q_0] - 1),$

where N_0 is the level of employment in the base case without extra protection.

Note that the 1987 bill called for protection using quotas rather than export restraints. On this basis, it might be appropriate to omit areas A and B from computation of the net welfare costs (equation 13), on grounds that the quota rents would accrue to domestic distributors (if quotas were granted on a basis of historical marketing shares) or the government (if auctioned) rather than foreigners, and would thus be domestic transfers rather than net costs to the nation. However, the bill also provided that foreigners would be compensated for the new quotas through reduced tariffs, indicating that much of this transfer from consumers to government or distributors would be offset by a transfer from government to foreign suppliers.

Chapter 9 reports the results of applying this model of consumer costs to the proposed limitation of global quota growth to 1 percent annually. For each future year, the baseline values of imports (M_0) and output (Q_0) are taken from the projections of chapter 10 under unchanged policy, while the forced level of imports (M_1') is obtained by permitting only 1 percent annual growth from the actual 1986 base.

Appendix D   Texts of Proposals for Textile and Apparel Trade Liberalization Submitted by the United States, Japan, and the European Community

1. Communication from the United States
February 5, 1990

The following communication has been submitted by the delegation of the United States for circulation to the members of the Negotiating Group on Textiles and Clothing.

Introduction

In a statement circulated to this negotiating group last December (MTN/ NG4/W/33), the United States delegation expressed views on possible modalities which would permit the eventual integration of the textile and clothing sector into the GATT on the basis of strengthened rules and disciplines. We indicated in that statement that we would be making more detailed proposals on alternative modalities at this time, and that we would be prepared to elaborate on the concepts suggested in W/33 in greater detail.

The United States delegation reaffirmed in December and will do so again that our objectives in these negotiations are to help bring about through negotiation the eventual integration of textiles and clothing into GATT on the basis of strengthened GATT rules and disciplines and to ensuring that this process contributes to the further liberalization of trade.

We would also like to reaffirm that the process requires procedures that ensure that all relevant trade measures affecting trade in textiles and clothing are integrated and that GATT rules and disciplines have been sufficiently strengthened to make integration viable.

Duration of Integration Process

As we stated in December, the successful integration of this sector into GATT will require a transition arrangement of sufficient duration to ensure an orderly and equitable adjustment in trade terms as well as in terms of the domestic production processes of each participant. We believe a transition mechanism, similar to those outlined below, of at least ten years duration would be appropriate to accomplish these objectives. In other words, assuming sufficiently strengthened GATT rules and disciplines exist, we propose that the transition mechanism start on January 1, 1992, and that the special safeguard arrangement for the textile and clothing sector end on December 31, 2001.

Criteria for the Integration Process

As we stated in December, it is important that any transition mechanism be evaluated by this group according to certain criteria. For the United States, it is important that the transition mechanism be simple, equitable, transparent, predictable and certain; that the mechanism allow trade patterns to be driven by market forces as early as possible and to the maximum extent possible, and that it allow an adjustment to GATT rules concomitant with the operation of market forces.

As we indicated in December, we believe that certain modalities for a transition mechanism offer certain concrete advantages to a mechanism based on the Multifiber Arrangement when evaluated according to these criteria. We believe a multilaterally agreed global, or non-selective, quota system or a tariff rate quota system, as elaborated below, offer substantial advantages for the transition to GATT; most significantly, the gradual opening of markets to competitive forces, transparency, equity and certainty. These alternatives also offer the progressive movement from selectivity to most-favored-nation (MFN) treatment for supplying countries.

We reiterate that the Swiss suggestion of the possibility that different participants could adopt different techniques or modalities is something which should be carefully studied.

Global-Type Quota System

The global, or non-selective, quota system that we envision is outlined by illustration in the attached graphics. We foresee a comprehensive quantitative limit, by product category, which would be divided among country allocations or guarantees (covering trade from those countries with whom we have bilateral agreements), and a non-selective "global basket" that would expand to provide growth. In the first year, the global basket would be increased by a certain uplift (or growth) factor, and would be open for competition from all parties, including those with country allocations. In addition, countries would be able to contribute their guarantees to the basket or to other countries.

Each year, over a ten-year timeframe, the country allocations would shrink by one-tenth of the original amount, and the global basket would increase by a growth factor and by adding to it the ten percent taken from each of the country allocations. The growth factor during the ten year transition would be determined through multilateral negotiation, but would vary depending on the import sensitivity of the product involved and would increase over time.

As illustrated, the global basket would gradually take over the country shares of the quota, and in the final year of the transition, the overall quota would be in place only in the form of the global basket. The transition system would end, under this scenario, at the end of the tenth year of the transition.

The product category coverage of a global-type quota system would be determined by individual participants; however, we intend that product classification under a transition mechanism be a contribution to liberalization of trade. For the United States, this would mean consolidating our existing product categories so as to allow more flexibility for exporters and possibly the removal of certain products from coverage during the transition.

Tariff Rate Quota System

As suggested in W/33, tariff rate quotas offer an additional modality for integration of this sector into the GATT. We envision a tariff rate quota system with a structure and duration similar to the global or non-selective quota system outlined above. The attached graphic illustrations therefore also show the structure of a tariff rate quota system, which would feature a two-tier tariff system with country allocations, and a global basket for the lower tier (with lower tariffs), shifting over time toward the global basket. Imports within the quantitative limits of the lower tier would enter at applicable duty rates. However, additional imports above and beyond these quantitative limits would be permitted at substantially higher penalty tariff rates.

We would offer one important caveat to the proposal for a tariff rate quota system, and that is the establishment of a special mechanism to ensure that exports from non-market economies are subject to equivalent tariff disciplines as those from market economies. We do not yet have definitive views on the form of this special mechanism, but believe it an essential part of any tariff-based transition modality.

Example 1A: Global Quotas
Category: Dresses
(Cotton and Man-made Fiber)

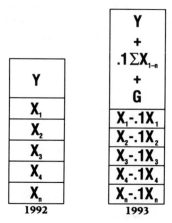

$$Y$$
$$+$$
$$.1\Sigma X_{1-n}$$
$$+$$
$$G$$

Y	Y + $.1\Sigma X_{1-n}$ + G
X_1	$X_1-.1X_1$
X_2	$X_2-.1X_2$
X_3	$X_3-.1X_3$
X_4	$X_4-.1X_4$
X_n	$X_n-.1X_n$
1992	**1993**

X=Country Allocation (Agreement Countries);
Y=Global Basket (Non-Agreement Countries Plus Growth in First Year);
G=Growth Factor

Example 1B: Global Quotas
Category: Dresses
(Cotton and Man-made Fiber)

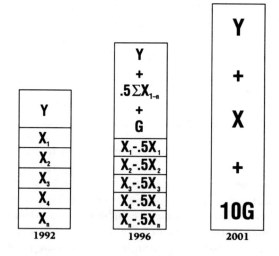

Y	Y + $.5\Sigma X_{1-n}$ + G	Y + X + $10G$
X_1	$X_1-.5X_1$	
X_2	$X_2-.5X_2$	
X_3	$X_3-.5X_3$	
X_4	$X_4-.5X_4$	
X_n	$X_n-.5X_n$	
1992	**1996**	**2001**

X=Country Allocation (Agreement Countries);
Y=Global Basket (Non-Agreement Countries Plus Growth in First Year);
G=Growth Factor

Figure D.1

QUOTA COVERAGE AND GROWTH RATES

PRODUCT SENSITIVITY	1992– 1994	1995– 1997	1998– 1999	2000– 2001
VERY HIGH	X	X+1	X+2	X+3
HIGH	X+1	X+2	X+3	X+4
MODERATE	X+2	X+3	X+4	X+5
NO COVERAGE				

X=Basic Growth Rate

Figure D.2

MFA-Based Transition System

As discussed above, we have carefully examined the range of proposals for
a MFA–based transition arrangement. We feel that we should take full
advantage of this existing multilateral forum by thoroughly considering
new and improved trading regimes for the transition back to GATT.

For this reason, we believe that alternatives to a MFA–type system offer
many advantages and must be seriously explored. Nonetheless, we are of
course prepared to continue work in this group on a system extrapolated
from the MFA, as suggested by many participants.

2. Communication from the United States
March 5, 1990

The U.S. submitted a proposal (MTN/GNG/NG4/W/37) at the February 1990 meeting of the negotiating group which offered options for the group to consider in order to attain the goal of eventual integration of the textile and clothing sector of trade into strengthened GATT rules. The U.S. proposal asked that participants examine two alternatives to a transition mechanism based on the existing structure of the Multifiber Arrangement (MFA), i.e., a global-type quota system and a tariff rate quota system, and discussed initial U.S. views on these mechanisms.

We have received a number of questions about one of our three options which we are still considering, the global-type system, and we would like to focus on this and use the occasion of the March 5–7 meeting of the negotiating group to answer some of those questions. To this end, the U.S. delegation would like to provide a further elaboration of its views on how a global quota-type system would operate with respect to certain key elements.

1. Method for Construction of Global-Type Quotas

Average of last three years of trade (1987–1989) plus uplift (to be negotiated) for the overall quantitative limit. Country allocations to be determined by the average of the last three years of imports, with no supplier to account for more than 15 percent of the total.

2. Product Coverage and Categorization

Existing product categories would be consolidated, perhaps by merging certain fiber classifications, in order to provide more flexibility for exporters. Certain outward processing trade (in the U.S. system, 807-A imports) could be exempt from global quota system. Possible formulae for reducing overall product coverage during the transition mechanism should be discussed in the negotiations.

3. Country Coverage

Comprehensive country coverage, the only exceptions to be partners in customs unions or in free trade arrangements.

4. Special Preferences

Special preferences for the least developed would be extended by allowing their country allocations to remain stable over the transition mechanism, i.e., the country allocations would not shrink as outlined in W/37.

5. Method of Allocation

Export shipments that are credited against country guarantees would be allocated by the exporting countries just as MFA quotas are presently administered. The global basket would be allocated by importing countries.

Related Issues: MFA Restraints Outside the MFA/Strengthened GATT Rules and Disciplines/Liberalization of Trade.

The U.S. delegation reiterates that successful integration of this sector into GATT will require procedures that: (1) ensure that all relevant trade measures affecting trade in textiles and clothing are integrated; (2) ensure that GATT rules and disciplines have been sufficiently strengthened to make integration viable (e.g., effective rules for dealing with trade from non-market economies and balance of payments derogations); and (3) provide for a process that will ensure an orderly transition from measures being applied following the end of the Uruguay Round to those which will be applicable when this sector is fully integrated into the GATT. In this respect, we remind participants of our specific proposals for addressing both non–MFA restraints and strengthened GATT rules and disciplines and invite reactions.

3. Communication from Japan

I. General Introduction

1. The textiles and clothing sector plays an extremely important role in the economic and social development of a large number of countries, *inter alia*, developing countries. The success of the negotiations in this sector is a key factor governing the outcome of the Uruguay Round, and it is essential that further liberalization of trade in this sector is achieved. Japan wishes to express its resolve to actively support the integration of this sector into GATT.

2. Japan considers it necessary to adopt a progressive and pragmatic approach to the issue of the integration of the textiles and clothing sector into GATT in order to attain the objective in a smooth integration process.

3. Japan, at the same time, considers it necessary that the process of integrating the textiles and clothing sector into GATT be accompanied by liberalization of this sector as a whole. To this end, it should be recognized that efforts by all participants to achieve liberalization on the basis of strengthened GATT rules and disciplines, which are being discussed in other negotiating groups, is also important.

II. Japan's Proposal

1. Scope of Integration

In order to expedite the negotiations and make substantial progress, this Negotiating Group should give priority to the discussions on the integration of MFA restrictions into GATT.

The decision of the Trade Negotiations Committee in April 1989 stipulates that the negotiations should *inter alia* cover the "phasing out of restrictions under the MFA and other restrictions on textiles and clothing not consistent with GATT rules and disciplines."

Since the issue of "restrictions not consistent with GATT rules and disciplines," is being handled by such negotiating groups as the Negotiating Group on Safeguards, it would be most appropriate that this Group, in the first place, limit itself to keeping a close watch on the progress of other negotiating groups.

2. Elimination of MFA Restrictions

The MFA should be terminated on July 31, 1991, at the expiration of the current Protocol of Extension.

The present MFA should not be extended, and all the restrictions based on the present MFA should, in principle, be eliminated by the end of July 1991. However, as regards bilateral agreements concluded under Article 4 of the present MFA, they may remain in force until the end of 1991, provided that both the importing and exporting countries concerned so agree.

3. Transitional Measures During the Integration Process

(1) *After the termination of the MFA, a transitional period should be established in order to facilitate a smooth integration of the textiles and clothing sector into GATT.*

A progressive and pragmatic approach should be employed in integrating the MFA into GATT. In view of the fact that the world textile trade has been in place for a long time under the regime of the MFA, it would be unrealistic to expect that the adverse effects of sharp increase in imports can effectively be coped with solely through the safeguard provisions of the General Agreement (hereafter "general safeguard provisions") during the transitional period.

(2) *Therefore, it is necessary to introduce transitional measures which are designed to deal with the specific problems of the textiles and clothing sector so as to facilitate a smooth integration of the MFA into GATT.*

Such transitional measures should be regarded as temporary arrangements to phase out the restrictive mechanism of the MFA so as to integrate it into general safeguard provisions.

Compared with MFA restrictions, such transitional measures should thus embody a higher level of objectivity, strict procedures, limited application, limited duration, equity, as well as an automatic mechanism for the phase out.

4. Time Span

The integration should be achieved as early as possible, by the end of 1999 at the latest.

III. The Transitional Measures During the Integration Process

Japan proposes the following as transitional measures during the integration process:

1. Summary

(1) For the purpose of ensuring an automatic and smooth phase out, objective criteria for invocation of the transitional measures will be made more stringent year-by-year, and the levels of restrictions will be liberalized year-by-year.

(2) When invoking the transitional measures, an importing country should request the exporting countries concerned for consultations. At the same time, the importing country should submit data to a multilateral surveillance body to be newly established (an organization similar to the TSB [Textiles Surveillance Body], for instance) for an appraisal of whether or not the imports in question satisfy the criteria to invoke such measures. The surveillance body should then examine the conformity of the measure in question to the criteria, based on the submitted data.

(3) In the event that an agreement is reached between the importing and exporting countries, restrictions will, in principle, be imposed by the exporting country. On the other hand, if no agreement is reached, the importing country may impose restrictions on exports from the exporting country.

(4) The transitional measures can be invoked from August 1, 1991 onward.

If any country proposes to invoke the transitional measures at an early stage after August 1, 1991, the surveillance body mentioned above shall be empowed to conduct examinations prior to August 1, 1991.

2. Five Principles Governing the Transitional Measures

The transitional measures should be governed by the following five principles:

(1) Objectivity and strict procedures.

(2) Limited application.

(3) Limited duration.

(4)　Automatic phase-out mechanism.

(5)　Equity.

(1)　Objectivity and strict procedures

The MFA stipulates that the determination of a situation of market disruption shall be based on the existence of "serious damage to domestic producers or an actual threat thereof." However, since the MFA only lists factors such as "market share," "profits," "export performance," with respect to factors determining "serious damage," actual application of MFA restrictions is left to the discretion of each participating country.

However, since transitional measures during the integration process should be applied only in a situation where emergency action is required, it is necessary to subject the invocation of the measures to objective criteria and strict procedures.

[Objectivity]
(a)　Of the factors causing market disruption, such as the market penetration of imports, the growth rate of total imports, the growth rate of imports from one particular country and its share in total imports, those which are capable of being quantitatively measured and agreed to by the participating countries should be established as universal and quantitative standards for invoking the transitional measures. Participating countries should also establish criteria in as objective a manner as possible for other factors which cannot readily be measured quantitatively. The transitional measures should not be invoked unless these quantitative and objective criteria are satisfied.

(b)　The above mentioned criteria should be drawn up during the UR [Uruguay Round] negotiations, and to this end, interested countries should submit data on recent production, imports of textiles and clothing etc. to the GATT Secretariat, which, in turn, should submit to the Negotiating Group proposed figures for such criteria.

[Strict Procedures]
An importing country proposing to take measures should submit the necessary data to the multilateral surveillance body mentioned above for an examination of their conformity with the criteria, while conducting consultation with the exporting country. Since the transitional measures warrant prompt action, the surveillance body should complete deliberation and notify its results to the countries concerned within a reasonable and specified period of time.

(2) Limited Application

Since the transitional measures are to be applied only in a situation where emergency action is needed, the scope of application of such measures needs to be limited as much as possible.

With a view to accelerating the social and economic developments of countries where the textiles and clothing industries play a key role in their exports, transitional measures should not be invoked against, for instance, LLDC's, new entrants and small suppliers.

The measures, when invoked, should be limited only to the necessary products, and accordingly, aggregate or group limits should not be introduced. Also, the measures should not be applied to products with no domestic production, or with under-utilized quotas.

(3) Limited Duration

The duration of the transitional measures should be limited and as short as possible.

(4) Automatic Phase-out Mechanism

The transitional measures should embody an automatic phase-out mechanism so as to ensure the integration of textiles and clothing sector into GATT.

(a) For this purpose, specific quantitative criteria, scheduled for each year during the integration process, and which will be made increasingly strict every year, should be established. For example, if the standard for market penetration of imports (or the growth rate of imports) are set at X_1% as the criteria for invoking the measures in 1991, it should be increased in the succeeding years as follows; X_1% + a% in 1992, and X_1% + a'% in 1993 ($a < a'$). In other words, the conditions under which the transitional measures may be invoked should be made increasingly strict by setting a higher threshold every year. The actual figures of X_1, a, and other relevant figures should be determined during the UR negotiations.

$$1991 \quad X_1$$
$$1992 \quad (X_1 + a)\%$$
$$1993 \quad (X_1 + a')\%$$

(b) Specific growth rates for the levels of restrictions and flexibility provisions are to be established for each year, and will become less restrictive every year. Those standards for growth rates and flexibility should be less restrictive than those stipulated under the present MFA.

The restraint levels for each year should be obtained by multiplying by the following growth rates the actual import performance of the previous year (the restraint level of the previous year if there is any quota), or the average import performance of the past several years, whichever is the higher:

the specific growth rate for each year

$$
\begin{array}{ll}
1991 & (100 + X_2)\% \\
1992 & (100 + X_2 + b)\% \\
1993 & (100 + X_2 + b')\%
\end{array}
$$

.
.
.

the specific rate of shift between quotas for each year

$$
\begin{array}{ll}
1991 & X_3 \\
1992 & (X_3 + c)\% \\
1993 & (X_3 + c')\%
\end{array}
$$

The actual figures of X_3, X_3, b, c, and other relevant figures should be determined during the UR negotiations.

The permissible levels of both carry-forward and carry-over should be increased every year in the same manner.

(5) Equity

Equity between exporting countries needs to be guaranteed. A country should not, in principle, be subject to restraints if there exists any other exporting country not under restriction through this transitional measure that has a larger market share, higher import growth rate, and lower import price in a particular importing country.

4. Communication from the European Community to the Negotiating Group on Textiles and Clothing

Introduction

1. The European Community's communication of 24 May 1988 outlined a number of key elements to help get the negotiations off to a smooth start, in accordance with the very clear indications in the Punta del Este mandate.

2. This new communication carries on from the previous one, and sets out an overall approach for establishing the broad lines of the future framework for international trade in textiles,[1] demonstrating thereby the European Community's willingness and determination to get the substantive negotiations off to a dynamic start.

3. Full compliance with all the elements of the Punta del Este declaration—and in particular with the parallelism between the gradual integration of textiles into GATT and the application of strengthened rules and disciplines within GATT—remains a vital condition for the success of this ambitious venture.

4. The Community is ready to grant special treatment to the least developed countries.

5. This communication looks at the *organization of the general framework* for the transition towards the integration of textiles into a strengthening GATT (see I below). It then examines *specific techniques and modalities* for integrating the sector into GATT (see II below). Lastly, it sets out our views on the *necessary strengthening of GATT rules and disciplines,* which is a vital basis for the integration process (see III below).

I. Organization of the general framework for integration into a strengthening GATT

1. The transition towards the integration of the textiles sector into a strengthened GATT must include both the progressive elimination of existing restrictions and the implementation of strengthened GATT rules and disciplines.

2. A process of integration of this type, covering the two components—the progressive elimination of restrictions and the application of strength-

---

1. Except where otherwise indicated, the term "textiles" includes both textiles and clothing.

ened rules and disciplines—needs to be organized within a general framework.

3. In order to ensure lasting results, the transition should be progressive, i.e., by successive steps towards the agreed final objective and should be *gradual*, i.e., consist of intermediate steps.

4. The *number, duration* and substantive *content* of these intermediary steps need to be determined during the negotiations.

5. As regards the *substantive content,* each step must include synchronized elements of the two components and must reflect the coordinated efforts of all the participants.

6. The *duration* of the transition will be determined by various political and economic considerations.

A number of preliminary points can already be made at this stage as regards dates for the beginning and the end of the integration process.

(a) It should first of all be stressed that, given the principle that the negotiations should be global, the integration process, referred to specifically in the Punta del Este mandate, cannot begin before the Uruguay Round has officially been concluded. In line with the Punta del Este Ministerial Declaration, the negotiations should be completed within four years, i.e., before the end of 1990.

The MFA, the future of which is so closely linked to our negotiations, will expire at the end of July 1991. It seems clear that international trade in textiles cannot become subject to all of the GATT general rules, immediately from 1 August 1991. Given the economic and political constraints, MFA IV will have to be followed, as from 1 August 1991, by arrangements whose precise content must be negotiated in the light of the situation prevailing at that time. It should also be borne in mind that Article 10(8) of the MFA lays down that the Textiles Committee "shall meet not later than one year before the expiry of this Arrangement in order to consider whether the Arrangement should be extended, modified or discontinued." This meeting must therefore be held before the end of July 1990, i.e., within one year from now.

Since the Uruguay Round negotiations are due to be concluded sufficiently in advance of the expiry of the current MFA, the beginning of the process of integrating the textile sector into GATT, which is the subject of our present negotiations, could therefore coincide with the entry into force of the post–MFA IV arrangements.

(b)   Deciding on a date for the *completion* of the integration process will be one of the most sensitive aspects of the negotiations due to the major importance of the textiles industry for the economies of many countries and to the impact which this date will have on businesses, and in particular on their investment activity. This problem can only be examined in detail once the Uruguay Round is drawing to a close and an overall view of the negotiations is possible.

7.   Movement through the successive steps of the transition process should take place subject to *multilateral verification* that commitments undertaken are being fulfilled.

8.   A specific body should be set up to *monitor the integration process*. It would need appropriate powers, including powers to verify that commitments undertaken have been respected. The role and composition of that body could draw on the precedent of the current Textiles Surveillance Body (TSB).

II. Integrating the textiles sector into the GATT framework

A. General considerations

1.   The integration process provided for in the Punta del Este Declaration must lead to a situation where eventually the *general* GATT rules apply to international trade in textile products. This entails the progressive elimination of trade restrictions incompatible with the GATT rules such as they will emerge from the Uruguay Round negotiations.

2.   The objective of the negotiations is the *integration into GATT* of the textiles sector. It is not limited therefore merely to restrictions under the MFA, but covers all other restrictions which are incompatible with GATT and which affect the patterns of trade in this sector. These other restrictions still have to be identified in detail and are not specifically dealt with in this communication.

The *Community has already made contributions* to a real lowering of trade barriers.

The customs tariffs it applies to textiles are low and a substantial proportion of its textiles' imports are covered by the GSP [Generalized System of Preferences].

In the 1986 negotiations on the renewal of the Multifibre Arrangement and the related bilateral agreements the Community proposed inter alia more favourable treatment for the least developed countries and special treatment for small exporters and newcomers. All the bilateral textile agreements negotiated by the Community with its partners in 1986 include provisions which are more favorable for exporting countries than those in previous agreements.

Moreover, the Community agreed that a number of agreements expiring in 1986 should not be renewed and should be replaced by an exchange of letters simply laying down a consultation mechanism. When renewing agreements with a number of countries, small or new exporters, the Community did not ask for existing quantitative restrictions to be continued.

From the beginning of the Uruguay Round, the Community has thus begun a progressive liberalization of its textile trade arrangements. This has resulted in major increases in imports into the Community from all textile-exporting developing countries. It might be difficult to pursue this process without a substantial strengthening of current GATT rules and disciplines.

4.   Appropriate modalities must be formulated to ensure the achievement of this component of the negotiating objective, i.e., the integration of the textiles sector into GATT. One can distinguish two sorts of modalities between which there is a clear political link:

(i)   modalities for the progressive elimination of restrictions (see B below); and

(ii)   modalities for a specific transitional safeguard mechanism (see C below), to be available only for the duration of the integration process.

B. Progressive elimination of restrictions

1.   As shown in the Canadian communication of 28 September 1988, there are *two basic techniques* for eliminating restrictions. The first consists in taking existing restrictions as a starting point and looking at ways of reducing and progressively eliminating them. The second consists in converting the restrictions into other forms of protection (e.g., tariffs) reducing in a transparent way the current state of restrictions, and then trying to reduce and progressively eliminate these newly created restrictions. The first of these techniques would permit the negotiation of a transitional regime which would be modelled on existing rules and mechanisms and which should allow for a progressive adjustment towards the final goal of the application of the general GATT rules.

2.   There have been several contributions from other participants in the negotiations regarding *possible* modalities for progressively eliminating MFA restrictions. They have set out a number of options, not all of which are

necessarily mutually exclusive, and which could be looked at together. The Community is willing to play a constructive role in any such examination.

3. In the context of the process of eliminating existing restrictions, the Community will be in a position to make a specific contribution as a result of the creation of the Single European Market without internal frontiers.

4. The measures finally decided for the progressive elimination of restrictions following the examination in paragraph 2 above should be *spread out over the various intermediate steps* of the integration process, taking into account particularly the situation of the industries concerned.

5. The *least developed countries* should be eligible for special measures compared with other textile-supplying countries.

C. A specific transitional safeguard mechanism

1. It is *vital* that a transitional safeguard mechanism be available in order to enable the progressive integration of the textiles sector into a strengthened GATT.

This mechanism is also needed to ensure the orderly development of trade, to avoid the disruption and to allow the restructuring of the industry to continue.

2. This safeguard mechanism should be developed in the light of the *experience gained in the application of Articles 3 and 4* of the current MFA. (This implies the examination of several possibilities some of which are not mutually exclusive.)

Should the market be disruptive by imports of a specific textile product from one or more countries, the mechanisms should allow for consultations to put an end to the disruption. Should agreement not be reached during these consultations, the importing country should be able, for a limited period, to restrict those textile imports causing the disruption of the market. Special provisions should be provided for situations requiring urgent action.

To avoid the disadvantages which would arise from too frequent an application of safeguard measures, it should also be possible to conclude bilateral agreements. Such agreements should not only remove the real danger of market disruption but also ensure the smooth growth and development of trade in textiles.

3. This transitional safeguard mechanism should in any case be more flexible than the present regime and should in particular take account of the differing economic and trade positions of the countries concerned.

4. The specific safeguard mechanism should be of strictly limited duration, not exceeding that of the transitional phase planned for the integration of textiles into GATT. This mechanism will in due course give way to the new general safeguard discipline to be agreed in the course of these negotiations (see III.C). The *possibility of relaxing* the transitional safeguard during the integration process should be examined.

5. As a general rule, the specific transitional safeguard mechanism *should not be applied to the least developed countries.*

6. Measures taken under the mechanism *should be monitored* by the surveillance body referred to at I(8) above.

III. Strengthening the GATT rules and disciplines as a vital basis for the integration process

1. Strengthening the GATT rules and disciplines should ensure:
—the effective and lasting opening-up of markets involving contributions from all the negotiation partners, particularly as regards tariffs, non-tariff measures, and derogations for balance of payments and infant industry reasons (see A below);
—the creation of fair competitive conditions, particularly as regards subsidies, dumping, access to raw materials and the protection of intellectual property (see C below).
—improved safeguard discipline (see C below).

This contribution gives only an initial indication of the objectives envisaged by the Community regarding each of the above subjects. These are suggestions for discussions within the Textiles Negotiating Group.

2. The new tighter rules and disciplines which will emerge from the negotiations will be applied across the board. They will therefore need to be negotiated primarily within the specific negotiating groups responsible for each area. The Textiles Negotiating Group will nonetheless have to follow other groups' negotiations very closely and, where necessary, itself discuss the guidelines and developments regarding issues of major importance to the sector.

The arrangements for the negotiations notably in part I.G. of the Punta del Este Declaration include general provisions for the inter-relationship between the different negotiating areas. The Textiles Negotiating Group will therefore have to "take into account relevant aspects emerging in other groups." But its link with the work of other groups is made more explicit by the specific reference to textiles in the Punta del Este Declaration, whereby the sector is to be integrated into GATT "on the basis of strengthened GATT rules and disciplines . . ." It will be for the Textiles Negotiating Group to assess whether the planned strengthening of GATT rules and disciplines represents a basis for integrating the sector into GATT, so that a timetable can be fixed on that basis for the synchronized implementation of balanced undertakings from all participants.

A. Contributions by all Participants Towards Opening Up the Markets

Contributions from all those involved, including from the textile-exporting countries according to their level of development, must ensure better access to markets through action on:

—tariffs and non-tariff measures

—derogations for balance of payments and infant industry reasons.

1. Tariffs and non-tariff measures

In order to ensure a real and lasting opening up of the markets of all Contracting Parties, close coordination is essential between tariffs and non-tariff negotiations in order to avoid tariff concessions being nullified or undermined by non-tariff measures. The Community is developing such a coordinated approach in new communications to the negotiating group specifically concerned.

(a) Tariffs

The fact that tariffs for textiles remain higher and less frequently bound compared to other industries gives some countries a certain degree of protection and flexibility of action equivalent to quantitative restrictions, which other countries can obtain only by recourse to the provisions of the MFA or GATT Article XIX. This situation is all the more unfair in that the competitiveness of the protected industries is often borne out by a rapid increase in their exports. All the participants should therefore contribute towards redressing the current imbalances. Within the framework of the Negotiating Group on Tariffs, the Community has just proposed a general approach to the tariff issue.

In this general context, a special effort is needed to reduce and harmonize tariffs in the textiles sector, which has become competitive in a number of countries. The levels of the duties to be bound should at any rate leave open real import opportunities.

2. Non-tariff measures

In a number of countries, imports of textiles and clothing products are seriously hindered by non-tariff measures, in such forms as excessive customs and administrative formalities, discretionary licensing, prior import deposits and discriminatory charges. An absolute ban can sometimes prevent importation altogether. Lastly, an opaque discretionary system for issuing foreign exchange can have an effect equivalent to prohibition and make quotas unusable.

The Community expects all partners to make genuine progress in eliminating and liberalizing non-tariff measures. As for measures which will remain applicable, greater transparency and the elimination of discretionary or discriminatory elements are essential. Suitable provisions should also be introduced to ensure that progress already achieved is not subsequently nullified or undermined by the new measures.

Within the framework of the Negotiating Group on Non-Tariff Measures, the Community has already stressed its interest in eliminating or scaling down non-tariff measures and in establishing multilateral disciplines in this area.

3. Derogations for balance of payments and infant industry reasons

Recourse to certain provisions of the General Agreement, in particular Articles XII and XVIII, and to the Decision of 28 November 1979 on safeguard action for development purposes, which provide for exceptions to the disciplines of the Agreement for countries with balance of payments difficulties, or for the promotion of infant industry, can worsen the international trade situation, particularly in the textiles sector. Recourse to the derogations for *infant industry* is scarcely compatible with the "mature" character of the textiles sector in almost all countries. The current situation can lead to the creation or maintenance of excess production capacity, running counter to the aim of an optimum international distribution of production.

It also involves a risk of unfair competition based on profits accruing from excessive protection of the domestic market.

Invocation of the *balance of payments derogations* can lead to distortions and the Community has already indicated the elements of the strengthened discipline which must be introduced into the working of these provisions in order to remedy such difficulties.

B. *Creating fair conditions of competition*

Substantial improvement is needed in:

(i) anti-dumping and anti-subsidy procedures;
(ii) access to raw materials;
(iii) protection of intellectual property; property trade marks, designs and models.

1. Dumping and subsidies

The relevant GATT subsidies should be adapted to make the required redress more effective in those sectors which are still characterized by

—seasonal factors and fashion, which provoke rapid changes in products, and

—a multiplicity of products, processing phases, producers and exporters.

(a) Dumping

The required adaptation should take account of the specific characteristics mentioned above and should include inter alia the following elements:

☐ provisions aimed at avoiding that the large number of products and of parties involved prevent a rapid opening, and an efficient execution of investigations;

☐ provisions aimed at avoiding that exporters making massive imports in anticipation of anti-dumping measures take advantage of the fact that anti-dumping investigations may take a considerable time before measures, even on a provisional basis, are taken;

☐ international progress on provisions to prevent the circumvention of anti-dumping measures.

Some of these points were brought up in the Community's memorandum of 21 March 1988 to the Negotiating Group on MTN Agreements and Arrangements. Additional elements will be provided very shortly.

(b) Subsidies

All participants will have to comply more fully with the obligations arising from the improved subsidy disciplines, according to the level of their competitiveness.

The Community will make its position known at a later stage.

2. Access to raw materials

It is not unusual for the production of marketing of raw materials in textile-exporting countries to be so arranged as to make those raw materials available to domestic producers at prices lower than those prevailing on the world market for raw materials of equivalent quality.

At production stages where the part of raw materials in total production costs is high, that is likely to distort competition to an extent which negates all the efforts towards structural adjustment undertaken in importing countries.

If fair conditions of competition are to be created, it is therefore vital that textile-exporting countries ensure that there are no artificially created price differences between raw materials for local production and those for export.

3. Protection of trade marks, designs and models

Considerable resources go into the conception and execution of new designs and models. This expenditure should be seen as genuine intangible investment. Only a small number of designs and models enjoy commercial success and it is these which are copied, often using lower quality materials. In addition to the direct commercial injury, this causes serious injury to the brand image of the company which produced the original design or model.

To remedy the situation, all the participants should subscribe to effective protective rules with a view to their incorporation into national law.

The Community has presented the Negotiating Group on Trade-Related Aspects of Intellectual Property Rights with initial proposals on commercial trade marks, designs and models, regarding both substantive standards and their enforcement.

This field is of particular importance to all textile producers and it is therefore essential that the negotiations on trade-related aspects of intellectual property rights produce substantial property results.

C. Safeguards

The Community has just presented a communication to contribute to the effects underway to produce a new general discipline on safeguards. It emphasizes the importance for textiles of achieving strengthened GATT rules and disciplines. This new discipline will also apply to the textiles sector, as soon as it is definitively integrated into GATT. Care must therefore be taken to ensure that the improved rules will serve, in due course, to solve also the problems arising in the textiles sector.

Index

Ghadar, Fariborz, 77n, 83n, 85n, 87n, 106n, 132n, 134n, 135n, 136n, 137n, 138n, 216n
Gibbons, Sam, 47
Global quota scheme, 17, 224–30, 247, 252, 273, 281, 283
Global quotas
  advantages and disadvantages of, 298–302
  consumer costs of, 311–17
  growth rate of, 295, 311
  employment effects of, 320–21
  features of, 292–95, 298
  revenues from, 321–23
  unresolved questions of, 296–97
  US apparel imports and consumer costs and, 324–25
Global tariff rate quotas
  advantages and disadvantages of, 298–302
  constrained, 332–35
  consumer costs of, 323–27
  features of, 298
  historical base, 330–31
Gregg, John, 265n, 266n
Gross domestic product (GDP), 25
Gross national product (GNP), 70, 72
Grossman, Gene M., 93
Gundersheim, Art, 266n

Haiti, 10, 77, 142
Hamilton, Carl, 153n, 165
Hayes, Philip, 131, 134n, 135n
Hickok, Susan, 165, 200–01
Hong Kong, 77, 81, 216
  comparative advantage, 8–10, 52, 56, 57, 101, 139–43
  industry size, 119
  liberalization policy, 224, 254, 261, 285
  MFA and bilateral restraints, 10, 14, 16, 146, 148, 151–54, 157, 159, 214, 220
  1985 textile bill, 17, 208, 209, 213
  price of quota tickets in, 300
  quota rights trading, 12, 165
  real exchange rate, 60, 233, 250
  tariff rate quota proposal, 259
  trade flows, 122
  US negotiations with, 303
Houthakker, H. S., 46
Hufbauer, Gary Clyde, 197–99, 201, 280–81, 294

ICF, Inc., study, 229, 230
Imperial Chemical Industries (ICI), 133
Import growth and penetration
  adjusted measure, 49–51
  apparel and textiles, 2–3, 34–44, 47–51, 64–65, 148, 151, 249, 255, 267–69
  footwear, 267
  international comparisons, 51–58, 123–28, 151
  MFA effects, 12–14, 169–73
  model assumptions, 231–32
  1983–84 surge, 13–14, 178–86
  nominal value of US nonoil imports, 59
  nominal value of US textile and apparel imports, 60
  sources of US imports, 1961–84, 54–58
Import license scheme, 208–09
Import penetration, as criterion in Japanese proposal, 304
Import sensitivity, differentiation according to, 295, 316–17
Import substitution, 26
Income distribution effects, 16, 201–06, 251–52, 273
India, 26, 56, 57, 77
  comparative advantage, 8, 9, 139
  export data, 142
  industry size, 119
  MFA-IV, 217, 220
  1985 textile bill, 209
  quota coverage and utilization, 159
  real exchange rate, 60
  tariff levels, 224
Indonesia, 77, 142, 165, 209
Industry performance
  Europe and Japan, 8, 113–18
  model projections, policy implications of, 254–56
  US sectors, 2–3, 25–34
Inflation, 188–89
Information exchange, 220
Input-output coefficients, 65–66, 242
Integrated Adjustment Program for Textiles and Apparel (IAPTA), 260–61, 264, 274
International Business and Economic Research Corp. (IBERC) studies, 208n, 210–11, 213, 229–30
International Development Association (IDA), 260
International Monetary Fund, 59n
Investment data, 29–30, 32, 33, 84
Isard, Peter, 93n

paths on apparel employment, 320
impact of textile quota bill on
imports, consumer costs and
employment, 338
item 807-A of the Tariff Schedules of,
295
MFA expansion proposal, 302–04
tariff rate quota surcharge for
imports, 300
Uruguay Round negotiations, 291–
344
Upgrading
MFA stimulation, 13, 36–37, 161,
173–78
US sectors, 36, 41, 44
Uruguay, 142
Uruguay Round, 1, 18, 207, 210, 221–
24, 247
AOTTA implementation, 288–89
GATT and, 306
goals of, 291–92
negotiations of Office of the US Trade
Representative (USTR), 292
US International Trade Commission
(USITC), 36, 174n, 176n
US Department of Commerce, SME
(square-meter equivalent) and, 327
USTR (United States Trade
Representative)
impact of global quota proposal on
US consumer costs, 316
item 807-A of the Tariff Schedules of
the United States, 334–335
options proposed by, 335–337
surcharge and, 299–301
Uruguay Round negotiations and, 292

USTR (United States Trade
Representative) tariff rate quota,
features of, 298

Vegetable fibers. *See* specific fiber types
Voluntary export restraints, 10, 146,
253, 270, 278

Waelbroeck, Jean, 150n
Wages
adjustment, 6, 33, 88–92
industry comparisons, 7, 103–04,
195–96
international comparisons, 8, 120
Williamson, John, 70
Wolf, Martin, 26n, 114n, 137n, 139n,
146n, 147n, 148n, 150n, 151n,
152n, 153n, 156n, 159, 161, 171n,
177n
Wool prices, 28
Woolen textiles
MFA coverage, 148–50, 248
tariffs on, 146
Women
labor force participation, 7, 106–7
World Bank, 50, 139n
Worker adjustment programs, 321

Yeutter, Clayton K., 219

POLICY ANALYSES IN INTERNATIONAL ECONOMICS

BOOKS

Dollar Politics: Exchange Rate Policymaking in the United States
I. M. Destler and C. Randall Henning/*1989*
$11.95   0–88132–079–X   192 pp

Foreign Direct Investment in the United States
Edward M. Graham and Paul R. Krugman/*1989*
$11.95   0-88132-074-9   182 pp

Latin American Adjustment: How Much Has Happened?
John Williamson, Editor
$34.95   0–88132–125–7   480 pp

SPECIAL REPORTS

1 **Promoting World Recovery: A Statement on Global Economic Strategy**
   by Twenty-six Economists from Fourteen Countries/*December 1982*
   (Out of Print)   0–88132–013–7   45 pp

2 **Prospects for Adjustment in Argentina, Brazil, and Mexico: Responding to the Debt Crisis**
   John Williamson, editor/*June 1983*
   (Out of Print)   0–88132–016–1   71 pp

3 **Inflation and Indexation: Argentina, Brazil, and Israel**
   John Williamson, editor/*March 1985*
   (Out of Print)   0–88132–037–4   191 pp

4 **Global Economic Imbalances**
   C. Fred Bergsten, editor/*March 1986*
   $25.00 (cloth)   0–88132–038–2   126 pp
   $10.00 (paper)   0–88132–042–0   126 pp

5 **African Debt and Financing**
   Carol Lancaster and John Williamson, editors/*May 1986*
   $12.00   0–88132–044–7   229 pp

6 **Resolving the Global Economic Crisis: After Wall Street**
   Thirty-three Economists from Thirteen Countries/*December 1987*
   $3.00   0–88132–070–6   30 pp

7 **World Economic Problems**
   Kimberly Ann Elliott and John Williamson, editors/*April 1988*
   $15.95   0–88132–055–2   298 pp

   Reforming World Agricultural Trade
   Twenty-nine Professionals from Seventeen Countries/*1988*
   $3.95   0–88132–088–9   42 pp

8 **Economic Relations Between the United States and Korea: Conflict or Cooperation?**
   Thomas O. Bayard and Soo-Gil Young, editors/*January 1989*
   $12.95   0–88132–068–4   192 pp

FORTHCOMING

The United States as a Debtor Country
C. Fred Bergsten and Shafiqul Islam

Equilibrium Exchange Rates: An Update
John Williamson

Global Oil Crisis Intervention
Philip K. Verleger, Jr.

The Debt of Low-Income Africa: Issues and Options for the United States
Carol Lancaster

Economic Sanctions Reconsidered: History and Current Policy, Revised Edition
Gary Clyde Hufbauer, Jeffrey J. Schott, and Kimberly Ann Elliott

Completing the Uruguay Round: A Results-Oriented Approach to the GATT Trade Negotiations
Jeffrey J. Schott, editor

Pacific Area Developing Countries: Prospects for the Future
Marcus Noland

Financial Intermediation Beyond the Debt Crisis, Revised Edition
Donald R. Lessard and John Williamson

Economic Policy Cooperation: Reflections of a Practitioner
Wendy Dobson

Reciprocity and Retaliation: An Evaluation of Aggressive Trade Policies
Thomas O. Bayard

The Greenhouse Effect: Global Economic Consequences
William R. Cline

The Costs of US Trade Barriers
Gary Clyde Hufbauer and Kimberly Ann Elliott

Energy Policy for the 1990s: A Global Perspective
Philip K. Verleger, Jr.

A GATT for Investment
C. Fred Bergsten and Edward M. Graham

International Adjustment and Finance: Lessons of 1985–1990
Paul R. Krugman

TO ORDER PUBLICATIONS PLEASE WRITE OR CALL US AT:

Institute for International Economics
Publications Department
11 Dupont Circle, NW
Washington, DC 20036
202-328-9000